TEAM TEACHING

Exploration Series in Education

*Under the Advisory Editorship
of
John Guy Fowlkes*

TEAM TEACHING

edited by

JUDSON T. SHAPLIN

and

HENRY F. OLDS, Jr.

with chapters by

JUDSON T. SHAPLIN

HENRY F. OLDS. JR.

ROBERT H. ANDERSON

JOSEPH C. GRANNIS

CYRIL G SARGENT

DAN C. LORTIE

GLEN HEATHERS

HARPER & ROW, PUBLISHERS

NEW YORK, EVANSTON, AND LONDON

Contents

Appendix: Bibliography and List of Team Teaching Projects

Foreword

FRANCIS KEPPEL

Former Dean of the Harvard Graduate School of Education

This book about team teaching comes at the right moment. As Mr. Shaplin points out in the first two chapters, the national commitment to exploring the possibilities of new ways of organizing schools is already substantial. Because of its actual and potential relationship to other reform movements in education, it is possible that team teaching will stand the test of time rather than slide into the footnotes of educational history. James B. Conant, who is not easily swayed by current fashion in education, has written the following about elementary education:

There is without doubt a ferment among educators with respect to the conduct of elementary education. The long-standing notion of a self-contained classroom of 30 pupils taught by one teacher is giving way to alternative proposals. One of these proposals is team teaching, which, as we have seen, has advantages in orienting new teachers.

If the idea of team teaching becomes widely accepted—and many elementary school principals predict that it will be—there will be places in classrooms for a wide range of instructional talent. How such schemes will work out over the years in practice remains to be seen, but team teaching seems to many the answer to the question of how to attract more of the ablest college students into elementary school teaching. The possibility of a teacher's having an opportunity to take advantage of her special field of interest is exciting.[1]

[1] James Bryan Conant, *The Education of American Teachers*, New York: McGraw-Hill, 1963, p. 147.

Mr. Keppel is now U.S. Commissioner of Education. It was during his service at Harvard that he urged the authors to prepare this book. Nothing in the book necessarily reflects the official views or policies of the Office of Education, which Mr. Keppel now heads, or of its parent organization, the U.S. Department of Health, Education, and Welfare.

ix

A detailed assessment of team teaching has been needed, and this is what the editors of this book have provided. The time has come to sharpen definitions, to puncture some balloons, and to put the movement—for that is what it has become—into proper perspective. The authors have tried to establish a detached tone, and this alone has been a major contribution. I can speak with some authority on this point for I have been an ardent supporter throughout the initiation and development of team teaching. Mr. Shaplin's description of some of the materials on the subject as presenting "a curious mixture of hortatory confidence and unsupported optimism" may have been prompted by some words of mine.

A decade ago my interests in encouraging new ways of organizing teachers and pupils grew out of a desire to recruit able young men and women into teaching and to keep them in the classroom. Three aspects of the teacher's career seemed to present serious obstacles: the low ceiling in salary, the lack of any clear path to increased responsibility and intellectual growth, and the lack of adult criticism and companionship. These elements appeared to be present in the career patterns of the other professions with which the schools were in competition for personnel. And the schools were not doing well in comparison.

It seemed sensible to try to do something about it. But, as so often happens, matters soon became complicated. Prophecy had to be replaced by planning, and planning brought unexpected factors to light. As Mr. Shaplin points out in the final words of the second chapter, sociological and psychological theories of small groups were largely ignored at the start. The effect of team teaching on curriculum had to be studied—and even wrestled with—under trying circumstances. Buildings and people had to be changed, and neither was found to be particularly malleable. In all this activity, basic purposes were easy to lose and detached assessment was hard to achieve.

The authors of this book have been a part of this history, as have I, and our qualifications as unbiased witnesses may reasonably be brought into question. In an area of controversy, the protagonist does not necessarily become a good judge. The reader will have to make his own estimate of the situation; it is only appropriate for me to record here my gratitude to Mr. Shaplin and Mr. Olds and their colleagues for taking on the task. At this stage of development, it seems necessary for those who are well-informed in theory and experience to report their observations. If team teaching is to be more than a fad, if it is to contribute to the increase in the quality of our education that the times so urgently demand, this book will be followed by others. Experiment should follow experiment; criticism should be made and should be followed by change. What has been needed is a point of departure for this process, and it is reasonable to hope that this book will serve that purpose.

One other point should be made. The reader will soon note that team teaching has been the result of collaboration between the personnel in schools and universities. Neither alone could have started the plan, and neither alone is capable of assessing its results. This type of relationship, long established in medicine and agriculture, provides a useful model. In order to strengthen many aspects of American education, a comparable relationship is needed to deal with the recruiting and training of teachers and the development of curricula. We can no longer afford the dichotomy between the interests of the schools and higher education which has so long marred the educational scene. Let the record of team teaching show, as the years go by, that it helped to forge new bonds between the schools and colleges. The senior editor of this volume, Mr. Shaplin, was for many years my close colleague at Harvard. I can report that his own life and thought have demonstrated the value of this approach in educational policy and the conduct of its affairs. This book is the result.

Editor's Introduction

For many years a favorite symbol for the perfect learning situation was a man (teacher) seated on one end of a log (school) and a boy (learner) seated on the other end. It was soon discovered that the economics of providing one teacher for each learner was impossible as the number of learners increased. Consequently the boy on the log was replaced by a group of pupils and a little red schoolhouse. The optimum number of pupils (learners) has never been established with sufficient validity to receive universal acceptance. Nevertheless the ratio of teachers to learners is a critical factor, not only in the educational activities of teachers and learners, but in the size and arrangement of rooms in school buildings and hence in the economics of schools with respect to both the amount of school expenditures and the value received. This view lacks a sound basis for defining, organizing, and utilizing educational staffs on the one hand, and the number and form of rooms in school buildings on the other hand.

The traditional insinuation that the focal point of educational institutions is the teacher seems open to serious question. Indeed to the writer it seems unfounded. For many years the levels of educational institutions and the individual differences of students (learners) have been emphasized to varying degrees. Cognizance of individual differences in learners has been in terms of homogeneous groupings of types and levels of learning capacity. Unfortunately there has been little evidence during the past years of recognition of individual differences among teachers and, therefore, no differentiation in their teaching assignments. Equally unfortunate is the failure to provide staff members other than teachers, e.g., secretaries.

When one considers the best method of organizing teachers and learners and establishing priorities between the two groups, an understanding of the words *teach* and *learn* appears essential. According to *Webster's New Collegiate Dictionary*, *teach* means "to make aware by information, experience, or the like," whereas *learn* "is to gain knowledge or understanding of, or skill in, by study, instruction, or investigation." An important synonym of learn is "discover."

It appears that learners and learning, rather than teachers and teaching, should be the focal point of school. Certainly learners and learning demand teachers and teaching, but it seems highly questionable whether any knowledge or skill can ever be imparted by one human being to another human being. Therefore it seems that teaching at its best is a process of stimulating, explaining, and consulting—as opposed to imparting.

As reported in the first chapter of this volume, the decade 1954–1964 has witnessed what in truth may be termed a revolutionary attempt in the conception, selection, organization, and utilization of a necessary staff for the stimulation and direction of learning; that is, for teaching.

In keeping with contemporary practice observed in many commercial institutions in which the need for learning, both general and specific is realized, this new movement toward the provision of more adequate and more effective instructional staff is a team affair—namely, the instructional team. Out of this inevitably has come what has become known as "team teaching."

To my knowledge this is a pioneer attempt to present a treatise on the fascinating educational venture of team teaching. Although this work is directed to the staffs of elementary and secondary schools, it seems that there is also much food for thought for college and university staffs. The volume itself is the product of a team since there are seven authors, all of whom are distinguished in the field of education. It is a pleasure to present this first volume on team teaching for the careful consideration of all those interested in human learning in any age group.

JOHN GUY FOWLKES

September, 1963

Preface

In the spring of 1960 the Graduate School of Education, Harvard University, received from the Fund for the Advancement of Education of the Ford Foundation a grant to be applied to the preparation of a book on team teaching by Dean Judson T. Shaplin. The editors wish to express their gratitude to the Fund and especially to its vice-president, Alvin C. Eurich, who has shown a continued personal interest in this book over the three years during which it has been in preparation.

The editors also wish to express their appreciation to their colleagues, Francis Keppel, Leonard M. Lansky, and David V. Tiedeman, for their encouragement and advice; to the School and University Program for Research and Development (SUPRAD) for making available to us their facilities and staff; and especially to Wade M. Robinson, Executive Director of SUPRAD, for his stimulating criticism and for his help in solving many of the problems encountered in preparing this book. We also wish to thank the administration and staff of the Lexington Public Schools, Lexington, Massachusetts, for their help and cooperation.

Early in the preparation of this book when materials on team teaching were solicited from projects across the country, the editors were greatly encouraged by the willingness of many school systems to readily provide materials describing their team teaching projects. Without their help and cooperation, this book would not have been possible.

To the many others who have contributed to the preparation of this book, particularly to Miss Jane T. Scott for her drawings and for her help in preparing the bibliography and to Mrs. Katherine Raff and Mrs. Ernestine Ciccolo for their assistance in preparing the manuscript, we express our gratitude.

J. T. S.
H. F. O.

TEAM TEACHING

Chapter 1

Description and Definition
of Team Teaching

JUDSON T. SHAPLIN

Graduate Institute of Education, Washington University

Team teaching, a new pattern of school organization which has emerged in American education since 1954, has rapidly assumed the dimensions of a major educational movement. Starting with a few pilot projects in 1956 and 1957, the movement has now spread to several hundred communities distributed widely throughout the country, and plans under development suggest increasingly rapid growth. A number of major universities are participating actively in the development of team teaching, and there is a high level of professional interest, both pro and con, expressed in meetings organized for the description and analysis of team teaching at local, state, and national conferences of teachers, supervisors, administrators, and school board members. In some communities programs have progressed far beyond the pilot stage and include the reorganization of entire schools, the spread of teams throughout the school system, and even the construction of school buildings designed to meet the requirements of the new program. Substantial sums of money have been allocated for these developments by local school boards and by one major foundation, the Fund for the Advancement of Education.

The national commitment to team teaching, in terms of the numbers of teachers and students now organized on this basis, is substantial. Since many of the programs include several schools and since the teams vary in size from 2 to 10 or more teachers, a very conservative estimate of the teachers now involved in team teaching is 1500; of students, more than 45,000. A few communities have mounted a major effort. In 1960–1961 Evanston Township High School, Evanston, Illinois, had 15 teams, involving 70 teachers and aides and 2700 students. During 1961–1962 Norwalk, Connecticut, planned 19 teams in 10 schools, both elementary and secondary, including approximately 90 teachers and aides working with 2500 students.

The communities engaged in team teaching are spread over twenty-four states with concentrations in Massachusetts, Florida, Illinois, Wisconsin, Michigan, Colorado, Utah, and California.[1] These concentrations are associated in some cases with the efforts of the universities. In Massachusetts, Harvard University has worked closely with the town of Lexington in the development of the Franklin School Project, an elementary school organized entirely on a team teaching basis. A second elementary school, its building designed specifically for a team teaching program, was opened in Lexington in 1961, and one junior high school adopted a similar program in 1960. The cooperation between Harvard University and Lexington was established through the School and University Program for Research and Development, a joint program financed in part by the Fund for the Advancement of Education. Similar joint programs have flourished with the help of the Fund at other universities: the Wisconsin School Improvement Program of the University of Wisconsin has worked with team teaching projects in numerous asociated school systems; the Claremont Graduate School Team Teaching Program embraces eight school districts; the School Improvement Program of the University of Chicago has been instrumental in establishing team teaching in a number of neighboring communities and supports an intensive program in its own Laboratory School; and Wayne State University in Detroit is in the process of developing an elaborate program in the public schools of Madison Heights, Michigan. George Peabody Teachers College and New York University have conducted related projects and have explored various aspects of team teaching programs. Faculty members at all of these universities have served widely as consultants to school

[1] For literature describing projects mentioned briefly in this chapter, see the bibliography and list of projects in the Appendix.

systems planning for team teaching. Conferences held during 1959 and 1960 at Harvard and Wisconsin devoted significant attention to team teaching. And the first moves toward the establishment of training programs for team teaching have been made: a seminar at Wisconsin in the summer of 1960, a training center and demonstration school at Harvard and Lexington in the summer of 1961, a workshop for teachers at Ohio University in the summer of 1961, and numerous summer workshops conducted by individual school systems.

More evidence of a substantial commitment to team teaching is found in the radical modification of old buildings and the design and construction of new school buildings to meet team teaching specifications.[2] New buildings adapted to team teaching are now being used in Wayland, Massachusetts; Carson City, Michigan; Lexington, Massachusetts; Greenwich, Connecticut; Lamphere, Michigan; Racine, Wisconsin; and Huntington, New York. Numerous others are on the drawing boards.

Though it is difficult to estimate the extent of enthusiasm for and commitment to team teaching within the teaching profession as a whole, observers at conventions have been impressed and even somewhat concerned by the widespread interest which team teaching has aroused. This interest has been so intense that, in addition to numerous panels and special meetings devoted to the subject, discussions of team teaching have occurred spontaneously in meetings formally organized for other topics. At the 1961 convention of the Association for Supervision and Curriculum Development, discussion of team teaching permeated many of the meetings although none of these meetings had team teaching for a specific topic.

Much of this professional interest has undoubtedly been stimulated by the Committee on Staff Utilization, appointed by the National Association of Secondary-School Principals and supported by the Fund for the Advancement of Education, and by its chief spokesman and secretary, Dr. J. Lloyd Trump. Each year since 1958 this Committee has issued extensive reports of projects which it has sponsored.[3] In 1958 team teaching was barely mentioned in the annual collection of these reports; only one school system appeared to have developed a team teaching project during the 1956–1957 period

[2] See Chapter 8.
[3] See Appendix.

reported. In contrast, in the 1961 annual *Bulletin* more than half of the reports specifically mention team teaching. Dr. Trump has written three pamphlets which encourage experimentation with staff utilization and which indicate ways by which experiments may be undertaken. Following his lead, many schools have started team teaching.

The Fund for the Advancement of Education has also supported numerous pamphlets and books which survey the changing atmosphere of public education and suggest methods of experimenting with new concepts of organization. Of major importance among these publications are *Time, Talent and Teachers; Schools for Tomorrow;* and *Schools for Tomorrow—Today.*[4] Descriptions of team teaching and its potential advantages figure prominently in each of these publications.

However, the literature specifically concerned with team teaching is still scarce, though it is constantly growing. The term *team teaching* is such a new addition to the vocabulary of education that it did not appear in *The Education Index* until 1957–1959 (Volume II). A number of professional journals have solicited articles on team teaching and in some cases have also published critical rejoinders. It has appeared, therefore, as an extremely controversial subject with ardent supporters and equally determined detractors. Apart from the few articles in the professional journals and an occasional article in the more popular periodicals, the main source of information about team teaching has been the documents developed by the projects themselves. These consist of proposals, annual reports or working papers, and descriptive articles in local publications of teachers' organizations, in state journals of education, and in newsletters and special pamphlets designed for public relations purposes. The tone of these publications, because of the special audience and the limited development of the projects they report, presents a curious mixture of hortatory confidence and unsupported optimism; and the contents are generally limited to brief descriptions and overgeneralized statements of objectives and results.

Team teaching has not been limited to any one level of public education. It occurs at the elementary, junior high, and high school levels, though the specific adaptations to each level differ consider-

4 See Appendix.

ably. Despite the severe reservations of many professional educators about the feasibility of team teaching in the lower primary grades, team teaching has been used throughout the elementary school. Though many of the customary practices of the colleges and universities are closely related to team teaching, developments at this level, with the exception of teams for the training of teachers, are not generally being labeled or reported as team teaching. The movement as a whole, therefore, appears to be mainly a phenomenon associated with the public elementary and secondary schools. Both suburban and urban schools have been in involved. As is true with most of our American educational developments, the lead has been taken by the more experimentally minded and wealthy suburban communities; but with team teaching the urban communities have been quick to share the leadership in this field, and substantial projects are under way in Pittsburgh, Baltimore, and San Diego.

What then is team teaching, this phenomenon which is rapidly becoming a major educational movement? Is it as diverse as the literature suggests, or are there basic similarities which can be identified and which may lead to the systematic development of both a definition and a rationale for team teaching? In the remainder of this chapter, both the diversity and the similarities will be examined, and a tentative definition, based upon the essential similarities, will be presented.

When comparing different team teaching projects, one is impressed by their great diversity in both methods of organization and aims. Their common properties are difficult to identify, both because each program tends to define itself in very general and, at the same time, exclusive terms and because no clearly recognizable group of projects seems to have the same objectives. Since it is equally difficult to point to one or two projects and say that they are the models for the typical or real team teaching, it is hardly an exaggeration to say that there are as many different types of team teaching as there are different school systems that have undertaken projects. This lack of conformity to any established norms would not be a matter of such grave concern if it were not for an accompanying atitude, which seems to be more and more prevalent in the literature, that uniqueness is a desirable end in itself. Many projects make special efforts to insure some kind of uniqueness for their work, one even going as far as admitting that it would not permit the staff to review the literature in the field for fear that the resulting program would be merely a copy of someone else's work Such an emphasis on differences obscures the very real similarities that exist from project to project and at times seems to be a conscious attempt to avoid the important problem of deciding what team teaching really is.

The tendency for team teaching to be presented in highly general terms reflects the aspirations, expressed as ultimate objectives and ideals, which are held for the future of modern education. Unfortunately, these objectives and ideals also characterize most other educational efforts, and thus the statements do little to clarify the nature of team teaching. For example, in the descriptive materials of one large project, three people closely connected with the direction of the program express three different views on what is the *primary* and *sole* justification for team teaching: to improve the quality of instruction, to develop improved teaching techniques, and to make better use of teacher time. Many projects, continuing to avoid concrete definitions and analysis, expand this list considerably in several forms: objectives, purposes, hypothetical advantages, rhetorical questions. Almost always they are global generalizations, expressing ultimate educational ideals, and virtually never do they incorporate any concrete description of the process by which the objectives might be attained.

Often, as a further way of avoiding definition and analysis, descriptions of team teaching attempt to establish a negative stereotype of present educational practices as a background for the favorable presentation of team teaching. Other promising approaches, old and new, to the same problems are ignored and labeled collectively "old-fashioned" or "unreasonable." The organization of classrooms in the typical school becomes an "egg crate"; the "self-contained" classroom begins to sound like a prison cell; the image of a typical under-trained, overworked, underpaid, isolated teacher is put on display; and a class of 25 students suddenly becomes educationally and financially impractical. Inadequately defined and described alternatives are thus offered to replace inadequately analyzed existing conditions, with the assumption that acceptance of the alternatives must be total and final. It is small wonder that many teachers and professional organizations have taken a critical stand against team teaching and have, under assault, adopted a similar indiscriminate negativism.

An attempt is also frequently made to surround team teaching with the aura of science. This creates a barrier between the projects and the potential critics who risk the label of "antiscientific" if they choose to assault the barrier. All projects have become "experiments," and objectives are frequently stated as "hypotheses." However, in most cases the projects are merely educational demonstrations of preferred practices with few of the variables identified, much less controlled in any experimental sense, and with the hypotheses stated so generally that it is impossible to establish operational conditions under which they can be tested. In fact, most team teaching projects have been established without the substantial planning period required, without a prior training period for participants, and without allowing sufficient time for on-the-job planning. Consequently, the specific organization and objectives go through a slow process of evolution from the general to the specific as the participants learn and develop in their thinking about team teaching and the problems associated with it. In the course of this development, description and definition become less general and enthusiastic and more concerned with specification of procedures and analysis of problems. There is a new note of sanity and objectivity and an appreciation of the difficulties which surround attempts to make basic changes in the educational system. However, even when this healthy kind of development is actively taking place, many projects still feel bound to state their results in terms of their original general objectives.

Without a doubt there are reasons for the enthusiastic, highly generalized overclaiming and the confused character of the literature on team teaching. All too many educators seem to be looking to team teaching as a kind of panacea for all the problems education faces and, at the same time, seem to feel it is synonymous with all that is new, exciting, and worthwhile in education. These educators are trapped in evangelism; a strong fervent devotion to some matter and a correspondingly weak attempt to define precisely what it is to which one is so devoted. By implication, school administrators are not modern, forward looking, or progressive unless they have accepted the new gospel. However, enthusiasm and devotion of this type, if not carried too far, may produce constructive results which might never have been obtained otherwise. During the past decade the schools have faced continuous critical attack and have countered with a proliferation of attempts to provide for constructive change. But any new proposal must have strong support from the public and from the school board if it is to be accepted in the face of so many competing alternatives for improvement. Also, with school financing so dependent upon the already overworked property tax, many people view all new proposals involving increased expenditure with a jaundiced eye. Then too, there is the inherent conservatism of school systems, often all too satisfied with the kinds of compromises which have been achieved with great effort over the years. Kenneth Boulding, in his fascinating book, *The Image*, has described this conservatism in the field of economics, and his revised laws of economic behavior apply equally well here, for they are really laws of human behavior in all fields of activity:

We will do today what we did yesterday unless there are very good reasons for doing otherwise.
The good reasons which are necessary if we do not do today what we did yesterday are derived from dissatisfaction with what we did yesterday or with what happened to us yesterday.[5]

To a large extent, then, it appears that the enthusiastic supporters of team teaching have succeeded in marshaling strong forces in education behind their banner and in making people dissatisfied with themselves if they are not part of the movement.

However, the immature, nonrational character of much of the literature on team teaching stands in the way of further constructive developments. Team teaching may become so meaningless that it turns into a mere fad, transitory and ephemeral, and the inevitable disenchantment with the fad will mean the destruction of all its real values and future possibilities.

Among teaching teams, the most obvious and important similarity, implied by the name itself, is that teachers are brought into a close working relationship for the joint instruction of the same group of students. This involves a change in the prevailing personnel structure of most schools. Prior to team teaching the assignment of in-

[5] Kenneth E. Boulding, *The Image*, Ann Arbor, University of Michigan Press, 1956, pp. 86–87.

structional tasks and student groupings were matters of administrative decision; with team teaching these matters become the joint responsibility of the members of the team. Implicit, if not explicit, in this working relationship is the assumption that the team teachers will share instructional tasks and goals; plan together; assign appropriate tasks to individual team members; see each other teach; have access to each other's classrooms; join together in the evaluation of instruction; share information about the students for whom they are jointly responsible; and hold discussions, based upon common observations, of teaching and the effects of teaching. An individual teacher is no longer asigned proprietary rights over *his* classroom and *his* students.

It is fairly common practice in many schools which are not organized into teaching teams for teachers to work together in the planning of the curriculum, in arranging for visitations of each other's classrooms, in exchanging information about students they teach in common, in planning common tests, and in trading teaching techniques among themselves. Often these activities are organized formally on a departmental basis as a regular part of the teachers' schedules. Team teaching differs from even the more formal organizations of this type because the joint activities are primarily concentrated upon a single group of students. The instruction of this group is shared among the teachers, and the teachers' schedules are closely correlated so that this working relationship can function within the normal structure of the school day.

As described in the literature, the quality and the formal organization of the working relationship among teachers varies enormously from team to team. At one extreme two or more teachers appear to work together rather loosely as associates, meeting occasionally and dividing up the responsibility for instruction and students so that a minimum of joint activity is necesary. There is a serious question whether this type of arrangement may properly be called team teaching. Often, when the formal organization of a team is loosely defined, it may quickly deteriorate into a minimum of cooperation if tensions develop among team members. Because many administrators fear that a carefully defined working relationship will infringe upon the strong feelings of autonomy held by many teachers, they often will ease into team teaching by starting with just such an informal associate relationship. In other teams *cooperation* is the key word, and emphasis is placed upon cooperative group planning, group decision, and volunteering for assignments. Even in many fairly large teams of this type, there is no formal designation of leaders or coordinators. Leadership either still resides outside the team in the principal or supervisor, or it is thought of as emerging out of group process and as rotating among team members to recognize competence in special areas. In still other teams coordinators are assigned to make sure that the working relationships among team members are established, that meetings are held, that assignments are made, and that all members of the team are fully acquainted with what is going on. And finally, at the other extreme, there are highly organized teams with several levels of responsibility, including team leaders, senior teachers, teachers, assistant teachers, student teachers, and aides of various kinds, all organized in a hierarchy of formal responsibilities with prescribed statuses and roles.

In view of this diversity of working relationships within teams, it comes as no surprise to find that many teachers and principals encountering or reading about team teaching for the first time exclaim, "Why, we have been doing this for years!" Certainly, to some extent teachers have always worked together informally, exchanging classes and teaching tasks and amalgamating their classes with those of other teachers for music, dramatic performances, athletics, and various other special activities. Teachers of the same grade level of the same subject have generally met together to develop curricula, and it has been common practice for older teachers to offer extensive help to new teachers. These and other informal cooperative arrangements among teachers with similar interests and goals and between teachers in adjacent classrooms tend to be permissively organized; that is they occur if the teachers want to work together and disappear if one or another of the group decides he prefers to work alone. Team teaching, as has been indicated, tries to insure the effectiveness and continuity of these working relationships by formalizing responsibilities and by restricting team members from returning at will to an independent classroom and schedule. Individual members may elect, within the terms of their contracts, to leave the team, but the formal organization and the formal delegation of responsibilities remains, to be taken up by new members as they join the team.

Another common characteristic of teaching teams is that they are composed of two or more teachers. Since the working relationship of a team involves joint instructional responsibilities, more than one professional member is necessary. Some projects which involve one teacher and one nonprofessional aide have, on occasion, been called team teaching, but it is more appropriate to think of them as teacher aide, clerical aide, or paraprofessional programs. Similarly, programs involving lay readers in high school English programs, usually consisting of one teacher associated with one or more readers, have generally not been called, and should not be called, team teaching. A team may, and often does, include a variety of secretarial or other technical, subprofessional members. There are also a number of team teaching programs, particularly those associated with teacher education programs in the universities, in which the team is composed of one fully qualified teacher and an intern teacher or a teacher still in the process of completing his professional training. These may properly be considered teams, for the intern teacher intends to complete his training, is under contract with the school system, shares with the fully trained teacher the responsibility for instruction which has been delegated to the team, and is paid for these responsibilities.

A third common characteristic of team teaching, a product of the assignment of the same students to a team of teachers, is the variety which may be introduced in the assignment, scheduling, grouping, and location in space of the students. Team teaching projects agree almost universally that their programs encourage flexibility in these areas. This flexibility is more difficult to obtain under general methods of school organization which tend to specify uniformity in length of periods, size of classrooms, and size of class groups. This assignment of time, space, and class size in standard units means that the grouping of children must be done on the basis of a limited number of criteria and, because of the organizational complexities involved, must remain fairly constant for an extended period of time—usually a year. Though the individual teacher may subdivide his basic group of students for various purposes, he will often find it difficult to teach one subgroup while the other is working in the same room with little direct supervision. Under team teaching the students may be assigned to the team for longer periods than the standard class length, in larger numbers than the standard class size, and often, where physical facilities permit, to rooms often larger or smaller than the standard classroom size. In effect, a team of teachers assumes responsibility for a substantial portion of the school schedule of a fairly large number of students. The team may then, within the limits of the time and space available to it, divide the students into several groups of various sizes for any desirable length of time. For some purposes it is possible to bring the entire group together for a lecture or demonstration; for other purposes the total group may be divided into a number of subgroups, the size of which will be determined by the teaching tasks.

A similar degree of control over grouping for instruction can be, and certainly has been, achieved occasionally by other methods of organization. Team teaching is not unique in its claim for more flexible grouping. Much the same results may be obtained by a highly efficient departmental organization which can watch individual progress closely and can reschedule individuals frequently on the basis of performance. A similar type of flexibility is also provided by a plan such as Paul Diederich's "Rutgers Plan" which proposes the construction of a large building to be used as a resource and study center, supervised by specially hired nonprofessional personnel. The teacher may, at any time, vary the size of his basic class group by sending any number of students to work in the resource center. The advantage of team teaching over such arrangements is that the team provides a convenient administrative unit, smaller than the department and larger than the individual class, for facilitating flexibility of grouping for instruction. However, it should be added that the advantages of flexible grouping are achieved only if the team can identify them and plan appropriate activities to attain them. Those who assume that team teaching, by providing greater opportunities for independent study; small-group instruction; large-group instruction; and diversified groupings by ability, achievement, and interest, automatically assures improved instruction are naive about the complexities involved. For the organization itself is unimportant and guarantees nothing. But the organization with its potential flexibility may offer a framework within which improved instruction may eventually develop. Team teaching thus focusses upon the responsibility of the team to take advantage of the opportunities offered to analyze the instructional needs of students, to provide optimum groupings for instruction, and to adapt curricula and teaching methods to these new arrangements.

Current teaching teams vary greatly in the extent to which they fulfill this responsibility. There are widespread attempts to vary the size of classes as much as possible on the assumption that some topics are taught more effectively or efficiently in groups of different sizes. It has become almost axiomatic that team teaching should include some large-group instruction in order to avoid the repetition of lessons by different teachers and to provide the opportunity for the most talented and specialized teachers to influence a larger number of students. In some cases the fact that team teaching encourages the use of large-group instruction seems to be the main reason for having the team. As yet, however, very little progress has been made in establishing criteria for the types of instruction which may best be used with large groups; criteria based on the kinds of learning which may be expected from students who differ in ability, achievement, and motivation. Considerable progress has been made in developing methods of presentation which utilize the latest technical equipment. But even so, the widespread demand, fostered by the Committee on Staff Utilization, that 20 to 30 percent of instruction should be presented in large groups seems to be based on unwarranted enthusiasm and optimism. In most teams much instruction still occurs in average size classes of 25 to 30, partially because the group tends to be assigned to the team in a ratio of about 25 students per team member, but also because teachers tend to continue old practices in the absence of firmly established justifications for new methods. Classes of small size and programs of individualized instruction and tutorial are achieved uniformly only in the best organized teams which have focused directly on these problems. Because most of the projects are so new and also because the full scope of curriculum problems has rarely been realized at the start of a program, curriculum revisions based on the new grouping procedures are just beginning to be developed and have not yet reached the stage of publication which would help new projects. All over the country teaching teams are going through the same process, facing the same problems, and seeking their own unique solutions; but no models capable of common application have as yet been developed.

Recently, an increasing number of educators have placed considerable emphasis upon the need for schools to individualize instruction. Many team teaching projects have interpreted this to mean that the individual student should be given increased responsibility for his own education. Just as the Committee on Staff Utilization has suggested that 20 to 30 percent of a student's time should be spent in large-group activities, it has also suggested that an equal amount of time should be spent in independent study. Almost without exception it has been accepted that the student can contribute more to his own education by taking on greater responsibility for its direction himself. There are obviously certain economies involved in such an arrangement, but few educators have felt it necessary to question whether or not and in what specific situations this arrangement is better for the student. A study recently completed in the University of Chicago Laboratory School indicates that without very careful supervision a student may become involved in serious difficulties while trying to work out his own program of study.

Perhaps the most characteristic groupings achieved under team teaching at the elementary school level have been based upon ability and achievement, or a combination of the two, in separate subject areas. These groupings vary in size depending upon the number of students who fall into the various classifications and upon the instructional methods to be used. At other times it is possible to regroup the students at random or according to special interests and thus to avoid the rigid, often cruel and arbitrary, separations which sometimes occur with ability and achievement grouping. In the secondary school, because the prevailing structure already provides for grouping on the basis of ability, achievement, and special interests, additional subgroupings of these types within the teams are much less frequent or appropriate. At times groupings at this level are attempts to promote the aims of liberal or general education by providing integration of education disciplines across subject lines. Similar efforts are also made in the elementary school to counteract the subject segmentation which may be fostered by ability and achievement groupings within subjects. In general, since the teams have tended to follow or select from accepted practices of their particular school system, the grouping practices followed within teams are similar to those of their neighboring nonteam colleagues. Of course, the size of the subgroups and the conditions under which teaching takes place may be very different. For example, in a team a low achievement group in reading may include as many as 10 or 15 students, taught in a separate room. In contrast, the regular classroom teacher might have only four or five of these students and would have to instruct them in the presence of his other students who would be given other occupations for the moment. Though general statements about team teaching often claim that the team organization makes it possible to follow the progress of the students much more closely, responsibility for justifying such statements remains the job of those involved in the projects.

In the foregoing pages the analysis and description of team teaching, based upon a broad survey of existing projects, has been concerned with those characteristics which team teaching programs have in common and which might be regarded as preconditions for a project's being classified as team teaching. As a result of this analysis, the formulation of a tentative definition of team teaching is possible. Because the field of endeavor is still developing rapidly and because any precise formulation must of necessity be arbitrary, the definition is framed in general terms to allow the inclusion of a wide range of projects. Though many features of team teaching, not mentioned in this definition, remain to be described and though proponents of one or another type of team teaching might insist that these features should be included, they are too often absent from significant projects and, therefore, do not seem to be critical for the kind of definition which can be formulated at this time.

Team teaching is a type of instructional organization, involving teaching personnel and the students assigned to them, in which two or more teachers are given responsibility, working together, for all or a significant part of the instruction of the same group of students.

No statement is made in this definition of the objectives of team teaching or of the special advantages which may accrue to those who undertake this type of organization. It is customary to include a statement that the aim of team teaching is to improve instruction.[6] Any definition of a plan for organization ought to be entitled to the assumption that its objectives are intended to foster the over-all intent

---

[6] See an earlier definition in Judson T. Shaplin, "Team Teaching," *Saturday Review*, vol. XLIV, May 20, 1961, pp. 54-55, 70.

of the institution and that the statement of such intent requires a systematic rationale which cannot be stated economically within a short definition.

By using the words *type of instructional organization* in the definition, attention is called to the formal organizational aspects of team teaching. Particularly when coupled later in the definition with the words *given responsibility,* this phrase conveys the idea that such an organization has formal status within the school, that it has had delegated to it certain responsibilities, and that it exercises through its personnel legitimate authority in carrying out these responsibilities. Therefore, excluded from team teaching are those efforts which are similar in many ways but which depend upon informal voluntary relationships among teachers and upon a permissive administrative attitude. Though the word "reorganization" has been used often in previous definitions, it was deliberately not used in this definition because it implies sweeping changes in organization with the elimination of prevous structures, whereas team teaching is actually a type of organization which may fit into regular organizational patterns and which may leave much unchanged. For example, there is no inherent conflict with departmental organization nor with the present pattern of administrative organization. The basic changes occur among teaching personnel where there is at present relatively little formal organization.

The use of the words *teaching personnel and the students assigned to them* indicates that team teaching is primarily concerned with the organization of relationships among teachers in conjunction with the organization and instruction of the students related to those teachers. Team teaching is not concerned solely with teachers or solely with students but with the combination of teachers and students. We may speak, therefore, of team teachers and team students, with the word *team* indicating in each case the basic unit of teachers and students. Projects which concentrate their efforts completely upon one aspect of this unity and which totally disregard the other are thus, by definition, not team teaching.

The phrase *teachers are given responsibility . . . for . . . the instruction of the same group of students* reiterates the formal delegation of responsibility discussed above and clarifies the direct relationship between the teachers and the group of students which they teach in common. *Responsibility* here means that the team of teachers has both a firm measure of autonomy and a duty to provide, through joint effort, an optimum instructional program for its students. A convenient, moderately sized administrative unit is created for the facilitation of grouping for instruction, and the team is given control, ordinarily possessed by the teachers for only a small number of students, for the scheduling, grouping, and location in space of the students assigned to them. The teachers have a responsibility to make maximum use of the opportunities which are offered to them by this type of organization.

The words *two or more teachers* define the team as a relationship between at least two professional teachers and is intended to exclude from team teaching any instructional group composed of only one teacher and other nonprofessional personnel such as clerical aides or technicians. If one of the major purposes of team teaching is to pool the talents of professional teachers to enable them to provide an optimum instructional program, a minimum level of professional preparation for teaching on the part of the principal members of the team is implied. The definition acknowledges as a teacher anyone so designated by the school system who is held responsible and compensated as a teacher and therefore includes intern teachers, beginning teachers, and part-time teachers. However, it is not intended to exclude nonprofessional aides from team membership as long as the minimum condition of two professional members is met.

The phrase *working together* specifies a close working relationship among the teachers of a team for planning, instruction, and evaluation. Teachers should have common instructional aims for the same students and should share the instructional tasks which are necessary to carry out these aims. The critical test of this relationship is the jointness which is displayed in actual classroom instruction. Joint planning may occur at the committee or departmental level, but if the teacher teaches *his* students and conducts *his* own evaluation, the conditions of joint instruction are not met. The definition intends to make a distinction between team teaching and the other forms of formal and informal cooperation mentioned earlier in this chapter. Included among the latter are those projects where cooperation and consultation are primarily concerned with scheduling. Many of these, often called team teaching, are attempts to work out parallel schedules to facilitate large-group instruction in separate subjects and, therefore, may be more properly considered projects in new types of block scheduling, not team teaching.

The phrase *for all or a significant part of the instruction,* while very general and permissive, is intended to set limits on the scale of operations which may justifiably be called team teaching. Many projects have started in a very small way with teachers cooperating in the instruction of one class, either regularly for a limited number of class periods or only for a few large group sessions. This may be an effective way of introducing teachers and students to the processes of team teaching, but if the program does not progress beyond this point and if, at the same time, it makes the grandiose claims so characteristic of team teaching projects, the label of team teaching is hardly justified. The project must involve a sufficient number of students for a sufficient length of time and must have sufficiently developed instructional objectives to permit some type of formal evaluation.

In addition to the characteristics covered by the definition, which in themselves allow considerable diversity of interpretation, four directions which some teaching teams have taken are worthy of particular attention: the development of further specialization in teaching, the improvement of supervisory arrangements in teaching, the utilization of nonprofessional aides for teachers, and the expanded use of mechanical aids to teaching. These may be described as the common, but not exclusive, characteristics of team teaching.

Team teaching provides an organizational vehicle for specialization in teaching. A team for an elementary school may consist of teachers in complementary skills, such as an expert in reading, one in social studies, and one in mathematics and science. At the secondary level teachers of a single subject like English may develop specialties within that subject and may become experts in grammar, literature, language, or other disciplines. Such specialization may lead to improvements in instruction and to more effective use of teaching talent. The next steps in training which are required of teachers who have not yet specialized become easier to identify and lead to a closer connection between training programs in the universities and the tasks of the schools. Other types of specialization which may have application in teaching teams include large group lecturers; television lecturers; teaching-machine specialists; and specialists in coordination, scheduling, and grouping.

Team teaching also provides a way of organizing for the improvement of supervision in the schools. Supervision has always suffered because principals and supervisors have not had enough time to help teachers improve their work. New teachers have taken their places side by side with veterans and have been given the same teaching loads and responsibilities. College students have been apprenticed to volunteer teachers who receive little or no reward for this additional work and who may or may not have the ability to train them. Within teaching teams it becomes possible to assign greater responsibility for the curriculum and for the supervision of other teachers to those teachers who are more knowledgeable, more expert, and more willing and able to accept leadership. Less expert teachers can study under the leaders and assume more responsibility and heavier teaching loads as they grow into the job.

Some teams take the next step and organize into a formal hierarchy of positions based upon ability, responsibility, and specialized training, with greater rewards and prestige assigned to the higher positions. New titles have emerged such as "team leader," "senior teacher," "master teacher," and "cooperating teacher." In the past our schools have had difficulty in creating attractive career patterns and in providing increasing responsibilities and rewards as the teacher advances in age, training, and experience. Advancement and increased salaries too often come only by leaving classroom teaching for promotion into administrative posts. Salaries, usually geared to length of service and the accumulation of course credits, have had little regard for ability. Many team teaching projects are deliberately trying to provide more satisfactory career conditions by defining new roles and responsibilities for teachers and by increasing salaries on the basis of performance in these roles.

Team teaching may also provide the kind of organization in which nonprofessional teacher aides and part-time professional personnel may be used with efficiency. There is now fairly widespread agreement that too much of the teacher's time is spent in routine chores, but there remains the problem of finding ways to introduce nonprofessional personnel into the schools to relieve him. Teacher aides can readily be assigned to teams, however, and, as the aide takes over the clerical functions performed by several teachers, it may even reduce the number of teachers required to handle a group of students. Teams can also make use of the large, untapped reservoir of qualified mothers and wives who cannot devote full time to the job but who can and will gladly work on a part-time schedule arranged by the team.

Finally, the teaching team may be a large enough unit to guarantee efficient utilization of its own audio-visual and other mechanical aids to teaching. Tape recorders, projectors, and teaching machines can be assigned permanently to teams in a way that is not possible under normal school organization. Areas for the team quarters can be set up permanently with this specialized equipment. And scheduling arrangements for the use of the equipment can be made within the team without requiring scheduling readjustments of large sectors of the school. Regular access to and systematic use of this equipment, already occurring in a number of team teaching projects, may lead to substantial advances in the contribution these aids can make to the instructional program.

As has been suggested by the analysis so far, team teaching programs, because they have chosen very different elements to emphasize, have created an impression of wide diversity in the field. A few examples will readily illustrate this situation.

In the Norwalk Plan of Norwalk, Connecticut, primary focus has been placed upon the improvement of the career opportunities for teachers.[7] An attempt has been made to make teaching more attractive through the creation of new teacher positions, different and more advanced than the usual teacher position, within a team teaching framework. Among the elements of this plan are the payment of higher salaries to the team leaders and the cooperating teachers than are paid to regular classroom teachers, the assignment of higher status and prestige through the use of new titles, the provision of clerical aides so that teachers may devote the majority of their time to professional tasks, and the opportunity for teachers to specialize and concentrate their energies in the areas of instruction in which

[7] *The Norwalk Plan, An Attempt to Improve the Quality of Education through a Team-Teaching Organization: A Two-Year Study Supported by the Fund for the Advancement of Education*, Norwalk, Conn., The Norwalk Plan, November 14, 1960.

they are most interested and competent. Though the Norwalk Plan meets all the criteria established in the definition of team teaching and, in addition, has made substantial progress in the use of mechanical aids to teaching, the published literature of the project has continued to emphasize the career opportunities for teachers which are being created.

The Easton Senior High School Team Teaching Program in Easton, Pennsylvania, is described as a means of providing for different levels of ability.[8] The program is limited to academically capable students in the last three years of high school. A block schedule permits the ninety students in the team to meet with any of the three team teachers in any type of grouping or for individual instruction as desired in the three academic fields of English, history, and mathematics. Emphasis is placed upon ability grouping, tutorial, college level seminar courses, extended period instruction, and individual help and consultation. Special efforts are made to offer rewards for scholarly interest and achievement. The team teachers meet at regular intervals both among themselves and with the principal and guidance counselor. In contrast with the Norwalk Plan where emphasis is placed upon teachers' careers, this program emphasizes almost exclusively flexible grouping for various types of instruction. In fact, the program is so completely aimed at the students that it is difficult to understand precisely what are the functions of the team of teachers, aside from coordinating schedules, and it is also difficult to see whether or not there is any attempt at coordinating the instructional elements common to all three subject areas.

The team teaching program of the University of Chicago Laboratory School attempts to provide well-qualified teachers in the subject disciplines and, at the same time, to make accommodations for student differences in ability, interest, and need.[9] The team is composed of 47 freshmen, 4 subject matter instructors covering the fields of

[8] Carl H. Peterson, "Easton Senior High School Team Teaching Program," Curriculum Publication SE-60-1, Easton, Pa., Easton-Forks Joint School System and Easton Area Joint High School System, 1960.

[9] Roy A. Larmee and Robert Ohm, "University of Chicago Laboratory School Freshman Project Involves Team Teaching, New Faculty Position and Regrouping of Students," *NASSP Bulletin*, vol. XLIV, January, 1960, pp. 275–289. Robert Hanvey and Morton S. Tenenberg, "University of Chicago Laboratory School, Chicago, Evaluates Team Teaching," *NASSP Bulletin*, vol. XLV, January, 1961, pp. 189–197.

English, science, mathematics, and social studies, and a "facilitator," who has specialized functions in the areas of guidance, small-group instruction, and administration. In particular, the facilitator is responsible for gathering information about the learning needs of individual students. The variables under control of the team include course objectives, class methods, materials used, learning activities, group size, group composition, period length, and teacher roles. An important element of the program is the constant evaluation of the progress and attitudes of students in each area of study and the subsequent attempt to vary educational procedures in accordance with the results of evaluation. Each year the specific focus of the project changes to study a new aspect of the educational potential of the team arrangement. The role of the facilitator, who teaches in all subjects in cooperation with the individual teachers, was developed; and, more recently, there has been increased emphasis upon collaboration across subject lines and upon the development of relationships among subject specialists. In contrast to the Easton High School project, with its emphasis upon grouping for specialized subject instruction and mastering subject matter, the University of Chicago Laboratory School project focuses upon ways of increasing the individual student's ability to inquire effectively, no matter what the subject matter.

Perhaps the most comprehensive elementary school team teaching project involving an entire school is the one established in cooperation with Harvard University at the Franklin School in Lexington, Massachusetts.[10] Among the elements included in the project are: the development for teachers of new career opportunities based on a hierarchical organization of the teaching staff with increased salaries for those who assume increased responsibility; increased specialization in subject areas by elementary school teachers; the provision of flexible grouping for instruction; revisions of a variety of curriculum areas as an adaptation to the new groupings; the introduction into teaching teams of clerical aides, part-time teachers, and lay resource persons; and a variety of attempts to increase the use of mechanical aids to teaching. If anything, the project suffers from

---

[10] Robert H. Anderson, Ellis A. Hagstrom, and Wade M. Robinson, "Team Teaching in an Elementary School," *The School Review*, vol. LXVIII, Spring, 1960, pp. 71–84.

its concern with a multiplicity of objectives and from the associated difficulties of concentrating in depth upon specific objectives and problems. A research team, associated with Harvard, has worked on all aspects of the program since its inception.

These illustrations of the diversity of objectives and emphases in different teaching teams have been drawn from among the minority of projects which have formulated relatively clear objectives and which have presented extensive reports in the literature. Other examples could be added to demonstrate that team teaching, as an administrative arrangement, is proving to be eclectic because it can serve so many schools of thought in education.

In this chapter an attempt has been made to sketch a picture of a new movement in American education called team teaching which is currently attracting widespread attention and enthusiasm. This movement has been shown to be distributed widely throughout the country, to involve a large number of communities, teachers, and students, and to have significant backing from the universities, from the foundations, and from at least one significant professional association. A tentative definition of team teaching has been presented which is based upon the underlying similarities displayed in the existing projects. Because individual projects tend to emphasize their uniqueness and the ways in which they differ from other projects, these similarities are not often given emphasis in the public announcements and descriptions. Common acceptance of a definition, with its exclusive categories, is an essential first step toward the elimination of the confusion, diversity, and generality which now characterize much of team teaching and inhibit its development.

The enthusiasm, the claim for uniqueness, and the expressions of discontent with present educational practices give the impression that team teaching is an isolated phenomenon, totally new on the educational scene and unrelated to other educational movements past and present. In Chapter 2 the relationships of team teaching to other current educational movements and to historic efforts to solve the same problems will be discussed. In the past, programs which present striking similarities to one or another aspect of team teaching have blazed brilliantly and briefly on the educational scene. Are the basic conditions or the available resources significantly different so that a permanent and productive future can be predicted for team teaching?

Chapter 2

Antecedents of Team Teaching

JUDSON T. SHAPLIN

Graduate Institute of Education, Washington University

The period in American education following World War II has been one of crisis, confusion of goals, controversy, and reassessment, with the emergence in the second decade of a variety of approaches to the improvement of the quality of education, among them team teaching.

Major aspects of the crisis in the schools have been the persistent shortage of teachers and the rise in the national birth rate, at first thought to be a war phenomenon but now known to be continuous, which have required enormous increases in both the size of the teaching force and in capital expenditures on school housing. The teacher shortage has been a qualitative as well as a quantitative problem. More than 300,000 teachers left their jobs during the war to take better-paid jobs, their places taken by substandard teachers.[1] The supply of new teachers from colleges and universities was not sufficient to meet the demands of the expanding schools, much less to allow for the replacement of underqualified teachers.

Early in the first decade following the war, the crisis was accentuated by a mounting crescendo of criticism directed against the schools which threatened their capacity to recruit and retain teachers and to obtain the funds necessary for development and expansion. Criticism reached a high point in 1953 and continues to the present.[2]

---

[1] For a discussion of the shortage of teachers and its causes, see I. L. Kandel, *American Education in the Twentieth Century*, Cambridge, Mass., Harvard University Press, 1957, pp. 217 ff.

[2] For an analysis and examples of the criticism and the type of defense which was made, see C. Winfield Scott and Clyde M. Hill, *Public Education Under Criticism*, Englewood Cliffs, N.J., Prentice-Hall, 1954.

The attack came from many sources and was directed toward almost every aspect of both the public schools and the colleges and universities engaged in the education of teachers. Paul Woodring has identified two main waves of criticism.[3] The first wave, which started immediately following the war in an atmosphere of anxiety about the international situation and about the spread of communism, attacked the loyalty of teachers and professors and attempted to purge the curriculum and the textbooks of potentially subversive content. This criticism created an atmosphere of fear and an avoidance of controversial issues in the schools and colleges. Often the critics were joined indirectly by others who were opposed to the mounting costs of education or were unsympathetic to public education for a variety of reasons. Occasionally they created an opposition sufficient to control school boards, to influence their employment and promotion policies, and to defeat school bond issues in local elections. The second wave of criticism, which started somewhat later and persists in much greater strength, has been a many faceted attack upon the educational philosophies and practices which the critics feel have come to control the schools. Professional educators, the quality of the supply and of the preparation of teachers, methods of instruction, the content of the curriculum and textbooks, and the major goals of education have all been foci of criticism from a variety of sources and points of view. One major long-term trend in American education, which attracted particularly sharp criticism, was the attempt to gain equality of educational opportunity through such institutions as the child-centered and community-centered school and the postwar life-adjustment education movement, all of which tended to encourage the development of school programs shared by all students of a given age irrespective of ability or achievement.

The intent here is not to provide a detailed analysis of all criticism of the schools but rather to show the relationship of the criticism to later developments in education. For the crisis in public education was real and was intensified by the criticism. The schools needed supporters, and support came in the form of a vast citizens' movement. In 1949 the National Citizens Commission for the Public Schools was founded. At that time there were as few as 17 known

[3] Paul Woodring, "Ten Years Acts as Prelude to Reform," *Better Schools*, vol. V, May, 1959, pp. 7–10.

citizens' groups concerned with the schools. By 1959 the Commission had assisted in the organization of 41 state and 18,000 local groups.[4] This growth was paralleled by growth in the organization of state and national school board groups and by the enormous growth of national, state, and local chapters of the Parent Teacher Association. The spirit of this citizens' movement was not one of unqualified support for the status quo in education or for the demands of the professionals in education. Rather, the emphasis was upon a re-examination and a reassessment of the practices and the directions which public education had adopted and upon a search for promising new practices for the improvement of education. In this period the public and the major foundations showed a willingness to support the quantitative expansion of the schools if it was accompanied by simultaneous measures to improve the quality of education. Criticism continued, but, largely through the efforts of citizens' organizations which have themselves remained critical, it became constructive and offered strong support for revision and innovation in education. Outstanding features of this movement were the efforts to seek a rapprochement between the critics and the professional educators and to encourage scholars in all academic fields to interest themselves in the schools and to join the professional educators and schoolmen in constructive action.

Thus, out of all the criticism has emerged a climate favorable to change, in which has developed a number of major new directions in American education, each with its own enthusiastic supporters and each directed toward the solution of one or another major educational problem. The over-all pattern of change, as is characteristic of American education, is still one of diversity rather than one of uniform acceptance of a few basic solutions. The impression of confusion and controversy over fundamental goals remains, but new patterns are rapidly emerging. We will review here five areas of development: improvements in the recruitment, training, and career prospects of teachers; the organization of small school districts and schools into larger and stronger units; fundamental revisions of the curriculum under new auspices; the widespread effort to provide new groupings of students for instruction; and dramatic advances in the

[4] "Citizens Movement Ten Years Old," *Better Schools*, vol. V, May, 1959, pp. 1–2.

technology of education. Though these efforts are all interrelated in many ways, the focus of the discussion in each case will be upon the relationships to team teaching.

Recruitment, Training, and Career Prospects of Teachers

Following World War II the school systems of the United States were in a poor competitive position with other markets for the services of college graduates. This had been true over a long period of time, but it was accentuated by the fact that teachers' salaries lost ground during the war and fell well below the average earnings of all employees in the United States.[5] Because of the shortage of teachers, strong public support developed for increasing teachers' salaries, and in the period since 1948 salaries have risen at the relatively constant rate of 5.5 percent per year.[6] At the present time the real income of teachers is higher than at any time since 1890 and has risen well above the average salaries of other state and local employees and the average earnings of all employees in the United States. However, several major weaknesses remain in the salary structure for teachers. Entrance requirements for teaching have risen in the same period, a bachelor's degree now being required in a majority of states. A major part of the increase in the average salaries of teachers is thus attributable to the higher salaries of beginning teachers resulting from higher entrance qualifications and thus higher placement in salary schedules. Minimum salaries have tended to rise more rapidly than maximum salaries because of the need to compete for new teachers. The period required to reach maximum salary has tended to shorten, so that teachers now reach the top of the salary schedule in ten years, with any future increases dependent upon general increases in the salary schedules. The most common form of compensation is the single salary schedule with equal payments to men and women teachers and with placement in the schedule based upon length of service. After ten years of service, teachers have rela-

[5] For an excellent discussion of salaries in education, see chaps. 13 and 14 in Charles S. Benson, *The Economics of Public Education*, Boston, Houghton Mifflin, 1961. Reference above is to p. 398.
[6] *Ibid.*, p. 396.

tively little to look forward to in terms of salary reward for excellence in teaching and are forced either to leave teaching altogether or to move into supervisory or administrative posts to obtain higher salaries. The compensation for teaching is still well below what a college graduate can expect from other occupations, particularly in the case of male graduates. Benson has stated that recent beginning salaries, in competitive terms, are perhaps $1000 too low and that maximum salaries, from the point of view of the alert male college graduate, may be from $3000 to $5000 too low.[7]

The inadequacies of the present methods of compensation of teachers have received increasing recognition by both laymen and professionals. Because of the heavy pressure on the local property tax, which is the main basis of support of the schools and other community services, and because teachers' salaries represent a major portion of the budgets of the schools, it has been increasingly difficult for school boards to provide the across-the-board increases which are required under the single salary schedule policies. There have been two general approaches to the solution of the problem. One, supported strongly by the professional associations, has been to lobby strongly for increased state and federal support of public education, for both school construction and teachers' salaries, in order to provide relief for local sources of taxation and thus to make it possible to advance all salaries. This approach has not yet been successful. A second approach has been to seek some way of distinguishing among teachers, on the basis of either merit or added responsibility, so that by paying some teachers more, higher ceilings would be established toward which teachers could work.

In the past decade there has been widespread controversy over the question of merit salary plans. Lay school board members have shown favorable interest in merit payments since many of them are familiar with merit provisions in business and industry. School board members and the public with whom they deal are also familiar with the widespread comments which are made about "good" and "bad" teachers, so that a system of compensation which rewards all teachers equally does not seem sensible to them. Though research studies have raised strong doubts about preparational-type single salary schedules by showing a relatively low relationship between either

[7] *Ibid.,* p. 404.

degree of training or length of experience and teaching proficiency as measured by the test performance of students,[8] there has been strong resistance to merit salary schedules among teachers and perhaps a majority of administrators because of inadequate means of measuring teaching efficiency and because of the practical difficulties of administering merit proposals. That merit provisions have not been widely accepted in the United States is indicated by their appearance in only 15 to 20 percent of the salary schedules reported by various studies.[9] A wide variety of practices are included in these schedules, some of which are more in the nature of penalty rather than merit systems and others of which merely pay lip service to the idea of merit. Providing suitable rewards in salary for teachers as they advance in training, competence, and experience remains as one of the persistent unsolved problems of the teaching profession.

The critical shortage of teachers in this generation also has revealed to the public that the teaching profession has been unable to attract a substantial share of the more able college graduates. In a major study of the characteristics of students entering various fields, Wolfe has shown that the proportion of students, both undergraduate and graduate, entering education who scored above the average on intelligence tests was well below that of other professions.[10] Similar results from older studies show that this is not a recent phenomenon, though it has come sharply to the attention of the public only in recent years.[11] The public has gradually been led to an understanding that the quality of education is fundamentally dependent upon the quality of the personnel entering the field and that no other measures can overcome deficiencies in recruitment. Critics, attacking the profession on a number of broad fronts, have claimed that the basic policies of the educational field stood in the way of the recruitment of high-ability personnel. Teachers colleges and schools of education were felt to be such poor institutions with such low

[8] David V. Tiedeman, ed., *Teacher Competence and Its Relation to Salary,* Cambridge, Mass., New England School Development Council, July, 1956.

[9] Benson, *op. cit.,* pp. 426 ff.

[10] Dael Wolfe, *America's Resources of Specialized Talent,* New York, Harper & Row, 1954, pp. 199 ff.

[11] For a general discussion of the intelligence level of the teaching profession, see Myron Lieberman, *Education as a Profession,* Englewood Cliffs, N.J., Prentice-Hall, 1956, chap. 8.

admissions standards that they could only attract poor-quality students. The teacher study program was considered too heavily concentrated on professional studies consisting of a proliferation of repetitive "methods" courses, and the professors were felt to be illiberally educated themselves. Certification requirements were attacked as being so specific and restrictive, that they prevented able liberal arts college graduates, past and present, from entering teaching. As the discussion of these issues became more calm and constructive, it was clear that over several decades the colleges and universities had become increasingly dissociated from the work of the public schools—upon which they depend for their students—and from the recruitment and training of teachers—upon whom the quality of the work of the public schools rests. Many of the proposed reforms, therefore, have aimed at increasing the participation of university academic personnel or have been initiated by the academicians themselves.

The decade of the 1950s has seen the development of several new trends in the recruitment, training, and certification of teachers, as well as the continuation of several long-term trends in these areas which happen to correspond with the new spirit of the times. The teachers colleges as such are rapidly disappearing from the scene and are becoming instead multipurpose state colleges and universities to which are attached departments, colleges, or graduate schools of education. This trend started in the 1930s but has accelerated in the period since 1950, during which time more than 40 teachers colleges have changed title and status, and the remaining ones supply only 15 percent of the new college graduates prepared for teaching.[12] The new multipurpose colleges are often able to offer greatly strengthened programs for teachers in both general education and in the academic fields. Increasing consensus has been reached among the lay public, school board members, academicians, and professional educators concerning the necessary elements in the training of teachers at all levels: a sound liberal or general education; a strong specialization in the subject or subjects to be taught; and the professional study of education, including a satisfactory practice or internship experience. Two important organizations have been instru-

[12] Lindley J. Stiles, *et al.*, *Teacher Education in the United States,* New York, Ronald, 1960, pp. 100–101.

mental in fostering this agreement. The Council on Cooperation in Teacher Education of the American Council on Education, representing 33 regional and national organizations having an interest in the improvement of the education of teachers, has worked for some years to bring together professional educators, state education officers, and the colleges. The TEPS (Teacher Education and Professional Standards) Commission of the NEA has made a similar effort on both a regional and nationwide scale. Programs for the training of teachers have slowly been changing, and the cumulative effect during the decade has been substantial. The proportion of training devoted to general education and to academic majors has increased markedly and has been accompanied by decreases in the proportion devoted to professional training and by attempts to improve the quality of this training by the elimination of repetitious courses, the more careful definition and development of essential elements of preservice professional training, and, in particular, the improvement of the quality of the apprenticeship or internship part of the training. Certification requirements for teaching have tended to change in the same direction as training programs, though somewhat unevenly and state by state, so that both the number of requirements and their specificity have been reduced. More recently, there have been attempts to increase and improve the requirements in general education and in the academic fields.

Substantial efforts have been made to develop programs for the training of teachers which will attract the new graduates of the liberal arts colleges into teaching and tap the reservoir of past graduates in the community who might be interested in teaching if suitable programs were available. Many universities have developed fifth-year graduate programs designed particularly for one or both of these groups. Characteristically, these programs involve cooperation of faculty members in both education and the arts and sciences; continued study in the academic field during the graduate year; professional studies carefully planned to the abilities of the students; and cooperation between school and university in developing intensive apprenticeship or internship programs, recognized by all as being of critical importance in teacher training. Similar trends are evident within the four-year undergraduate programs for teachers. Increasingly, members of academic departments have taken a responsible role in encouraging, advising, and instructing able liberal arts students who are interested in teaching, and members of both the education and the academic departments have come into a closer relationship with the schools in their joint effort to recruit and train this new supply of teachers.[13]

The changes in the recruitment, training, and certification of teachers which have been described above have been important as a context for the development of team teaching. The joint concern of the schools and the universities in the recruitment of able potential teachers and the increasing collaboration between the two types of institutions in the training of the new recruits has brought with it new confidence in the kinds of working relationships which can be established and a new vision of common purposes. A number of the more significant team teaching projects have developed in schools which have had a close association with universities, and frequently it has been the personnel engaged in the preparation of teachers who have first seen the potentialities of team teaching. A growing willingness and desire on the part of university personnel to establish working, not merely consulting, relationships with the schools has made possible university training programs that are functionally related to work going on in the schools, whether it be team teaching or some other form of activity. A concern for working conditions in the schools and for new types of in-service training has provided much of the impetus which a new type of school organization like team teaching needs to enable it to take hold in the formal structure of the schools. And the climate of re-examination and change in certification requirements has made possible consideration and development of new assignments in teaching through the greater differentiation of roles and responsibilities which is characteristic of team teaching.

The broad-scale public and professional interest in the recruitment of a more able and better-educated corps of teachers for the schools has led quite naturally to a complementary interest in the kinds of career prospects which are open to teachers. To attract able people into teaching and hold them, there must be attractive career prospects, not only in terms of salary but also in terms of the kinds

[13] For a summary of many of these new programs, see Paul Woodring, *New Directions in Teacher Education,* New York, The Fund for the Advancement of Education, 1957.

of increased responsibility and prestige which most professionals can expect to attain with increased experience, training, and competence. The fact that teachers must leave teaching and enter the supervisory or administrative ranks if they want to obtain increased responsibility, higher salaries, and professional recognition has been widely deplored. In recent years attention has turned from attempts to provide merit salary increments to efforts to create new positions and new ranks within teaching. These new plans have aimed at simultaneously increasing efficiency in the utilization of the professional teaching force and providing more attractive careers and salary incentives. Benson, contrasting these efforts with the usual types of preparational and merit salary schedules, terms them "position and rank" systems of classification.[14] In their emphasis upon such things as the analysis of the tasks to be performed, the recognition of a hierarchy of skills and responsibilities, the assignment of personnel to tasks on the basis of skill and training, and reward based upon the level of complexity of the tasks and the quality of the performance in the assigned role, these "position and rank" systems resemble the workings of most business and industrial organizations.

There are many types of efforts to provide through "position and rank" systems of classification more attractive and satisfying career opportunities in teaching, and of these team teaching is merely one of a group that have been generally classified together as "staff utilization" studies. Indeed, it is unlikely that team teaching could have taken root unless it had been directly preceded by other projects devoted to similar aims but less comprehensive in scope. In the early 1950s there was a great increase in the use of the term *master teacher.* This usage appeared in at least three different contexts, some controversial but all aimed at providing recognition and an expanded sphere of influence for outstanding teachers. First, many of the new teacher education programs financed by the Fund for the Advancement of Education placed heavy reliance upon apprenticeships and internships under the guidance of "master teachers" in the schools.[15] Subsequent reports do not use the same words, but at the time the label had wide currency, probably because it partly justified the heavy emphasis upon field experiences in the programs by extolling

[14] Benson, *op. cit.,* p. 435.
[15] Woodring, *New Directions in Teacher Education, op. cit.*

the qualities of the teachers involved. Few of the programs provided financial rewards for the teachers, but all had the general effect of enhancing the status of the teachers involved, and they all helped to spread the idea that there are many teachers in the schools capable of assuming greater responsibility for the training of new teachers.

Secondly, a number of significant projects explored the possibility of using teaching assistants or aides to free the teacher from clerical and other nonteaching duties as well as from some of the more routine aspects of teaching. There have been, and still are, a large number of these projects in all parts of the country, the most notable of which are the Bay City, the Yale-Fairfield, and the George Peabody College projects.[16] The basic effect of these projects has been to show that there are a large number of extremely time-consuming tasks performed by the average teacher which are not instructional in nature and which can be more effectively performed by readily available and talented nonprofessional personnel under the guidance of the teacher. The Contract Correcting Project in Newton, Massachusetts,[17] where educated women served as readers for English teachers in order to permit heavier writing assignments for students, was one example of the use of teaching assistants rather than clerical assistants. This and similar projects have demonstrated the potential for expanded teaching opportunities and for relief from routine nonteaching tasks that can be realized through the use of nonprofessional personnel.

Finally, there has been a widespread effort to provide a wider audience for the highly skilled teacher by allowing him to lecture to large groups of students. Schools like Newton High School in New-

[16] For the Bay City study, see *A Cooperative Study for the Better Utilization of Teacher Competencies,* Mount Pleasant, Mich., Central Michigan College, 1955. For the Yale-Fairfield study, see John J. Howell, Constance M. Burns, and Clyde M. Hill, *Teacher Assistants,* New Haven, Conn., Yale-Fairfield Study of Elementary Teaching, 1958. For the George Peabody College study, see David T. Turney, *The Instructional Secretary as Used by Classroom Teachers,* Nashville, Tenn., Peabody Research and Development Program, 1959.

[17] Edwin H. Sauer, *Contract Correcting: The Use of Lay Readers in the High School Composition Program,* Report to the Cooperative Research Program of the United States Department of Health, Education, and Welfare and to the School and University Program for Research and Development, rev. ed., Cambridge, Mass., SUPRAD, 1962.

ton, Massachusetts, and Evanston Township High School in Evanston, Illinois, have concentrated upon developing large group lectures, and, in the latter case, closed-circuit television has also been used.[18] All such projects are faced with the problems of identifying those elements of the curriculum which can be taught effectively and economically to large groups and of assigning specialist teachers to teach these elements. Often even the most talented teachers need to be trained in the special techniques of large-group instruction before they can present their lessons. Consequently, there has been some tendency within projects of this type to provide special status and salary increments for teachers who become particularly competent in this method of instruction.

The three trends described above may be considered both direct antecedents of team teaching and concurrent movements which are both discrete and merged with team teaching. The over-all effect has been to help to create an environment of acceptance for some of the elements which team teaching, in many of its forms, involves: the assignment to master teachers of responsibility for supervising other teachers and interns, the use of nonprofessional personnel, the assignment of teachers to specialized teaching roles, the use of large-group instruction, and the establishment of a "position and rank" salary classification system based on the new roles which have been defined.

It should be remembered that the presence of subordinate teaching personnel has been a familiar feature of the American educational system since its inception. In all periods of rapid expansion of enrollment, underqualified teachers have been brought in as assistant or substitute teachers with lower status than qualified teachers and often under their direct supervision. However, a development of this decade that is relatively new for elementary and secondary education, though familiar to higher education, is the creation of superordinate positions that are above the rank of fully qualified teachers yet still within the teaching ranks.

[18] Henry S. Bissex, "Newton Plan Challenges Traditions of Class Size," *The Nation's Schools*, vol. LXV, March, 1960, pp. 60–64. Barbara S. Pannwitt, "Evanston, Illinois, Township High School Reports on Five Years of Projects, Including Television, Team Teaching, and Large and Small Group Instruction," *NASSP Bulletin*, vol. XLV, January, 1961, pp. 245–248. Also see other articles in the Appendix.

During discussions of team teaching, teaching aides, and other staff utilization plans, occasional reference is made to similarities between these plans and the monitorial system which was in vogue in England and America during the early nineteenth century. For example, Griffiths, urging school administrators to make use of past research, says:

> . . . Take the problem of teacher aides, for instance. Some of the evidence which should be used in making a decision on this problem is to be found in historical research. The administrator should know that there is nothing new in the proposal to have a teaching team composed of a master teacher and several ladies of the community. This is essentially the teaching system practiced in the early 1800's in England, and even earlier by Comenius in the 1600's. In England it went under the name of the Lancasterian Monitorial System and earlier it was called the "simultaneous system." The system introduced visual aids to learning such as wall charts, blackboards and slates. It managed to teach larger numbers of students at low cost. Teaching was characterized by imitation, memorization, and just plain rote learning. Brubacher comments that it was more significant as an administrative device than as an instructional device. The system gave way to the Pestalozzian method which stressed flexibility and insight into child nature. The administrator should be able to see that the teacher aide and the team-teaching plans advocated today differ little from their ancient predecessors and should look for substantial departures which might ensure success when failure has been their historical fate.[19]

This statement, apart from the cavalier linking together of teacher aide and team teaching plans in an oversimplified way, is itself an example of poor use of historical information in criticizing present-day administrative practices. The monitorial system, developed principally by Bell and Lancaster, was a way of organizing a school so that one master with the help of the more advanced pupils as monitors, could teach a large number of students.[20] The pupils were first divided on the basis of their level of performance into classes, each with a chief monitor. Then these classes were divided into smaller groups of about ten pupils, each with a monitor who had teaching

[19] Daniel E. Griffiths, *Research in Educational Administration: An Appraisal and a Plan*, New York, Bureau of Publications, Teachers College, Columbia University, 1959, p. 35.
[20] David Salmon, ed., *The Practical Parts of Lancaster's Improvements and Bell's Experiment*, London, Cambridge University Press, 1932. Joseph Lancaster, *Improvements in Education*, New York, Collins and Perkins, 1807.

duties as well as such custodial duties as taking attendance and supervising the distribution and collection of slates and books. There was, then, a complex hierarchy of monitors, all under the direction and instruction of the principal master, who served to instruct extremely large numbers of pupils.

A knowledge of the history of the meteoric rise and fall of the monitorial system can contribute little to our ability to predict the future of present organizational schemes, for conditions in the nineteenth century were very different. In the 1800s there was an enormous expansion of formal schooling despite the lack of a corps of trained teachers and of institutions to train them. Today, though surging enrollments have produced a teacher shortage, there is still a large corps of teachers trained to the highest educational level in our history. In 1800 there was no one to man the clasrooms; today, there are large numbers of well-trained teachers to whom other well-educated but less well-qualified persons can be attached under supervised conditions. The monitorial system found its manpower pool in the pupil population; today many plans have developed a hierarchy of teaching positions within the teaching staff and attach to this staff able, well-educated, responsible adults as teaching assistants and clerical aides. The monitorial system in New York City, which handled the instruction of some 600,000 students in the period from 1806 to 1853, collapsed for very different reasons than those cited by Griffiths. Charleson suggests that there were inherent weaknesses in the system which brought about its downfall.[21] The pupil monitors were themselves inadequately educated, and a formal educational system could not succeed which depended so heavily upon children teaching children. The advocates of the Lancasterian system insisted upon adherence to their own standards in the face of changing times and public willingness to provide a more adequate educational system. These standards were based more upon principles of economy than upon principles of learning. Further, the Lancasterian system was operated by a private corporation which depended upon public funds at a time when there was a demand for public control of the expenditure of public funds. The monitorial system, or pupil-

[21] In this discussion the author is indebted to an unpublished paper by William R. Charleson, "The Lancasterian System of Education in the State of New York, 1805–1860," prepared for History 172, Harvard University, Fall, 1961.

teacher system, is still in existence in such remote underdeveloped areas of the world as the smaller islands of the West Indies, where extreme poverty and an extreme shortage of educated persons severely restrict educational development.

The Organization of Schools into Larger Units

There has been a continuation and intensification in the past decade of a long-term trend in American education toward larger and larger school units. This trend takes two forms: the consolidation of small school districts into larger administrative units, and the construction of larger school units within districts. In 1931–1932 there were reported to be 127,442 school districts, with an average enrollment per district of 200 pupils; in 1960 the total number of school districts was estimated at 40,605, with an average pupil enrollment of 900.[22] The intent of this reorganization has been to develop more economical and efficient school units at both the elementary and secondary school levels. That the problem is still by no means solved is shown by the twelfth-grade enrollment statistics provided by Conant: approximately 74 percent of the schools offering the secondary school diploma enrolled fewer than 100 students in the twelfth grade, and approximately 32 percent of twelfth-grade students were enrolled in these schools.[23] Conant's voice is merely one of many that have spoken in favor of the consolidation of small schools into larger and more efficient units. On the other hand, it is true that in urban and suburban areas an increasingly large proportion of pupils is being housed in relatively large schools. Elementary schools with enrollments in excess of 500 pupils, junior high schools of over 1000, and high schools of more than 2000 have become quite common.

Large school units, both elementary and secondary, offer many educational advantages, and it can be argued that they are necessary if optimum educational resources and a rich and varied educational program that approaches the ideal of the comprehensive school are

[22] "Bigger and Fewer School Districts—Make Many Improvements Possible," *NEA Research Bulletin*, vol. XXXVIII, February, 1960.
[23] James B. Conant, *The American High School Today*, New York, McGraw-Hill, 1959, pp. 132–133.

to be provided. With an enlarged staff it becomes possible to offer specialist assignments to teachers and thereby to reduce the heterogeneous assignment of many subjects and age levels to a single teacher. It also becomes economical to offer other specialized services requiring both specialized personnel and facilities such as guidance and library programs. Economic utilization can be made of such expensive facilities as science laboratories, physical education facilities, specialized audio-visual equipment, lunch rooms, and the like.

On the other hand, as schools approach the size mentioned above, many disadvantages appear, particularly if the schools have been built in the traditional pattern of equal-size rooms, one per teacher. Scheduling of classes becomes rigid and tends to control the choice of programs by students and the assignments of teachers. The teachers, bound into their teaching schedules, become relatively isolated from their colleagues and from the principal and supervisors. Many generally informal school procedures become formalized, and the school loses much of the spirit of spontaneity and congeniality which characterizes smaller units where the administrative officers, teachers, and pupils can come to know each other well.

With the advent of the staff utilization studies, described in part in the preceding section and including team teaching, there has been increasing dissatisfaction with the working arrangements provided in the typical school building.[24] This has led to renewed interest in various plans, such as the campus school and the house plan, for the decentralization of the large school. Smaller units have greater flexibility for the accommodation of instructional innovation and provide a more intimate environment for the close working relationships between teachers which the new staff utilization programs require. In addition, the programs require new kinds of space: larger rooms for large-group instruction; small conference rooms for discussion groups; small study spaces for individual projects; resource areas, such as language laboratories, centers for programed instruction, and the more common science laboratories for specialized

---

[24] For a popularized and more complete account of the work of the Commission on the Experimental Study of the Utilization of the Staff in the Secondary School, see J. Lloyd Trump and Dorsey Baynham, *Focus on Change: Guide to Better Schools*, Chicago, Rand McNally, 1961.

activities; working areas for the teachers; and decentralized libraries for readily accessible sources of information. The typical school building has many physical barriers to the introduction of the new programs, and the possibilities of suitable renovation are limited. In the construction of new buildings exciting new vistas are opened, and many architectural plans for new schools incorporate elements of the new utilization plans (see Chapter 7).[25]

Thus, team teaching can be seen as one of many efforts to create smaller working units of teachers and pupils within the larger school. Teams may well be both a way of achieving close working relationships among a relatively small number of teachers associated with a manageable number of students and a way of achieving a continuity of relationships between teachers and students which is difficult in larger units. Teaching teams also frequently require the same types of working spaces and facilities as other staff utilization projects and may be of sufficient size to justify the economical assignment of such spaces and facilities for the exclusive use of the team.

Fundamental Revisions of the Curriculum Under New Auspices

A third major trend in American education in the past decade has been the major revision of the curriculum in several areas of study. A major example is the work, started in 1956, of the Physical Science Study Committee in the revision of the secondary school physics course. Other significant groups have been at work in mathematics; chemistry; biology; and, more recently in English.[26]

The various curriculum revision groups, following the lead of the Physical Science Study Committee, have certain characteristics in common. The major initiative has come from university scholars in the academic disciplines, and the main centers of activity have been established in the universities or in affiliated institutions. Most of the projects have been careful to include teachers from the public and private schools and from the schools of education in the working

[25] *New Schools for New Education,* New York, Educational Facilities Laboratories, 1961.
[26] *The School Review,* vol. LXX, Spring, 1962, contains a series of articles describing the developments in mathematics and the sciences.

parties, but the basic leadership has not come from these sources as has most often been the case in the past. The objectives of the projects have been national in scope; that is, the new courses of study are intended for wide use throughout the country at particular grade levels. Furthermore, attempts are made to develop a complete "packaged" course, with textbooks, teachers' guides, supplementary reading materials, sequential films, laboratory equipment, and other materials. Most of the curriculum efforts have been in the sciences and in mathematics and have been directed initially toward academically talented students. Very quickly, however, the attention of the projects has turned to all intelligence and grade levels, even to the early elementary grades, and it appears that major new efforts are to be directed toward nonscientific fields.

In the past, curricula have usually been developed either for particular school systems, and therefore have been too specific for broad application to other systems, or for the textbook publishers, and therefore have been too general to be of optimum value in any specific situation. The current projects have been conducted on a scale hitherto unknown in American education. They involve dozens of scholars and teachers in long-term working groups, numerous trials of the materials in the schools, and revisions based upon these experiences. In most cases the next step is the systematic retraining of the teachers in summer and year-long institutes established specially for this purpose. The size of the expenditure for the purpose of curriculum revision is also larger than has hitherto been made in American education, the bulk of the funding coming from federal sources, principally the National Science Foundation. The College Entrance Examination Board, an organization with nation-wide interests in education, has also sponsored three major curriculum revision efforts: the Advanced Placement Program, the Mathematics Commission, and the Commission on English.

A curious phenomenon of the times is the fact that the major curriculum efforts appear to be almost totally dissociated from the staff utilization projects, though the two have developed simultaneously and often in the same schools. For example, many of the outstanding school systems associated with the Staff Utilization Studies of the National Association of Secondary-School Principals are also participants as cooperating schools in the Advanced Placement Program and in one or another of the major efforts in mathematics and science. Yet seldom in the various reports of the Commission or in individual project reports on team teaching is there any mention of a combination of the two types of projects! This situation probably reflects the enormous amount of energy which is required of the teachers in either type of project. The teacher who undertakes to introduce one of the new courses must study at one of the institutes and then must return home to introduce the course usually on an individual basis. Teachers involved in the staff utilization studies, on the other hand, become deeply involved in establishing effective working relationships with their colleagues. However, the dissociation of the two types of developments probably reflects a more fundamental difference. The staff utilization studies, including team teaching, have most frequently been primarily concerned with administrative reorganization and the adaptation of the existing curriculum to the new organization. The curriculum projects have been primarily concerned with the introduction of a new curriculum and the retraining of teachers within existing organizational patterns.

It seems clear that the staff utilization projects, and paricularly team teaching, have suffered from their initial preoccupation with staff organization; in most cases the specialist teachers and team teachers have been surprised to find the existing curriculum inadequate and have had to undertake major revisions of the curriculum with totally inadequate resources. The major project still remains to be formulated which undertakes to organize part of the staff of a school, perhaps into a teaching team, for the purpose of teaching a new and fully developed course of study which has been differentiated in terms of the teaching skills and the types of instructional groupings which are required. As many team teaching projects have already realized, this seems to be the next and most urgent step to be taken in the further development of team teaching (see Chapter 5). Perhaps this will occur as curriculum revision moves from mathematics and the sciences to English, the social studies, and the elementary subjects where team teaching and other utilization studies have a firmer foothold.

New Groupings of Students for Instruction

One of the persistent problems of American education since the advent of the graded school in the early nineteenth century had been its inherent structural rigidity. The trend has been toward an age-graded school with promotion based upon social and physical growth characteristics rather than upon the passing of specific academic standards. From the very beginning of this system, educators have recognized its disadvantages, particularly for talented children who may be held back in their academic progress by such rigid organization. Thus, each generation has seen the emergence of a variety of new administrative and instructional plans designed to bring flexibility into school organization, to allow for a greater variety of groupings of students for instruction, and to provide opportunities for individualized instruction. The period 1900–1920 was a particularly active one with the appearance of such notable plans as the Pueblo Plan, the Platoon School, the Winnetka Plan, and the Dalton Plan.[27] The 1930s witnessed widespread attempts to develop more satisfactory grouping practices and open conflict between those educators who favored homogeneous groupings and those who favored heterogeneous groupings. The verdict in that decade appeared to go to heterogeneous grouping, though the research evidence favored neither side in any conclusive way. In spite of the strong trend toward heterogeneous grouping,[28] ability grouping did persist strongly in many schools, particularly at the secondary school level with college preparatory students.

The past decade has been one of major turmoil in grouping practices. At both the elementary and secondary levels there has been a major movement toward the provision of both special programs for

[27] For a detailed description of the various plans, see Henry J. Otto, *Elementary School Organization and Administration*, 3rd ed., New York, Appleton-Century-Crofts, 1954.

[28] For a summary of grouping practices in the 1930s, see *The Grouping of Pupils*, Thirty-fifth Yearbook of the National Society for the Study of Education, Part I, Bloomington, Ill., Public School, 1936. For an evaluation of research on grouping practices, see J. Wayne Wrightstone, "Class Organization for Instruction," *What Research Says to the Teacher*, No. 13, Washington, D.C., Department of Classroom Teachers, American Educational Research Association of the NEA, May, 1957.

academically talented students, those frequently called "the gifted," and systems of ability groupings.[29] This movement has been motivated by a widespread feeling that the progress of the most able children has often been sacrificed to the interests of average and below average children. At the elementary level extremely talented children are often separated completely from the regular grade organization for all or at least a major part of their instruction. At the secondary level such separation has been formalized into the Advanced Placement Program with its own special curricula for highly talented students.[30] It is fair to say that the public interest and demand for this type of program has been so great that no school superintendent can afford to be without some method of providing for differences in ability in his school system.[31] The result, of course, has been a proliferation and diversification of programs which defies tabulation and description. Shane, for example, has identified 32 different plans for grouping at the elementary school level.[32]

Most of the new grouping programs attempt to fit into existing patterns of school organization, or, if they vary sharply from these patterns, they become additive organizations and leave the basic school organization for the majority of students unchanged. Though fewer in number and less widespread in immediate impact, a number of programs have developed which attempt to provide new grouping procedures associated with a substantial reorganization of the school, notably the Dual Progress Plan, the nongraded primary school, and many of the team teaching plans and proposals.[33] The distinguishing characteristics of these programs, in contrast to the majority of grouping plans, are a concern for regrouping all children, a reor-

[29] For a recent survey, see Elizabeth Paschal, *Encouraging the Excellent: Special Programs for the Gifted and Talented Students,* New York, The Fund for the Advancement of Education, 1960.

[30] *Advanced Placement Program,* Princeton, N.J., College Entrance Examination Board, 1957.

[31] Conant, *op. cit.*

[32] Harold G. Shane, "Grouping in the Elementary School," *Phi Delta Kappan,* vol. XLI, April, 1960, pp. 313–319.

[33] For a recent comprehensive analysis of grouping practices and school organization, see Robert H. Anderson, "Organizing Groups for Instruction," in Nelson B. Henry, ed., *Individualizing Instruction,* The Sixty-first Yearbook of the National Society for the Study of Education, I, Chicago, University of Chicago Press, 1962, pp. 239–264.

ganization of the basic structure of the school to accomplish this purpose, and a new pattern of staff utilization as a part of the structural change. With the recent emergence of a strong interest in programed instruction, more emphasis is placed upon the individualization of instruction and the invention of organizational patterns which will make this possible.

A notable characteristic of the schools' response to the demand for flexibility of grouping practices has been the enormous increase of voluntary cooperative activity among teachers who are attempting to attain some of the same grouping objectives without the benefit of formal organization.[34] Frequently, in order to avoid duplication of instruction, teachers will combine subgroupings of pupils at a given performance level to form one group of reasonable size which may be taught by one of the teachers. Another pattern is for adjacent teachers to develop specialties. For example, one teacher may teach all of the arithmetic for two classes, while the other might handle social studies. There are many other similar practices, all of which require close cooperation among teachers, careful planning and scheduling, the informal exercise of leadership by one of the teachers, and in most cases an analysis of the strengths and weaknesses of the cooperating teachers which leads to functional specialization. Clearly, one of the primary factors underlying the strong interest in team teaching is the widespread growth of voluntary cooperation activity in the schools.

Of the systematic grouping plans developing in this decade, the Dual Progress Plan stands out as one of the most comprehensive and most carefully designed. The plan was developed by George D. Stoddard and his staff at New York University in cooperation with the Long Beach and Ossining, New York, school systems.[35] In this plan distinction is made between subjects designated as "the cultural imperatives" (English, social studies, health and physical education) and "the cultural electives" (mathematics, science, art, music, and foreign languages). The school day is divided into two halves, one half devoted to the cultural imperatives under a single teacher and the other half devoted to the cultural electives under a

[34] *Ibid.*

[35] George D. Stoddard, *The Dual Progress Plan*, New York, Harper & Row, 1961.

number of specialist teachers. The cultural imperatives are offered in grade units, with sectioning according to ability at each grade level. The cultural electives are nongraded and are organized in systematic subject sequences into which the individual student is placed in accordance with his interests, ability, and performance. The teachers of the cultural imperatives, while specialists in English and social studies, serve the general function of homeroom teachers at a particular grade level and are responsible for registration and counseling. The teachers of the cultural electives are subject specialists who offer their subjects on a longitudinal basis throughout the grades. Scheduling is handled by a platoon system; each homeroom teacher has two groups, each for half a day. The specialists receive half of the children in the school in the morning and the other half in the afternoon, and they work together as a team to develop a schedule for each pupil in accordance with his interests and abilities. This brief description gives only a rough outline of the structural elements of the Dual Progress Plan and does not do justice to the elaborate rationale for the plan which is based on a cultural analysis and on learning theory. The Dual Progress Plan has close kinship with many team teaching plans because of the mutual concern for specialization in teaching, ability grouping, and sequential, nongraded progress in certain subjects, but the Dual Progress Plan has not as yet concentrated upon the team possibilities. Stoddard does mention that the specialists work together as a team and that team arrangements between homeroom teachers may modify the graded nature of their assignments, but the specific details of the structure and operation are not given. Because the Dual Progress Plan is a synthesis of many important features of earlier programs directed toward the same types of problems, it has much merit as a model for team teaching projects with similar objectives.

The platoon school, also known as the work-study-play school or the Gary Plan, was developed by Wirt in 1900.[36] The plan gained widespread acceptance between the two World Wars and still exists in various modified forms in many city school systems. In this

[36] For a description and evaluation of the platoon school, the Pueblo Plan, the Winnetka Plan, and the Dalton Plan, see Otto, *op. cit.*, pp. 137–147. Also see J. R. McGaughy, *An Evaluation of the Elementary School*, New York, Bobbs-Merrill, 1937, pp. 225–240.

organization plan, the school program was divided into two halves or platoons, with one half devoted to academic subjects and the other half to those activities such as manual arts, physical education, art, and music which require special facilities or laboratories. The purposes of the program were twofold: to break down the traditional academic emphasis of the elementary school by making a place for work and play-related activities, and to provide for economical use of school facilities. The academic subjects were taught in the homeroom, and the other subjects were taught by specialists, often on a highly departmentalized basis. The grade level structure was preserved with the exception of auditorium and gymnasium periods, and with a few exceptions there was little emphasis upon continuous sequential learning. Though its educational emphasis is very different, the Dual Progress Plan has adopted the platoon system, and modified forms of it are common within team teaching plans as ways of handling scheduling problems.

Other early grouping plans were more concerned with the problems of continuous sequential learning and the adaptation of instruction to the abilities of individual pupils. In the Pueblo Plan, instituted in 1898, the school was organized on a multiple-track basis. Standards were established for each grade, and tracks were developed which required different rates of progress depending upon the abilities of the pupil. Able pupils proceeded through the grades in a shorter time, while slow pupils spent a more extended time at each grade level.

The Winnetka Plan and the Dalton Plan were both developed around 1920. Though differing in their philosophical outlooks, both emphasized individual rates of progress through the successive stages of the curriculum. In the Winnetka Plan the curriculum was divided into two parts, "the common essentials" (the knowledge and skills needed by everyone, including most of the basic subjects), and "the group and creative activities" (literature, music, art, manual arts, physical education, and projects in many subjects). In the common essentials program the pupils worked on individual assignments at their own rate and passed tests to measure whether or not their achievement met the standards established for the successive units of work. A pupil would move on to the next unit when he passed the standard. In the remainder of the program, the emphasis was placed on self-expression and on the development of the special interests and abilities of each individual pupil without the requirement that specific standards be met. Homeroom placement was on the basis of age and social maturity, but easy transfer was possible because progress was individual rather than by grade placement. The plan depended heavily upon the preparation of detailed, sequential curriculum materials and very little upon organized group instruction.

Similarly, the Dalton Plan placed emphasis upon individual effort and progress, but it also placed great emphasis upon group life. Again there was a two-fold division of the curriculum: one part considered academic subjects in which there was individual progress in a sequential curriculum, the other part consisting of those elements of the curriculum more appropriately taught by class or group methods. In contrast to the Winnetka Plan with its homeroom teachers, the Dalton Plan provided for specialized teachers and facilities, and it mingled age groups on a nongraded basis. The pupils had great freedom of choice of the units of work they undertook.

The broad similarities between the Winnetka and the Dalton Plans, on the one hand, and the more recent Dual Progress Plan, on the other hand, are apparent from the above description. All three plans have a dual separation of the curriculum, though there are philosophical differences among the three approaches. The organization of instruction in the cultural elective subjects of the Dual Progress Plan resembles the individual progress systems of the Winnetka and Dalton Plans, though different subjects are chosen for the treatment. The Dalton Plan and the Dual Progress Plan share the idea of specializing teachers and facilities and of teaching nongraded groups. Many of these features are found incorporated in a number of team teaching projects, but they have not received the formal expression and organization found in the Dual Progress Plan.

The most widespread current organizational plan for continuous, sequential progress in the school curriculum is the nongraded elementary school.[37] This plan is also the most direct forerunner of team teaching of all the plans mentioned so far. A nongraded plan has been in effect in Milwaukee since 1942, but the movement has be-

[37] John I. Goodlad and Robert H. Anderson, *The Nongraded Elementary School*, New York, Harcourt, Brace & World, 1959.

come especially vigorous in the last few years. Though some programs emphasize the importance of an established sequential curriculum, while others emphasize a curriculum more closely geared to the individual interests, needs, and abilities of the pupils, all programs agree that continuous pupil progress is essential in a nongraded school. The nongraded school plan tries to eliminate the structural rigidity of the present graded school, to make better provision for the wide range of individual differences in intellectual, physical, and social development which occur within any age group, and to develop systems of continuous pupil progress at varying rates of speed. The close relationship between the nongraded elementary school movement and the team teaching movement has been furthered by the active participation of a number of educators in both fields, notably John I. Goodlad and Robert H. Anderson. For example, at the Englewood School in Florida, where both Goodlad and Anderson have served as consultants, there has been an active program of team teaching within the context of a nongraded elementary school.[38]

Before turning away from this discussion of grouping practices, we should examine one further early plan, the Cooperative Group Plan developed by James F. Hosic in the early 1930s, which appears to have had a close affinity with present team teaching activities but which quickly disappeared from the educational scene and left no known descendants. Hosic outlines eleven basic propositions, to be taken in their entirety and not piecemeal, as the basis for his Cooperative Group Plan.[39] Its primary purpose was to provide for individual differences, not only of pupils, but also of teachers, principals, and communities. Each teacher was responsible for only a part of the education and guidance of individual pupils and groups of pupils, and each teacher was a specialist in a group of subjects or activities, with a classroom designed for the specialty. Teachers who were responsible for the same pupils worked together as a group. One of the teachers was designated as group leader or chairman and was given supervisory responsibility. Each teacher was expected to

[38] John M. Bahner, "Team Teaching at Englewood School," Englewood, Fla., Englewood Elementary School, October, 1960.

[39] J. F. Hosic, *The Cooperative Group Plan: Working Principles for the Organization of Elementary Schools*, New York: Teachers College, Columbia University, 1929, as cited by Otto, *op. cit.*

relate his work and the work of his pupils to the activities of the other teachers. The groups of teachers were ordinarily composed of three to six members, and each teacher, meeting with each group for more than an hour, was expected to teach not more than two hundred pupils in the course of a school day. Since the pupils in the group usually covered more than one grade, cross grade instruction and some degree of continuous pupil progress was possible. The children often remained with the same group of teachers for two or three years and thus benefited from continuity of instruction over a relatively long period of time. In effect, as far as scheduling was concerned, the plan was a multiple-platoon system. It was a new organizational pattern, not a plan for curriculum revision. If the Cooperative Group Plan were in existence today, it would be called team teaching; in fact, it would be considered an outstanding plan in terms of its carefully detailed planning and its clear objectives. Curiously, though the plan was adopted for a time in the New York City Schools, it appeared to have very little impact on the educational scene. The reasons for this are not clear because of a paucity of published literature, but it is clear that the plan came before its time. It was to be many years before the slow movement toward quality education would create a climate that would be favorable for such a plan.

Dramatic Advances in the Technology of Education

A fifth major development in American education in the past decade has been the explosive growth of educational technology, including educational television, improved audio-visual devices, tape teaching, and programed instruction. Each of these separate developments has required new adaptations in school organization, including the creation of specialized jobs, the adaptation and change of existing teaching roles and responsibilities, the creation of new cooperative working groups within teaching, and major curriculum revisions and innovations. The pace of the movement has accelerated in recent years, and vast sums of money have been directed toward these developments, particularly from the Ford Foundation, the Fund for the Advancement of Education, and the National Defense Education Act.

Ruark has identified two major trends in the way the new educational media affect instruction.[40] The first trend is toward mass instruction through the use of such devices as lectures, demonstrations, movies, and television. The second trend is toward individualized instruction through the use of such devices as the language laboratories and teaching machines.

The use of films and television to instruct large groups requires a careful analysis of the objectives and content of the curriculum, wise decisions regarding those elements most appropriate for presentation to large groups, and extensive knowledge of the characteristics of the potential audience. These requirements demand the cooperation of a number of subject specialists. The actual production of the film or telecast involves elaborate studio facilities, electronic technicians, production specialists, and teachers with special abilities for film and television presentations cooperating together as a working group. Additional effort is required to bring the classroom teachers into effective working cooperation with the production team and to change school organization and scheduling to arrange for the proper student audiences at the proper times.

Many films have been developed by the major curriculum revision projects. The curriculum is produced outside of the school by working groups of specialists and is presented to the school as a package. The introduction of the new program to the schools is facilitated by training programs for teachers. Thus, the whole process has been dissociated from the team teaching movement in the schools. However, the development of closed-circuit television within the schools presents an entirely different picture. Here we have the development of new working groups of teachers and technicians, and these working groups are frequently identified directly with team teaching. For example, in Evanston Township High School, Evanston, Illinois, the closed-circuit television courses in English-speech and typewriting were developed by a working team composed of an experienced teacher, a television engineer, several cadet teachers, and a clerical aide.[41] The use of closed-circuit television was seen as stimulating

[40] Henry C. Ruark, Jr., "Technology and Education," *Phi Delta Kappan*, vol. XLII, June, 1961, p. 387.

[41] William G. Carpenter, Jean E. Fair, James E. Heald, and Wanda B. Mitchell, "Closed-Circuit Television is Used at Evanston Township High School," *NASSP Bulletin*, vol. LXII, January, 1958, pp. 19–54.

the development of teaching teams. In Dade County, Florida, the arrangement is somewhat different.[42] In 1958–1959 there were 12 specialist television teachers offering a wide variety of courses. The teachers occupied special studio facilities and were associated with specialists in art and television production. Several teams were formed among the studio teachers, one of which was composed of a history teacher, a science teacher, and an aide, working on a course combining these subjects. Opportunities were created for the studio teachers to work with the associated classroom teachers and to visit classrooms, and elaborate guides were prepared to assist the classroom teachers in the interpretation and follow-up of the television programs. Perhaps the most extensive closed-circuit school television program is that in Hagerstown, Washington County, Maryland.[43] The type of programing involved requires the formation of many working groups of teachers, aides, and technicians. The possible advantages of a team approach in television teaching, as now practiced widely throughout the country, are summarized in a report by the Ford Foundation as follows:

In addition, experience to date has shown that the "team" approach to teaching, particularly at the elementary and secondary levels, opens up exciting new possibilities for capitalizing on the varying teaching skills in any given school system. Televised courses have been much more carefully planned and organized than conventional courses, and the combinations of the skills of the studio teacher and of the classroom teacher has made possible a cooperative teaching effort far better than either teacher could achieve alone. At the elementary and secondary levels, for example, the usual practice has been for the studio teacher to "meet" only one class a day, generally for twenty or thirty minutes. The teacher then has the rest of the day to prepare tomorrow's lesson. This opportunity to plan carefully, combined with the unique possibilities that television affords in the presentation of visual materials that reinforce learning, has stimulated the studio teachers to do a much better job of teaching than they had done in their conventional classes. In the meantime, the classroom teachers, relieved of the burden of planning and presenting the

[42] "Educational Television Experiment, 1958–59," Miami, Fla., Dade County Public Schools.
[43] "Washington County Closed-Circuit Educational Television Project: Progress Report," Hagerstown, Md., Board of Education, March, 1959, pp. 44–45. See also Arthur D. Morse, *Schools of Tomorrow—Today*, Albany, University of the State of New York, The State Education Department, 1960, pp. 81–99.

principal material in several different subjects during the course of a day, are free to concentrate on other important aspects of teaching—such as eliciting student participation, answering questions, leading discussions, reinforcing when necessary the main concepts presented in the telecast, providing individual help where needed, and stimulating the students to do something with what they have learned. Studio teachers and classroom teachers who have mastered the techniques of the "team" approach say they greatly prefer it to the conventional method of teaching.[44]

Team teaching projects have made extensive use of various types of projectors, with associated slides, films, and teacher-produced materials, as well as tapes, records, and other devices for instruction in groups of all sizes. In fact, one of the most valuable contributions of team teaching may be the more effective and economical use of these technical aids to teaching. For example, the Norwalk Plan reports significant increases in the use of overhead projectors, tape recorders, controlled readers, and open-circuit educational television; and heavy use has been made by the team teachers of the resources of the system's curriculum-material center.[45] The Wisconsin School Improvement Program reports that instructional team arrangements have "consistently stimulated a more premeditated and widespread use of equipment. . . ."[46] Similar results have occurred in the Franklin School Project in Lexington, Massachusetts.

The association of team teaching with individualized instruction by means of technical devices such as programed instruction is not a particularly strong or direct one. Programing, both of texts and materials for teaching machines, requires the combined efforts of several types of specialists. Porter, for example, in discussing the uses of instructional devices in foreign language teaching, points out that three types of personnel are required to prepare the special types of materials needed: content specialists; psychologists with a knowledge of instructional materials; and technical personnel, including native-language speakers, to prepare the actual materials.[47] Thus,

[44] *Teaching by Television*, New York, The Fund for the Advancement of Education, May, 1959, p. 11.

[45] Bryce Perkins, *et al.*, "Teamwork Produces Audio-Visual Techniques," *Grade Teacher*, vol. LXXVII, June, 1960, pp. 55–72.

[46] *The Wisconsin Improvement Program Reporter*, vol. II, April, 1961, p. 3.

[47] Douglas Porter, "A Report on Instructional Devices in Foreign Language Teaching," in A. A. Lumsdaine and Robert Glaser, eds., *Teaching Machines and Programmed Learning: A Source Book*, Washington, D.C., NEA, 1960, p. 188.

the further development of programs for use in the schools depends upon the recruitment and training of substantial numbers of content specialists and learning psychologists.[48]

The present trend is for the programed materials to be developed mainly outside of the schools by working groups similar to the curriculum study groups. In a few cases, as at the Franklin School, short-term experimental trials or pretests of programs have been conducted within team teaching. It would appear likely that programed instruction may demand its own forms of school organization with newly defined roles and relationships for teachers and special resource centers for the use of the programs. Ruark, looking into the future, has the following vision: "The teacher will no longer be principally a communicator, presenting facts, constructing concepts, and guiding skill development; increasingly, the teacher will work with individual students on a tutorial basis, directing their learning and using machines for much presentation and routine exposition, pointing out further resources, and encouraging the student to accept increasingly higher levels of responsibility for his own educational growth."[49] Before such conditions exist tremendous efforts will have to be made to produce programs that are technically adequate and educationally appropriate.

Conclusion

In this chapter an attempt has been made to provide a brief review of the major changes that have taken place in American education during the past decade and to indicate the place of team teaching within this context. In a few cases brief descriptions have been given of programs with similar objectives which appeared in earlier historical periods. Viewed in this way, the diversity of aims and organizations which appear under the title of team teaching no longer seems so puzzling. In an explosive era of American education, team teaching has been merely one element in a broad pattern of innovations and changes, all aimed at improving the quality of instruction.

[48] For a series of articles on the role of psychology in new audio-visual media, see "Learning Theory and AV Utilization," *A. V. Communication Review*, Supplement no. 4, vol. IX, September-October, 1961.

[49] Ruark, *op. cit.*, p. 390.

In this pattern, certain major directions are clear: a search for ways to create for teachers attractive new positions with greater status, rewards, and responsibility; a search for ways to improve the utilization of the present teaching staff and facilities; a search for ways to revise the school curriculum in almost all areas; a search for ways to create smaller human organizations within the large-size structures which have become characteristic of our schools; a search for ways to change existing school organization to provide for more efficient instruction in certain areas and for continuous pupil progress in others; and a search for ways to apply technological innnovations in instruction in the schools. As has always been the case in American education, but with particular intensity in this historical period, there has been a multiplication and diversification of efforts. In reality the elements identified overlap at many points and often are merely facets of the same larger problem. So it is with the innumerable projects; one project may take a discrete course, emphasizing a single element, while others of the same type may select another element, and still others may choose a combination of elements. A large number of unique projects are possible because of the large number of possible combinations. Team teaching projects have tended to make a selection among procedural goals rather than curricular goals. They have been concerned with the relationships among the members of a working group and with the definition of new roles and types of specialization, and they have assumed that this will lead to greater efficiency in carrying out already existing instructional goals. Other projects which are more curriculum oriented have tended to work with individuals and have ignored the possibilities inherent in group organization. It would seem that both types of projects could well afford to learn from each other.

Will team teaching in its various forms follow the fate of past projects which have challenged the traditional organization of the American schools and the teaching profession? Our analysis suggests that the times are different, that the impetus and technology for change along with broad societal participation of both laymen and specialists in other fields has sufficient force and support to bring about lasting innovation. Of itself, as a way of merely organizing teachers to work together, team teaching would perhaps be doomed. But, linked as it is with other major directions of change, team teaching may make a sustained and permanent contribution to the improvement of education. This will occur, however, only if the aims and goals of team teaching are clarified. In the next chapter, we will attempt to provide some clarification by presenting an approach to a theoretical rationale for team teaching that is based upon administrative theory and upon sociological and psychological theory of small working groups, both of which have been largely ignored during the initial development of team teaching.

Chapter 3

Toward a Theoretical Rationale
for Team Teaching

JUDSON T. SHAPLIN

Graduate Institute of Education, Washington University

In Chapter 1 team teaching was defined as a type of instructional organization, involving teaching personnel and the students assigned to them, in which two or more teachers are given responsibility, working together, for all or a significant part of the instruction of the same group of students. This definition is essentially a descriptive one, based upon similarities which exist among the majority of projects called team teaching. The description is concerned primarily with the common organizational aspects of team teaching and not with the goals of such organizations. Furthermore, the discussion of team teaching and the review of the movement dealt with the claims of team teaching and did not provide a systematic, theoretical analysis of team teaching, nor did it include a basic justification for group organization. To develop a theoretical rationale for team teaching, it is necessary to examine the nature of the groups involved and the goals for which the groups have been organized. And it is also necessary to inquire whether this type of organization is more effective or more efficient in the achievement of these goals than existing forms of organization or other possible forms.[1] Is team teaching just another move toward the bureaucrati-

---

[1] The author is greatly indebted to his colleague, Wade M. Robinson. Much of the content of this chapter is drawn from an earlier, unpublished, paper, Judson T. Shaplin and Wade M. Robinson, "Toward a Definition of Team Teaching," January, 1960.

zation of American life, thought by many to be a threat to our democratic ideals? Is team teaching just another move in the vast trend toward group action, group decision, and the diminution of individual initiative, described so vividly by Whyte and Riesman?[2] Are the reasons advanced in support of team teaching sufficiently compelling to justify major changes in schools which have long resisted the bureaucratic organization of the teaching force?

We have seen in Chapter 2 that team teaching is not a radical educational innovation but rather a concatenation of a number of long-standing trends toward improved quality in education. Likewise, when viewed from the broader perspective of the organization of large enterprises such as industry, business, and government, team teaching certainly does not appear to be a radical organizational innovation. Basically, teams in teaching are small working groups, organized on a formal basis for the accomplishment of certain goals. Therefore, in at least one sense, we do not need to create a new and special theory of team teaching, for as a first step we can turn to both existing sociological and psychological theories concerning small-group action and to administrative theories. There are many incomplete and conflicting theories in these fields, and this presentation will at best be an incomplete eclectic borrowing of selected elements. Nevertheless, this represents an important forward step in thinking about team teaching. With a few minor exceptions, there has been little attempt in the literature to relate team teaching to relevant theories in other fields.[3] In most cases those responsible for team teaching organization have been practicing superintendents, principals, and teachers who have not been trained in the recent theories of psychology, sociology, or administration. When university personnel have been involved, they have been drawn mainly from the teacher training staffs where there is strong interest in the curriculum and the role of the teacher but relatively little interest in or experience with organizational theory.

---

[2] William H. Whyte, Jr., *The Organization Man,* Garden City, N.Y., Doubleday, 1957. David Riesman, Nathan Glazer, and Renee Denney, *The Lonely Crowd,* Garden City, N.Y., Doubleday, 1953.
[3] One exception is Robert E. Ohm, "Toward a Rationale for Team Teaching," *Administrator's Notebook,* vol. IX, March, 1961.

In only a few isolated cases have professional psychologists, sociologists, or administrative theorists been directly involved in projects.

The Meaning of "Team"

The literature on team teaching does not give any rationale for the choice of the word *team*. Each individual is free, therefore, to choose any connotation of the word and evoke any image of "team" which is salient for him. A common image, that of a team of horses pulling together, often omits the fact that such a team is in harness and is being guided and directed. Another common image evoked by the word is that of a baseball or football team where individual star performers have specialized assignments and, with varying degrees of direction from the bench, cooperate together to win a competition. Thus the image evokes a sense of both cooperation and external control. Also evoked is a strong sense of in-group cohesiveness and loyalty. Since no rationale for the use of the term is offered by the originators, we might assume that the choice was made with just such a popular image in mind in order to help provide a popular incentive for the enterprise and to encourage an initial *esprit de corps* within the new groups.

Let us examine the ways in which the term *team* has been used in the psychological and sociological literature and within other professional groups to see if a similar image prevails.

Dubin distinguishes three types of organized groups on the basis of the degree of initiative left to the members of the group in executing their tasks: (1) team group, (2) task group, and (3) technological group.[4] In the team group the team members may take the initiative in designating the positions to be filled and the people to fill them, and within such a group there may be interchange and rotation of jobs as a consequence of the decision of the members. Management controls the assignment of the task, the tools, and the number of men to accomplish the task but leaves it up to the members of the group to determine how best to accomplish their work. In the task group the jobs are clearly defined, and each individual

[4] Robert Dubin, *The World of Work*, Englewood Cliffs, N.J., Prentice-Hall, 1958, pp. 104–105.

is assigned to one and only one job within the group. However, the individual may often choose his own method of executing his task, and the general pace of work may often be determined by the group as a whole. In the technological group, best exemplified by the assembly line, the job pace and the method of executing the task are both clearly specified and controlled by management, and very little is left to individual choice or group decision. The technological group becomes a kind of human machine.

Many teaching teams would fall within Dubin's team group classification. However, where there is an attempt at task differentiation or specialization, particularly in the designation of nonprofessional assistants, the teaching team falls within the task group classification, though it still retains elements of the team group. Rarely in team teaching do we find anything approaching the technological group.

Goffman presents a more general case of the team. Within a general dramaturgical framework he speaks of "performance teams" or "teams" to refer to "any set of individuals who cooperate in staging a routine."[5] In his definitional system a "performance" is defined as "all the activity of a given participant on a given occasion which serves to influence in any way any of the other participants; a routine is the pre-established pattern of action which is unfolded during a performance and which may be presented or played through on other occasions. . . ."[6] Some of the important qualities that Goffman sees in a team performance are cooperation, cohesion, mutual dependence, and familiarity. The concept of team as he develops it has widespread application wherever two or more people interact to create some common impression upon others. Because his system was developed to handle the analysis of social encounters, it is extremely useful in thinking about team teaching in a relatively novel way. For Goffman the constraint of formal organization is not placed upon the concept of "team," as in the case with Dubin and with the definition of team teaching given above. Goffman's concept easily embraces the informal interchange patterns of teachers which we have excluded from team teaching.

---

[5] Erving Goffman, *The Presentation of Self in Everyday Life*, Garden City, N.Y., Doubleday, 1959, p. 79.
[6] *Ibid.*, pp. 15–16.

Klaus and Glaser attempt to distinguish the team from the small group:

Teams, on the one hand, are usually well organized, highly structured, and have relatively formal operating procedures—as exemplified by a baseball team, an aircraft crew, or a ship control team. Teams generally:

1. are relatively rigid in structure, organization, and communication,
2. have well defined positions or member assignments so that the participation in a given task by each individual can be anticipated to a given extent,
3. depend on the cooperative or coordinated participation of several specialized individuals whose activities contain little overlap and who must each perform their task at least at some minimum level of proficiency,
4. are often involved with equipment or tasks requiring perceptual-motor activities,
5. can be given specific guidance on job performance based on a task-analysis of the team's equipment, mission, or situation.

Small groups, on the other hand, are rarely so formal or have as well-defined specialized tasks—as exemplified by a jury, a board of trustees, or a personnel evaluation board. As contrasted with a team, small groups generally:

1. have an indefinite or loose structure, organization, and communication network,
2. have assumed rather than designated positions or assignments so that each individual's contribution to the accomplishment of the task is largely dependent on his own personal characteristics,
3. depend mainly on the quality of independent, individual contributions and can frequently function well even when one or several members are not contributing at all,
4. are often involved with complex decision making activities,
5. cannot be given much specific guidance beforehand since the quality and quantity of participation by individual members is not known.[7]

Klaus and Glaser and their colleagues at the Team Training Laboratory of the American Institute for Research have established a dichotomy between the team and all other small groups in order to limit strictly the concept of a team to a highly structured, goal-oriented small group, an ideal type which approaches the concept

[7] David J. Klaus and Robert Glaser, *Increasing Team Proficiency Through Training: A Program of Research*, Pittsburgh, Pa., American Institute for Research, 1960, pp. 2–3.

of a human machine. Their definition is very rigid because it represents an appropriation of the term for their own specific research purposes, the training of task-oriented groups. The strict definition of conditions and the specificity of tasks permits them to undertake more easily the manipulation of variables. Clearly, most small groups outside of the experimental laboratory would be classified somewhere between the two extreme types described above. This would be the case with teams in teaching. There are no teaching teams that would approach the Klaus and Glaser concept of the team principally because of the lack of specificity of tasks and the diffuse nature of the differentiation and analysis of tasks which has been made so far. The work of the Team Training Laboratory, however, is of greatest importance to the whole team teaching movement because of the group's precise thinking and their concentration upon goal-directed behavior so notably lacking in team teaching.

The team concept has frequently been used by other professional groups, notably the medical profession. Within medicine we have the diagnostic team, the clinical team, the surgical team, and others. The diagnostic team is a loose group of doctors, often specialists from several different fields of medicine, who pool their knowledge and opinions to diagnose the ailments of the patient and to propose a strategy of treatment. Such teams have characteristics of both Dubin's team group and his task group. Clinical teams in the mental health field are frequently composed of a psychiatrist, often serving as the leader; a clinical psychologist; and a psychiatric social worker. In the psychiatric treatment of a child, for example, the psychiatrist usually handles the therapeutic treatment, the clinical psychologist is responsible for diagnostic testing and often for the treatment of learning difficulties, while the social worker consults with the parents. There is some interchangeability of roles, for the clinical psychologist sometimes conducts the therapy with the patient. Coordination and planning is achieved through case conferences which are held by the team, often in the presence of the larger staff of the institution. Clearly such a team is closer to Dubin's task group than his team group. The surgical team, on the other hand, has the human machine quality of Dubin's technological group and of Klaus and Glaser's rigidly defined team. The tasks of the operation are extremely specific, and each member of the team has his specific task to perform. The leadership of the surgeon insures the perfect timing that is required.

The nursing profession has recently developed a plan for team nursing which corresponds in many ways with plans for team teaching.[8] As with team teaching, the nursing team has sprung up independently in many parts of the country and takes many forms. One of the main objectives, to try to achieve maximum performance with a minimum staff, reflects the personal shortages in the nursing field. "A concept of the team as here described is a concept of leadership, or organization, or partnership, of group response to goals, of integrated action, of inservice training, of supervision."[9] The teams are composed of a graduate nurse as leader and varying combinations of other personnel, including general staff nurses, private duty nurses, licensed practical nurses, and nursing aides. There are many direct parallels between the descriptions and aims of team teaching and those of team nursing. It is very likely that the original impetus for team teaching came from the medical profession rather than from industry or from previous efforts within teaching. Early statements about team teaching frequently used the medical analogy, and many school administrators, school board members, and citizens are much more familiar with the organization of hospitals than they are with the organization of industry.[10]

Though there are many small working groups within universities, they are generally referred to as staffs rather than teams. Instruction in large courses is often conducted by a staff which includes a professor, several instructors, teaching assistants or fellows, and readers. Laboratory instruction in the sciences similarly makes use of groups of personnel with different specialties and degrees of experience. Frequently the term *team* is applied to research groups within the universities and also within industry. Bush and Hattery discuss single and multidiscipline teams and note that "teamwork is one of

[8] Dorothy Perkins Newcomb, *The Team Plan: A Manual for Nursing Service Administrators*, New York, 1953. Eleanor C. Lambertsen, *Nursing Team Organization and Functioning*, New York, Teachers College, Columbia University, 1953.

[9] Newcomb, *op. cit.*, pp. vii–viii.

[10] For example, see Francis Keppel and Paul A. Perry, "School and University: Partners in Progress," *Phi Delta Kappan*, vol. XLII, January, 1961, p. 175.

the essential ingredients which can be improved through research, training, and improved communication—all of which will protect and aid an effective spirit of inquiry."[11] Teams are "the assignment of research problems to groups of scientific personnel, who may be supported by a contingent of aides and by expensive equipment and who are supervised and evaluated by an administrative structure above and alongside them."[12] They discuss problems of coordination, of the balance between freedom and control, and of maximizing the productive capacity of a limited supply of adequately trained professionals. And they note that one only need look at the large number of research reports that have joint authorship to see the marked trend for research to be done in teams.

This brief review of the meanings of the term *team* in the psychological and sociological literature and within professional groups reveals that there is no standard usage. Only a few examples have been given. Additional types of small groups called teams do appear occasionally in the literature on small groups. For example, there have been studies of two- or three-member working teams in factories, and experiments have been conducted with competition between two or more teams in the performance of an experimental task.[13] But the team concept does not have any consistent application in either the psychological or the sociological theory of small groups.

However, in the literature on small groups a distinction is made between the affective, expressive, or primary group and the working, task-oriented, instrumental, or secondary group. In the former type, there is an emphasis upon localism, friendship, kinship, and other personal factors. In the latter type, there is some form of organization, formal group goals, and stress upon the principles of universalism and achievement. Olmstead makes the distinction as follows:

> The former emphasis may be described in terms of the principles of *particularism* and *ascription*, the latter in terms of *universalism* and *achievement*. The first pair stress the primacy of the traditional bonds of

[11] George P. Bush and Lowell H. Hattery, "Teamwork and Creativity in Research," *Administrative Science Quarterly*, vol. 1, December, 1956, p. 372.

[12] *Ibid.*, pp. 362–363.

[13] Henry W. Riecken and George C. Homans, "Psychological Aspects of Social Structure," in Garner Lindzey, ed., *Handbook of Social Psychology*, vol. II, Reading, Mass., Addison-Wesley, 1954, chap. 22.

sentiment that grow up among persons sharing a common habitat or name; they stress the unifying factors which are "given" or *ascribed* without any act of volition on the part of the individual; the resulting bonds involve special or *particular* other persons. The principles of universalism and achievement embody the opposite and complementary emphases: on impersonal and abstract bases for evaluation and on the importance of *what* a person can do (achieve) rather than on *who* he is. A belief that a person deserves "fair" treatment regardless of his color, his creed, or who his friends are, is a belief in universalism and achievement. These sets of principles are by no means always as sharply opposed as the above definitions might suggest. They are, nevertheless, contrary tendencies which underlie much of the strain and controversy constantly besetting man's attempts at civilization.[14]

By looking at teaching teams as instrumental or secondary groups, we can begin to remove some of the magic and mystique that surrounds the team teaching movement and that has been promoted by the popular belief that teams are expressive or primary groups. We may also be able to show why no team teaching project is unique and why, on the other hand, it is foolish to search for one particular ideal type of team organization that can be applied in all situations. To do so, we must turn to theoretical, analytic, and experimental work in the study of small groups and their administration, and we must begin to isolate some of the basic variables of team action. Our attention must turn to problems of social structure, organization, communication systems, goal behavior, leadership, morale, etc. Identification and systematic treatment of these problems have been completely neglected by the team teaching movement. Though it will not be possible in this book to deal comprehensively with the application of small-group research to team teaching, we may be able to indicate a few fruitful directions for analysis.[15] A starting point will be to examine a model for the analysis of the team as a social system.

[14] Michael S. Olmstead, *The Small Group*, New York, Random House, 1959, p. 53.

[15] For collections of significant papers on small-group research and on small-group research as it applies to administration, see the following: Paul Hare, Edgar F. Borgatta, and Robert F. Bales, *Small Groups: Studies in Social Interaction*, New York, Knopf, 1955; Dorwin Cartwright and Alvin Zander, *Group Dynamics: Research and Theory*, White Plains, N.Y., Harper & Row, 1958; and Mason Haire, *Modern Organizational Theory*, New York, Wiley, 1959.

The Team as a Social System

Getzels and Thelen have developed a model for the analysis of the classroom as a social system.[16] A schematic diagram of the model is reproduced in Figure 1. Though the model was developed for the analysis of the classroom situation, it can be applied equally well to the analysis of a teaching team or to any other working group whether large or small. For our purposes we can apply it to the team of teachers only, to the students in the team, or to the combination of teachers and students in the total team. The model distinguishes between two major dimensions of a social system, the nomothetic and the idiographic.

The nomothetic dimension is concerned with normative behavior, that is with the establishment of norms for the rational definition and control of behavior in relation to desired goals. An institution is created for the accomplishment of certain goals; the institution is defined by the roles which are established within it, the roles are defined by the expectations which are held for the role incumbents, and the expectations are determined by the nature of the desired goal behavior. Because the nomothetic dimension emphasizes the rational organization of human behavior toward certain desired goals, it provides a model for bureaucratic organization.[17] In a bureaucracy an attempt is made to develop a well-defined division of labor so that specialized persons can be assigned to the particular positions and roles for which they are qualified and so that the individual can be held responsible for the performance of his part of the work. The concept of a hierarchy of authority is also included; each role incumbent is under the authority and supervision of a higher role incumbent. Rules and regulations are developed to govern the performance of the tasks and to develop standards. In

[16] J. W. Getzels and H. A. Thelen, "The Classroom as a Unique Social System," in N. B. Henry, ed., *The Dynamics of Instructional Groups*, The Fifty-ninth Yearbook of the National Society for the Study of Education, prt. II, Chicago, University of Chicago Press, 1960, pp. 53–82. See also J. W. Getzels, "Administration as a Social Process," in Andrew W. Halpin, ed., *Administrative Theory in Education*, Chicago, Midwest Administration Center, University of Chicago, 1958, pp. 150–165.

[17] For a discussion of the concept of bureaucracy, see Peter M. Blau, *Bureaucracy in Modern Society*, New York, Random House, 1956, pp. 28–33.

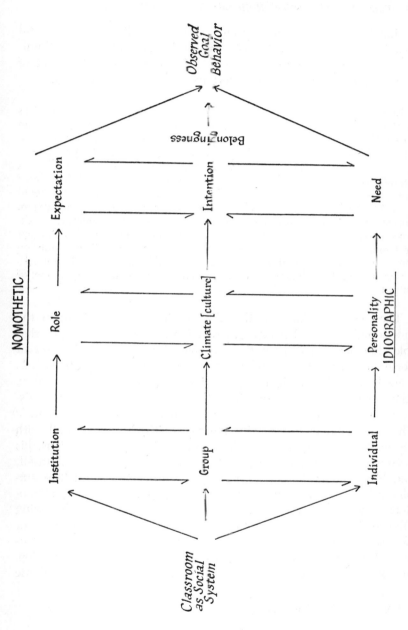

FIGURE 1. The Team as a Social System.

an ideal type of bureaucracy an impersonal attitude prevails, and individuals are assigned to tasks and evaluated on the basis of universal rather than personal criteria. Efficiency in the attainment of goals is the major criterion of performance. As Blau suggests:

> Bureaucracy, then, can be defined as organization that maximizes efficiency in administration, whatever its formal characteristics, or as an institutionalized method of organizing social conduct in the interest of administrative efficiency. On the basis of this definition, the problem of central concern is the expeditious removal of the obstacles to efficient operations which recurrently arise. This cannot be accomplished by a preconceived system of rigid procedures . . . but only by creating conditions favorable to continuous adjustive development in the organization. To establish such a pattern of self-adjustment in a bureaucracy, conditions must prevail that encourage its members to cope with emergent problems and to find the best method for producing specified results on their own initiative, and that obviate the need for unofficial practices which thwart the objectives of the organization, such as restriction of output.[18]

The major emphasis in the idiographic dimension is upon the individual's personal needs and reactions. This is a reminder that roles are performed by individuals who bring to the job a set of personal characteristics and needs which affect their performance. Getzels and Thelen define the individual in terms of personality, "the dynamic organization within the individual of those need dispositions that govern his *unique* reactions to the environment."[19] The individual identifies with the role, with the group, and with the goals of the organization in terms of his need dispositions, his personal aspirations and expectations, his needs to express himself, and his peculiar demands for rewards and satisfactions. The emphasis here is not upon rationality but upon the affective or emotional needs and demands of the individual. Earlier, following Olmstead, we made a distinction between the instrumental or secondary group and the affective or primary group. The instrumental group is principally defined by the nomothetic dimension, but because the Getzels and Thelen model presents the nomothetic

---

[18] *Ibid.*, pp. 60–61.
[19] Getzels and Thelen, *op. cit.*, p. 68.

dimension in relation to the idiographic dimension, it also illustrates the fact that the affective needs of the individual, though often at variance with the rational goals of the organization, remain important elements moving in the direction of primary group affiliation.

The model presents a third dimension, group culture, which illustrates the interaction between the institutional and the individual dimensions. This dimension represents the way in which the group establishes its own climate or culture in adjustment to the demands of the formal organization and cf the individuals which make up the group. Group intentions, rather than formal role expectations or the particular needs of the individuals, develop and define this climate. Individuals differ in the extent to which they share a sense of belongingness to the group and its intentions as it emerges as an organization.

The Getzels and Thelen model is a powerful one for the analysis of team teaching and provides a number of fruitful directions for study as well as a number of primary lessons which have been largely ignored in the team teaching movement:

1. The focus of the model is upon goal-directed behavior and suggests that a first step in the creation of any new organization is the careful delineation of the desired goals, for the establishment of formal roles and role expectations depends upon the nature of these goals. Conflicts often arise because roles established for the accomplishment of one goal may not be suitable for the accomplishment of other goals. Since the goals of teaching teams are often diffuse and comprehensive, as noted in Chapter 1, conflicts are extremely frequent. The subject of goals in team teaching will be given further treatment later in this chapter.

2. The model shows that the personalities and need dispositions of individuals have an important effect upon the way in which role expectations are met. The individual's needs may be in conflict with the role assigned to him. If he holds multiple roles within the team, these roles may be in conflict. In the presence of diffuse goals and ill-defined roles, the possibilities for conflict with personal needs is greatly increased. Chapter 9 provides a further analysis of the needs and satisfactions of teachers. Administrators of team teaching projects have had very few, if any, reliable criteria or measuring devices

for the selection of suitable team members for the various roles involved. Nor have they had techniques for handling the personality difficulties and the conflicts among individuals which have been revealed in the teams.

3. The group may take on a climate and intentions which are at variance with the formal objectives of the team. In fact, the initial organization of many teams has been based on the personalities of members assigned without reference to goals. Within the prevailing professional atmosphere of democratic cooperation, a dominating ideal among teachers, teams often become affectively oriented primary groups with the effective purpose of satisfying individual needs rather than formal goals.

4. The formal organization must be created with the needs of the individuals in mind. The role expectations must be reasonably congruent with the talents, values, and training of the individuals; and they must be clearly identified and defined so that they can be communicated to the individuals and so that the process of group identification with goals may occur. Following Getzels and Thelen, the ideal system is one in which each individual identifies with the goals of the system because they fulfill some of his own needs. Consequently, he believes that the expectations held for him are rational, and he feels that he belongs to a group with ideals and beliefs similar to his own.

5. The standard organization of the American educational system, where teachers are assigned to a single classroom and to one or more groups of pupils who come to that classroom, minimizes the formal relationships among teachers and likewise limits the opportunities for conflicts among teachers. Since the accent is upon pupil-teacher and pupil-pupil relationships, the common conflicts which arise in the school setting are pupil-teacher and pupil-pupil conflicts. Getzels' and Thelen's model suggests the types of conflicts which are likely to arise when teachers work together in groups. Team teaching must consider carefully whether or not the constructive or productive aspects of group organization outweigh the increase in problems arising from potential teacher-teacher conflicts against which the school is now protected by its general form of organization.

The Managerial Functions and Goals of Team Teaching

Parsons has made an analysis of formal organizations with respect to *managerial, technical,* and *community* functions, and the relationships among these functions, which is useful in developing a rationale for team teaching.[20] We will be concerned here primarily with some of the managerial and technical functions. The *technical functions* are the processes of teaching, including the development of the curriculum, the organization of instruction, the specific methods of teaching, and the assessment of the needs and progress of the students. The technical suborganization is oriented toward the materials and human skills which are required to accomplish the tasks. In contrast, when an organization reaches a certain level of complexity, *managerial functions* arise which are oriented toward the terms on which the product or service is offered and the provision of the resources necessary for the performance of the technical functions. In an educational system decisions of two main types have to be made. The first type, which Parsons labels the "disposal" function includes decisions concerning what educational services will be offered to what pupils at what age, what kinds of groupings of pupils will be made, and what the disposition of the teaching force will be with respect to pupil groups. The second type, called the "procurement" function, includes decisions concerning what resources in the form of personnel, classrooms, books, and materials will be provided. In a complex institution where significant division of labor exists, managerial decisions take precedence over many technical decisions. In an educational system, for example, the teacher's classroom and pupil assignment and his allotment of books and materials are all largely determined by management before the teacher even starts to provide his technical services. Such decisions, of course, involve technical knowledge, and there are many types of mechanisms for coordinating the managerial and technical systems so that the needs of technical personnel receive consideration in managerial decisions.

[20] Talcott Parsons, "Some Ingredients of a General Theory of Formal Organization," in Halpin, *op. cit.*, pp. 40–72.

In terms of the disposal function, team teaching projects represent an attempt to transfer certain managerial functions to the technical staff, particularly the grouping and scheduling of pupils and the assignment of teachers within that complex in accordance with their special interests and talents. In fact, this may be stated as one of the major goals of team teaching. In most cases this leads to a greater degree of division of labor and technical specialization within the teaching force as well as a different distribution of authority. These topics will be discussed in greater detail later in this chapter. At this point it is important to raise certain fundamental questions concerning the transfer of managerial responsibilities to the teaching staff.

This transfer assumes that certain members of the teaching force have both the managerial and technical skills to make decisions regarding the allocation of teachers and pupils to instructional tasks. It may be argued that a team can hardly fail to do a better job of allocation than the present rigid administration system with its extremely limited range of possible assignments for both teachers and pupils. The fact is, however, that even the smallest team leads to an increase in managerial complexity, new possibilities for difficulty and confusion, and a loss of the security found in ordinary arrangements, however inadequate. The early history of many team teaching projects suggests that although many teachers may excel in the performance of regular classroom duties, relatively few have well developed managerial skills. They simply have no experience with or training in the problems involved. Further, most teachers lack connection with expert colleagues and peers outside their system who might serve as professional reference groups. Parsons, in analyzing the managerial and technical functions of the professional, stresses the importance of such reference groups. It may also be said that few principals and supervisors possess managerial skills in sufficient degree to give effective assistance to teams in the process of formation. New teams go through a long process involving the identification of new problems, both managerial and technical, and the solution of these problems by trial and error. The claim, therefore, that team teaching will bring immediate increases in efficiency in the allocation of teachers and pupils to their tasks is false. Team teaching, however, does represent a new constructive force in the identification of problems and the search for solutions. Many teams have reported that one of the main advantages of team teaching is the professional growth that it stimulates among team members. As a result, Ohm suggests that the instructional team may well have few peers as a form of in-service training.[21] Experience so far suggests that the in-service training and problem-solving functions of team teaching should receive more emphasis in any statement of a rationale. Also, more emphasis on these functions might partially relieve the evaluation dilemma facing many teams. At the outset, when the team is just beginning to learn about its new managerial and technical functions, it might be more interesting and informative to evaluate teacher achievement instead of pupil achievement.

Team teaching and other staff utilization plans have revealed the inadequacy of the past performance of managerial functions. The usual disposal functions have been based upon gross criteria and judgments. The transfer of managerial functions to the teaching staff has not brought with it, either from administrative or university sources, the detailed operational goals and plans which characterized the Dalton Plan, the Winnetka Plan, and other plans in the past.

Another unrealistic claim frequently made about team teaching is that there will be a great saving of time which can then be spent on further teaching and on increasing productivity. This claim occurs most frequently when clerical and other nonprofessional aides are a part of the team. However, as a result of the transfer of managerial functions to the teachers, there are enormous increases in the amount of time required for planning, communication among team members, supervision, and evaluation; and these increases quickly absorb any saving of time in other areas. In dysfunctional teams the time spent on such managerial duties may actually bring about a reduction in teaching time and productivity. Any rationale for a team operation must consider the allocation of time necessary for these new managerial functions.

And, finally, we must examine carefully the claim for flexibility in teaching assignments and pupil groupings. Is it possible for teaching teams to make changes at will as is often claimed? In fact,

[21] Ohm, *op. cit.*, p. 4.

the opportunities for flexibility, while expanded considerably over the normal self-contained classroom situation, are quite limited.[22] In the first place, the transfer of managerial functions to the team may be quite circumscribed. For example, a small team may be restricted to a single grade level or to a single subject. The team may be assigned only a small block of the time schedule of the students, as is the case with those plans which seem more like block scheduling plans. And the team itself may be composed of teachers who are not specialists in any area. Secondly, even in larger teams an application of the simplest concepts of game theory in decision making reveals that each decision made limits the scope of successive choices and decisions.[23] This often leaves many unfavorable residual problems to be solved when no rational choices remain to allow a solution. For example, a four-member team with one hundred pupils may decide that it is going to have two of its teachers teach reading in ability groups of ten pupils each for periods of one half hour daily. This will occupy two teachers in a complicated pattern for two and a half hours a day out of an available six hours. A parallel plan must be developed to occupy the other teachers and the other pupils when they are not reading. The ability pattern in reading poses problems for other subjects. If there is to be parallel scheduling in arithmetic, problems will undoubtedly arise in obtaining "pure" groups. Further grouping by ability in other subjects will increase the problem of getting the right student into the right group at the right time with the right teacher. An alternative procedure might be to have all the teachers teach reading for a period and then regroup the next period for arithmetic. This plan tends to restrict class size to an average of 25 and denies the possibility of strong subject specialization on the part of teachers. As whatever plan chosen evolves into a working arrangement, the idea of changing at will is quickly lost. The concept of flexibility changes to another concept, that of *the establishment of rigorous priorities among choices with a full knowledge of the consequences which follow from alternative strategies*. The teacher

[22] For a detailed description and criticism of the self-contained classroom, see George D. Stoddard, *The Dual Progress Plan*, New York, Harper & Row, 1961, pp. 48–70.

[23] Herbert A. Simon, *Administrative Behavior*, 2nd ed., New York, Macmillan, 1960, pp. xxvii–xxix, 67–73.

in the self-contained classroom practices this kind of strategy but with highly limited possibilities and resources and without the problem of coordinating his activities with other teachers.

So far we have concentrated on the disposal functions at the managerial level. Let us now turn to what Parsons has defined as "procurement" functions, including the procurement of both personnel and resources. In Chapter 2 we have already discussed the problem American education has in attracting a reasonable share of the well-educated members of our society and in paying them salaries comparable to earnings in other fields for which they might qualify. Once such an able person has entered the field, there is still the major problem of retaining him in teaching. One of the procurement functions of educational management is to create a personnel and salary structure, a career pattern in teaching if you will, sufficiently attractive to compete with other professional fields for able employees. One of the major goals of team teaching is to provide such attractive career patterns by creating positions of increased responsibility and rewards within teaching. As Benson has pointed out, however, haphazard personnel plans or specialization which seeks temporary relief from an inflexible salary schedule or personnel structure may be harmful.[24] If a permanent solution is to be reached, team teaching must be affiliated with a rank or position type of classification system which brings order to the staffing arrangements of the school. Such a system must specify monetary rewards adjusted to various levels of responsibility and job difficulty, an orderly division of labor, and standards for role differentiation. A team teaching plan which emphasizes a new and attractive career pattern without having a personnel classification scheme is likely to be short lived and may hinder the accomplishment of larger objectives.

Two basic problems of procurement remain to be discussed: the procurement of subprofessional personnel within teaching (as distinct from the secretarial, clerical, and custodial force of the central staff), and the procurement of material resources for the support of teaching. In the face of a shortage of well-qualified professionals, management in other fields has characteristically handled the per-

[24] Charles S. Benson, *The Economics of Public Education*, Boston, Houghton Mifflin, 1961, p. 440.

petual economic problem of effectively allocating scarce resources by examining job requirements and by attempting to make a division of labor so that the professional or specialist could be located strategically in the organization and could be supported by a corps of technicians and other types of assistants. Where such division of labor occurs, training programs are also found which are aimed at increasing the effectiveness of various types of personnel. Historically the field of education has been slow to respond to this type of division of labor, for it has been preoccupied with the problems of improving the qualifications and status of the teaching force and of recruiting a qualified corps of teachers for an ever-expanding system. In this generation, however, it has become increasingly clear that a large fraction of the teacher's time is spent in nonprofessional duties—in some cases up to 40 percent of the total time spent in school. Such duties as collecting milk money and other funds, patrolling corridors, keeping attendance rosters, typing stencils, running the mimeograph machine, and supervising the lunchroom help account for this ludicrous state of affairs. Also, it has become clear that other tasks, more closely associated with teaching, such as the routine grading of papers and tests; the administration of tests; the preparation of classroom materials and exhibits; and the supervision of study halls, of independent study, and of study with the help of mechanical teaching aids can be performed by well-trained nonprofessional aides under the direction of the teacher.

There is a large reservoir of skilled labor in our society, particularly part-time labor, for which educational institutions can successfully compete. At the clerical and secretarial levels there are large numbers of women for whom the schools could provide an exciting work environment. There is also a large pool of college educated women in the community who could quickly become qualified to assist teachers as aides, technical assistants, readers, etc. In a number of cases where teacher aides and clerical assistants have been recruited, the response has been overwhelming, and it has not been unusual to find that the nonprofessionals who have been hired have had a better educational background than the teachers for whom they have worked. There is a strong likelihood that many of the people who become involved in these duties may undertake to prepare themselves for professional posts. Thus, a reorganization of the schools to include nonprofessional personnel might provide a lively new basis for recruitment.

Unfortunately, the general organizational structure of the schools makes the type of division of labor discussed above virtually impossible. The relatively isolated position of each individual teacher and the absence of working groups of teachers and of working spaces other than classrooms makes it extremely difficult, if not impossible, to create an efficient working situation for the aide or assistant. Clearly the resources available to education and the competing demands within education at the professional level will not allow the introduction of nonprofessional personnel to be on an additive basis. Some way must be found to associate aides with teachers so effectively that the number of professional teachers needed is reduced and yet not so radically that the instructional services suffer. In this sense those teaching aide experiments which have used one teacher and one assistant to do the work of two teachers are radical experiments and do not appear a viable form of organization. What is needed within teaching is a method of suborganization, a grouping of teachers into small groups with common work objectives and shared working space, to which the teaching aides and clerical assistants can be attached in such a way that a sufficient amount of work will be absorbed efficiently from the teachers to allow a reduction in the teaching force. One of the principal justifications for team teaching may be that it answers this need.

The argument with respect to the procurement of material resources for teaching is similar to that presented above. The typical school budget for books, teaching aids, laboratory equipment, and other supplies and materials is quite restricted, and under present organizational arrangements fundamental problems exist in obtaining efficient allocation of materials and maximum utilization of equipment. It has not been possible to equip each classroom with the necessary projectors of various types, with tape recorders, and with other types of equipment because of the high cost and the low utilization involved in such an arrangement. As an attempt to minimize cost and maximize efficient allocation, schools have tended to establish central resource facilities, and often a corps of specialists operate these centers as a service to the teachers. However, because of the routine problems of requisitioning, scheduling, moving, and operating equipment, maximum utilization is often not obtained, and it becomes a major task to persuade teachers to use many of the available aids. Again, small-group organization presents an alternative solution to the problem, and many teaching teams have already demonstrated both an increased and a more efficient use of a variety of teaching materials and mechanical aids to teaching. Within a group organization it becomes possible to establish both stations for the use of mechanical aids and centers for the collection of instructional materials and books which provide for convenient access and high utilization. In fact, this facet of team teaching has created several new problems for the schools. Because of more efficient utilization, teaching teams have occasionally increased their consumption of materials so drastically that they have monopolized the supplies of a given school. However, centralization is not the only reason for the increased efficiency in the use of resources in teams. Many teams have also devoted considerable energy to training some of their members in the use of these resources in order to insure efficient utilization.

One caution should be entered at this point with respect to group organization of teachers for the utilization of both nonprofessional aides and technical materials and aids. Subgroup organization of a reasonable size is required to meet the criteria of efficiency which have been given. Teams of four or five members or larger may be required for the assimilation of an aide without significant loss of professional teaching time and for the proper utilization of expensive technical equipment and resource centers. It does not seem likely that two- and three-member teams can be justified on the same basis.

In this section we have developed a number of reasons for organization of the teaching staff into teams, and in some cases a detailed justification has been offered. To summarize, then, a major goal of team teaching is the transfer of certain managerial functions, particularly the disposal functions of teacher assignments and pupil grouping, to the technical staff. A major justification for this goal remains to be given in the following section. A secondary goal of team teaching, derived from the fact that relatively few professional teachers are prepared to exercise the new managerial functions, is the use of the team as an in-service training and problem-solving unit. The need for such training and for such a concerted attack on fundamental problems is one of the primary justifications of small-group organization in teaching. Another concern of the team in the exercise of the disposal function becomes the establishment of rigorous priorities among available choices with a full knowledge of the consequences which follow from alternative strategies. At the managerial level one of the major goals of team teaching is to provide an attractive, competitive career pattern in teaching. Desirable though this may be, it can only be justified in terms of a workable division of labor within teaching. One subgoal, related to the problem of the division of labor, is the more efficient use of the teaching force through the utilization of nonprofessional aides. This goal seems fully justified, under certain conditions, by the relief from nonteaching duties which it affords the teacher, by the resulting increases in individual productivity, and by the quality of the pool of talent from which the nonprofessionals can be drawn. Finally, an important though rarely major goal of team teaching, which has already been fully justified by the performance of many teams, is the efficient utilization of materials and technical resources in education. This can become a major goal in the case of certain technological innovations such as television, which require special types of working groups as a precondition for operation.

The Technical Functions and Goals of Team Teaching

In the previous section we examined the transfer of managerial functions, particularly the disposal functions, which occurs when a team organization is established. A further justification of team teaching is needed, in terms of administrative organization and efficiency, for the accomplishment of technical functions and goals. Technical functions, as noted before, include the development of the curriculum, the organization of instruction, the specific methods of teaching, and the assessment of the needs and progress of the students. Though teaching teams, as developed so far, are relatively simple small-group organizations, nevertheless they present many of the same administrative complexities as larger organizations and are susceptible to description and analysis in the same terms. In the discussion that follows, we will rely heavily upon the descriptive and analytic framework developed by Herbert Simon.[25]

Simon's analysis is concerned with the processes of decision making as well as with the processes of action. An administrative organization is characterized as purposive; the reason for organizing a group is to get something done, and the purposes of the organization provide the principal criteria for deciding what things are to be done. This introduces the notion of a "hierarchy of decisions," based upon the purposes of the organization. "Behavior is purposive in so far as it is guided by general goals or objectives; it is rational in so far as it selects alternatives which are conducive to the achievement of the previously selected goals."[26]

Administrative activity is concerned with group activity. When the purposes and tasks involved become too complex for individuals to handle them and several individuals are required, it is necessary to develop organized group effort. As Simon notes, this involves developing for the organization a plan which substitutes organizational decision-making processes for some of the decisional autonomy of the individual. The organization specifies the general scope and nature of the duties of the individual, allocates authority for making decisions for the individual, and sets other limits on individual choice which are necessary to coordinate the activities of the group.

An organization is characterized by specialization; different parts of the work are delegated to different parts of the organization. Simon distinguishes between two main types of specialization: "horizontal" specialization, or the division of work, which is given by most authors as the basic characteristic of organizations and even as the reason for their existence; and "vertical" specialization, or the division of labor, which involves a division of authority and decision-making functions and a distinction between operative and supervisory personnel.

Regarding the establishment of administrative organizations, Simon states that "over-all efficiency must be the guiding criterion."[27] This involves balancing of mutually incompatible advantages and

[25] Simon, *op. cit.*
[26] *Ibid.*, p. 5.
[27] *Ibid.*, p. 36.

judging the relative efficiency of alternative choices. *"The criterion of efficiency dictates that choice of alternatives which produces the largest result for the given application of resources."*[28] Simon shows that his concept of efficiency is analogous to the economic concept of maximization of utility and that both concepts rest on the following three assumptions:

> The first of these is that there is a scarcity of applicable resources. A second assumption is that the activities concerned are "instrumental" activities—that is, activities that are carried on for the positive values they produce, in the form of some kind of "result." Third, both propositions involve the comparability, at least subjectively, of the values in terms of which results are measured.[29]

Thus far an attempt has been made to introduce the reader to the main ideas which Simon uses in his analysis of administrative behavior. In the following sections three of Simon's concepts (horizontal specialization, vertical specialization, and coordination) will be elaborated and applied to team teaching. In the process we will inevitably be forced into the difficult position of trying to compare team teaching with an overgeneralized model of school organization as it is presumed to exist under normal conditions.

Horizontal Specialization

"To gain the advantages of specialized skill in a large organization, the work of the organization is sub-divided, so far as possible, in such a way that all processes requiring a particular skill can be performed by persons possessing that skill."[30] The work is divided up along functional lines, and persons with the appropriate skills and knowledge are assigned to separate tasks. According to Simon the conditions of effective functionalization are: "(1) It must be technically feasible to split the work activity, as well as the objective, along functional lines; (2) these segregated work activities must not affect, to a substantial degree, values extraneous to the specified functions."[31] Group organization is necessary to coordinate

[28] *Ibid.*, p. 179.
[29] *Ibid.*, p. 182.
[30] *Ibid.*, p. 137.
[31] *Ibid.*, p. 192.

the work of the various specialists and to guarantee that their objectives are compatible with the over-all goals of the group.

Amongst the large number of goals and activities of team teaching which provide examples of attempts at horizontal specialization, we can distinguish at least two major types for which a rationale for team teaching will have to provide justification.

The first major type of horizontal specialization is the development of more highly specialized teaching assignments based upon the special knowledge and competence needed in particular subject areas. This type of specialization is common within the usual forms of school organization, especially in departmentalized secondary schools. But similar attempts at departmentalization do occur in the upper grades of the elementary schools and were even more common several decades ago. One of the major goals of many team teaching projects has been to increase the amount of subject specialization among teachers at all levels of the school system. At the secondary school level this means further division of a broad subject area. An English teacher, for example, may become a specialist in language, in some phase of literature, or in developmental reading. At the elementary level the teacher becomes a specialist in a single subject over a number of grade levels. This increase in subject specialization through team teaching seems to occur in two stages. The first stage occurs when specialized teaching assignments are made on the basis of a teacher's interest and desire to teach in a certain area rather than on the basis of more objective standards of special knowledge or competence. This may be regarded as a developmental stage which may lead to true specialization under proper conditions. The second stage is the division of the work among teachers because they possess special knowledge and skill prior to the assignment.

The first stage of specialized subject teaching assignments represents an attempt to subdivide the total teaching requirements into reasonable individual assignments based upon a limited age range of pupils, a limited segment of the curriculum, and a limited number of pupils. Much of the present organization of the schools is based upon this type of subdivision of tasks. Since there is no subject specialization at all in most elementary schools, teaching subdivisions are attained through the graded structure, which is based upon age, social maturity, and achievement. In the junior high school the teaching assignments are characteristically limited to a single subject or to combinations of subjects with which the teacher has at least some familiarity. In the departmentalized senior high schools teaching assignments are based upon age and curriculum groups rather than upon the possession of further specialization within the subject. The tasks of teaching are further subdivided at all levels by limits that are placed on class size. It seems, then, that the present organization of our schools is based on the assumption that an increasing degree of task subdivision is required at each more advanced stage. Team teaching projects have adapted to this basic structure; at the lower levels one of the major objectives is to subdivide the tasks of teachers to create more reasonable loads, whereas at the higher levels team teaching projects frequently attempt to attain further specialization of teaching within the present task subdivisions. In this discussion we shall be more concened with the subdivision of tasks than with the more intensive forms of specialization, and, therefore, the following remarks apply primarily to the elementary school.

At the present time the elementary school teacher has an enormously complex and overdemanding job, for she is expected to teach all subjects to a given group of pupils at a given grade level.[32] Though most elementary school teachers in our culture have a substantial background in English and social studies, relatively few have a thorough understanding of and training in mathematics, science, music, art, and foreign languages. The amount and quality of the training a given pupil receives in a given year is dependent upon the constellation of abilities and interests of a single teacher. One year the instruction in arithmetic may be excellent; the next year it may be barely acceptable, even with teachers who are considered to be generally outstanding. In our society, where knowledge is expanding at an enormous rate, where advances in specialization require better and better early training, and where the expectations of an educated public are constantly expanding, the range of abilities required of any single teacher to handle the total education of a child is far too great. There are several ways to solve

[32] For a more extended discussion of the demands placed upon the elementary school teacher, see Stoddard, *op. cit.*

this dilemma. One is departmentalization, and another is the type of program represented by the Dual Progress Plan. Team teaching tries to simplify teaching assignments by subdividing teaching tasks on the basis of the interests and competencies of the team members. The teacher is required to teach fewer subjects and thus has fewer preparations to make. If there is some continuity in the arrangement, such a limitation of the teaching task also simplifies many of the problems of training and supervision, for it becomes more feasible to identify the weaknesses of the teacher and to select training programs which apply specifically to his needs. Likewise, supervisors will be able to provide more intensive help to a less diverse group of teachers.

On a rational basis one might expect in team teaching increments in learning from pupils if the teacher is relatively free to concentrate on a single area of knowledge. However, there are many other variables involved. Usually, the total teaching time is not reduced, additional duties, particularly those involving cooperative efforts in scheduling and planning, are added, and the total number of pupils with whom teachers work is increased. Increments in pupil learning are unlikely to occur until specific program developments can be made, and these are not likely to appear until teachers have developed their specialties through further training and supervision.

The need for a second stage of specialization, extensive subject specialization, has been recognized in many elementary school systems by the introduction in such subject areas as art and music of specialist teachers who serve a number of schools and many teachers. But in too many cases this is merely a gesture toward solving the problem. Frequently these specialists are overworked, and their activities are seldom well coordinated with the rest of the school program.

Stoddard's case for increased subject specialization rests in part on a distinction between an area of common knowledge necessary for all citizens (cultural imperatives) and an area of specialized knowledge and skills that is not essential for all people in our culture (cultural electives).[33] He emphasizes the need for specialist teachers in the cultural electives (mathematics, science, music, art, and foreign languages). However, many of the proponents of team

[33] *Ibid.*, pp. 5–8.

teaching would argue that the requirements for teaching the cultural imperatives (English and social studies) are just as specialized as those for teaching the cultural electives.

Perhaps the most compelling argument for specialization can be made on the basis of the direction that the new curriculum studies have taken at all levels of the educational system. The courses of study are developed by specialists and in most cases require specialized knowledge on the part of the teacher to understand them and to teach them. This has been particularly true of the mathematics and science courses developed so far, and it is likely to be equally true for other courses as the curriculum revolution spreads. Unfortunately, far too many teachers have serious deficiencies in their substantive preparation for teaching. College and university training programs present a bewildering variety of elective courses, and students select among these courses on the basis of their general interests rather than on the basis of a systematic plan designed to prepare them for teaching. Prospective elementary school teachers receive very little training in mathematics, science, music, and art, and little improvement can be expected as long as the field requires teachers to be generalists. A similar case can be made for the secondary school level. The training program of a prospective high school English teacher, for example, seldom includes the study of composition, and the study of literature may be restricted to a smattering of survey courses. If specialist teaching assignments were defined and established in the schools, the pattern of training for teaching could be made more orderly.

A very strong case for specialization in the schools can be made in terms of the requirements of innovation and change. If any fundamental changes are to be made in our schools, it will be necessary to be able to communicate with all teachers quickly and efficiently. To do so, new communication channels must be opened and new chains of influence must be established. If there were specialist teachers in each of the major subject areas with responsibility for communicating information to their associates, the process of change would be enormously simplified.

The second major type of horizontal specialization is specialization in particular methods of teaching or in one of the forms of technology in education. This topic has already received an extended discussion in Chapter 2. Large group instruction, for example, would undoubtedly improve if an expert made the decisions about what material can most effectively be presented in a large group and assumed responsibility for the preparation and presentation of the large-group lessons. Such a specialist would also increase the efficiency and economy that large-group instruction affords. Technological specialists, such as audio-visual specialists and programed learning specialists, can also be justified on the same grounds. In fact, it is hard to see how any of the new techniques of teaching will be very effective unless teachers receive special training in their use.

Before turning away from the topic of horizontal specialization, it is necessary to introduce a word of caution. As noted before, Simon states that one of the conditions of effective functionalization is that the "segregated work activities must not affect, to a substantial degree, values extraneous to the specified functions."[34] Attempts to introduce special subject teaching are not new in American education. The tug of war between the specialist and the generalist, between general education and special education, has been a characteristic of educational discussions over many generations. The dangers of excessive specialization are well known; the specialist tends to retire into the narrow confines of his specialty and to disregard the connections between his specialty and other areas of knowledge. Part of the protest of the progressive movement was against the segmented subject curriculum of the time, and since then there have been many efforts, such as the core curriculum, to develop a curriculum which gives proper emphasis to the relationships among subjects. Thus, there is certainly a danger that further specialization may lead to a proliferation of discrete curriculum elements which are dissociated from other elements of the program. But a concern for this danger does not discredit the justification of specialized teaching within teams given here. In most cases where horizontal specialization is developed within teams, one of the primary purposes of the team organization is to encourage relationships among specialists. Furthermore, we would take the position that an understanding of the interrelationships between subjects requires a knowledge in depth of the subjects involved. One of the major diffi-

[34] Simon, *op. cit.*, p. 192.

culties faced in the introduction of the core curriculum and other similar efforts was the scarcity of individuals with sufficient depth and breadth of knowledge and skill. Surely we should be in a better position to achieve the objectives of general education when the job of relating various areas of knowledge is undertaken jointly by teachers with special training in particular subjects.

Vertical Specialization

Simon defines vertical specialization, or the division of labor, as "the division of decision-making duties between operative and supervisory personnel."[35] The reasons for vertical specialization in an organization are given as follows:

First, if there is any horizontal specialization, vertical specialization is absolutely essential to achieve coordination among the operative employees. Second, just as horizontal specialization permits greater skill and expertise to be developed by the operative group in the performance of their tasks, so vertical specialization permits greater expertise in the making of decisions. Third, vertical specialization permits the operative personnel to be held accountable for their decisions. . . .[36]

In other words, Simon suggests that effective group activity requires coordination among group members. Furthermore, he suggests that in order to obtain maximum coordination the functions of decision making must be allocated to specially trained supervisory personnel.

Simon distinguishes two types of coordination, substantive and procedural. Substantive coordination is concerned with the content of the work. Procedural coordination is concerned with the operation of the group; with lines of authority, spheres of activity, and relationships among personnel. Within the field of education we may equate substantive coordination with the area of curriculum decisions and procedural coordination with the area of supervisory decisions. Though these areas obviously overlap at many points, we shall consider them as distinct for the purposes of the discussion which follows.

[35] *Ibid.*, p. 9.
[36] *Ibid.*, p. 9.

Substantive Coordination—Curriculum Decisions

The organization of teachers into teams represents a new attempt to achieve effective substantive coordination within our schools. The distinctive feature of the new form is the transfer of authority for making curriculum decisions from both the individual teacher and the higher supervisory staff to the team. The rationale for such a transfer rests first upon the development of horizontal specialization within the team so that the requisite knowledge and skill is present to make the necessary decisions, and secondly upon an analysis of the present methods of substantive coordination within the schools. For purposes of analysis we shall divide the discussion of substantive coordination into two parts, inseparable in practice: (1) the development of curriculum plans and materials, involving decisions about what is to be taught and (2) the allocation of pupils to instructional groups, involving decisions concerning who is to be taught what materials, when, where, and how.

As most schools are now organized, the responsibility for developing curriculum plans and materials rests largely with the individual teacher, who spends the major part of his professional life in relative isolation from his colleagues. The novice usually has just as much of this type of responsibility as his more experienced associates, for few effective mechanisms exist to enable the more knowledgeable, better-trained, and more experienced teacher to exert his influence on curriculum matters in any legitimate formal way.

To be sure, our present system often assigns responsibility for curriculum development and continuity to certain individuals. These may be principals, curriculum directors, directors or supervisors of special subjects, department heads, grade chairmen, and others. There are several difficulties here. First, fiscal authorities have been reluctant to provide the funds necesary to finance a proliferation of curriculum activities. A system that possesses a full complement of officers representing all the significant specialties is indeed fortunate. Less fortunate and far more common is the system which must count on a few officers to influence the behavior of large numbers of teachers. Often these officers barely know their teachers well enough for purposes of tenure evaluation, and they have virtually no opportunity to influence their teachers' work in any way. Secondly, given the relatively few positions now possible, the tendency is to develop generalists or coordinators rather than specialists and to promote these individuals out of the classroom. Generalists, operating outside of the classroom, do not have sufficient special knowledge to influence the curriculum content in specific areas. The position of the department head is somewhat better, but rarely is he released from teaching and administrative duties for a sufficient length of time to allow him to do effective curriculum work with his teachers. It is even more rare for his teachers to be released from their duties long enough to participate in such work. Clearly, everyone is locked into a heavy teaching schedule as though there were a basic principle at work—when students are in school all teachers must be teaching all the time.

To try to solve its curriculum problems, a school will often appoint a curriculum committee. Such committees must meet after school hours and without remuneration. The research necessary to do satisfactory curriculum work is neglected because it requires too much time which a teacher needs to plan for his own classes. Consequently, inferior materials are produced, and, even when the materials are valuable, the members of the committee are without the authority to introduce their product into all classrooms. They must begin a long process of persuading individual teachers to use the materials.

The present system, then, is inefficient because it places heavy responsibilities upon a small number of curriculum specialists who are removed from classroom teachers, because it gives equal responsibility to all teachers irrespective of their competence and of the specialized knowledge and skill they may possess, and because it lacks the leadership necessary to insure direction and continuity for any program. The inefficiencies of the present system may be able to be improved by team teaching. Teams can be formed which include teachers with specialized knowledge and skills in a given area of the curriculum. These teachers can be given responsibility to plan the curriculum work of the team and to oversee the work of the other teachers in carrying out the objectives of the curriculum. The curriculum leaders from a number of teams can work together, serving as an "instructional cabinet" for a school, with specific responsibility for developing curriculum and maintaining the necessary coordination between levels of instruction and between subject areas. Thus the team becomes the functional unit for the introduction of innovations (see Chapter 5).

A suggestion might be made that instead of forming teaching teams, it might be simpler, for example, to give the department head and the teachers in the department the necessary free time to devote to curriculum work. If this were done, however, the result would be a working group that would undoubtedly have to split itself up into teams or committees that would concentrate their efforts on a specific area of the total task, say English for the tenth grade. From that point it is only a few short steps to a full team teaching program. Clearly, team teaching can be arrived at in a number of ways. In fact, the wide variety of courses that have been pursued to get to team teaching suggests that at some point in the search for improvement in education, the formation of teaching teams may be a necessity.

The allocation of pupils to instructional groups and the adaptation of the curriculum to the groups involved are two of the principal types of substantive coordination within the schools. In our definition of team teaching we restricted the application of the term to those groups of teachers who are given responsibility for all or a significant part of the instruction of the same group of pupils. By this definition a primary function of team teaching is the allocation of pupils to instructional groups. At least four major problems of substantive coordination are involved. First, there is the problem of providing for continuous pupil progress through a sequential curriculum of increasing complexity and difficulty. The ideal here might be an individually tailored program through which the student proceeds at his own rate (see Chapter 5). The second problem is that of coordinating the various elements of the curriculum so that the interrelationships among the various subjects are taught. This is one of the principal objectives of the proponents of the core curriculum. Thirdly, there is the problem of deciding what elements of the curriculum should serve the ends of general education; that is, what common elements there should be in the education of all students of a given age. Stoddard has called these elements "the cultural imperatives." A subsidiary question here is whether such general education should be taken by all students together in heterogeneous groups as a part of the process of teaching democratic ideals, or whether it too should be taught in ability groupings. A fourth problem is that of determining what particular aspects of the curriculum lend themselves to what particular sized groups. If certain materials can be taught just as well in large groups as they are taught in small groups, then by using some large groups there may be a saving of teaching time which can be used productively elsewhere, either for planning or for other instruction which requires small-group or individual teaching.

Some elements of the rationale for team teaching with respect to instructional groups have already been presented in Chapter 2 and will receive further treatment in Chapter 6. The present graded structure of the school and the present methods of assigning instructional groupings within the graded structure are rigid and inflexible solutions to the problems outlined above. Grade placement has come to reflect the age and social maturity of the student rather than his academic achievement and progress. Groupings within grades are based upon gross criteria such as IQ scores and achievement scores on standardized tests rather than upon performance criteria in specific curriculum areas. Standards of economy dictate that few variations in groups at any grade level are possible, and, therefore, even ability groupings display a wide range of aptitudes and abilities on the part of students. Furthermore, once the schedules for pupil groupings and teacher assignments are made, variations and changes become difficult, if not impossible. The term and the year become the basic time units, and little allowance can be made for changes in rate of progress or changes in direction of interests that occur in shorter time intervals.

In view of the complexity of the problems involved and the basic limitation that some form of grouping is necessary most of the time, it is doubtful whether any solution can approach an ideal. As was shown in Chapter 2, each of the grouping plans, such as the Winnetka Plan or the Dual Progress Plan, stresses one or more discrete elements and leaves other problems unresolved. One must choose among alternatives, and each combination of alternatives has its own set of consequences. So it is with team teaching. Teams have been established as ways of solving each of the major problems outlined above or combinations of these problems. Many represent efforts to introduce flexibility into the assignment of teachers and pupils to groups; they hope that by allocating these decisions to the teaching staff, more frequent variations in pupil groupings may be made on the basis of more immediate criteria. In this way grouping changes may more immediately reflect changes in performance. Furthermore, within a team any savings that can be made through variations in groupings can be more readily put to use than would be the case under a more rigid method of organization.

Procedural Coordination—Supervisory Decisions

We will define the scope of procedural coordination as the definition of roles, the allocation of tasks, and the description of relationships between the teaching and the nonprofessional members of staff.

One type of vertical specialization involves the separation of the work of the teacher into professional tasks appropriate for the professionally trained teacher and nonprofessional tasks more appropriate for individuals of lesser training and qualifications. This has already been described in the section above on the procurement functions of management, and it is the simplest case of the subdivision of tasks in contrast to task specialization.[37] The primary objective of subdividing tasks, according to Dubin, is to break a job down into its simple component parts and to distribute these task parts to individuals who perform them exclusively. Such tasks are relatively simple, can be learned readily, and do not require a high degree of training. There seems to be widespread agreement in the teaching profession that many of the clerical and custodial tasks of education can easily be separated from the teaching tasks and assigned to nonprofessionals. However, controversy occurs when the nonprofessional category includes functions that are closely related to the teaching process, such as grading papers, supervising study periods, preparing teaching materials, and supervising numerous types of child activity. Nonetheless, it seems reasonable to make such divisions of tasks and to assign them to qualified persons who fall short of full teaching qualifications. It may, in fact, be possible to have several levels of

[37] Dubin, *op. cit.*, pp. 78–80.

nonprofessional personnel, who vary in degree of education and past types of experience, and to provide several types of training programs within the schools for these people.

Strictly from the point of view of efficiency, it may well be that this type of task division under team teaching could lead to a reduction of the number of professional teachers needed to teach a given group of students without an increase in cost for the school. But such a viewpoint is not common. More frequently a school system assumes that any attempt to increase the quality of instruction will lead to an increase in costs, and, therefore, the addition of aides is an attempt to reduce the over-all loads of teachers and to allow them some released time for instructional tasks which could not be undertaken under normal teaching loads. This problem of excessive teaching loads is one of the most pressing in our whole educational system, and its solution is complicated by the public image of the teacher as a part-time worker who works a short day and a short year. In many schools, particularly in overcrowded schools and in schools attempting to offer extensive programs, secondary school teachers are expected to teach six or more periods and handle several subjects at different age levels. Elementary school teachers are asked to teach all subjects to 35 or more students. Loads like this are extremely exhausting, and, if the teacher does a conscientious job, he has no time for personal or professional development. Of course, when teachers' loads are reduced, it will be necessary to determine whether or not the time made available is used productively. Increments in pupil learning can only be expected when the released time or reduced load has allowed the development of specific educational programs that will produce outcomes that can be measured.

Task division may also be employed to vary teaching loads in terms of the amount of experience, the energy levels, and the work capacities of individual teachers. Teachers, like all individuals, vary enormously with respect to these factors. In the typical school organization teaching tasks are defined very rigidly by the demands of mass scheduling. Where the only category of teachers consists of fully qualified, full-time teachers, the only problem of scheduling is to arrange equitable programs; the schedule of each teacher should have the same number of classes, the same number of preparations, and roughly the same number of pupils. In practice, however, assignments are often made on a seniority basis. This situation has been described elsewhere as follows:

To illustrate the stress conditions of teaching, let me describe the rather typical experience of a beginning teacher. Common sense would suggest that his beginning load should be lighter, that is should include fewer preparations, with free periods for planning. Not at all. Given a few months warning of his assignment, armed with a sketchy curriculum guide and an assortment of textbooks, he enters upon a full teaching schedule of five or more classes a day, and a bewildering complement of extra duties. He is treated as though he were a full-fledged, fully-certified teacher, and in theory, at least, the same expectations are held for him as for his neighbor of twenty-five years experience. Usually his senior colleagues have chosen the favorite courses and the ablest students, so the novice quite often faces the more difficult classes of slow, bored, and belligerent students. If he has standards for himself, his work is never done—he can never know enough, plan enough, or know the feeling of completion.[38]

Variation of teaching loads on more rational grounds has been a feature of a number of teaching teams, particularly those which include beginning teachers and interns and apprentice teachers involved in training programs. Characteristically these plans assign a two-thirds or three-quarters time load to the beginner, and salaries are often adjusted to the load level. However, there has been little variation in teaching loads outside of the teacher training programs because such changes inevitably involve increased costs. Since the average work loads of teachers are already heavy and cannot be increased, lighter loads cannot be achieved for either inexperienced teachers or those with marginal energy levels without an increase in total personnel costs or a major change in the salary schedule.

Thus far we have offered a rationale for the vertical division of authority in teaching, and in team teaching, in terms of a definition of nonprofessional roles and a more rational system of allocation of the work loads among teachers. Horizontal specialization, described in the preceding section, also dictates new vertical authority arrangements among teachers. Efficient operation in all three cases requires the establishment of working groups of teachers and aides and the

[38] Judson T. Shaplin, "Practice in Teaching," *Harvard Educational Review*, vol. XXXI, Winter, 1961, p. 35.

supervision of some members by others. Still further justification for team teaching proceeds from a more general analysis of present supervisory arrangements within the schools and the nature of the supervisory process.

Supervision, as applied to the process of teaching, is concerned with the ability of the individual teacher to translate the curriculum into action, to motivate learning in his students, to plan his lessons and execute them with competence, to measure the progress students are making, and to adapt his instruction to the conditions facing him so that optimum learning conditons prevail. In this whole area we are plagued by a lack of valid criteria for measurement and a lack of reliable research evidence. The qualitative and quantitative shortages of teachers dictate that substantial efforts should be directed toward improving supervisory practices. Teaching receives a small proportion of the ablest individuals entering the professions. There is a very high turnover rate, largely because many women stay only a few years in teaching, or, if they stay longer, their primary obligations and responsibilities lie elsewhere. Many stay in teaching because there are no other alternatives for them, not because they have achieved a marked degree of success. Indeed, a very small proportion of the teaching force can be characterized as successful career teachers. Teachers, then, vary enormously in their technical teaching capacity.

The schools, as typically organized, are poorly prepared to offer help to teachers of limited experience and capacity and to those who are having technical difficulties or management problems. The situation with respect to responsibility for the supervision of teaching is similar to that which we have described for the curriculum. Principals, supervisors, and department heads have so many teachers under their charge or so little available time that they can pay little attention to the majority of the staff. They are involved with "putting out fires" most of the time rather than with systematic supervisory practices. Proper supervision requires a substantial amount of time. It should include an examination of the planning process and sustained observation of teaching so that sufficient samples of behavior under varying conditions are available to make a diagnosis possible. Evaluation sessions, where the diagnosis is presented and constructive suggestions are made, should follow these sustained observations. Often the process must be repeated many times if the teacher is to be helped to improve his performance.

The task of supervision is not well regarded or well understood by many school personnel, particularly by teachers. The helping role of the supervisor is too frequently confused with the judgmental-evaluation role. Supervision is seen as a threat to the autonomy of the individual teacher, as an invasion of his classroom where he is "king." Many of the issues relevant to this conflict are clouded by high-minded and idealistic statements about the art of teaching and about the difficulty of judging teacher competence. Even on a very simple level of analysis, it is clear that teachers vary enormously in various modes of behavior that are susceptible to change: their speech habits, their capacity to observe and analyze classroom behavior, their tolerance for certain types of pupil behavior, their routine techniques of classroom management, and their attitudes toward planning. Teachers also vary enormously in their capacity for self-improvement. Under present conditions, where the teacher works in isolation, rarely seeing others teach, where shop talk is frowned upon, where supervisory help is sporadic, and where little support from colleagues can be expected, one should not be surprised to note that performance does not improve and poor practices often become habitual.[39]

Because of this situation, the major trend in the field of supervision in American education has been toward group work and cooperative efforts that are detached from the functional classroom performance of the teacher.[40] This trend emphasizes group process as a way of changing attitudes and implementing the spirit of democracy in the schools, the emergence of leadership in place of the exercise of authority, and the importance of group morale. Thus, supervision theory has become closely linked to developments in the fields of group dynamics and human relations. This spirit is not incompatible with that of team teaching, but there is one crucial difference; team teaching permits supervision through group work and cooperative efforts

[39] For a more extended treatment of this problem, see Shaplin, *op. cit.*

[40] For examples of approaches which stress group work and cooperation in supervision, see Kimball Wiles, *Supervision for Better Schools*, Englewood Cliffs, N.J., Prentice-Hall, 1955; and William S. Burton and Leo J. Brueckner, *Supervision, A Social Process*, New York, Appleton-Century-Crofts, 1955.

within the context of the working situation and direct observation of the performance of the individual on the job. Within teams provision may be made for teachers to see each other at work and to join in the evaluation of instruction and learning after observation. Teachers with greater technical competence can be made responsible for influencing the performance of their less expert colleagues. Talk about teaching becomes legitimate because it is based upon common observations and because its purpose is constructive. Viewed in this way, team teaching may have as cne of its major goals the introduction of functional, on-the-job supervision by able career teachers.

A Multiplicity of Goals

In the preceding sections, an analysis has been made of the major goals of team teaching. There are a large number of possible goals, serving a variety of organizational and instructional purposes. Since the majority of present team teaching projects are small, involving only a few teams of two to four teachers each, it is also clear that the multiplicity of goals is a source of confusion and contradiction. A small working group can only hope to achieve progress in a few directions; it cannot hope to be the instrument of reorganization of an entire system. Any full statement of the goals of the whole team teaching movement proves to be a critique of present types of school organization and a statement of the possible directions of change for American education. One of the difficulties for beginning team teaching projects has been the tendency to develop all-embracing statements of objectives and goals, phrased in the most general terms. All too often the ultimate goals receive the greatest emphasis and mask the more immediate and possible goals. In most schools the introduction of fully developed specialization of both horizontal and vertical types must be a long-term objective; a more immediate objective would be the introduction of a carefully planned in-service training program. As noted in Chapter 1, emphasis upon long-term goals leads to exaggeration of objectives and overclaiming.

A second source of difficulty is the attempt to claim certain goals as the exclusive property of team teaching and to state that certain changes can only be brought about by team teaching. In the above discussion an attempt has been made to show that team teaching is but one of many ways to achieve these goals. The accomplishment of any objective requires specific planning and operations directed toward the achievement of that particular goal, and there are many types of suborganizations that can be established to accomplish the same purposes, many of which remain well within the framework of present school organization. Claiming multiple goals of far-reaching implications and exclusive rights and capabilities to attain these goals often puts team teaching in the ridiculous position of trying to shoot elephants with a pea shooter.

The goals of a specific team teaching project, then, should be consistent with the size of the reorganization which is contemplated. A small team, working in isolation, can only hope to progress toward a few specific objectives. Larger teams, or a complex of interrelated small teams which are firmly linked to the basic salary schedule, personnel classification, and recruitment policies of the system, may hope to make progress with a more complex pattern of goals.

If we look at the goals of team teaching from another point of view, we can see that they are improvement goals; they are aimed at improving the career pattern and status of the teacher; the conditions of work of the teacher; and the patterns of curriculum development, training, and supervision of education in general. Improvements have their price! Rarely can improvements be brought about while maintaining a stable cost pattern. In the above discussion there were only a few situations described in which there might be increases in efficiency without increases in cost. It is safe to make the generalization that teams which are limited to prevailing expenditure patterns for personnel, equipment, and materials will also be limited in the goals which they may reasonably hope to accomplish. Like other attempts to improve the quality of education, team teaching constantly reveals new weaknesses in the present educational structure and makes large demands for additional resources. Clearly, the improvements that can be attained through team teaching will be directly proportional to the investment that is made in its behalf.

Chapter 4

A Taxonomy for Team Teaching

HENRY F. OLDS, JR.

Graduate School of Education, Harvard University

In Chapter 1 a definition of team teaching was presented for two purposes: to clarify the concept of team teaching and to set limits upon the types of organization which can legitimately be considered team teaching. Obviously, this definition does not attempt to make clear-cut distinctions between projects that are team teaching and projects that are not, nor was it intended for such a purpose. Too strict a limitation upon the concept of team teaching might strangle it. Consequently, though concern is expressed in the first chapter about the wide variety of activity which has been labeled team teaching, the definition was framed in terms that would include at least all those activities which closely approximate team teaching or which are seriously interested in becoming fully developed team teaching projects. After such a definition, then, a classificatory system, a taxonomy, is needed which will permit intelligent description of existing projects and which will provide a terminology appropriate for this description.

In developing a taxonomy for team teaching, it is important to realize that team teaching is neither as unitary or as various a concept as has been claimed. As was noted in Chapter 1, there is tremendous variety among team teaching projects, and this variety seemingly increases in direct proportion to one's inability to describe consistently what is taking place in each project. With no consistent scheme for describing team teaching, the variety may seem incomprehensible. On the other hand, it is a drastic oversimplification to try to reduce team teaching to some unitary concept which says, in effect, that team teaching is precisely this or that and accomplishes precisely this or that. The assumption behind such a unitary concept is that an experience in a high school in California can be generalized with an experience in an elementary school in Massachusetts. It is all too clear at this stage in the development of team teaching that any kind of general statement about team teaching will have to be extensively qualified if it is to make any sense at all. Also, we have no perfect models. Since most teaching teams are imperfect demonstrations, it is clear that the full potentiality of this type of organization is yet to be realized. An adequate descriptive scheme, therefore, will have to take into account the developmental nature of team teaching and should indicate as many lines of development as possible. Any taxonomy should probably cover at least three areas: it should indicate differences among teaching teams, including those which are likely to occur because of conditions beyond the control of the team, it should indicate and explore areas in which significant similarities among teams exist, and it should indicate lines of development by bringing within its scope as many of the theoretical potentialities of team teaching as possible.

This chapter is by no means the first attempt to develop a workable way of talking about team teaching. In an article published in 1960 Luvern L. Cunningham claims that teaching teams can be divided into four categories: team-leader type, associate type, master teacher-beginning teacher type, and coordinated-team type.[1] Cunningham makes a distinction between the team-leader type and the associate type on the basis of the authority structure involved. The team-leader type has a hierarchical authority structure with a designated leader and the possibility of other roles in the chain of command. The associate type has no designated leadership and is, therefore, generally smaller in order to be manageable. The next type of team mentioned by Cunningham is the master teacher-beginning teacher type. In placing this type of team teaching in a separate category, Cunningham drops his original basis for distinction among teams, that is, the basis of their authority structure. For a master teacher-beginning teacher type team could also be either a team-leader type or an associate type and, therefore, is not distinct from these. Never-

[1] Luvern L. Cunningham, "Team Teaching: Where Do We Stand," *Administrator's Notebook*, vol. VIII, April, 1960.

theless, Cunningham does make an important point by noting that some teams have embraced a training function for beginning teachers and that others have not. The fourth category, a coordinate-team type, is described as a method of joining together for planning and large-group presentations but with each team member retaining personal responsibility for a single class of normal size. After describing this type of team, Cunningham says, "It is questionable whether this should be included as a team type. The relationships appear to be so loose and informal that little can be expected from an organization of this character."[2] No criteria are presented for deciding to what extent a coordinated-team may actually be a team.

The clearest distinction Cunningham makes is between his first two categories, between a team with a set authority structure and a team without one. His third category merely points out an aspect of team teaching, and his fourth category raises a problem but does not solve it. Furthermore, distinguishing among teams solely on the basis of the degree of authority structure they embody does not provide much information about them. Cunningham's pioneering attempt to provide categories for teaching teams is valuable in suggesting some possibilities and in setting a task for those concerned about team teaching. It points out the need for a classification system which will permit adequate communication on this subject.

Will Hemeyer and Jean B. McGrew, in an article describing the team teaching project at Rich Township High School, Park Forest, Illinois, make another important distinction between two types of teaching teams.[3] They divide teams into two types, one which is doing coordinate teaching and the other which is doing associate teaching. In coordinate teaching the typical classroom unit, one teacher with 25 to 30 students, is preserved, but classes are rescheduled so that they may be combined at certain times for certain purposes. "When the purpose of combining classes has been accomplished, the large unit is broken up into its component classes, and each goes about its work under the direction of one teacher."[4] Obviously, coordinate teaching in this sense is very similar to Cunning-

<hr/>

[2] *Ibid.*, p. 3.
[3] Will Hemeyer and Jean B. McGrew, "Big Ideas for Big Classes," *The School Review*, vol. LXVIII, Autumn, 1960, pp. 308–317.
[4] *Ibid.*, p. 309.

ham's coordinate-team type, and, similarly, it runs the danger of not meeting minimal requirements for consideration as a teaching team. Associate teaching, on the other hand, assumes as its basic unit the total group of pupils assigned to the team. Each teacher no longer has his own class and must think of himself as one of a number of teachers of a large group. When the group is subdivided, it is done on the basis of needs that exist within the large group for particular types of subgroups, and it is suggested that "the flexibility of this approach is limited only by the imagination and the initiative of the teachers involved."[5] The authors seem to make their distinction on the basis of the degree of autonomy which the team possesses. The two types they describe appear to occur at the two extremes of a possible scale of autonomy with degrees of autonomy which range all the way from coordinate teaching to associate teaching, to use their terms. This is an important distinction and one which Cunningham must have felt when he was describing his coordinate-team type.

It is regrettable that Robert E. Ohm does not further develop some of the ideas which he presents in his brief article, "Toward a Rationale for Team Teaching."[6] Though it is extremely short, it is one of the best analytical articles on team teaching to date. Ohm does not specify any particular types of team teaching, but in the course of his article he points out all of the areas where distinctions need to be made before one can adequately describe a team teaching project. He indicates that a team is autonomous to the extent to which it accepts and carries out decision-making responsibilities, that the degree of coordination that exists within a team may be one of its distinguishing characteristics, and that there is an important distinction to be made within teams between specialization and subdivision of tasks. This latter distinction is a more highly complex approach to the distinction made by Cunningham between hierarchical and nonhierarchical teams. It can be understood by considering that in order to have specialization one must have specialists, whereas in order to have subdivision of tasks one merely needs to divide the job that is to be done into those tasks which require a

---

[5] *Ibid.*, p. 309.
[6] Robert E. Ohm, "Toward a Rationale for Team Teaching," *Administrator's Notebook*, vol. IX, March, 1961.

special degree of competence and those tasks which can be delegated to less well-trained and less competent people.[7] Ohm concludes, "A team can be categorized along a simple to a complex continuum depending on the nature and scope of the instructional variables for which it is responsible. The problem of complexity and the limits within which the team will be expected to work needs to be considered."[8] Though Ohm does not make any attempt to create a formally structured taxonomy, he does point the way to the construction of such a system.

Interestingly enough, Ohm was one of the first to indicate that there are distinctions that have been made in fields other than education which may be helpful in describing teaching teams. As has been noted in Chapter 3, a teaching team, generally considered, is merely a goal-oriented working group, and, therefore, studies which have been made of working groups in other fields should be helpful to those interested in teaching teams. Of particular value is Herbert A. Simon's *Administrative Behavior*.[9] In an attempt to describe administrative behavior of working groups, Simon makes some important distinctions among types of groups and presents some extremely helpful terms by which some of the types may be described. The presentation in this chapter of a taxonomy for team teaching is in considerable debt to Herbert Simon for many of the distinctions made and many of the terms used.

Before presenting this taxonomy it is necessary to review briefly a few of the major points of the definiton of team teaching presented in Chapter 1. First, a teaching team is a close association of professional teachers, not an association of nonprofessionals or of one professional teacher with one subprofessional assistant. Secondly, this association of professional teachers takes on certain types of responsibilities that have normally been the responsibilities of the school administration, namely the allocation of teachers to tasks and the allocation of pupils to tasks. And third, this professional association with the responsibility for accomplishing certain tasks is a formal

---

[7] Ohm draws his distinction between specialization and subdivision from Robert Dubin, *The World of Work*, Englewood Cliffs, N.J., Prentice-Hall, 1958.

[8] Ohm, *op. cit.*, p. 3.

[9] Herbert A. Simon, *Administrative Behavior*, 2nd ed., New York, Macmillan, 1960.

organization and, as such, is one administrative unit within a larger unit, the school.

Also, it should be pointed out that the subheadings under each major category in the taxonomy are not intended to exhaust the possible points which could be mentioned. Rather, they are meant to give a broad coverage of each topic and to suggest further descriptive features to each reader. Only when team teaching is a much more firmly established concept than it is at this writing will an exhaustive classification be possible.

Taxonomy

 I. Structural requirements of specific situation
    A. Gradedness
    B. Departmentalization
    C. Size of school
    D. Resources
       1. Financial
       2. Human
    E. Goals and special plans
II. Autonomy or span of control within existing structural requirements (to be expressed in degrees: none, little, some, considerable, complete)
    A. Pupils
       1. Degree of control over the use of a variety of types of groupings for a variety of purposes
    B. Teachers
       1. Degree of control over size and composition of team
       2. Degree of control over time available for cooperation and coordination
       3. Degree of control over use of available time
       4. Degree of control over operation without external supervision
       5. Degree of control over nonteam activities of teachers
    C. Curriculum and methods
       1. Degree of control over establishing curriculum goals
       2. Degree of control over choice of materials and methods

      3. Degree of control over study and development of curriculum materials

      4. Degree of control over allocation of finances and other resources of instruction

   D. Schedules

      1. Degree of control over group size and composition

      2. Degree of control over frequency of grouping changes

      3. Degree of control over time allocation

      4. Degree of control over space allocation

      5. Degree of control over teacher allocation

III. Authority structure and degree of specialization (to be expressed in degrees: none, little, some, considerable, total)

   A. Degree of vertical authority structure

      1. Degree of task subdivision

         a. Degree of differentiation in abilities among staff

      2. Degree of hierarchy in administrative structure

         a. Degree of specialization of decision-making functions

         b. Degree of expertise in decision making

   B. Degree of horizontal authority structure

      1. Degree of task specialization

         a. Degree of expertise in special task areas

IV. Coordination (to be expressed by degrees: absent, rare, occasional, frequent, extensive)

   A. Degree of procedural coordination or concern for the organization of the team as a social system

      1. Degree of coordination concerned with behavior and relationship of individuals in terms of authority

      2. Degree of coordination concerned with behavior and relationship of individuals in terms of roles

   B. Degree of substantive coordination or concern for the task

      1. Degree of coordination concerned with pupils

      2. Degree of coordination concerned with curriculum

      3. Degree of coordination concerned with methods

The first major section of the outline, structural requirements of the specific situation, holds a prominent position at the beginning of the taxonomy because it is necessary to consider these factors before attempting to describe the team itself. Virtually every school differs in some respect from every other school, and it is important in trying to describe a team teaching project to be completely aware of the structural conditions which existed in the system prior to the advent of team teaching. Many of these conditions do not come under the direct control of any one individual in the system. Often, being a part of the system's tradition or of the image the system has of itself, they are far more elusive. It is assumed, therefore, that in virtually all cases where a team is introduced into a school system, it is fitted into the existing conditions of that system. These conditions represent external controls that are imposed upon the teaching team and that limit the team in certain ways. Any descripion of a team, therefore, should always be prefaced by a statement of the special requirements the school system has for the organizations that are a part of it.

Under this heading the first item which merits attention is the amount of gradedness which exists in the school. Most high schools and junior high schools today are completely graded, that is each successive year of a child's education is denoted by a specific grade. At the elementary level the fixed grade sequence is less strongly upheld, partly because of the influence of the nongraded school movement. In many elementary schools two or more years of education are combined into a single grade, and, even within this structure, there is often enough flexibility to permit a child to move between groups. At any level the more rigid the concept of gradedness held by the school system, the more difficult it will be for the team to exert any influence in this area, and, among other things, the more difficult it will be for the team to provide an adequate educational environment for extremely talented or extremely retarded children.

Departmentalization is another form of organization, much more characteristic of the high school and junior high than of the elementary school. At present, however, there is considerable study being done on the degree of departmentalization desirable at all levels. On one hand, there has been a movement to departmentalize the elementary school and, on the other hand, there has been a movement to break down departmental barriers in the high school. Many junior high schools have adopted a core program, which preserves departmental structure but which plans considerable overlapping between departments. Once again, though the departmental pattern is less fixed than the grade pattern and may, in situations where the matter is under consideration, be influenced by team teaching, on the whole team teaching will have to accommodate itself to the pre-existing pattern whatever that may be. Therefore, elementary level teams will represent most subjects, junior high school teams will tend to be composed of teachers from two loosely related subject areas, and most high school teams will be single-subject teams.

The size of the school also exerts considerable influence in pre-determining the nature of the team. First, it is fairly evident that a small school will tend to have small teams. Also, smaller schools, that is fewer teachers and fewer pupils, will often have a more favorabe teacher-pupil ratio. In such a situation the creation of small groups may present little difficulty, and the team may concentrate more effort on the use of larger combined groups. But often in such a small school the creation of a truly large group is impossible. In large schools the reverse is more generally true. The teams will tend to be large, the teacher-pupil ratio will tend to be high, and there will be considerable pressure to provide small groups, often with a proportionate increase in the use of large groups.

Obviously, the financial resources of the community are going to place certain controls upon the activities of any organization within the community. A school system in a depressed area that wants to try team teaching will have to work under numerous financial re-strictions. It certainly will have a difficult time providing adequate spaces for the various activities which may be undertaken in a team arrangement. In fact it may have adopted team teaching as a method for handling more successfully already overcrowded situations. In such cases it will probably make extensive use of large groups and will accommodate them in cafeterias, auditoriums, and gymnasiums even though the lighting and accoustics in these places may be in-adequate and even though the school cannot purchase the tech-nological aids which might make such rooms somewhat acceptable. As has been noted before, team teaching, as one step in a move toward quality education, is expensive, and school systems that can-not afford the expense will have to settle for many compromises.

Even in communities that can well afford to make large steps toward increasing the quality of education, teams often have to work under severe financial restrictions. Many school systems have an unwritten rule which says that no extra expenditure may be made for any experimental program. Each student, teacher, department, and grade must receive an equal proportion of the budget of the school no matter what the circumstances. However often this rule may in fact be violated in particular cases, such school systems are very reluctant to bring any violation before the public to the extent which team teaching would demand. True, no matter what the school system and no matter how liberal its financial policies may be, disproportion in the amount of money spent in one school compared with another school of equal size will be a serious matter, one which will require an intelligent public relations effort by the system (see Chapter 8). It seems quite clear, though, that if the effort is made, the results may be surprisingly good.

It is true that the human resources—teachers, administrators, aides—a school can command may, in part, be an aspect of the financial resources it can bring to bear to attract competent personnel. However, there are other aspects of this matter, not directly related to financial resources, which play a large part in determining the pre-existing nature of the school's staff. The competitive position the school holds in the hiring market may be influenced by its geographical location, its reputation, its proximity to institutions of higher learning, and its own peculiar hiring policies. It must be remembered that most schools will not hire completely new personnel for their teams but will form them out of personnel already in the school. It may turn out that many teachers, who were considered thoroughly competent in their individual classrooms are not as adequate in a team situation as it was originally thought they might be. Such inadequacies, as they are exposed, will also place restrictions upon the activities of the team. An elementary school team, for instance, may find that it has four teachers who are adequately trained to teach social studies and the language arts but that it has no teacher who is adequately trained to teach science and math. Such an extreme situation would have to be solved both by a relocation of teachers and by a retraining of some of the available teachers. If the school finds that it does not have the right kind of personnel to put in the team, it will find itself faced with a complex in-service training problem.

The last category under this first heading of the outline is intentionally vague and meant to cover considerable territory. It incorporates all those special goals, programs, projects, plans, and predispositions which the school system has before the advent of team teaching. A few examples should suffice to indicate the kinds of restrictions which are covered in this category. A school may decide that there is a certain grade level or a certain subject area upon which it wishes to concentrate its work with team teaching. It may decide, for instance, that team teaching can only be done after the child has reached a certain age. Or it may decide that it wants to use team teaching as a way of implementing a program for the education of specially talented students.[10] It may wish to limit the amount of time a teacher or a student spends in the team teaching setting. In such a case the teacher and student may find that they spend two fifth of their day working in a team and three fifths of their day in the regular school program. The scheduling problems involved in this kind of part-time team teaching limit the kinds of activities that can take place. In fact the school may select any one of a variety of goals for team teaching and concentrate its efforts upon achieving that particular goal. However, such concentration upon a single goal necessarily imposes certain limitations upon the activities of the team. It is not meant to suggest here that such limitations are bad. To the contrary, they are undoubtedly necessary and wise in all cases. But, in describing a team teaching project it is necessary to recognize the limitations under which it is working, whatever they may be. Only then can one begin to get a clear picture of what a particular team is doing.

Having indicated, then, those pre-existing conditions in a school system which may act as limiting factors upon the organization and function of teaching teams, one may now attempt to examine the degree to which the team assumes control over the variety of factors that make up an educational program. The amount of control which the team does assume will be limited both by the administration of the school and by the team itself. In the early stages of development of a team teaching project, the school administration will often want

---

[10] Carl H. Peterson, "Easton Senior High School Team Teaching Program," Curriculum Publication SE-60-1, Easton, Pa., Easton-Forks Joint School System and Easton Area Joint High School System, 1960.

to restrict the team's area of control until it is sure that the team is ready to assume some degree of autonomy. Such early restrictions will often save the inexperienced team from trapping itself in organizational schemes that quickly become unmanageable. The administration will also want to restrict the autonomy of the experienced team to some extent because a completely autonomous team would undoubtedly be administratively unfeasible. Such restraint is clearly wise in most cases, but, if it is extended too far, it may severely restrict the possible value of team teaching.

However, the school administration is not the only source of potential restraints upon the span of control of the teaching team. Even within an area in which the team has been given complete freedom of control by the administration, it will often unconsciously place severe restrictions upon its own autonomy. As was noted in Chapter 1, teams differ greatly in the degree to which they are willing to assume control over the various factors of education which confront them.

The autonomy of a teaching team, then, may be described in terms of the degree of control that the team can exercise in four interrelated areas: pupils, teachers, curriculum and methods, and schedules. Each of these areas can be divided up into a number of smaller areas for purposes of description, and each subarea may be thought to have associated with it a continuum of control expressed in degrees: none, little, some, considerable, complete. Although it might be inferred from what has ben said that a certain degree of autonomy should be a goal of all team teaching projects, it must be kept in mind that this descriptive framework does not intend value judgments. An evaluation of a particular team teaching project might discover that, given certain pre-existing conditions in the school system, a lower degree of autonomy for one team might be more appropriate than a higher degree of autonomy would be for another. It will be difficult to find a team that has complete autonomy, and, likewise, it will be difficult to find a team that has no antonomy at all and still meets the minimum requirements for being a team.

Each team may be able to control to some extent the various ways in which its pupils are grouped. Team teaching can permit extensive exploration of a wide variety of criteria for combining students, some of which have yet to be explored, so that each student may obtain maximum benefit from instruction. The responsibility for exploration in this area lies with the team. Even if it merely considers the most widely recognized types of grouping, it will still have to decide between heterogeneous and homogeneous grouping, or it will have to decide what combination of the two is appropriate for various purposes. And then, within homogeneous grouping, it will have to decide to what extent it will make use of ability grouping, achievement grouping, interest grouping, and other special groupings. Many elementary school teams have a guiding principle which enables them to say that they are going to group by ability in reading and mathematics and that other subjects will be taught by the homeroom teacher in homerooms of heterogeneously grouped students. Once having made such a decision, the team has placed severe restrictions upon its ability to vary these groupings for any special purposes. A team seldom realizes that the fewer arbitrary decisions it makes about grouping procedures, the greater will be its control over the use of a variety of groupings as it becomes aware that such variety may be desirable to provide for those individual differences which it becomes more and more capable of assessing. Autonomy in this area consists of a team's maintaining control over the types of groupings that can eventually be used and not restricting its control by imposing upon itself arbitrary groupings before any rational basis for these groupings exists.

The next item to be considered is the degree of control that the team can exercise over the teachers that are a part of it. The five points listed under this heading in the outline should be self-explanatory, but some clarification on each point is perhaps necessary. A team may have some control over its own size and composition. This assumes that the team probably has a better idea than anyone else of its own personnel needs. If it decides that it needs another professional member on the team for a given amount of work, it may be able to obtain a new teacher. On the other hand, it may decide that its excessive work load could be relieved by the addition of a nonprofessional assistant of some variety. When the size and composition of the team is decided by the administration and cannot be changed by the team, restrictions may be placed upon the team's ability to fulfill its potentialities. Most beginning teams are generally understaffed, and, unless they have some control over obtaining assistance of one form or another, they will have some difficulty in being thoroughly effective.

It is similarly true that beginning teams are not provided with sufficient time for cooperation and coordination. Virtually all teams can exert considerable control over the time that is available because they are always able to use after-school hours for this function. However, a team may be able to control its schedule so that it can provide for itself the necesary time for cooperation and coordination during the school day. Probably over the course of a few years, less and less time will be necessary for this function, and the team, if it has control over this time, can then allot the time to other purposes. (See the discussion below of section four for further treatment of the problem of coordination.) Of course, even given some control over the amount of time available, the team may not have control over the way in which it uses its time. If the team or the school administration has decided that the team should have three team meetings per week, there will be a strong tendency for the team to hold these meetings even when there is no reason for them. This is just another way in which teams will often restrict their own autonomy.

To have considerable autonomy teams must function on their own without continual external supervision. If, as may often be desirable, the principal or some other ranking member of the administration attends all team meetings and supervises all activities of the team, the team's span of control will be limited.

Finally, there is an extremely important matter which is seldom recognized. If the team has no control over the nonteam activities of its members, it may soon find that it can no longer function as a team because the energies of its members are being consumed in other activities. This seems to be particularly true of team leaders, who often find that their new position of prominence within the school organization entails a heavy demand upon their time from both the school and the community. All too often these teachers, who in the beginning have the demanding job of working out the operation of their team, are suddenly called upon to participate on system-wide committees, school committees, and extracurricular committees. In short, they become celebrities of the community. The teaching team should be able to exert some control over the extra-team activities of its members.

The third major area over which the team may have control is curriculum and methods. Team teaching has been notoriously effective in exposing weaknesses in the materials and in the sequence of materials that have been the curriculum in the schools. It has also raised serious questions about many long-established teaching methods. Therefore, teaching teams, almost without exception, have been faced with the problem of revising the old curriculum (see Chapter 5). To do this job most effectively, decisions must be made about what are to be the goals of the new or revised curriculum. Curriculum work that is not directed toward goals is liable to be extremely haphazard and inefficient. Old curriculum goals, seen in the light which team teaching sheds upon them, appear ill defined and inadequate. Teams generally discover, and undoubtedly will continue to discover, that they can exercise considerable control over the shape and content of the new curriculum and over the choice of appropriate methods for teaching the new materials. But it is a common complaint of teaching team projects, when they find themselves faced with major curriculum revisions, that not enough free time has been allotted them to pursue this extremely time-consuming curriculum work. Control over the development of curriculum and methods will be of little benefit to a team that has little control over the amount of teacher time than can be used for curriculum work.

A new or revised curriculum invariably requires new teaching materials, new texts, and new technological aids. The team may have some control over the choice of these new materials within the restrictions that may be imposed by the financial condition of the system and by the selection policy already in effect. Often teams will find that no published materials are available that meet the needs of their curriculum. In such cases the team may decide to make use of its clerical help to prepare and process the materials that are necessary. In other cases the team may find that the use of audio-visual aids may make available to the students instructional materials that would be otherwise unobtainable. A team, working on its own budget, would be able to choose among a wide variety of alternatives.

Though the topic of schedules is broken down into a number of subheadings, it is difficult to consider any one of these subheadings without relating it to several of the others. Therefore, the following discussion will consider the general problem of scheduling as a whole and will touch upon the individual aspects of this problem as they come up.

Once decisions have been made about what types of groups of pupils the team will employ and about the purposes for which various types of groups will be used (see II A on the outline, and the related discussion above), decisions will have to be made about the exact size and composition of each group, the frequency of grouping change that is possible, time allocations, space allocations, and teacher allocations. In schools where the team teaching project is a very small part of a larger and more conventional organization, many schedule decisions will have to be made by the administration. This is also true to a lesser degree of schools that have adopted team teaching completely but do not have an ideal physical plant within which to work. However, this fact need not seriously restrict a team's area of control. Far more restrictive are the questionable assumptions under which many teams work.

There is a very strong tendency, pointed out elsewhere in this book, for teaching teams to think of their group of students as being composed of a certain number of conventional classroom groups. If the conventional class size in a school is 30 pupils, a team which works with 90 pupils will be inclined to look at them as three groups of 30, and it will tend to split the large group up on this basis. Thus, medium groups would be groups of 30, and small groups would be groups of 15. Such a procedure has its limitations. If the team could look at its group of 90 pupils without thinking of it as three groups of 30, it would quickly see that there are many different ways to subdivide this group. Of course, decisions about group sizes will have to be guided by the size and number of the spaces that are available to the team. If the largest space available to a team of three teachers and ninety students is a classroom with a maximum occupancy of thirty students, the team will be extremely limited in the variety of sizes that can be obtained. However, if the same team has access to two classrooms with a maximum occupancy of 45 and one room that accommodates all 90 pupils, the potential for a wide variety of group sizes is greatly increased.

It is also generally asumed that a period length of one hour, more or less, is somehow optimum. Elementary schools are far less restricted by this assumption than are secondary schools. The latter show a strong reluctance to think in terms of some other basic unit of time, say a half hour. Since two-hour sessions are fairly common in science courses to allow sufficient time for laboratory work, there seems to be no good reason why larger chunks of time could not be employed profitably in other subjects.

The one-hour assumption is often found closely linked with the every-day assumption; each class must meet an hour a day. Though there are many deviations from this pattern, it is, nonetheless, generally accepted. Alternative arrangements are not only entirely possible, but also may prove to be of great value. For certain purposes two two-hour classes in one week might be much more valuable than five one-hour classes.

Many teaching teams asume that once groupings and allocations have been established at the beginning of a school year, they should be relatively fixed for the remainder of the year. Rarely does a team realize that if it arranged the program with extreme care, it would be theoretically possible for the team to form new groupings every day. Naturally, such an extreme measure would be virtually impossible because of the inordinant amount of team time it would consume in order to make the necesary grouping decisions on a daily basis. However, it is extremely important for teams to see such an arrangement as being theoretically possible. Such a realization may encourage the team to plan to have a certain number of check points throughout the year when the team will meet to review the grouping procedures that have been used during the previous period and to make any changes that are thought necessary for the next period.

If assumptions like those noted above are made by the team or form the basis for the administrative policy within which the team must operate, the grouping possibilities that are open to the team are extremely limited indeed. Curiously enough, it is an observed fact that teams do far more than administrations to restrict these possibilities. They forget all too often that flexibility is not inherent in a team teaching form of organization It must be carefully planned for and built into the everyday operation of the team. In this regard, few teaching teams have even begun to realize the potential for planned flexibility that is available to them.

Beginning with Section III of the taxonomy, "Authority Structure and Degree of Specialization," we are in considerable debt to Herbert A. Simon for the descriptive framework used. Simon's approach, mentioned above and described in some detail in Chapter 3, distinguishes between vertical and horizontal authority structure. Both types may be present in a team to some degree; none, little, some, considerable, total. Vertical authority structure has two basic subdivisions: there is task subdivision, and there is specialization in decision-making functions. Task subdivision occurs when teaching tasks are separated from nonteaching tasks and can be seen in a team that incorporates such positions as teacher aide, clerical assistant, audio-visual specialist, and laboratory assistant. A team which has created special roles for the specialization of decision-making functions may have such positions as team leader, team coordinator, senior teacher, teacher, and intern or student teacher.

Figure 2 is a diagram of the teaching team model used in the Lexington Public Schools, Lexington, Massachusetts.[11] This team would probably be described as having considerable vertical au-

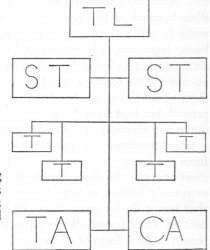

FIGURE 2. The Lexington Teaching Team Model. TL: Team Leader; ST: Senior Teacher; T: Teacher; TA: Teacher Aide; CA: Clerical Aide.

[11] Beverly S. Stone and John M. Bahner, "The Teaching Team Project: Lexington, Massachusetts," Cambridge, Mass., SUPRAD, April, 1962, p. 6.

thority structure. On the other hand, a team composed of two professional teachers who make decisions jointly would be described as having no vertical authority structure. Often teams are formed of four or five professional teachers with aides of one kind or another assigned to the team but with no hierarchy of authority among the professionals. The teachers insist that decisions will be made by the total professional group by democratic process. Often they feel that it is best to let authority in any given situation evolve out of group process. Such teams could be described as having some vertical authority structure. It should be emphasized at this point that authority should not be understood as simply a matter of giving orders. It is equally as much a matter of seeking advice from the right people at the right times and of exercising persuasion when necessary. In other words, authority is synonymous with a very high degree of administrative skill. As is suggested in the outline, the fact that a team may have established certain roles for the specialization of the decision-making function does not necesarily mean that the decision-making function is any more specialized than it was before these roles were established and filled. In order for such specialization to be effective, considerable expertise is necessary in the ability to perform in the established roles. One of the major problems in team teaching has been defining these new roles and training experienced teachers to fill them.

If a teaching team contains a wide variety of specialized tasks for the teachers that are a part of it, it may be said to have considerable horizontal authority structure. The general task of an elementary school team may be to teach sixth graders. This general task may be divided up into many specialized teaching tasks: language arts, social studies, math, science, art, music, physical education, etc. And, of course, these tasks could be even further specialized. Likewise, in a high school the general task of teaching English can be divided up into a number of specialties: prose, poetry, drama, composition, speech, etc. It is evident that the size of the team will limit the degree of specialization that can exist within it. It is also evident that though a team may claim to embrace a number of specialized tasks, it will not rank high in degree of horizontal authority structure unless the teachers who assume these tasks are extremely competent in their specialized area. Like new roles of authority, new roles of specialization will generally require extra training before they will be optimally effective.

Though subject matter specialization may be the most common form of horizontal authority structure, there are two other forms that are worth noting. The first is methodological or technological specialization, and the best examples of such specialization in today's schools are the large-group lecturer and the television instructor. Other such specialties may soon develop so that in the future we may have teaching-machine specialists, tape-teaching specialists, etc. It would be unlikely that any single team would command the total services of any one of these specialists, but it is conceivable that three or four teams could share the services of one specialist. Secondly, as noted above, nonteaching tasks may also be specialized, and the special functions may be distributed among two or more full or part-time, specially trained personnel. Thus a team might embrace a full-time teacher aide to help with supervision of pupils during nonteaching activities, a half-time clerical aide to handle the paper work of the team, and a quarter-time audio-visual specialist to prepare materials for large-group presentations and to operate the various technological aids at the disposal of the team. Each team will have a variety of nonteaching functions to be handled by nonprofessional assistants, and the number and variety of these aides will have to be determined by the individual team, perhaps in cooperation with other teams in the same school. .

Looking at teaching teams throughout the country, one will find that in the majority there is some combination of vertical and horizontal authority structure. They are certainly not to be considered mutually exclusive categories. Indeed, though it is possible for vertical authority structure to exist without horizontal structure, it is impossible for horizontal structure, as described above, to exist without some vertical authority structure. Simon is very firm on this matter: ". . . If there is any horizontal specialization, vertical specialization is absolutely essential to achieve coordination among the operative employees."[12] As mentioned before, many team teaching projects have suggested that cooperation is all that is necessary for a team to function. Simon raises an important objection to this theory: "In cooperative systems, even though all participants are

[12] Simon, *op. cit.*, p. 9.

agreed on the objectives to be attained, they cannot ordinarily be left to themselves in selecting the strategies that will lead to these objectives; for the selection of a correct strategy involves a knowledge of each as to the strategies selected by the others."[13] The authors suspect very strongly that if all teaching teams that claim to work on a purely cooperative basis were carefully studied, a very clear vertical authority structure would be apparent. The only exception would be in a case where the team has most of its decision-making functions assumed by administrative personnel outside of the team. Pseudo teams which begin their life as pure cooperative ventures very quickly become nonteams as soon as any kind of conflict arises; the participating teachers withdraw and re-establish their individual autonomy.

In talking about any team teaching project, probably the most important aspect to be described is the type and degree of coordination that is present in the team. More than all the factors noted thus far that are important for the functioning of a teaching team, coordination seems to be crucial. In any formal working group it is important for the members of the group to understand and at least partially accept the goals and the structure of the group. And it is equally important for lines of communication to be established and kept open so that these basic understandings are furthered and so that new understandings can be established as the team performs its task.

As noted before, in Chapter 3, Simon gives us an important distinction between two types of coordination—procedural and substantive.[14] Within procedural coordination he includes the description of the behaviors and relationships of the members of the organization, the definitions of the roles of the individual members, the lines of authority that are to exist within the organization, and the communication channels that are to be used. Clearly, when you have any organization with even the smallest degree of vertical specialization of decision-making functions, a certain degree of procedural coordination is going to be necessary to see that each person knows his job and does it. Substantive coordination is necessary to determine who is to be taught what, when, where, and why.

[13] *Ibid.*, p. 73.
[14] *Ibid.*, p. 10.

Obviously, when a teaching team is first formed and while it is developing into an effective working group, there is going to be a large amount of procedural coordination. Furthermore, it is going to make large demands upon the available time of the team because never before has it been necessary for teachers to handle procedural coordination except in a very limited sense. For the individual teacher who maintains his autonomy in his own classroom, there are few encounters with procedural coordination outside of faculty meetings and occasional committee meetings, and there is almost no demand for him to have to take a direct hand in facilitating whatever small amount of procedural coordination he may experience. In a teaching team procedural coordination becomes an everyday experience and at least a small part of every professional teacher's job.

However, as the team develops in its capacity to run itself efficiently, the amount of time needed for procedural coordination should become less and less, eventually reaching a very low level. Few teaching teams have reached this point yet, and there appears to be some danger that teams will continue to consume large amounts of time and effort in working out procedural matters. As has been noted earlier, effective vertical authority structure does not just happen when you assign certain teachers to certain roles. First, a teacher who has not received special training is not going to adjust easily to being in a position of authority. All too often such a person will not exercise the authority that he has been given. Sometimes he will express his doubts by saying that exercise of authority seems to him undemocratic and therefore distasteful. When this situation occurs, the team tends to fall apart, and extensive procedural coordination is necesary to set things right again.

Likewise, few teams spend much time in their planning stages defining carefully the roles that are to be filled within the hierarchical structure of the team. Consequently, when a teacher is assigned to his role, he often has a very poor and incomplete idea of what his function in the team is to be. Without such knowledge, he is incapable of doing his job effectively, and again the team will suffer until, through extensive procedural coordination, the situation is rectified.

It is clear, then, why so many teams have spent so much time working out procedural matters and why so many teams complain that when they began they did not have sufficient time allotted to them to coordinate activities as much as necessary. But if teams have complained of not having enough time for procedural coordination, they certainly have not had enough time for substantive coordination, for, given a limited amount of time, more attention to procedural matters means less attention to substantive matters. If one accepts as one of the major goals of team teaching the opportunity for a group of teachers to get together to improve the substantive quality of the teaching task (see Chapter 5), there is a very real danger that teams will lose sight of this goal if they are overwhelmed with procedural problems. To any teaching team on the job, procedural problems always seem much more immediate and important than substantive problems, and it takes strong leadership and an effective working organization to either solve these problems quickly or put them aside in favor of the more important job of improving the quality of instruction.

In virtually every teaching team project across the country, the substantive problem has been the same; as soon as a group of teachers get together and find time to think and talk about what they are going to teach, whom they are going to teach it to, when they are going to teach it, what teaching situation is best for its presentation, and why they are going to teach it, they quickly realize that they don't have very good answers to any of these questions. Some teams have made the assumption that the curriculum goals of the team should be the curriculum goals previously used in the school and supposedly adhered to by each and every teacher. Such an assumption has invariably been proven to be naive. When the teachers get together, they find that they haven't had the same goals, haven't pursued them in the same way, and haven't considered carefully the reasons for their own actions. With this realization a movement for change is started, and substantive coordination becomes the major concern of the team.

A few teaching team projects have tackled the substantive problem immediately because they were established for exactly that sole purpose. With a limited substantive goal clearly defined, they have been able to avoid many of the distractions of a procedural nature that have plagued other teams. Indeed, there might be a lesson to be learned from these projects. Teaching teams might fare much better if they were more sure of where they were going before they started.

As is perhaps already apparent to the reader, substantive coordination is clearly related to horizontal specialization, just as procedural coordination is clearly related to vertical authority structure. The more training each specialist has in his particular specialty, the more effective will be the results of the substantive coordination that takes place. But also, in terms of the degree of substantive coordination, well-trained specialists, adequately prepared in the areas to which they have been assigned, are more likely to be willing to tackle substantive problems.

In part this chapter has been an attempt to establish a framework within which teaching teams can be more adequately described. But it has also served as a heuristic device for suggesting what is believed to be the necessary path of development of the teaching team as it is seen by the authors of this book. Consequently, though an attempt has been made to suspend value judgments as much as possible, it is inevitable that they have often been implicit, if not explicit, in the manner in which the taxonomy has been structured and explained. Nonetheless, it is felt that an understanding of this taxonomy will be of great benefit to anyone interested in discovering and describing team teaching.

Chapter 5

Team Teaching and the Curriculum

JOSEPH C. GRANNIS

Graduate School of Education, Harvard University

In team teaching two or more teachers share decisions for a significant part of the instruction of students assigned to them and for decisions required to organize efficient action. This rewording of the basic definition of team teaching (see Chapter 1) stresses two focuses for decisions: the curriculum and the organization of a team. Scope and sequence of content, instructional materials, learning activities, and evaluational procedures are all determined to some extent by any team. Other decisions involved are the assignment of teachers to specific lessons, the grouping of pupils, the division of space, the coordination of groups, the use of equipment, and so forth. These are by no means mutually exclusive categories. The decision to allow a certain group to dwell longer than had been planned on a topic in science has both a curricular and an organizational aspect. Not only does it represent a choice of content, but it also commits the team to various adjustments of its schedule. Probably, most of a team's decisions as they are commonly worded have both a curricular and an organizational aspect. Nevertheless, it is essential to realize that each aspect requires its own justification and that the central problem confronting a team is to balance the demands that both create.

We shall examine in this chapter how these two focuses of a team's decisions interact, and we shall see some of the opportunities and difficulties that this interaction can present. The first part of the chapter will barely sketch some of the most general characteristics of the complex of decisions involved in team teaching. Later parts will then take up in greater detail several more substantive questions in order to illustrate the points advanced in the first part and in order to provide a few guide lines for those who are prepared to explore further some of the various problems that a team must solve.

Our approach will, of necessity, be more clinical and formal than empirical. The research literature which would be both relevant and helpful is, in many of these areas, either scarce or nonexistent. However, the author has been engaged for several years in a revision of the social studies curriculum in the Lexington team teaching project, Lexington, Massachusetts, and this has at least served to define some major questions. The experience has been clinical in the sense that one must cope with practical problems that do not appear to be easily replicable because of both their complexity and their relationship to historical accidents. It has been formal in the sense that analysis of what is to be learned and of the various resources for instruction can suggest the range of alternatives that research may then help us to evaluate. Some persons prefer to play with theory before data, while others proceed with equal reason in the opposite way. The author frankly confesses to being one of the former, if a choice must be made, but he hopes that the reader will perceive that the theory has been chastened by brute fact and will join in testing more widely what has been developed in a highly specific situation.

The Decisions Matrix

Let us observe first that team teaching involves the individual teacher in making many more decisions than does the self-contained classroom. Most of these decisions, to be sure, may be shared with other teachers. Some decisions which normally occupy a teacher in the self-contained classroom may, in team teaching, be delegated to a colleague. Specialization and the differentiation of new roles are intended to redistribute the teachers' decisions, sometimes even to university personnel. Nevertheless, many added decisions are occasioned by team teaching. These develop not only out of the more complex organization of a team but also out of a team's altered view of the curriculum. Knowing in advance only that team teaching stresses efficiency, the novitiate may be shocked and, for a while at least, disillusioned when he discovers the true proportions of the demands that team teaching makes upon him.

But it is putting the cart before the horse to say, as we almost did above, that the more complex organization of team teaching is the *cause* of new decisions confronting the teachers. We shall see later on in what sense this is true, but here we should reverse the proposition. The more complex organization of team teaching, whether in one form or another, *results* from the desire to give teachers more options than they would have if they operated alone. Because we tend to reify unknowns, we tend to think of team teaching as a strange new creation of some sort which has been found to contain all sorts of unwanted or unexpected problems requiring decisions. It would be more appropriate to say that team teaching is a structure of givens and alternatives, deliberately fashioned to create certain options that require decisions and also entailing other decisions that might not have been anticipated in the original design. The advantage of this second formulation is that it emphasizes the necessity for considering from the very beginning of a project the decisions that one does and does not want to demand of the teachers. Such considerations will strongly determine the structure that one proposes to establish.

Review very briefly just a few of the many features that could be built into a team teaching situation. Specialization could run the gamut from a teacher's advising his colleagues on a brief series of lessons to a teacher's replacing his colleagues for a major part of the curriculum. Cooperative planning could be an occasion for in-service training as well as a means of redistributing, if not actually lightening, responsibilities. With a larger complement of both teachers and pupils, team teaching permits many more grouping arrangements than are possible in the self-contained classroom, and space and materials can be coordinated on a broader basis. As the reader is already aware, this only scratches the surface.

Clearly, each of these features would almost inevitably thrust a team into a host of decisions unfamiliar in degree, if not in kind, to the teacher in the self-contained classroom. Which lessons will we ask a specialist to handle? What sort of planning should the teachers not do collectively? When is it desirable to conduct large-group instruction? When we remember that for every such decision the team must juggle both an argument for instructional effectiveness and a rationale for organizational efficiency, we begin to respect the dimensions of the central problem the teachers face.

Not only are there many additional decisions to make in team teaching, but also every decision, clearly every major decision, affects many other decisions in the immediate or more distant future. If a team decides to release one of its teachers from language arts instruction in order to prepare science lessons, this then restricts the grouping possibilities in language arts. Presumably the team must have taken into account a number of questions concerning the relative competencies of the teachers, the optimum grouping arrangements for language arts, and so on. Furthermore, if unanticipated difficulties arise in executing the language arts plans, the team— now minus the person delegated to science planning—will not have remaining the same range of alternatives that was available at the outset. Multiply this oversimplified example by the number of leading decisions to be made, and you will have an intriguing problem of the sort that game theory might investigate.

One aspect of the problem is that a team generally wants to keep open as many viable alternatives as possible for potential decisions in the future. This is a major part of the much vaunted flexibility of team teaching, which many teams are very jealous of preserving. There was a stage in the development of the Lexington project when all of the pupils in the Franklin School (Grades 1 through 6) were studying farming simultaneously in social studies; it was intended that this be followed by studies of water, oil, and space as they relate to man. This was a bold and imaginative plan, which had a multitude of possibilities for combining teachers and pupils from different grade levels for various purposes and yet which left the several teams comparatively free to determine the specific content for pupils at different achievement levels. The succeeding stage in the project, however, saw the teachers return to grade levels in social studies and adopt a sequence of units that did not allow many of these alternatives to be realized (although still other possibilities were opened up).

In order to account for this strategic retreat, let us turn over the coin. If sustained effective action is desired, it is imperative to cut down on the alternatives confronting a team at certain junctures. The first scheme mentioned above broke down in practice partly because the teams had not yet worked out a planning strategy that could cope with all of the alternatives the scheme presented. It required systems of communications, recording, and scheduling, without which the teachers at different levels could not establish direction.

This apparent paradox can be related to a suggestion advanced by Bartlett in his analysis of thinking.[1] He distinguishes between "closed" and "open" systems of thought and argues that in a closed system, moves that reduce the number of probable next moves are preferred, whereas in an open system, there is a tendency to maximize possibilities. In education, as in all realms of action, we are continuously involved in both types of systems. The art is to keep them properly phased. The literature on team teaching has laid so much stress upon the flexibility created by its myriad potential opportunities that we have neglected the very real possibility that certain arrangements might lead to even more rigid states than those with which we began. We will observe later on how this can materialize in a team's scheduling as a consequence of making decisions in response to immediate needs that render the schedule unresponsive to needs that develop subsequently. Likewise, we will notice how attempts to involve a maximum of teachers in the collective planning of a set of lessons can force the teachers to close the system more on the basis of their own need for consensus than on the basis of the needs of the pupils.

Another general characteristic of the complex of decisions that confront a team is the embarrassing fact that there is no adequate rationale for many of the decisions that a team is required to make. Who knows, even intuitively, what kinds of learnings are best suited to large- or to small-group instruction? Some persons have recommended that various proportions of the total instruction be conducted in large, average, and small groups respectively, but this does not tell us when one or another size is more appropriate. Some have pushed the argument further to claim that those learning activities involving socratic discussion, individual recitation, com-

[1] Sir Frederick Bartlett, *Thinking: An Experimental and Social Study*, New York, Basic Books, 1958.

mittee work, and the like are more adaptable to small groups than to large, and that activities adaptable to either large- or small-group instruction include lectures, demonstrations, films, silent independent study, and so on. Now there is some validity to this approach, but not enough. To the extent that one can say that the behaviors of discussing x or viewing a film or demonstration of x are the behaviors of the desired learning outcomes, then one might determine the size of a group on this basis. It is more likely, however, that the question has merely regressed from, "When are large or small groups more appropriate?" to "When should we use discussions, films, or demonstrations?" These are not the same question, but they are interdependent. We will consider this problem further in a later section, and our ignorance will force us to be more charitable to the approach suggested above. Let it suffice at this point to indicate that when a team must choose and justify its choices without enjoying the security of convictions based on public knowledge, it is faced with a major dilemma. The teacher in the self-contained classroom is in the same predicament in some respects, but he does not have to deal with the same range of alternatives and does not have to rationalize his position to his colleagues.

A more subtle aspect of this problem is one that has plagued for years the whole area of supervision in education. In brief, it is that a teacher might be by intuitive standards a whiz in the classroom and yet not have the capacity to describe objectively to others just what it is that he does that makes the difference. We have all had the experience of hearing a master teacher tell us that he uses filmstrips, three texts instead of one, committee work, and so forth, but seldom do we hear him analyze what it is in his behavior that succeeds where so many others fail with these same techniques. It might be, for example, that the type of question he asks in the classroom is a more fundamental consideration, but even some of the best teachers often cannot verbalize about such things. This, of course, will cramp our style when we are attempting to utilize team teaching for in-service training. A far more pervasive effect, however, is to be noticed throughout discussions among teachers. Plans are often cast mechanically at that level of gross techniques on which the teachers manage to communicate, and the kind of behavioral articulation that is implicit in terms like *preparation* and *follow-up* does not get specified for collective action. Indeed, those teachers who are threatened by proposals that they feel they cannot handle can become a serious drag on their colleagues who cannot specify what it is that they want to accomplish, and who must accommodate, therefore, to the others to maintain team morale. This suggests that a high priority should be established for the training of team leaders in the clinical analysis of teaching behavior. Though some teachers may very well be master teachers in the classroom, they are often unable to foster substantial growth among other teachers with whom they work.

Still another general characteristic of the decisions complex that confronts a team is that the teachers frequently do not have the hardware—the reading materials, achievement tests, personality inventories, and so on—that may be necessary to carry out their intentions effectively. This is especially relevant for curriculum revision and for the differentiated assignments that are associated with the nongraded school and the individualization of instruction. Other schools or scholars may have developed the tools a team needs to implement its intentions, but it is a notorious fact in education that a group of teachers must often start from scratch because we do not have a cumulative system for distributing the results of educational studies.

This was another reason for the breakdown of the original social studies revision in the Lexington project (see above). The teachers felt that they did not have the instructional materials that were essential to the variety of attacks they had proposed for studies on various levels. This can be construed to some extent as an adverse comment on the teachers' resourcefulness at that early stage of the Lexington project, and we will attend to this problem when we discuss a planning strategy for a team. At the same time, however, it raised the larger question of whether the teachers could legitimately be expected to create all of the materials that a curriculum revision might require. It was this question that led to the Harvard consultants' stepping in to assist the teams more actively in the further revision of their curriculum. The University had originally perceived its role in the curriculum affairs of the Lexington teams as that of a midwife, ministering to the painful birth of the expected progeny of team teaching. Only much later was it fully realized that successful curriculum revision could not come from the teachers alone.

It might be supposed that a school could easily keep a damper on the teams' ambitions to revise their curriculum by attempting to provide an interim period for the stabilization of new roles, the working out of schedules, and so forth. In other words, a school might try to focus first on the efficiency of the teams' operations before releasing the energies of the teams to concentrate directly on the effectiveness of the instruction and whatever revision in the curriculum that might entail. Ironically, however, if the reorganization of the school makes substantial demands upon the teachers for collective action, a doubly frustrating situation is likely to ensue. The teachers will initiate curriculum revision even though sufficient allowance has not been made for the time and resources it requires. And the resulting confusion may well offset the increased efficiency and effectiveness that might be obtained with those elements conserved from the old curriculum.

This impulse to revise the curriculum is not simply the consequence of the teachers' exchanging more ideas with each other in team teaching than in the self-contained classroom, although this phenomenon will not be underestimated by anyone who has experienced it. Neither is it sufficiently explained by the tremendous impact that nationwide programs of curriculum revision are having upon the schools. *The teachers in team teaching must revise their curriculum because, more often than not, they have hitherto not perceived in it the texture of intentions which they now require in order to rationalize their decisions.* They must ask, out loud and far more frequently, "What are we trying to accomplish with the children, and why?" The results of the teams' efforts to revise the curriculum on their own may look to others more like "more of the same" than like the splendid products of a PSSC or an SMSG. The teachers alone cannot muster anything like the resources of these larger efforts. But to the teachers themselves, their own handiwork appears very different from the curriculum with which they began. In varying degrees they are discovering the underlying rationale of the curriculum which has been in their books for several decades or more.

Perhaps this should caution us, as we develop in the future more radical departures from the standard courses of study of the era now passing, that we must specify much more clearly how the intentions of the curriculum relate to the decisions that must be made at various points by both teachers and pupils. This is perhaps another way of saying that we must specify our criteria for learning, but it says also that these criteria, in addition to providing the basis for the final evaluation of learning outcomes, must serve to regulate the process of inquiry at every turn along the path. A curriculum requires the continual interplay of long- and short-range intentions. Too often, however, it becomes embalmed in an assortment of textbooks and teachers' guides. These may then overdetermine many of the particulars which should be most responsive to the immediate contingencies of the learning situation, while the generalities, lying in state, fail to govern the teachers' tactics. Team teaching exhumes the curriculum. It forces the teachers to confront decisions that in the self-contained classroom they may have surrendered or executed unwittingly. This is not to say that team teaching necessarily copes effectively with the problem, but rather that it cannot avoid it.

We have been suggesting so far that team teaching tends to generate a demand for new materials and techniques of instruction because the teachers revise the curriculum in the process of trying to define their intentions. It is also the case, as we have implied all along, that their demand for materials and techniques reflects the organizational requirements of the teams. This is nowhere more evident than in the need for tests and inventories in team teaching. It is widely recognized, for example, that instruments for the evaluation of learning with respect to behavioral objectives are sorely lacking in many areas, notably in science, social studies, and certain areas of language arts—in short, at all those points where we have been accustomed to speak of "understandings" and "appreciations." This now poses an acute problem for the teams in their grouping of pupils and evaluation of pupil progress. Given that teachers must evaluate pupils collectively to some extent, they do not ordinarily enjoy in team teaching the conditions that one has in the self-contained classroom for acquiring information about a pupil in a relatively constant environment.

In the first place, each teacher is likely to be dealing with more pupils than he would handle in the self-contained classroom. (These remarks may not apply in quite the same way to a departmentalized situation as they do to an elementary school, but there is a similar problem in both.) This means that the teacher will not have as many encounters with a given child as he would if he were teaching alone and, furthermore, that the encounters he does have will not fall as neatly as before into recurrent patterns like "the boy in the third row," "the girl who always wants to work with so-and-so," etc. Therefore, the teacher cannot rely as heavily as he might in the self-contained classroom on his more casual strategies for picking up information on the run.

Secondly, the pupils themselves are interacting with more than one teacher. This raises the familiar question of whether or not the children need a mother-surrogate in the classroom or at least a single adult with whom to establish a special emotional relationship. Unfortunately, the issue has been debated along the somewhat misleading line of trying to determine the possible effects upon the child's personality of having more than one teacher. The research which has been addressed to the question defined in this way seems to confirm our expectations that only a small fraction of the school population needs to be the object of this kind of concern. At the same time the argument has practically ignored the broader issue which has been extensively explored under the heading of *classroom climate*. Here we have begun to recognize that children (and all of us, for that matter) must understand an elaborate structure of expectations and procedures in order to function both as independent individuals and as members of a group, in a classroom or in another social context. The danger is not so much that we might damage the core of a child's personality by involving him with more than one teacher simultaneously, but that our expectations and procedures might be conflicting in such a way as to reduce the child's capacity for regulating autonomously his own processes of inquiry. Consider a relatively simple matter just to illustrate what is involved here. If the several teachers with whom a child is involved have very different tolerances for interruptions, noise, and so forth, the child might adopt a defensive posture of waiting to be told what to do when it might be more desirable for him to ask the teacher or another child. We will go into this question somewhat more deeply in later parts of this chapter, but it has been raised here to underline still another complication in the decisions that teachers must make. Especially if a team has not worked out a common policy for these matters, it will have difficulty grouping pupils and evaluating pupil progress.

We used to speak of the "report-card trauma" in the Lexington project because for a time the grouping patterns were so unstable that, for the reasons discussed above, it was very hard to assess the pupils with any confidence. Let it be urged that this is not to be construed as a pitch for the self-contained classroom. Evaluation by a single teacher can be more sloppy and more unfair to one child or another than it is in team teaching. What emerges from this is, rather, that a team needs a whole arsenal of instruments in order to render its decisions more objective. Team teaching also requires a far more sophisticated system for tracking individual pupils through their assignments to various teachers than we have developed in the self-contained classroom.

Up to this point we have been discussing some of the general characteristics of the decision-making process in team teaching in such a way as to imply that the behavior of the teachers is always highly rational in determining a course of action. In fact, a great deal of irrational behavior can be expected, particularly when the teachers' roles are not well defined. Indeed, another major characteristic of team teaching, especially at this time, is that the various roles of the staff *are* vaguely defined, even in those projects which have established a hierarchy of several roles with differential status and pay. When this is compounded with the considerable increase in the sheer number and complexity of the decisions that have to be made, it leads to confusion and anxiety. Our qualifying phrase, "at this time," might seem to indicate that this proposition does not have the same generality that we have ascribed to those that have been developed earlier in the discussion. However, we have interjected the qualification merely to emphasize the exaggerated nature of the situation at present. It is reasonable to anticipate that the roles of the staff will always be defined with a certain degree of vagueness because the abilities and personalities of the individuals who are engaged in team teaching will never exactly fit the repertoire of job descriptions that we build into a model for a given school. It is one thing, for example, to describe a specialist ideally but quite another thing to integrate his efforts with those of his fellow teachers. Perhaps if the whole responsibility for a given area of the curriculum were to be turned over entirely to a specialist, then his role would not pose any particular problem for the team. More often, however, we can expect to find a specialist being asked to lead his colleagues, and here there must be an adjustment to the capacities of all concerned.

The irrationality of human beings can take as many bizarre forms in team teaching as in any other realm of life. We are more interested here in noting how it may effect the decision-making process of a team. The teachers may overextend themselves in their commitment to very demanding intentions, as we saw above, and then may attempt to recover their balance or their morale by disengaging themselves from the interdependence of team plans. They drift into their own rooms, or, more subtly, they seek a weak level of planning consensus that does not require that the behavior of any one teacher be materially contingent upon the behavior of the others. A team may isolate a difficult teacher by giving him a special responsibility for preparing lessons or materials or even a special group of pupils that are to be handled separately from the rest. With respect to curriculum development a team may become quite quixotic in charging now in one and then in another direction, both within and across subject areas. Midway through a period when the development of new social studies units commands all the energies a team can summon, it may decide to overhaul its arithmetic program. All of this suggests that certain regularities should be built into the structure of a team teaching situation.

This brings us to the most challenging and exciting problem in team teaching, what is actually the sum of the problems we have separated for the purpose of analysis. *Who* makes *what* decisions, and *when* does he decide? This question does not merely concern teachers. For any school, many major decisions are made at the community level, including the scholars of the universities as well as the general public and school administrators. At the same time certain decisions are made by the pupils themselves. Team teaching redistributes these decisions and creates new ones in the process. Clearly, it tends to place in the hands of a group of teachers a number of decisions that are usually made "up above" for the teacher in the self-contained classroom. On the other hand, the teachers individually may feel a loss of freedom with respect to various decisions they once made on their own. Likewise, team teaching may create more options for the pupils by offering a greater variety of persons and situations to which they can relate at a given time. But it is also possible for the pupils to have less control over the course of inquiry than in a self-contained classroom if the teachers' plans become more responsive to the exigencies of their schedule and team meetings than to the needs and interests of the pupils.

The basic question can be approached in two ways. First, it is a classic problem in curriculum design. The following statement by Hanna, who in turn quotes Dewey, is representative of any number that can be found in the writings of educators:

> The assertion that the elementary school curriculum must be designed or organized rather than formless or haphazard is basic to any improvement in the curriculum. As the educator must understand the nature and needs of his society and survey the interests and capacities of his pupils, so John Dewey says he must also: ". . . arrange the conditions which provide the subject-matter or content for experiences that satisfy these needs and develop these capacities. The planning must be flexible enough to permit free play for individuality of experience and yet firm enough to give direction towards continuous development of power."
>
> When we speak of planning or designing the curriculum, we refer to a proces that has at least two stages. Some aspects of the curriculum must be carefully planned in advance, while others are best planned just prior to or during the educative experience.[2]

The question of which aspects of the curriculum are to be planned in advance and which during the educative experience has been answered in many different ways. Some have placed more stress upon the child from the viewpoint of developmental philosophy and psychology. Others have emphasized more the knowledge and values of society. Both Dewey and Hanna attempt to mediate these extremes, and the author strongly shares in many of their convictions. A new approach to the problem has recently come to

---

[2] Paul R. Hanna, "Society—Child—Curriculum," in Clarence W. Hunnicutt, ed., *Education 2000 AD*, Syracuse, N.Y., Syracuse University Press, 1956, pp. 173–174. The statement by Dewey is quoted from John Dewey, *Experience and Education*, New York, Macmillan, 1938.

the surface, however, that both men foreshadow in their writings. This is the current emphasis on the organization of knowledge in the disciplines, which is being discussed under the heading of "structure." The power of this approach does not come merely from the possibility that it might help us to identify those learnings which would be most valuable to the child. It derives also from our realization that the organization of knowledge in the public domain, we can say "in the books" for convenience, might be a major point of departure for the exploration of how knowledge is organized in the private domain, say "in the head." We must stress that it is only a point of departure because the conditions for receiving, storing, and recovering information are not the same for the public and the private domains of thought. Books, for example, do not forget in the same sense that heads do. Nevertheless, some of the most striking contributions to education in recent years stem from the attempt to relate the structure of thinking in these two realms, which, it must be emphasized, are in fact intimately interrelated although we can separate them to some extent in order to analyze them.[3] What we would propose here is that the decisions which are made at various junctures in a team's planning of its curriculum might also be structured in terms of the organization of knowledge in the respective disciplines or subject areas. This immediately suggests, for instance, that a team would not plan in the same way for arithmetic or mathematics as it would for social studies. Our subsequent sections on planning will be written from this point of view.

The second approach to the question of who makes what decisions focuses on the problem of exploiting and maintaining the

[3] A few of the names that come to mind from very different corners of this field are Bloom, Bruner, Piaget, B. O. Smith, and, of course, Dewey. We can see best in this light why How We Think has been so influential in education. Granted, it should have been entitled How We Ought To Think, or, as Schwab has suggested, The Schoolbook Version of How We Ought to Think. Even so, it stimulated much fruitful consideration of thought processes, while at the same time it resulted in wooden problem-solving units. The structure that Dewey propounded served as a model for our conception of thinking, and it would have been an especially valuable one if we had taken heed of his reservations about the actual sequence of the steps he had defined. It should be recognized as an ancestor of the very stimulating book by George A. Miller, Karl H. Pribram, and Eugene Galanter, Plans and the Structure of Behavior, New York, Holt, 1960, which has heavily influenced the conception of planning developed in this chapter.

efficiency of a team's operations. Here it will be important not only to differentiate between the roles of the various members of a team, the pupils included, but to establish a rhythm of long- and short-range decisions. Rather than subject the team at all times to an ever-changing frame of reference as now one and now another policy is attempted, we can set up a system of priorities, and we can specify certain occasions for the consideration of those decisions which involve a greater number of alternatives and consequent decisions. Thus we might set up our priorities for curriculum development on an annual basis and make certain decisions about grouping on a semiannual or quarterly basis. Removing major decisions to a high level of policy planning would control the alternatives a team must deal with at a given time. Similarly, it is essential to displace those decisions which are more contingent upon the immediate circumstances of the learning situation downward in the hierarchy to a level closer to the actual circumstances. Again, this implies that at certain points the pupils themselves will be the best governors of their own course of inquiry. It means also that the teachers must be permitted to make various decisions without having to seek the consensus of their teams. Individual teachers would thus receive that freedom of action which they require in order to capitalize on their own special interests and capabilities and in order to relate the instruction effectively to the particular groups with which they are working at any time. It would also serve to break up the log-jam of decisions that piles up upon increasingly frequent team meetings where teachers are trying to determine every specific course of action collectively. The reader might imagine at this point that we are recommending a sort of alternation between team teaching and the self-contained classroom, and perhaps there is a certain degree of truth to this. However, we will develop later a principle of negotiable assignments that would remove certain decisions from the team meetings but still preserve the possibilities for cooperation as particular circumstances develop.

On some occasions when the going has been very rough and tempers have flared, we have been tempted to conclude that team teaching requires a special personality, possibly something that could be determined by a personality inventory administered to applicants for a team teaching school. The author cannot state too strongly his own conviction that idiosyncratic ways are as much to be prized as to be feared in team teaching and that we would do well not to ascribe too many of our troubles to the fact that the teachers are not all dealt out of the same deck. In other organizations, not all to be sure, the conditions of work are structured to facilitate the productivity of creative individuals and to recognize that they may be mild or aggressive, ornery or sweet. When the emotions start to smolder, we should look first to the tangible problems the teachers are confronting, not merely to their interpersonal relations as such. Inventories will have their place in helping to predict potential leadership and so on, but we must first understand clearly what the requirements of the various roles are to be.

These two approaches to our fundamental question about decisions have been distinguished in terms of their rationale but are actually two aspects of a single complex of decisions. It will be noticed that a number of their features run somewhat parallel to each other, for both are concerned with long- and short-range plans, with distinctions as to who is in the best position to make various decisions, and with the necessity of preserving freedom of play within the structure. The author is persuaded that team teaching does indeed offer us a wealth of opportunities for improving both the effectiveness and the efficiency of instruction. At the same time, it is evident that if we are to accomplish our intentions as teachers, the reorganization of the school must proceed hand in hand with the reorganization of the curriculum. The task is hardly begun.

Constructs and Contexts

In the last section of this chapter we will examine the planning of the social studies curriculum in the Lexington project in order to illustrate the application of the ideas sketched in the first section to a specific team teaching situation. First, however, it is necessary to underline several points which any social studies curriculum must take into account and which present special problems for social studies planning in team teaching.[4] For this purpose we can examine a somewhat futuristic scheme. We say it is futuristic be-

---

[4] These points may apply to other curriculum areas as well but not in precisely the same ways.

cause it would require a lengthy program of research and development to make it effective. Yet the reader will perceive that the components of the scheme stem from a variety of already familiar approaches to curriculum such as the Winnetka and Dual Progress Plans and programed instruction (see Chapter 2).

Suppose that we were to establish within social studies (in contrast to other plans) a two-track curriculum and that each pupil proceeded simultaneously in both tracks, throughout Grades 3 to 12. Track I we might call the "constructs track" and Track II the "contexts track," although social studies constructs and contexts will be seen to be inseparable in many respects. We could also label our two tracks the "literacy" and the "problems" tracks respectively, but again this does not describe either one very well. The constructs track would systematically develop a repertoire of concepts, skills, and strategies of reasoning and judgment that is required in the investigation of social studies contexts. The contexts track would be concerned with the extensive exploration of historical periods, geographic and cultural areas, political and economic problems, and so forth, all representing various chunks of the existential matrix of human events.

Track I would be nongraded, that is each pupil would proceed in it "at his own pace" (we shall develop our special meaning for this concept further). Track II would be graded, but each pupil's study of a context would be articulated with his progress in the constructs track.[5] Thus a 4th-grade class might be strung out all along Track I but would be studying together in one context or another, say modern India. Each pupil's study of India would be related to constructs that were available to him at this point, although we shall see that this would by no means be a ball-and-chain relationship.

Track I would employ a variety of materials and techniques of programed instruction, team learning, and highly directive tutorial.[6] It would be quite specific as to learning outcomes. A pupil

[5] We say Track II would be graded partly to emphasize the relative arbitrariness of the pacing in this track. A team which comprises more than one grade level, as in Lexington, might cycle its offerings in this track so that some pupils would study context A before context B, and others B before A.

[6] We owe the phrase "team learning" to Professor Donald K. Durrell of Boston University, who has systematized the practices of Carleton Washburne and others.

would not be expected to achieve in this track alone what we would consider a full-fledged concept or a fully developed skill. Rather, he would be led to differentiate and generalize a given concept or skill with enough precision so that he could then augment its meaning in contextual situations where his feedback was less didactic. For instance, the pupil would learn how to distinguish the referents of the terms *import* and *export,* or *institution* and *constitution,* and how to read maps, charts, and graphs. The materials of Track I would be designed to facilitate the progress of the pupils with as little active intervention by the teachers as possible. To put it differently, the instruction would be built into the materials so that when the teachers intervened, it would be for clear strategic purposes.

It might be difficult for the reader to envision what kinds of materials and techniques would be appropriate for this sort of instruction in social studies. Programed instruction, in the conventional sense that applies to programed texts and teaching machines, has only begun to develop in social studies. Team learning in social studies has emphasized primarily the acquisition of information and skills through relatively dysfunctional tasks, and many fear that this will also be the case with programed instruction. Stoddard quotes Heathers and Kaya on this matter:

> An important question is whether the self-directed learning can be effective for other than fact or tool-skill learning. Pupils questioned about *why* they were studying a particular unit had difficulty in answering the question. It seems that the program (a team learning program), to date, does not sufficiently emphasize pupil planning, analytic thinking, and acquiring the sorts of understandings that permit applying what is learned to *new* problem situations.[7]

There are two attacks that we can make upon this problem. The first is to design materials for self-directed learning which are geared to small, manageable problems that will make the pupils' efforts in Track I more purposeful. (It is for this reason that we qualified our description of this as the "literacy track.") Secondly, as we have already implied, we can relate a pupil's learning in Track I to his

[7] George D. Stoddard, *The Dual Progress Plan,* New York, Harper & Row, 1961, p. 192.

studies in Track II. Let us suggest how each of these attacks might be carried out.

We are now beginning to develop in Lexington (partly with an eye to this more futuristic curriculum) a wide variety of exercises that have a number of features in common. Each type of exercise (more than 40 at the time of this writing) is distinguished from other types in terms of the specific combination of logical operations it requires of a pupil; these include various approaches to categorizing, the drawing of inferences, the testing of generalizations, the construction of series or sequences, and so on. Each exercise can be presented to the pupil as a problem or a game, each can be partially adapted (through the use of picture material and oral instructions) to nonreaders, and each can be employed either with individuals or with teams of two pupils. Correct or suggested solutions can be provided with the exercises for a pupil to compare with his own, or these solutions can be withheld when the exercises are being used for evaluation. Although we have not yet tried it, it seems reasonable to expect that the exercises can be programed in sequence, with "branching" to provide further instruction where a given exercise presents special difficulties to one pupil or another.[8] Finally, the exercises can be constructed in the classroom by the teachers or by pupils themselves when this would help clarify a problem encountered in the study of a context.

Let us look at just one exercise that might be included in a cluster of exercises designed to teach a pupil a working definition of the concept of *role*. As is the case with all of our exercises, the pupil would receive a "package" of materials. In this case let us suppose

[8] In these exercises we do not anticipate having to dole out information to the pupils in "bits" as tiny as standard linear programing techniques seem to require, though this would be useful for some purposes in our proposed Track I. The question of what kind of reinforcement is necessary to shape appropriate behavior is very confused in the programing literature, not the least in the writings of B. F. Skinner and his associates. Let us simply observe that most behaviorists have not distinguished adequately between the reward and the information components of reinforcement and that they have thereby neglected to capitalize on man's strategies for combining bits of information to yield far more powerful information. The Skinnerians employ only a minimum of formal reasoning in their programing, with the result that it seems far less effective than it might be, at least for most of our purposes in social studies. Whether or not our own procedures will be more effective will have to be determined empirically.

that he receives a card with printed instructions, six numbered cards each describing a different job and specifying whether the job is or is not performed by women in tradtional Navaho culture, and a response sheet on which the pupil is to record his solutions. If the pupil has played this type of game before (as he might have many times before he came to the concept of role), his instructions can be relatively brief. First, he is to sort the cards into two groups: jobs that he thinks women are capable of doing or learning and jobs they cannot do whether they belong to the Navaho culture or to any other culture. Secondly, he is to sort them into two groups again: jobs that Navaho women actually perform and jobs they do not perform. Finally, he is to sort them into jobs performed by women in Lexington and jobs not performed by women in Lexington. Each time he records his solution by circling numbers corresponding to the paragraphs or pictures, as the case may be, on his response sheet. If his solutions are correct, the pupil may proceed to another exercise of this type (perhaps having to do with the games women play) and then to an exercise to test or correct a generalization, all designed to contribute to his concept of role. If the pupil's first sort does not check with the suggested solution (available on another card), he may be branched off to an exercise about what jobs women can be trained to perform, though the jobs in question would have to be familiar enough to the pupil to prevent his having to be branched off indefinitely. The pupil could be referred to a particular reading at this point, or more writing might be required of him than we have indicated above. There seem to be countless possibilities (and difficulties, we admit).

It will be noticed that a pupil developing rudimentary concepts in ways like those suggested here would at the same time be learning basic strategies of reasoning that apply in virtually every social studies context. The growing body of research on children's thinking might help determine an appropriate sequence in which to introduce these various constructs through Track I. Indeed, this track could itself be a valuable instrument for research as well as a clinical tool for the teachers' study of individual cases. However, even when all the research is done (which, of course, it never will be), it will still not dictate a sequence of learnings that is superior *a priori* to all others. For too many years now we have restricted unduly the child's alternatives by assuming that he was by nature capable of only certain learnings at one age or another—the too narrow view of the "widening horizons" frame of reference in social studies. We may next find ourselves subscribing dogmatically to a sequence that the disciplines seem to prescribe for the child's learning. In truth, any number of sequences could be employed in social studies, each with equal justification. *The advantage of a given sequence, whether it is derived from developmental psychology or from the disciplines, lies not in its inner logic alone but in the use that we make of it in our teaching.*

In the first place, because we cannot simply assume that a child's ideas and experiences will add up over the years, we must employ our own knowledge of the sequence to help the child relate what he has learned at different times. Secondly, sequence in the curriculum not only enables us to control the child's studies in terms of a progression of learnings that we plan for him, but, equally, it can also facilitate our helping the child to plan for himself so that he can break through the bounds laid down for him by our own beliefs and expectations. Let us consider how these objectives might be realized through Track II of our futuristic curriculum.

It will be remembered that Track II involves the pupils in the exploration of a variety of contexts (we might say somewhat arbitrarily between two and four a year). At one time a class might be studying the Peace Corps; at another time the history of Boston, the origins of World War I, or the excavations of ancient cities. Now it will be asked what a pupil is supposed to learn in these contexts, or what he is supposed to get out of them. As a rule of thumb, we shall answer "anything." Any question goes. Any line of inquiry that a pupil chooses to follow is the line we want to encourage. Any problem that he defines is worthy of his investigation. Of course, the teachers would propound key questions or some of the classical problems in various contexts, but the object would be to lead each pupil to examine that which is problematic for him personally. The structure of the social sciences, if that is to be a guide for our teaching, is partly defined by the major ideas in the several disciplines. Even more fundamental, however, is the process of inquiry through which these ideas are set forth and examined.

By no means would such a policy need to result in chaos. On the contrary, it is essential to insure the continuity and purposefulness of the learner's inquiry. For each context we would try to provide a rich array of resources, many more than any single pupil could be expected to exploit. On some occasions the pupils would be studying independently, on others they would be studying in teams of two or three or in larger groups. From time to time the whole class or several classes would convene to share questions or findings or to examine together some resource or problem. Since the teachers would have a record of each pupil's progress in Track I, they could assist the pupils in their use of previously developed relevant constructs to tease out and organize different dimensions of the context in question. If a pupil should pose a problem that requires command of constructs that he has not yet begun to develop, the teacher might try to help the pupil channel his inquiry toward one aspect of the problem that he could handle with more ease. The teacher might equally be able to refer the pupil to exercises somewhat in advance of his present position in the constructs track.[9] Likewise, it would be necessary at times to refer a pupil back to exercises he had worked through earlier in order to review certain constructs that he required at the moment. Finally, the broad sequences of both Tracks I and II could be correlated to some extent so that materials would be available for each context that were especially appropriate for various levels of achievement in the constructs track.

The materials for Track I would have to be centralized in several places in the school, and teacher aides might be responsible for the general management of these centers. Tutorials required by one pupil or another could be handled by the teacher responsible for him at that time in Track II, and grouping within grade levels for

[9] In order to understand the mechanics of this tactic and also the general management of Track I, it is necessary to realize that the exercises in the track would not all be rigidly in sequence so that each depended upon every exercise that preceded it. Instead, the over-all sequence would be divided into achievement levels, and each level would include a number of clusters of exercises. Each cluster would be a miniature program in itself, but the relationships among the clusters and between levels would be somewhat looser. Thus, the pupils at a given level would not all have to work through the clusters in the same order, and it would be possible for a pupil to skip ahead in the sequence to at least some of the exercises on a more advanced level without his finding them too difficult to justify the effort.

Track II might take into account (but not exclusively) the pupil's progress in Track I. Many patterns of collective action by the teachers, both within and across grade levels, would be both possible and necessary to make the curriculum effective.

On a typical day, or at least within any week, a pupil would spend part of his time in both tracks. Ideally, he himself would regulate the proportion of effort he devoted to one or the other, and he would move freely back and forth between the two. In practice, we would have to study the situation carefully in order to gauge what proportions seemed to be more appropriate for each individual.

No doubt, this is a very complicated scheme! Why, then, have we advanced it in an essay about team teaching? Our reason again is that the problems with which the scheme attempts to cope are the very same problems that face any social studies curriculum and which our planning in Lexington even now must try to resolve. Because we are operating only a single track at the present time, we have to make many compromises. Still, we must ask ourselves these questions:

1. What does it mean in social studies to say that each pupil should proceed at his own pace? The answer frequently given, that enrichment is preferable to advancement in social studies, does not seem to recognize the problem.

2. How can we teach social sciences constructs without continually using (and abusing) the contexts of the pupils' inquiry for didactic purposes? When we are attempting to teach rudimentary concepts and skills through examples afforded by one context or another, our representation of the context itself is likely to be filtered through a screen of oversimplified questions that grossly distort the lines of inquiry that the disciplines would be inclined to follow. Again, constructs and contexts are inseparable in many respects, but how can we do justice to both?

3. How can we foster independent thinking among pupils and at the same time engage them in the ideas, the values, and the concerns of their culture and the world? We are all painfully aware of the problems of selecting content for a social studies curriculum from the infinite array of possibilities that the social sciences offer. More often than not, however, the crisis is concluded by defining the curriculum for the books and teachers instead of by confronting

the pupils themselves with both the opportunities and the limitations of social sciences inquiry.

A Planning Strategy

At this point, a few remarks are necessary about the background of the social studies curriculum in Lexington. We do not claim that the pattern of curriculum development that we have followed in Lexington is the best for any school to follow. On the contrary, there is consensus among everyone concerned that the university, in particular, should play a much larger role than has been possible in our situation to date. At the present time this is especially evident in the inadequacy of the materials available to the pupils despite a major effort to take advantage of books and periodicals to supplement, and often to replace, the tetxbooks.[10] It is encouraging that many scholars now recognize the need for preparing materials of high quality that are expressly tailored to the needs of a more powerful curriculum. At the same time, however, our experience in Lexington has confirmed the necessity for involving the teachers themselves in the construction of the curriculum. Their own questions and concerns have led to many considerations that would not have been anticipated by the university consultants alone, not the least of which is the point that we emphasized in the first section of this chapter—in the final analysis it is the intentions of the teachers, their interpretation of the nature and purposes of the curriculum, that determine what occurs in the classrooms.

The social studies area was the first to come under heavy fire in the Franklin School and has been in almost continuous revision since.[11] Following a year of preoccupation with roles and techniques (especially for large groups), there were in 1958–1959 frequent discussions of the purposes of the social studies, and there was an

[10] As of December, 1962, it must be reported that the revised social studies curriculum is barely in effect in Grades 1 and 2 in Lexington. This reflects chiefly the combination of inadequate materials for both teachers and children and a high turnover of teachers since the previous year. It would be premature to claim that the units for Grades 1 and 2 either are or are not appropriate.

[11] In September, 1961, the newly opened Estabrook School in Lexington joined the Franklin School in this project. The new social studies curriculum is now in effect in both schools.

exchange of papers among the teachers and the Harvard Research and Development staff. Their discontent focused on the manifest gap between the alleged objectives and actual practices of the standard text-based curriculum. Fairly conventional notions of critical thinking and concept formation, together with an effort to find a fruitful formula for curriculum revision, were the essence of these communications. The first concrete result was the proposal, alluded to in the first section, to develop four successive themes (farming, water, oil, and space) throughout the grades simultaneously. Following a summer workshop, all six grades started strongly in September, 1959. At Christmas time, however, they were still on the farm with little feeling of accomplishment. During the balance of the year they straggled back to the old curriculum a team at a time, and the cries for revision were now joined by others calling for stability.

The reasons for this failure were both numerous and complex. Rather than detail them here, we will simply observe that this entire chapter, by implication, is addressed to the problems that began to emerge at this time. While the first revision was foundering, the research and development staff was exploring possible ways of giving it more substance. One approach that was considered at some length was the specification of skills throughout the grades. Another tack dealt with current problems. Our main concern, however, centered on concepts and generalizations, clearly an outgrowth of the earlier trend in the school. Much time was devoted (both then and ever since) to clarifying the staff's own comprehension of conceptual thinking and to surveying previous efforts to identify social studies generalizations.[12] Toward the end of the school year 1959–1960 a proposal began to take shape, based on a six-year sequence of generalizations.[13] At the same time there was a decided urge for closure from the school faculty. After an extensive but futile search among curriculum guides published for other schools, the staff's proposal was rushed into the breech. We had not anticipated and were not prepared for so swift a trial.

The proposal was presented in May to the Instructional Cabinet,

[12] See, for example, the article by Hanna, *op. cit.*
[13] The original author of this proposal was Beverly Simpson Stone, who has since been one of the leaders in its implementation.

composed of the principal, the team leaders, and the senior teachers of the school. It was a lengthy, rather forbidding outline of generalizations, arranged under six themes with some commentary on what sorts of contexts might be appropriate for each level. The cabinet was interested but asked the staff to spell out what "content" the proposal entailed.

A week later the staff made another presentation, this time suggesting at each grade level units through which appropriate generalizations could be explored. The proposal was adopted, and it was arranged to begin the planning in a workshop to be held only two months later. Roughly half of the curriculum was to be developed on the run during the year 1960–1961, and the remainder during 1961–1962.

We have sketched this chronicle of the curriculum's inception so that the reader can appreciate the significance of the following development: it was not until the summer of 1962 that teachers from all of the grades were prepared to think through together the specific rationale and substance of the curriculum as a whole. By that time most of the proposed units, some of them designed by the consultants, others worked out by the teachers alone, had been tried in the classroom at least once. In the summer of 1962 a draft curriculum guide was written, but it was not, nor could it have been, a sheer compilation of our earlier efforts. Many different approaches to planning had been attempted during these two years as we strove to come to grips with our central problem, the necessity for harmonizing the requirements of the curriculum with the organization of the teams. When a guide was finally produced, it was written from the viewpoint of a clear-cut planning strategy. This guide is not now, and will not become, a blueprint for teaching. Rather it is a resource that has been designed to support the kind of planning that the teachers must do every time they embark upon a unit, whether for the first or for the fiftieth time. The details of the strategy will vary, and perhaps even the broad outline of it will change over time. Nevertheless, none of its considerations seems superfluous in terms of the curriculum and the teams *in Lexington* as these are now constituted.

We will now list the themes and units of the curriculum as it is projected at present, and then we will examine in detail the planning of a single unit. Brevity must be purchased at the expense of consistency here; it is simpler to refer to some units by their context, to others by their conceptual focus, and to still others by a combination of these. We might comment that material dealing with distant lands and times is extensively involved at all six levels.

I. Man has many ways of meeting similar needs. (In each unit our own ways and those of some other culture will be considered simultaneously.)

Schools around the world
Workers in Indonesia
Celebrations in Japan
Art and Play in Mexico
Homes and Families in Nigeria

II. Man has learned to survive in his natural environment. (The main emphasis in each case will be on the traditional culture, but the transition to present-day patterns will not be ignored.)

Introduction to physiographic concepts
The Navaho
The Copper Eskimo
The Pioneer in the Eastern American Woodland
The Masai

III. Man has found ways to improve his relationship to his environment.

Water Control
Agriculture
Mining
Fishing and Whaling
Textiles

IV. The Industrial Revolution has changed the production and distribution of goods and services and has created new opportunities and problems for human society.

Power and Technology
Natural Resources
Trade
Food and Population
Cities

V. Man's acts of inquiry, creation, and expression evolve from and influence his total way of life. (Each unit will relate a context from ancient or medieval European history to the world of today.)

    Archaeology
    Writing
    Architecture
    Law and Government
    Education

VI. There are a variety of patterns of development and interdependence within and among the Americas. (Each unit will examine a region of the United States and/or a period from United States history in conjunction with an equivalent context from elsewhere in the Americas.)

    Physiographic survey of Americas through study of representa-
        tive explorers
    The cultural geography of two regions
    Two revolutions
    The economic development of two regions
    The Alliance for Progress, O.A.S., and Peace Corps

Much groundwork remains to be completed to develop these units at all levels and to insure the articulation of learnings from one level to the next. The sequence is basically conceptual rather than historical or geographical, although there are strands of both the latter as well. Ironically, in view of the fact that it is the conceptual sequence that we prize most in our curriculum, it is this very feature of the curriculum that poses the major unresolved problem for the organization of the teams in Lexington. Each team comprises two grade levels, 1 and 2, 3 and 4, or 5 and 6. Thus, as long as the curriculum is graded, each team must divide its efforts at any given time between two social studies units. This circumstance creates numerous obstacles to the optimum scheduling of teachers, classes, meetings, and so on, not only in social studies but in science as well.[14] We are currently experimenting with a re-

[14] Several of the Lexington teams have scheduled a single block of time for both social studies and science (which are taught separately) with the result that grouping decisions in one area tend to affect the other area as well. For instance, if social studies is graded and science is cross-graded, it is not possible to teach both social studies and science at the exact same time of day within a

arrangement of the units at grade levels 3 and 4 in one school to create a two-year cycle that would permit the entire team to concentrate on a single social studies unit at a time.[15] However, this solution promises to be much less satisfactory than something like the two-track program proposed earlier. Let it suffice here for us to observe that where the requirements of the curriculum and those of the organization of the teams have appeared to be irreconcilable for the present, the curriculum has predominated. In Lexington we have virtually reorganized the teams in social studies. To have done otherwise would have resulted in the tail wagging the dog.

Candor requires that we reveal an ulterior motive for our having graded the curriculum, which is very pertinent to the theme of this chapter. We felt that it was necessary to deal with smaller complements of the Lexington teams—with three or four teachers and the pupils assigned to them at a given time in social studies rather than with six or seven teachers and all of the pupils on a team—to work through the problems of planning. Now that we have defined a planning strategy in Lexington, it seems to us to apply as well to the larger as to the smaller complements (if we omit the problem of sequence), and we will be using it to plan both occasional lessons and whole units for an entire team. Therefore, as we discuss this planning strategy, we shall not specify exactly how many teachers or pupils we are involving in a unit. Let us assume that at least two teachers and about 50 pupils are involved. We shall use the word *team* to cover many different possibilities and the word *leader* to

---

given team, since some pupils would belong in both a social studies and a science group simultaneously. Nevertheless, there is no arrangement which does not involve conflicts of this nature, and we have found the use of blocks of time within the school day far more flexible than the attempt to get an optimum combination of groupings throughout the entire day (by scattering social studies, science, and other groups throughout every hour). Secondary school administrators will recognize immediately the problem that the latter policy would entail. Once the optimum combination had been determined, one could not make major grouping changes within any one area without affecting all of the other areas at the same time. By dividing the school day into blocks, we can at least contain this interaction to the areas of the curriculum within each block.

[15] For instance, the following two years might be cycled:
   A. Water Control, Agriculture, Fishing and Whaling, Food and Population, Cities
   B. Mining, Textiles, Power and Technology, Natural Resources, Trade

refer either to a team leader or to a social studies specialist. This will make it easier for the reader to perceive the possible relevance of the strategy to another situation, provided that the objectives of the curriculum in question are consistent with the basis on which the teachers establish consensus in their planning.

The following outline of our planning strategy applies to all of the units in the curriculum:

1. Teachers read on the general topic of the proposed unit.
2. Teachers survey written materials and other resources available to pupils for unit.
3. Teachers individually, and then together, consider possible scope and sequence of generalizations and contexts relating to unit. Unit is now divided into phases.
4. Teachers together stake out key lessons for collective planning. The teachers need not know the actual plans for the lessons at this point but should be individually committted to doing some research and preplanning in preparation for ensuing planning sessions.
5. Teachers and consultants begin construction of team learning and evaluation exercises in accordance with specific objectives of unit.
6. Periodic meetings for collective planning to accomplish the following: (a) critique of previous key lesson, i.e., consideration of how it worked out in individual follow-ups; (b) presentation and discussion of plan proposed for next key lesson by individual teacher(s) responsible—this will lead to the individual's preparing a written plan in advance of the lesson's being taught so as to coordinate preparation and follow-up and to serve as a record for the resource unit; and (c) discussion of possibilities for individual, small-group, and class studies revolving around generalizations highlighted in proposed key lessons.
7. Daily planning on a contingency basis. Pupil-teacher planning recommended especially for individual and small-group projects within the frame of reference established for the unit or unit phases.
8. Coordination of team's daily plans. Teachers can share activities, materials, space, and pupils, provided (a) that plans are made public in advance and (b) that leaders encourage cooperation.
9. Leaders help teachers set up conditions in classrooms to facilitate planful behavior of both teachers and pupils. This involves strategic use of leaders' teaching commitments, clinical analysis of teaching style, help with grouping, help with record keeping on pupil progress, etc.

Let us reiterate that all nine of these planning steps are essential, despite the fact that the curriculum guide offers suggestions that are pertinent to each step. We should also observe that these steps overlap. They have been listed roughly in the order that a team would take them up initially, but the actual planning process moves back and forth among these steps. We will now consider the planning of a unit on mining (at Level III in our Lexington curriculum). This exposition will attempt to clarify what each of the steps entails and some of the reasons for these steps. However, we must presume at this juncture that the reader himself will do the major job of relating the strategy to the points we have developed earlier in this essay.

1. The primary purpose of having the teachers read in advance is to stimulate their thoughts anew, irrespective of how well informed on the topic they may or may not be already. For each unit we have purchased at least one book (in more than one copy) at a junior high reading level or above—for instance, June Metcalfe's *Mining Around The World,* Oxford University Press, 1956. Almost invariably articles pertaining to any of the units can be found in current periodicals, and we have set up for each unit a resource folder of clippings and other information, which ought to be reviewed and added to at this point.

Many teachers do surprisingly little reading outside the classroom. This recommendation, therefore, is not as simple as it appears and may require a long period of encouragement and suggestion before it even begins to take hold. The observation applies equally to Step 2 of our planning strategy. The traditional role of the teacher as the dispenser of wisdom in the classroom is extremely hard to break down in some cases. The teacher may feel he already knows all that the pupils need to learn, and he has been supported in this belief by his professional training and the standard curriculum. One cannot overestimate the proportions of this problem. A curriculum revision as drastic as ours in Lexington may produce a healthy shock effect to counteract it, but it may also drive some teachers into retreat or open rebellion. Another dimension of the problem is time, which we will consider in the conclusion of this section.

2. For every unit beyond Level II, many readings have been provided for the pupils, far more than any one pupil would be likely to read thoroughly. Some are in textbooks which can be used for several units. For example, *Old Ways and New Ways* by Todd, Cooper, and Sorenson, Silver Burdett, 1954, has chapters appropriate

for all of the units on Levels III and IV. A variety of other books have been purchased for the pupils such as Markum's *The First Book of Mining*, Franklin Watts, 1960.

Partly with a view to preventing the instruction's being based on a single source, we have rarely obtained more than 15 copies of any one title. This means, of course, that the teachers must be famiilar with a number of books with respect to reading level, illustrations, and general pertinence to various lines of inquiry. The teachers need not always assign books to pupils on this basis, but they can help adjust the situation when a pupil's own selection seems inappropriate (easier said than done!).

Fewer readings will be available to most pupils at Levels I and II, but it will be no less necessary to review them at this time, as well as the considerable variety of picture materials that have been provided for these units. We have had to write much of our own material for the pupils at this level, and this might be an opportune time for the teachers to try adapting some of the reading they have done for classroom purposes.

Although it might seem too obvious to mention, we have found that many of the books available for a given unit are never discovered when they are needed unless a copy of each has been collected in some central place before the planning commences. In this way the teachers, and later on the pupils, can examine them cursorily with ease, though one might be referred to some other place for a copy to withdraw for further study. Incidentally, it is already almost too late (several weeks before the unit is to commence) to order films and filmstrips unless they are owned by the school.

3. The process of dividing a unit into phases is very difficult and has no apparent rules. It is a question of each teacher's trying to size up the unit's possibilities and then agreeing with other teachers on a frame of reference that makes sense to all of them. The problem is to get a good *gestalt*.

This is where the conceptual sequence of a curriculum can pay off in planning. In our case the theme for Level III and its relationship to previous and subsequent levels provide some major leads as to the directions the mining unit might take. We can quote from the guide:

The major understandings which run through the units at Level III are especially salient in the context of mining. These understandings are concerned with the geographic distribution of natural resources; the skill, fortitude, and inventiveness required of the men who deal with the natural environment; the importance of the technology of science and industry in the modern exploitation of the environment; the need for conservation; etc.

At Level IV "understandings" (a conveniently vague term for our purposes at this point) will be drawn together under the headings of Power and Technology, Natural Resources, etc., and larger questions will be posed about rich and poor nations or urbanization. At Level III these understandings will be antcipated in a more concrete form, building on the earlier studies of man's needs and his ways of fulfilling them. Some of the phases of the mining unit that might result from these considerations are the value and uses of minerals, finding minerals, types of mines, and the life of miners. The teachers might agree to structure these phases (or others) in this or some alternative sequence.

While this process is going on, the teachers must also be considering generalizations that would be appropriate to develop through these phases. *These generalizations are not to be construed as a summary of content to be mastered at this time.* Rather, they are hypotheses which are to be treated as points of convergence and departure for the process of inquiry. They will not be true in the same way for every specific context the pupils study, and thus they must not be used to blur the differences and details of one particular context or another. This is crucial to the fit that must obtain between our conception of the curriculum and the planning strategy. As recently as the summer 1962 workshop, the teachers found they could not get consensus in their planning until they were agreed that they were not trying to define the truth in these generalizations but were only seeking to propose fruitful lines of inquiry to be explored through the pupils' studies. A few of the generalizations suggested in the guide are the following:

Minerals have unique properties which make them of varied value to man.

Early man could obtain only certain minerals that he found on the earth's surface. Modern machinery and technology allow man today to exploit minerals far below the surface.

Miners' towns and lives, especially in the coal mining industry, have often had little opportunity for beauty, rest, and alternative kinds of work.

The objective for the mining unit, and for the curriculum as a whole, is to develop the ability to formulate and test ideas like these, not simply to memorize them. This requires both a knowledge of relevant contexts and a repertoire of constructs. It demands fundamental values of respect for individuals and commitment to the processes of free and open inquiry and decision. These must be reflected both in the curriculum and in the organization of the teachers and pupils for learning.

4. The next step in the strategy—still at least two weeks before the unit is to begin—is for the teachers to divide the responsibility for planning at least one key lesson for each of the phases that they have determined. One teacher may have a special interest in the value and uses of minerals, another in the lives of miners, and so on. Each teacher might be assigned more than one key lesson, the actual number being dependent upon the number of phases and the number of key lessons per phase.

We call this a "staking out" process because it sets up major guideposts throughout the course of the unit. It has been our experience, over and over again, that teachers are inclined to attempt to plan a unit straight through from the beginning. The first lessons are planned in great detail with the expectation that they will give the teachers a strong start. Later lessons are more hazy, if this initial planning even gets to them. This has two unfortunate results. The first two or three weeks are overplanned, and at the same time no clear direction has been established for the unit as a whole. By staking out key lessons we do not overdetermine the details of instruction during any phase of the unit, but we do establish points of reference for what we call our "contingent planning"—the planning that must respond to the immediate circumstances of the classroom. The key lessons thus serve a number of purposes:

a. They pace the several subgroups of a team as the groups lead up to and away from these lessons.
b. They focus on major ideas that are to be explored in various phases of the unit.
c. These lessons are an occasion for special research and preparation by the teachers, which they cannot be expected to be doing at all times during their teaching.
d. The key lessons can be employed to present material that is not readily accessible to the pupils in the classroom.

e. The planning and the critique of these lessons present an opportunity for the teachers to share their thoughts about the progress of the unit and the effectiveness of their teaching on a regular and systematic basis.

As the reader will have inferred from our outline of the strategy, the key lessons are not all planned before the unit is begun. The teachers are expected to meet formally about once a week (or perhaps every other week). At this time they criticize the previous week's key lesson(s). The key lesson for the week of the meeting has presumably been discussed earlier, and the critique of this lesson will take place later. As soon as the lessons have been staked out during the preplanning, teacher X will know that he must present plans for discussion with his colleagues in perhaps the second and the fifth weeks. Of course, the exact time for actually teaching the lessons can be adjusted, or the team might find that an additional key lesson is required that was not anticipated in the preplanning.

The key lessons do not have to be large group lessons, but they are to be carried out along approximately the same lines for all the pupils of the team. Likewise, the key lessons do not have to be taught exclusively by the teacher who prepares the plans, though this teacher would need to work closely with the colleagues with whom he shared the instruction. Again, these lessons need not be employed only to introduce a phase of the unit; they can serve equally to culminate a phase or to bring a phase into focus somewhere in the middle.

It is essential that the teacher responsible for a key lesson write up the lesson plan after his colleagues have discussed it but before it is to be taught. Otherwise, the preparation and follow-up will not be well articulated, and the work and thinking which has been invested in the lesson will not be available to the team in successive years. It is also advisable that a summary of the critique of the lesson be filed with it. In this way the team can build a very useful resource unit from one year to the next.

5. The teachers should begin their construction of team learning and evaluation exercises even before the unit commences. This will help them think through their objectives specifically and will also provide some materials that can be used at the start of the unit. We cannot pretend that this will be easy, and it is for this reason that

we are involving our consultants from the university most directly at this point. We have referred earlier to the variety of exercises that we are developing for this purpose. Each type of exercise has been discussed in the curriculum guide, but that alone will not guarantee that the exercises will be employed effectively. We are dealing here with a pervasive attitude toward evaluation, compounded of reliance on testing for facts and frustration in trying to evaluate more complex processes of thinking.

6, 7. We have already discussed the planning of the key lessons in weekly meetings. Here we need to elaborate to some extent on the rationale of the contingent lessons. When a teacher presents to his colleagues his tentative plan for a key lesson, we are also asking him to suggest classroom activities that could be built around the lesson. These also will be discussed in this meeting and should be listed briefly on the written plan which is prepared subsequently. However, they are not binding on the team in the way that the key lessons themselves are.

It is our general policy that a single teacher should be primarily responsible for each pupil in social studies for the duration of an entire unit, if not longer. It is a common practice in team teaching to rotate the pupils among the teachers, chiefly so that a teacher can repeat his lessons with more than one group. In effect we are doing this through our key lessons, and we shall notice in Step 8 other possibilities for cooperation among the teachers. However, the nature of the curriculum itself, plus the difficulties of following an individual pupil's progress closely, recommend that a consistent learning environment be maintained for at least the course of a unit. This means that each teacher will be responsible for a defined group of pupils during this time and that the activities in the several groups will vary according to the particular needs, resources, and interests of the teachers and pupils from one group to the next. The picture that we have drawn so far in this discussion shows the several (two or more) subgroups of a team converging and diverging rhythmically.

Let us comment at this point on a phenomenon observed many times during the initial stages of our project and which, more than any other single problem, drove us to examine the whole rationale of planning. The teachers were planning furiously, and often quite inventively, but they seemed unable to get their units going effectively. Plan was compounded upon plan, with erratic switches of direction, while the pupils followed along almost impassively. As we analyzed this situation, two factors emerged which seemed to account for it.

First, it was frequently the case that much of the instruction, sometimes most of it, was being conducted in large groups. We will recognize later some of the advantages of large-group instruction, but here we need to notice one of its drawbacks. Under usual conditions the teacher of a large group receives very little immediate feedback from the individual pupils to indicate what makes sense to them, how they are interpreting a lesson, and so on. For this reason the teacher cannot very well exploit the pupils' reactions to the lesson while it is in process, and so he must rely almost entirely on the material he has prepared in advance and hope it is hitting the mark. (Or else he is dimly aware that the lesson is missing, but he does not have enough feedback and control of the situation to replan the lesson "on his feet.") This characteristic of large-group instruction puts a premium on very detailed preparation of the material of a lesson and on the inclusion of a dramatic element. The lessons tend to become big productions unless they are simply films or filmstrips without supporting instruction.

Secondly, we noticed that often when the teams were in the doldrums, they had developed various devices for rotating the pupils through highly structured sets of lessons (both large-group and small) and for rotating the teachers' planning responsibilities simultaneously. One or two teachers were released from instruction at a given time to prepare the next set of lessons, while the remaining teachers rotated the pupils through the present set, say two small- and two large-group lessons. Then one or two other teachers were released for the next go-round, and so on.

A number of unhappy consequences ensue from these procedures. The plans are largely out of touch with the pupils and in various ways are geared more to the teachers themselves. Secondly, the teachers frequently find themselves executing lessons for which they had little or no share in the planning. From a psychological standpoint alone, this is a very difficult task, since one must internalize a plan in order to govern his teaching behavior effectively. Perhaps the most serious consequence of all is that the instruction fails to sustain the momentum of inquiry of the pupils, and the teachers must crank up the works from a dead halt every time a class convenes. This leads into a vicious cycle—more planning needed, more released time, more large groups, more out of touch, etc.

It is to break this cycle that we have advocated teacher-pupil planning in relatively stable groups in between the key lessons of a unit. To be sure, the notion of pupil-teacher planning has been much abused. Some of its advocates have not distinguished between decisions pertaining to the basic frame of reference of the curriculum and decisions among alternative lines of inquiry within this framework. Others have used pupil-teacher planning as a transparent gimmick for foisting their own decisions upon the pupils covertly. In another sense, however, the sense of planning which is being employed through this essay, *the pupils must participate in the planning in order to regulate their own behavior as learners.* When they do not, both the pupils and the teachers are handicapped.

Suppose a phase about types of mines and mining has been introduced by a key lesson about how various American Indian groups obtained gold, silver, copper, flint, salt, and other minerals. Here are just a few of the many individual and small-group activities that could lead out of this:

a. Study gold panning procedures of forty-niners and make and experiment with equipment.
b. Construct diagrams and models to show how ore is removed from today's open pit and shaft mines.
c. Engage in dramatic play about work in shaft mines following study of various jobs.
d. Invent machines to replace human workers in different jobs and follow by research on recent automation.
e. Study measures taken to prevent mine disasters.

It is one of our assumptions, not without precedent, that different pupils can be engaged in different activities at a given time and that both the teachers and the pupils will find this more rewarding than if everyone in a class or team is doing the same things at all times. Nevertheless, it should be anticipated, especially during the earlier stages of a team teaching project, that the pressures for conformity may be very high and may lead even to a regression in the technique of some teachers. This adds to the classical problems of managing different classroom activities simultaneously and is all the more reason for a planning strategy.

8. We have been speaking so far as if the several subgroups of a team were isolated from each other during the intervals between key lessons, but this need not be the case at all. Once a teacher has assumed the primary responsibility for a group of pupils, he is in a position to initiate many kinds of cooperation with his fellow teachers without involving the entire team (in which case too many opportunities are passed up altogether). If teacher X and teacher Y find they are planning a similar activity with their groups, they may pool their efforts, share their resources, or combine their pupils. If teacher X learns that Y is stressing a certain skill at some point that some of his own pupils especially need (as he has ascertained through an inventory), or if a topic is being explored in one classroom that could be shared with a research committee from another, small groups can be temporarily exchanged. One teacher might supervise pupils from another group as well as his own in independent study or library work. The possibilities are almost limitless.

Bearing in mind our earlier observations about the necessity for a fairly consistent learning environment, we should re-emphasize that the teachers' primary responsibilities are to the pupils in their groups. The pupils are not to be shuttled back and forth indiscriminately, but, if you will, sent on clearly purposeful missions that relate to the basic lines of inqury they have established in their primary groups.

These spontaneous arrangements among the teachers are what we have called "negotiable assignments." They will be facilitated by ease of communication among the teachers, not only within one team but also among teams. In addition to the informal exchanges that occur in the team offices and elsewhere, large public team planning boards are advisable for this purpose.

9. We need not add to our remarks on why the leaders need to help their colleagues establish appropriate learning conditions in the classroom, but let us comment on how it might be done. One must take into account the limitations of many teachers in talking about their classroom practices. It is characteristic of many complex skills, in the laboratory for instance, that one must learn them to a large extent by working through them with a more experienced colleague or tutor rather than by learning a set of rules for a skillful per-

formance. For this reason team leaders should take advantage of the negotiable assignment possibilities, if not actual released time, to share various responsibilities with their colleagues. Even brief periods of cooperation may be very valuable to the teacher who has never really seen it done.

One circumstance that seems especially to stand in the way of this cooperation is, paradoxically, the necessity for maintaining group morale. The leaders may be afraid that they will threaten their colleagues or invade their privacy. Naturally, they will have to be patient and genuinely helpful, but even so, they may still find it very difficult in some cases. A more subtle aspect of the problem is that the leaders often take upon themselves the team's meanest tasks or left-over assignments so that they will not have to saddle their colleagues with them. This is a waste of leadership because their time would be much better spent with another teacher in a classroom or a planning session. It may be argued that these tasks just have to get done by somebody, but if it has to be the leaders, then something is wrong.

Another point needs to be stressed about the leaders' assisting their colleagues. Many times in Lexington one or another senior teacher has protested, "But I am not a social studies specialist; I can only claim a special *interest* in social studies." Clearly, we have invented the role of specialist before we have persons who are fully prepared to fill it. The specialist is caught in a double conflict. His colleagues expect him to justify his position, and yet his role has not been specifically defined. Furthermore, the specialist's colleagues may expect him to produce plans and materials that are really beyond his present capacity. Some of us who have worked in Lexington are convinced that the specialist should have special clinical and curriculum training, as well as further study of his subject, beyond the level of the master's degree. Realizing that one could not have such persons in every subject on each team, we would appoint one specialist in each field to the faculty of the elementary school as a whole. These persons would not be included in the pupil-teacher ratio calculations for the school and would have roving assignments. They would work mainly with one team at a time to improve the curriculum, to train the teachers, and to make studies of the pupils. Moreover, we conceive of this position as a joint appointment of some sort which would allow the specialist access to the resources of the university for research and development. Such an arrangement is not as far in the future as one might suppose. For the time being, we have agreed in Lexington that the specialist's role is to ask the embarrassing questions, not necessarily to answer them. With reference to the planning strategy, the leader (whether team leader or senior teacher) of each grade level complement must be inquiring continually about the team's opportunities and obligations. Otherwise, the strategy will fall apart.

We have saved until last a question that has probably been uppermost in the reader's mind. Where do the teachers get time for all of this? As of this writing, we would have to say emphatically that they do not get time enough. The shortage of time enters into virtually every discussion and is a ready explanation for the incompleteness of any task or project. Not every aspect of the question, however, adds up to the same conclusion. Some can be classified as disappointed expectations. A second heading subsumes those features of team teaching which seem to be extraordinarily time consuming at present but which can be expected to require less time as they are refined or improved. Thirdly, team teaching confronts a swiftly developing situation that makes unreasonable demands upon the teachers' time and that cannot be expected to improve without still more fundamental changes in the organization of instruction.

Perhaps the most basic disappointment for many of the teachers at this time concerns certain expectations that hover about the notion of professionalization. Some who were accustomed to the long grind of the teacher's working day, as well as others who were not, anticipated that team teaching would result in something vaguely defined as more professional hours. It has not yet worked out in this way, and it seems likely that team teaching will demand as much time as the self-contained classroom, if not more, for a long while to come. This time may be spent more profitably than before, but that is a different story.

It has been widely supposed that large-group instruction would create a considerable amount of released time for teachers. Our experience with literally hundreds of large-group lessons in Lexington has led us to reject this expectation, at least in its most obvious sense. Not only do these lessons require a great deal of time to prepare, but it is also generally necessary for teachers who are not directly responsible for the lessons to be present anyway, or at least to be involved in the planning, in order to insure the articulation of these lessons with others that precede and follow them.[16]

A related matter concerns the planning that one teacher can do for others. Teachers have often tried to parlay a little released time into much more released time by having one teacher plan for others, who would in turn have more planning time when they put the lessons into effect. This rarely works out very neatly, as we saw above in examining the preparation of sets of lessons for a rotating scheme.

[16] It seems to us that there are two stages in the justification of large-group instruction for a particular lesson. First, the lesson will be the same for all of the pupils who receive it. Therefore, the rationale for it is closely allied to the rationale we have developed for key lessons: pacing, introduction of inaccessible material, definition of major ideas, etc. But the teacher cannot control the lesson in terms of feedback from the pupils or, at most, the feedback is limited to mass responses like laughter and hand raising and to whatever information the teacher can glean from brief conversations with a small sample of the total number of pupils involved. (We are not considering here the feedback that one can obtain in smaller groups after the large-group lesson is over.) The question at this point, therefore, is whether the lesson can be controlled adequately without this feedback. A study of many large-group lessons in Lexington arrived at the following rather straightforward, perhaps deceptively simple, conclusion: those large-group lessons seemed to be most successful which (1) told the pupils what the lesson was going to be about, (2) presented the lesson, and (3) told the pupils what the lesson had been about. A somewhat less prosaic way of saying this is that the lessons should have a great deal of conceptual redundancy. This does not mean sheer repetition, but it does mean that the basic message should be communicated in a variety of ways that support each other. Concrete examples, visual aids, and so on may be combined to tell the pupil that he is on the right track as well as to bring out complementary details of the argument. A derivative question that must be asked at this point is whether or not the pupils can respond appropriately to the lesson while it is in progress. By this we mean vicarious participation, response to visual and auditory stimuli, meaningful responses to vocabulary, and emotional responses. It is a truism about learning that we remember only our responses to stimuli, not the stimuli themselves. In summary, we would argue the following. If all pupils need the same lesson, and if the lesson can be prepared so as to include high conceptual redundancy and to provide opportunities for continuous response by the pupils (even a lecture can do this if properly fashioned), then it might be appropriate to offer the lesson in a large group. Only at this point does one ask if the large group would be more efficient in terms of the utilization of teachers, space, and equipment. Or, if one is absolutely bound by this last, logistical consideration, when an outside resource (a person, film, etc.) can be employed only in a large group, for example, then the lesson must be constructed so that it does meet the aforementioned requirements.

Despite these strictures, there is a different sense in which we can expect large-group instruction and cooperative planning to yield more time. The teachers will be developing resources for each other and for the future through what we have been calling key lessons and also through their suggestions for related activities. However, the condition which must be met in order for this gain to materialize is that each teacher must exploit these resources for himself and with his pupils. He cannot do this without internalizing the intentions of the curriculum at every point in his teaching.

There is another sense in which a planning strategy can pay off. The problem of time is partly a problem of good timing. Plans can be developed much more efficiently when a system of priorities is observed in the order and extent of the decisions that one makes at various stages. The teams which have already employed our strategy in the past year report that it is in fact more efficient than their former practices in social studies, and we can expect it to become even more so as it is mastered.

Yet another feature of the situation at present that can be expected to improve eventually is curriculum revision. The curriculum will always be subject to further development, and new teachers will need at least a year to orient themselves. Still, we can distinguish between the initial and later stages of curriculum revision and argue that the latter will be considerably easier. A complicating factor that we have not considered is that other areas of the curriculum will be in the process of revision at the same time. It will be necessary to co-ordinate these projects so that their initial stages do not overlap, though inevitably the later stages will.

Simply finding the time in the schedule for weekly meetings of the teachers in a given curriculum area may be difficult for some teams. We do not expect to hit this stride in all of our Lexington teams for a year or two and may be scheduling only one meeting for each phase of a social studies unit until the strategy is in high gear.

We have alluded to a third category of problems which arise out of the rapidly accelerating demands that our society is making today upon education and the schools. Until our traditional conception of the school is altered still further than it has been so far, we cannot begin to accomplish all that we should, and that we must, through education. This is the underlying implication of our two-track proposal or, rather, the import of numerous developments over the past 70 years or more that emphasize the learner's capacities for governing his own inquiry. Often this concern appears to run counter to another trend which seeks to command more and more of the learner's effort for his mastery of the exploding universe of knowledge. But it is for this reason that educators have been intrigued by the structure of thought as an approach that relates the learner's control of his own inquiry to the organization of knowledge. Can we now be as daring as we ask about the organization of the school and its relationship to our society?

As soon as we emphasize education as a process of inquiry, rather than the sheer acquisition of knowledge, it becomes apparent that we have made many arbitrary distinctions in setting up the school as the seat of education. Why *this* knowledge from *these* teachers in *this* place at *this* time of one's life? We can imagine some alternatives.

Time and again in this century it was urged by the progressives, but not by them alone, that the school should be more closely related to the conditions of modern life. At first their emphasis was placed largely on creating a miniature society within the school with the intention of nurturing the growth of individuals who could function autonomously and creatively within, one might almost say in the teeth of, the complex and impersonal patterns of an emerging industrial culture. Later the emphasis seemed to shift to the reconstruction of society through education, and the group seemed to gain ascendence over the individual in progressive programs. A third phase saw some educators, apparently despairing of this reconstruction, stress life adjustment, while others moved on to propose that the school share with other institutions (civic groups, unions, and agencies of government) planning and action to reconstruct society. Today we are witnessing a full-scale reaction against many features of this whole development. Ironically, it does not stem from our having solved any of the basic problems that were posed in these successive phases of progressivism, but rather it comes in good part from our frustration in having met them inadequately and from our response to still other problems confronting our society.

At the root of all these problems is the development of increasingly complex patterns and organizations of human activity. While these developments have greatly enlarged the scope of man's life, they have at the same time tended to remove him, as an individual, further from the sources and ends of human activity. Decisions that affect our daily lives seem more and more intangible as they issue from government, or corporations, or science, or from the vast matrices elaborated by communications, commerce, the specialization of tasks, and the differentiation of knowledge itself. Likewise, we see less of the results of our activity, in many respects, as we produce pieces of goods, give to charities, vote for others who must act on our behalf, and wrest fragments of personal knowledge from the awesome known and unknown. Surely a legitimate concern of some of those (including this author) who have been wary of team teaching, is that our reorganization of instruction might itself become a further accommodation of education to the exigencies of corporate life (see Chapter 9). That this could happen is very evident from the patterns that develop in team teaching when one does not carefully work out the relationships of the individual pupil or teacher to the total enterprise. It is suggested by the very connotations of the word *team*, which, in its apparent consistency with other aspects of our life today, has been accepted uncritically by many persons who have not really considered the basic rationale of team teaching (see Chapter 3). It is for these reasons that we are in deadly earnest when we speak of a strategy for planning. We can all too easily submit to the impersonal mercies of organization if we are not constantly on guard to protect and nourish the rights and capacities of the individual in education.

Indeed, our stance must be aggressive, not merely defensive. We are asking here how the reorganization of instruction can bridge some of the discontinuities between the compartments of modern life, not only for the child but for the adult as well. Perhaps progressive education attempted to assume in the school responsibilities which could only be shouldered by the society as a whole. Today we must recognize that the fulfillment of the individual in a world of overwhelming complexity demands that we shift the locus of inquiry from the school to the society for persons of every age and that we redefine the purposes of the school to support the efforts of society. Thus we should not ask, though we habitually do, how the school is to make good citizens of our children. In this endeavor the school plays but one part which must be integrated with other parts. Suppose that the people of an American town or school district set themselves the task of trying to understand the people and the way of life of an Asian community. The many forms of cultural exchange, the seminars of young and old alike, the accomplishments and the rebuffs and frustrations of such an effort, these would be the proper setting for a study of the world in the school. Or suppose that the lay public of a community, as well as its officials and professionals, were to explore its problems of urban renewal, or crime, or segregation, or public welfare, or of maintaining civil and political liberties. The point is not that this would enhance the specific utility of a unit about cities in the classroom but that it would place the function of the school in its rightful relationship to the inquiring community. Education, in a larger sense, is not the business of the schools alone.

What about the increasingly dysfunctional role of the adolescent in our society, for whom we seem to be able to find few responsibilities more purposeful than taking courses and doing summer jobs and domestic chores? *They could teach with us;* that is, they could engage in all aspects of the process of inquiry if we arranged the conditions of instruction so as to free them of certain artificial didactic impediments (of the sort which are more apparent to anthropologists than to learning psychologists). Suppose, for instance, that we asked some high school youngster who was especially interested in and knowledgeable about Mexico to come into the elementary school for a few hours a week when Mexico came up in our hypothetical Track II. He would be asked to converse with the children, or with one child, as the case might be. Of course, we would have to encourage the young to develop special lines of inquiry, but would we not find them eager to share their ideas in this way? What elementary school science program would not profit from having some of today's high school students come into the classroom to share laboratory know-how and science projects with the children? We have already seen that college students can contribute to the school, but we have tied this too closely to preparation for a teaching career. The author has been told of a recent project at Hull House in Chicago where adolescent girls who had dropped out of high school were asked simply to read to children of preschool age. These girls discovered that society needed them in a way that the school itself had failed to communicate.

One can envision inviting many persons from the community to participate in the affairs of the school. Our older citizens have experienced continuity and change that would enlighten and fascinate the young. Not all of their skill and knowledge is as dated as our conception of the curriculum sometimes leads us to believe. In most other cultures the old are deeply involved in education through the family. If they do not belong in the modern home, do they not belong all the more in the school? Would not the old gain equally from this experience? Again, we could apprentice youngsters to persons outside the school when their questions overreached the resources of the teachers. We have in mind not the vocational apprenticeship of the past, but an inquiry apprenticeship. It could be handled as an extension of Track II. The function of the apprenticeship would not be simply to exploit a larger labor pool for education, but rather to further the integration of the community on an inquiring basis. An architect could say to a youngster, "Go look at these buildings and their surroundings. Walk around them and wander through their rooms. Then come back, and we will talk about them." Our whole notion of the pupil-teacher ratio becomes absurd when we contemplate these possibilities.

We started by talking about the teachers' not having enough time in the schools. Yet our society faces the problem of too much time in our lives. The problem of leisure calls for our raising the most basic questions about the place of inquiry in the whole fabric of man's career. The problems of the world demand that we ask anew, what are knowledge and leisure for? The role, the very nature of the school cannot be properly determined beforehand.

Chapter 6

The Organization and Administration
of Team Teaching

ROBERT H. ANDERSON

Graduate School of Education, Harvard University

Educational change does not come about by accident. Because of the conservative role played by the educational system in most societies and especially because the American public school enterprise has such a large and well-established structure, even minor changes come about only as a result of widespread recognition of the need for change, accompanied by an enormous effort to define and implement the plan which may fulfill the acknowledged need. The adoption of team teaching, it seems reasonable to indicate, is by no means a minor change. Therefore, the nature and the amount of thinking and work that must necessarily precede any attempt to adopt team teaching must be unusually great.

This chapter attempts to examine some of the factors that should be taken into account by a school or school system if it has sensed the need for reorganization. Since the available experience of pilot projects has been too diversified and too brief to offer definite clues to the experiences that future adventurers will encounter, the material that follows is necesarily somewhat speculative. This is not to imply that lessons have not been learned or that useful warnings and assurances cannot be given. However, the fact remains that most pilot projects have not yet examined their own experience with the necessary care and objectivity; nor have accurate readings been taken of the profession's general attitude toward cooperative organization plans.

Although it seems to the authors that a more informed and receptive climate exists now than existed in earlier years (1957, for example), it is nevertheless impossible to predict whether or not a given community will react to a proposal for team teaching with the same relative mixture of interest, excitement, doubt, and confusion, as that which existed in some of the early pilot communities. However, it does seem reasonable to assume that all of these elements will be present to some degree in every situation. Further, it seems prudent to assume that the elements of doubt and confusion will be great enough in any situation to warrant very careful study and planning.

General Background[1]

Team teaching and the nongrading of pupils have had a number of philosophical and practical characteristics in common. Deriving as they do from an underlying concern for individual pupil progress, and both representing an effort to increase flexibility and efficiency in the arrangement of instructional groups, they have inevitably dealt with (or been frustrated by) the same problems of staff and program. To some investigators it seems that nongrading and team teaching are so closely linked together in theory and in operation that the initiation and development of one of them must ultimately lead to adoption of the other arrangement as well. It may be helpful, therefore, to consult the experiences of pilot projects in nongrading, which predate team teaching by at least a decade or more, in order to gain some perspective on the initiation and development of team teaching.

Goodlad and Anderson in their book on the nongraded school have drawn in part upon data submitted at various times since 1957 by school administrators in pilot nongraded projects.[2] In addition, because of their subsequent (or simultaneous) experience with pilot team teaching projects, these authors have utilized evidence gathered

---

[1] The information and viewpoint of Chapter 8 are related to the following material.

[2] John I. Goodlad and Robert H. Anderson, *The Nongraded Elementary School*, New York, Harcourt, Brace & World, 1959.

from both team teaching and nongrading in their more recent discussions of school organizations.[3]

A 1957 questionnaire study, which included 34 communities with pilot nongraded programs, asked the respondents to describe (in open-end form) the factors which had in their judgment contributed most to the successful development of their programs. Of some 20 items mentioned, the most frequently noted were (in order): strong interest and desire on the part of the teaching staff (13 mentions); careful staff study and research (12 mentions); effective use of PTA and other public relations channels (10); staff concern about pupil retentions and related problems of pupil adjustment (8); special interest and leadership shown by a teacher, principal, superintendent, or supervisor (8); parent conferences and parent meetings (8); and continuous parent-education emphasis.[4] Noteworthy is the obvious conclusion that success in the 34 projects was seen as closely related to the understanding gained (both in advance, and as the project progressed) by both teachers and parents.

A second question dealt with the problems or difficulties that had been encountered in establishing the nongraded program. Three out of the first four problems noted by the respondents had to do with the *limited flexibility or enthusiasm on the part of teachers*, as distinct from parents.[5] Specifically, there were mentioned (in order): (1) grade-level-expectation habits of teachers; (2) reluctance of traditionalists among teachers to try something different; (3) general problems of informing parents; and (4) problems of retraining or orienting staff members.

The same authors polled a larger sample (89) of pilot nongraded programs in 1960, and, although the same specific questions were not repeated, the obtained data tend in various ways to confirm the impressions of the earlier study.[6] Of at least equal importance is the strong impression conveyed by the 1960 study (and certainly hinted

---

[3] See in particular chaps. XII and XIII of Nelson B. Henry, ed., *Individualizing Instruction*, The Sixty-first Yearbook of the National Society for the Study of Education, pt. I, Chicago, University of Chicago Press, 1962.

[4] Reported in further detail in Goodlad and Anderson, *op. cit.*, pp. 170–172.

[5] *Ibid.*, pp. 172–174.

[6] See Robert H. Anderson and John I. Goodlad, "Self-Appraisal in Nongraded Schools: A Survey of Findings and Perceptions," *Elementary School Journal*, vol. LXII, February, 1962, pp. 261–269. See also a second article in *Elementary School Journal*, vol. LXIII, October, 1962, pp. 33–40.

at by the 1957 study) that the great need for fundamental curriculum reform is seen as both a major stimulant to organizational change and one of the greatest problems that emerges as the staff carries out the new organization.

The experiences of nongraded pilot projects have something further to say to those who would become involved in organizational reforms such as team teaching. Again in the context of the 1957 questionnaires, they suggest that the understanding and the enthusiasm of the teaching staff is the real key to success for any venture of this kind. Also prominent among the specific recommendations offered were comments such as: "Take time to get full parental understanding and consent." "Get the cooperation of *all* teachers and staff members, see that they develop a common philosophy and have access to common knowledge." "Move slowly, evaluate every move."[7] Clearly, the experiences of the profession with nongraded schools have proved very useful in suggesting some factors that might lead to success or difficulty in team teaching.

Comments on the Initiation of Team Teaching

As in the case of other innovations and reforms, team teaching must initially be based upon someone's recognition of a problem and concomitant perception of a particular mechanism which is potentially related to the solution of that problem. Who is the "someone" with this role of recognizer and initiator? Such recorded history as we have available and the relevant literature on the processes of effecting changes within institutional settings tell us that changes or ideas that lead to changes can be initiated by almost anyone within the setting, or even by persons external to it.

Team teaching is rather unique among current educational trends in that it seems to have received its original stimulus and much of its continuing energy from certain universities. Many of the theoretical studies and promotional activities carried on by the philanthropic foundations, by the federal government, and even by some of the national associations appear to have been directly stimulated by university activities in this field. Also, a large proportion of the specific

[7] Goodlad and Anderson, *op. cit.*, pp. 171–172.

projects begun between 1955 and 1960 can trace their origins to the "ivory tower."

The present authors, for example, trace much of their own interest and activity in team teaching to a series of theoretical discussions during the 1955–1956 school year. Without reference to any specific school systems and their needs, and long before the idea of SUPRAD (see Chapter 8) had been suggested to neighboring school systems, a small group of faculty members in the Harvard Graduate School of Education sat down together to consider some extremely tentative proposals for school reorganization. These proposals had first been sketched informally by Dean Francis Keppel in a mimeographed memorandum to which reactions were solicited. Finding that the proposals embraced both some exciting theoretical concepts and a promising new structure for school operations, the faculty group developed and refined the Dean's proposals to a point where it soon proved feasible to approach several school administrators and to consider plans for testing the new arrangements.

The mechanism of Harvard's SUPRAD came into being at least in part to enable a clinical partnership to be established between a school system and the university so that promising ideas such as team teaching could be tested under favorable conditions. Inherent in the SUPRAD type of arrangement is the principle that the ideas generated by both parties to the agreement have equal chance of acceptance and support. Whatever success there has been in realizing this goal, it remains that the inventions and suggestions of anybody within the affiliated institution, including the often neglected class-room teacher, are heard and considered.

The experience of the Harvard group was by no means an isolated case, for during this same general period a number of other university faculties are known to have wrestled with many of the same problems and proposals and to have developed similar arrangements with school staffs.[8]

[8] For the Wisconsin Improvement Program of the University of Wisconsin, see *Making Teaching and Learning Better: The Wisconsin Improvement Program, 1959–1961*, Madison, Wis., Wisconsin Improvement Program, 1962. See also their own publication, *The Wisconsin Improvement Program Reporter*, all issues. For the School Improvement Program of the University of Chicago see their *Newsletter*, published by the Department of Education. For the joint program of the Claremont Graduate School, see John A. Brownell, *The Clare-*

Since only a small handful of school systems have as yet an organic connection with college or university agencies, we had best proceed to the question of initiation and implementation within the typical school setting. There, of course, are found persons in a variety of roles within the hierarchical structure. Sometimes the structure actually includes persons with responsibility for research and development of new ideas or arrangements. Usually, however, research and development is merely one of the countless duties of the people concerned with teaching and administration.

The classroom teacher may actually be the first to become interested in an arrangement such as team teaching. Apparently the growing literature on team teaching is now commanding the attention of rather large numbers of teachers. Regional and state meetings planned for teachers have included in the last several years discussions or presentations of team teaching or topics related to it. In the colleges and universities some classes in which teachers are enrolled are spending time on these same topics. In fact, a number of universities have already begun to offer course work dealing with the topics of curriculum, organization, and supervision in relation to team teaching. Therefore, the teacher group is likely to be exposed to ideas which appear to merit further discussion in the local setting.

School administrators and supervisors are perhaps more likely to be the first to become aware of and interested in team teaching since the conferences, courses, and magazines serving this group are more directly tuned to the whole field of organizational reform. Also, it is the function and responsibility of administrators to contemplate and plan for change, and they have been invested (as teachers on the whole have not) with the authority to make changes.

Brickell takes a rather strong, and on the whole plausible, position with respect to the initiation of change. General opinion to the contrary, he states that teachers are extremely unlikely to suggest changes, especially if the changes involve distinctly new types of working patterns for themselves.[9] Their power to initiate instructional change without dependence upon administrative initiative or

mont Teaching Team Program, Claremont, Calif., Claremont Graduate School, 1961.

[9] Henry M. Brickell, *Organizing New York State for Educational Change*, Albany, New York State Department of Education, December, 1961, pp. 22–23.

approval seems to Brickell to be limited to changes in their own classroom practices, in the relocation of existing curriculum content, and in the introduction of special (usually advanced) courses in the high school.[10] Such changes can usually be made without disturbing the work of others. When it comes to structural changes, however, the work of many persons is affected, and the teacher encounters various types of opposition.

What matters most about the initiation of team teaching is not whose idea it may have been in the first place, but whether or not the entire staff comes to understand and accept the idea as relevant to its most cherished ambitions. That all teachers must reach this stage, as noted earlier, is to be taken quite literally. All teachers in the school system, whether they be those who are directly involved in the first efforts at local implementation of the idea, whether they be those whose involvement in the near future is predictable, or whether they be those who might conceivably become involved at some distant point, need to have at least a minimum understanding of what is to be done and why.

It may be that the complete endorsement, or even intellectual involvement, of an entire staff is too much for which to hope. Sometimes it becomes necessary to take a stand and move ahead even though some may object or even wish to obstruct. Such a move must of course be taken knowingly, and in such cases the energy and commitment of the group proceeding with the project needs to be unusually great. Certainly it is necessary to have the wholehearted understanding and support of at least the status leaders (especially, of course, the superintendent and his assistants), as well as the persons working most closely with the project.

If an opposition group should develop and if the basis of opposition is primarily a lack of understanding, then an appropriate strategy for the project's supporters would be to open as many lines of communication to this group as possible. For that matter, even if the opposition group does have an apparently accurate understanding of the project and its purposes, it is highly desirable to provide that group with an internal channel of criticism and communication. In other words, every reasonable effort should be made to furnish information and to ensure discussion and debate within the family.

[10] *Ibid.*, pp. 24–25.

Too often the zealous proponents of an idea such as team teaching have resorted to strong-arm tactics and have imputed malevolence or stupidity to those who have not joined or supported them. The results are unfortunate; the issues separating the two groups become personal and must be resolved outside the family to the ultimate disadvantage of both sides.

That two opposing camps should exist in a school system is of course to be avoided as much as possible. This is not to say that divergent viewpoints cannot be tolerated—on the contrary, disagreement is a strong sign of health—but a basic split on some major aspect of a school system's operations can make excessive demands upon the energy and the effectiveness of that system. It is perhaps better to devote extra years to planning and discussion until workable compromises can be achieved rather than to risk a house divided.

Related to this general problem is evidence which suggests that team teaching has sometimes been championed by superintendents and others not because they fully understood and appreciated its relevance to fundamental school problems but because they were enchanted by its uniqueness, its fashionableness, and its superficial glamour. The very fact that it is different has seemed to some a sufficient reason to get on the bandwagon.

"How do you do?" one educator might say to another on the boardwalk in Atlantic City. "I'm superintendent Doakes of Blankville and we have team teaching in our fair city!" Thus that cheery gentleman would be announcing in one convenient statement his identity, his virtue, and his modernity.

While patently unfair to the 99.44 percent of superintendents with purer minds and motives, this fictional episode has at least a grain of truth in it. At a time when the literature on team teaching was primarily promotional and optimistic, the situation caused this author so much concern that he inserted the following notice, what must have seemed to the editor an unusual request, alongside an article published in June of 1960:

> Teaching teams and other forms of reorganization are attracting widespread attention, and in recent months a surprisingly large number of communities have taken steps toward launching such programs. In *The Nation's Schools* for May, I described several pioneer ventures in team teaching. I pointed out that this pattern of school organization is extremely

complicated and has not yet been well demonstrated with the necessary care and rigor. Because team teaching has a certain logical appeal and, at least in the present climate, an arresting glamour, there is now a real danger that some enterprising administrators will jump on the team teaching bandwagon to the ultimate sorrow of the profession. . . .[11]

That the understanding and support of the school administration is vital to the welfare of any new project is already a major assumption of our general argument. While a merely permissive or tolerant attitude on the part of administration may suffice if other vigorous leadership and enthusiasm exists to give the project its needed momentum, a fair trial is far likelier if top administration takes a clearly positive position both publicly and internally. Summarizing his own views on this matter, Brickell notes:

. . . authority is a critical element in the shaping of institutional decisions. Schools depend heavily upon administrative authority in decision-making. Consequently, the control center of the institution, as schools are managed today, is the administrator. He may not be—and frequently is not—*the original source of interest in a new* type of program, but unless he gives it his attention and actively promotes its use, it will not come into being.[12]

Like nongrading, team teaching is more likely to begin in a small way in a selected pilot school. It will then spread only as the rest of the school system comes to the persuasion that the pilot operation is working well and that the scheme has relevance to the needs of other schools.

The hazards of being a pilot school amidst conventional schools are well known. Such a school may be the object of envy, resentment, and misunderstanding on the part of other schools; the publicity involved, the invidious comparisons sometimes made or implied, the nonconformity of the pilot school, the threat it represents to established ways of doing things, even the suspected motives of the participants become a source of threat or annoyance. As a result, there is danger of a schism within the staff unless top administration has the desire and the skill to define the problems in universal

[11] Robert H. Anderson and Donald P. Mitchell, "Team Teaching, New Learning Concepts Demand Changes in School Plant Design," *The Nation's Schools*, vol. LXV, June, 1960, p. 75.
[12] Brickell, *op. cit.*, p. 24.

terms, to involve the people from other schools in planning and development work, and to prevent potential problems of competition and poor communication from arising.

One of the greatest dangers is that people may become so personally involved that the issues come to revolve around personalities rather than philosophies. There is "a tendency of some leaders to become inextricably identified at the personal level with the causes to which they are dedicated. Sometimes a leader's enthusiasm for an idea . . . is so strong and so contagious that the idea spreads, more because of the affect on or trust felt by the leader's colleagues for him than because of the intrinsic appeal of the idea itself."[13]

Also, it may be that a staff will find itself persuaded to go along with a proposal not primarily because the proposal is uniquely attractive to them, nor even because the leader is personally admired, but because that leader is known for getting things accomplished and for the general respect with which his views are held. In passing we may note that the opposite situation may also prevail; if the leader's ideas do not have much value in the administrative hierarchy, his enthusiasm for team teaching may be of little significance.[14]

However flattering may be the implications for a leader who has the aforementioned positive influence upon his staff, it behooves him to avoid mistaking staff loyalty for staff understanding. The intrinsic merits of team teaching must serve as the chief bases for exploring and developing it. If such is not the case, the project is headed for troublesome times should the leader leave the community, shift to some other favored cause, or lose some of his influence and prestige. Evidence to this effect is quite widespread in the history of nongraded schools.[15] Also, there are already several sobering examples in the brief experience of team teaching.[16]

[13] Goodlad and Anderson, *op. cit*, p. 189.
[14] See Nelson B. Henry, ed., *In-Service Education for Teachers, Supervisors, and Administrators*, Fifty-sixth Yearbook of the National Society for the Study of Education, pt. I, Chicago, University of Chicago Press, 1957, pp. 96, 177, and *passim*.
[15] Goodlad and Anderson, *op. cit.* p. 190.
[16] Several personal communications in the authors' files indicate that changes in administration have been responsible for the discontinuation of healthy team teaching projects. Such information is not available in the published literature. See Chapter 8, the section on frank and complete reporting.

Getting Team Teaching Underway

Study and Planning

We turn now to the steps that might be taken by a staff after it has come to the conclusion that team teaching has potenial value in the local setting and that information about team teaching should be gathered, sorted, weighed, and then perhaps applied.

TO VISIT OR NOT TO VISIT?   One of the ways a staff may choose to inform itself about the advantages, disadvantages, and characteristics of team teaching is to observe it at first hand in one of the pilot communities. Stemming in part from a typical disinclination among school people to deal with problems in theoretical or abstract terms, the urge to visit other schools may also be motivated by a tendency to imitate the practice of others rather than to invent unique procedures and by a feeling that much additional information and insight can be gained from face-to-face contact with the persons who are engaged in team operations. More immediately, the visit offers an opportunity for verification of arguments and data which have been received in written or verbal form.

On this latter point it must be admitted that much of the available information about team teaching has been not only incomplete but also somewhat untrustworthy. As is noted elsewhere (Chapters 1 and 8), a tendency to propagandize and over-claim has contaminated much of the reporting of team teaching. Questions may legitimately be raised at times about the accuracy and even the sincerity of the spokesmen for these projects. Especially suspect, it appears, are the claims that have to do with the morale and the welfare of the teachers and the children.

The fact that most of the available published information comes from administrators or their counterparts in the universities and foundations makes it difficult for teachers to accept it. Many teachers and principals feel more confident about information obtained directly from teachers and, where appropriate, from children. Since access to the ideas and feelings of teachers from pilot projects is more limited than access to the administrators (through correspondence, through their appearances as speakers, or through their writings), it seems necessary to search out the teachers in their own setting.

After interviewing hundreds of teachers and administrators about the factors that might influence them to adopt a particular program, Brickell concluded that "the most persuasive experience a school person can have is to visit a successful new program and to observe it in action. Speeches, literature, research reports and conversations with participants outside the actual instructional setting are interesting but relatively unconvincing."[17] Certainly the prevalance of this sentiment is corroborated in the experience of pilot projects. The authors do not contest Brickell's data nor the conclusion as he has phrased it. However, we submit that *actual visiting may provide neither a valid nor a useful experience, nor is it usually an efficient and economical approach to the fundamental issues at stake.* That so much reliance has been placed upon it has very distasteful implications for the integrity and the intelligence of the profession.

The authors have had extensive experience with visitors, and it is only fair to admit that this experience has prejudiced them against the practice of visiting projects, especially when they are in a formative, struggling stage. In many ways the ceaseless demands of visitors upon the time and the energies of pilot project personnel have, in fact, tended to prevent research and development activities from being carried on. Clearly, visitor fatigue, strongly felt by many other pilot projects as well, has motivated the foregoing statement. However, there are more important considerations involved, and these are (hopefully) much more objective in nature.

Team teaching can exist in many forms and for various reasons. Each community will have its own specific reasons for undertaking team teaching and must work out an essentially unique solution to its recognized problems. Though knowledge about several pilot projects may indeed be helpful and though fairly intimate acquaintance with one of them might by accident have special relevance, nonetheless each community needs to look inward rather than outward if it is to do more than gamble on that relevance through imitation. The primary need is for a deep understanding of one's own institution.

Turning to the experiences and models of others can also be an illusory or evasive device. Very few teachers and administrators are such skilled observers and questioners that they can visit a pilot

[17] Brickell, *op. cit.*, p. 27.

project for a few hours, or even a few days, and come away with all the understanding and information necessary for their own purposes. Furthermore, team operations are often varied, so that many weeks may be required to witness the whole range of team activities. Also, much of the important work of teams goes on behind the scenes. To assume that one knows how a team works, unless he has been a direct witness to dozens of separate episodes in the staff's life together, would be to severely delude oneself.

Some visitors appear quite willing to delude themselves. Arriving with a preconceived idea (whether hostile or friendly, it does not matter), they will seek visible evidence in support of their preconceptions and then hurry home with their data. Inasmuch as one could probably find every kind of evidence, both terrible and wonderful, in almost any school in the United States, whether team-organized or not, it goes without saying that this sort of visitor is rarely disappointed. It also goes without saying that he is not a very useful and reliable source of information to the people to whom he reports. In a sense there is little protection against such foolish people, and all we can hope is that their numbers and their influence will diminish in time. There is a more numerous and better-motivated group, however, whose behavior is almost as disturbing.

A number of sponsors of team teaching projects gathered together during a recent national meeting to compare notes on their experiences. As might be expected, the matter of dealing with visitors was one topic of lively interest. While it should not be implied that visitors have been uniformly unwelcome and troublesome, it seems worth recording here that many visitors were perceived as not being honestly concerned with the theoretical and intellectual problems to which team teaching addresses itself. Roughly four out of five revealed in questioning or comments that they had not bothered to consult, especially in depth, the general literature or even the informative materials made available to them in advance. In the same vein they seemed rather uninterested in approaching fundamental questions or in organizing their daily observations with a view to examining specific issues. Rather, they seemed primarily concerned about minor details of scheduling, financing, equipping, and other low-level problems. This was regarded by the project sponsors as a most discouraging situation.

STAFF STUDY. One is therefore tempted to ask whether far better results might be obtained for each local situation if the inquiry into team teaching could be conducted at the level of discussion, study, and local soul searching. The time and money that might be wasted on travel might better be devoted to thoughtful inquiry, including not only the reading of the literature but also the examination of locally recognized problems as they might relate to staff reorganization.

This is not to say that travel to pilot projects ought never to be considered. On the contrary, it seems that eventually a local staff would probably profit from, and might even be desperately in need of, first-hand informaiton about some other project and the way it has solved a particular set of problems. In general, however, the argument of the previous section has indicated that visits which are not preceded by exhaustive and introspective studies of local needs and of how the broad theory of team organization bears upon them are a great waste of everybody's time.

Staff in-service study of professional problems is one of the primary sources of a school system's health and progress. As the vast literature on this topic attests, school systems have long been attempting such studies (see Chapter 2). On the whole, however, only very modest beginnings can be reported for all but a handful of places. The budget in support of local research and development activities is usually negligible if not nonexistent, and the number and variety of consulting specialists in most school systems are similarly restricted. Only in very recent years has a trend appeared whereby the employer district subsidizes such in-service staff pursuits as extended workshops, summer curriculum studies, university studies undertaken at the employer's specific request, and participation by teachers in national or regional meetings of professional associations directly concerned with the school program.

For the most part, therefore, each local staff finds whatever time and energy it can conserve for fundamental in-service program studies by squeezing it out of an already overloaded working schedule. Little is to be gained here by bemoaning the prevailing situation, but it does seem necessary to point out that the prior existence of a well-supported and well-organized plan of in-service staff activity can serve as a major plus factor when studies of team teaching are contemplated. If a staff really wants to study team teaching, if it has the necessary energy and resources upon which to draw, if leadership and consultation services are assuredly available as needed, and if other favorable conditons exist generally, then it seems reasonable to expect that good progress can be made. Conversely, a history of chronic undersupport, with all the attending fatigue and frustrations, can be a brilliant red light warning of impending disaster.

ASSESSMENT OF THE LOCAL SITUATION. At some point, in light of what has been said above, the study group and the administration will have to pool their efforts in taking inventory of the local situation and its susceptibility to major change. In general, such an inventory will uncover three kinds of information: (1) factors and elements which appear to indicate the need for change become the subject of staff analysis at the initial study level; (2) factors which indicate readiness and receptivity become the elements in strategic planning for moving ahead on whatever scale seems warranted; and (3) forces or factors representing resistance, hostility, or other opposition also have strategic implications and will influence every decision that is made.

Let us take a moment to survey a few areas that deserve examination in connection with the second category, conditions propitious for change. While some of these are quite obvious, their mention may at least prove helpful. The first group of favorable conditions has at least one characteristic in common, *superior financial support*.

One such condition is the existence, for a number of years prior to any of the current thinking about reorganization, of a strong tax-supported kindergarten program. This is especially important in those states and localities where kindergarten service is not usually provided. As Goodlad and Anderson have pointed out, kindergarten programs are often a reflection of effective leadership in the past, and it is probably not a coincidence that nearly all of the pilot nongraded programs (and here we may add, pilot team teaching programs) have been launched in communities where good kindergartens have long existed.[18]

Adequacy of supervisory and administrative services, especially

[18] Goodlad and Anderson, *op. cit.*, pp. 186–187.

the principal-to-teachers ratio, is a very good clue to the community's past appreciation of the need for leadership. A sufficient central office staff to prevent overburdening of the superintendent and, more important, to insure the availability to the schools of adequate consulting and supporting services is certainly a major need in a situation as potentially complex and explosive as team teaching creates.

Not only is there an obvious need for secretarial service in the office, but also long overdue is a better arrangement for meeting many of the routine secretarial needs of teachers themselves. Evidence that this fact has been recognized and met through some definite provision or arrangement would seem to be a most encouraging sign.

A generous and well-chosen supply of instructional resources of all kinds (textbooks and source books, library collections, audiovisual equipment of many types, expandable supplies) appears to be an important factor. Certainly as team teaching gets underway, the needs of the school's inhabitants for these resources will be multiplied. If the usual supply is submarginal or barely adequate under conventional conservative conditions, it is certain that a crisis will be created when the need suddenly increases.

An amusing example comes to mind from the experience of one pilot school. Based upon past practices of budgeting supplies, the supplies closet in late August contained one quart of art paste for each class in the school. This was intended as the full year's supply. In a single large-group art lesson in September one of the teams of three classes used one and one-half quarts of paste, or roughly half the year's supply. The temporary crisis created by this situation came later to be regarded as a symbolic event, the import of which could be truly serious.

The suitability and flexibility of the physical plant is another factor. Many communities have been so hard pressed to accommodate the burgeoning pupil population that they have made continuous compromises in their architectural planning. If classrooms are generally packed, if special facilities for various purposes have been skimped or omitted, if furnishings and equipment have been of limited quality and adaptability, then the space demands made by team teaching will sorely strain such buildings.

The community which has made a sincere and ungrudging effort to maintain attractive teacher salary levels seems on the whole to enjoy a tremendous advantage over communities which have not. Especially important, it would seem, is the community's history with respect to merit pay or to other systems for rewarding superior staff performance. For one thing, it should shed light upon the prevailing attitude within the community toward the conventional pattern of equal-salary-for-equal-training-and-service. Even more important, it affords clues to the feelings within the staff on this same issue. In general, it seems reasonable to expect that team teaching, especially of the hierarchical variety, will seem far more acceptable and desirable in communities where there has been in the past a serious effort to acknowledge the fact that some teachers have greater competence and are capable of exerting greater influence than others. In such a community the idea of assigning a more responsible and better paid role to teachers of outstanding skill may appear to be a desirable solution to a long-recognized problem.

While it is sometimes difficult to measure, the quality of the relationship between the school district and the community it serves can usually be described in strategically useful terms. Part of the history of this relationship is marked by the successive elections held in connection with tax rate increases, school building bond issues, and the selection of board of education members. These votes have been either favorable to the schools, mixed in meaning, or unfavorable. This in turn has some relationship to the esteem and confidence in which school officials and educational administrative policies are held. Probably the support which has been given or withheld by the power structure of the community, the business leaders and the press, also can be described along a continuum of favorable to unfavorable. Furthermore, it may be possible, though it will certainly be more difficult, to assess the attitudes of parents toward their children's school and to rate them as being somewhat favorable, neutral, or hostile.

In addition to a measure of the school-community relationship, some measure also needs to be taken of the community's tolerance of innovation. In some communities each new idea is greeted with suspicion or resistance, while in others there may be a high degree of acceptance of new ideas. It is well to know the local situation on this point before a beginning is made.

As in the experience of pilot nongraded schools, where parent resistance appears to have been a negligible factor, especially by comparison with teacher resistance, it could be that team teaching projects may be safely launched without undue concern for parent reaction. If the history of school-community relations has been reasonably harmonious and constructive, if the school staff is held in relatively high regard, and if normal care is exercised to inform and explain, it would seem that the professionals could safely proceed to initiate the desired changes.

Of interest here is one other aspect of the Brickell study noted earlier. Brickell came to the conclusion that "parents and citizens groups in most communities do not exert a direct influence on the adoption of new types of instructional programs."[19] However, he also notes that active parent opposition, when it does occur, can often be a decisive factor. Brickell even goes as far as to state that the board of education in most communities is not likely to be a strong factor in determining the path of educational innovation, though again its influence is decisive when exerted.[20] This is a plausible argument because the board of education is, in the final analysis, the community in microcosm, and in general we may expect board members to represent and reflect the general attitudes of the community toward the schools.

Some Considerations of Structure

In the early stages of planning and preparation for team teaching, the school system will encounter certain structural problems which will require careful examination. The size and the type of teams to be organized, the extent to which all teachers are likely to become involved, and the ways the proposed structure will influence the professional behavior and the morale of participants will each in turn merit detailed analysis. In the conversations which grow out of these studies, two topics will probably be especially prominent: the sovereignty of the individual teacher, and the hierarchical or-

[19] Brickell, *op. cit.*, p. 20.
[20] *Ibid.*, p. 21.

ganization of the team. These are of course interrelated, although here they will be discussed separately.

SOVEREIGNTY. In conventional organizations there is little doubt that the individual teacher has complete control (to the extent any teacher does) over the classroom situation and the pupils assigned to him. Though certain school-wide rules and regulations establish a general atmosphere and a code of goals and operations, the teacher is largely free of interference and restrictions as he turns to the tasks of planning, teaching, and evaluating. Especially at the moment of confronting the pupils, he has considerable freedom in his choice of language, strategies, and other teaching behavior. As long as no standards of ethics or good taste are violated and as long as his work results in appropriate achievement by his pupils, the likelihood of intervention or objection by any professional colleague is very remote. He enjoys, in fact, a remarkable degree of freedom.

It is suspected by many that participation in a team organization means a surrender of this freedom. Probably this feeling arises both from the realization that joint decisions are not necessarily unanimous and from the further suspicion that the risk of censure and disapproval, in a situation where teachers are free to observe and criticize each other freely, may encourage conformity.

The right to be idiosyncratic is cherished by workers in nearly all fields. The nonconformist, the inventive and creative worker, the person of unusual insights and talents is often the one who reveals new truths or brings the art to a higher level of excellence. Ethical codes usually exist to prevent such a person from doing harm, but even the codes are subject to re-examination, and ultimately the justification of a procedure must reside in its intrinsic validity.

In medicine, for example, a physician may employ a diagnostic or therapeutic technique within certain limits prescribed by his profession. These limits are subject to revision as research and experience may allow. Whether the physician who knowingly violates or extends those limits is reproved or lauded by his colleagues depends upon the outcome of his performance and the scientifically confirmable theories upon which it was based.

Frequently, too, a physician turns to fellow physicians for expert advice on a particular problem with which he is confronted. Upon concluding that a colleague's skills are superior to his in a given instance, he may transfer his authority to that colleague—in other words, surrender his sovereignty in the case. This is done frequently in the case of referrals to specialists in various branches of medicine.

On the other hand, a physician may discuss his case with his colleagues and then may reject their skills and advice. The patient is his own responsibility, and he proceeds on the basis of the best judgment he possesses—in other words, he chooses to retain his sovereignty. Later he may be required to defend his procedure in debate with his colleagues or his superiors.

The medical analogy is quite relevant to team teaching. In a team we assume adequate professional judgment and competency in each teacher until the evidence proves otherwise. Teachers remain the "physicians" to their own "patients," and in each specific teaching situation the teacher is therefore free to proceed on the basis of his own best judgment. There may have been a prior compromise about the nature and purpose of the lesson, to be sure, but presumably no teacher would ever be placed in a position where he is doing something he feels should not be done. Whether or not he has chosen to avail himself of the opportunity for consultation and advice, the manner in whch he teaches will be essentially his own private decision. In the final analysis his right to continue using a particular procedure will depend upon its essential validity.

Thus our argument indicates that the team arrangement allows each teacher to retain his sovereign individuality, subject only to the defensibility of his performance. Since this asks nothing more of a teacher than ought to be asked under any circumstances, it may well be said that team organization costs the competent teacher nothing he cannot afford to pay.

HIERARCHY. Schools have long been organized on a hierarchical basis, with authority and responsibility flowing down the organization chart from superintendent to principal to teacher to pupil. While it might be erroneous to suggest that all teachers approve of this arrangement, it seems probable that all understand the necessity for it.

Typically, the salary schedule in American schools applies uniformly to teachers of various degrees of competency, to men and to women, and to workers at the various school levels, regardless of their relative influence and competence. A teacher with ten years of experience and x hours beyond the BA will receive exactly the same salary as another teacher with the same background, though one may be the best teacher in the county and the other barely capable of holding his job. In recognition of this situation much discussion in recent years has been devoted to the idea of merit rating —assigning higher financial and symbolic rewards to the superior teacher, and eliminating the illogical system of automatic salary progress for the substandard performer.

It is well known, of course, that many excellent teachers suffer not only a financial injustice but also an unfortunate restriction in the influence they may exert. Ordinarily, a superior teacher performs the same teaching duties as a marginal teacher, and, except in small indirect ways, his influence upon other teachers and pupils is scarcely felt. If such a teacher wishes to get ahead in the profession or to exert greater influence, about the only alternative is to leave the classroom for an administrative post.

As noted elsewhere in this volume, team teaching has been offered as a means of establishing within teaching a hierarchy of roles and thereby providing attractive career opportunities for superior teachers who qualify for leadership roles. Now we shall return to that discussion to ask how such a hierarchy might affect the morale and well-being of teachers who may not ever qualify for leadership assignments (see also the discussion of this problem in Chapter 9).

For the moment let us assume that the hierarchy of a teaching team is a matter of satisfaction to the leader. The question is whether or not the nonleaders of the team will also be happy about the hierarchy. Will they not feel inferior if they are assigned to a role of lower status? Will the children not regard them with less admiration and affection because of that lower status? Will they not resent the decisions and the power of the leader? Will not the team become a competition of leader-aspirants rather than a community of friends?

The final answers to these and related questions are not yet available, though certain generalizations may be drawn from the experience of pilot hierarchical teams. On the whole, the evidence suggests: (1) the existing corps of teachers finds it difficult to accept hierarchy before having direct experience with it; (2) veteran teachers who join hierarchical teams usually develop positive attitudes toward hierarchy, though some do not; (3) young teachers who begin their careers in hierarchical teams find it to be both helpful and desirable; (4) there is a strong relationship between the competence of the leader and the team members' feelings about the hierarchy; (5) pupils, especially at the elementary level, tend to value and approve of all the members of the team regardless of their role; and (6) competition for leadership roles does become evident in some teams, but the effect of this seems to be generally constructive rather than destructive.

It is interesting to note that veteran teachers in highly paid school systems seem to be less attracted to the hierarchical concept than are teachers in average or below average systems. This may be true in part because of their relative financial security and in part because they perceive themselves and their colleagues to be of generally high professional calibre. A salary supplement appears to be less of an incentive to them, and they sense the prospect of internal strife and dissension if the administration attempts to select some of them as leaders.

To the authors' knowledge, there is as yet no evidence to support the widespread professional wariness about hierarchy. The morale of teachers appears to be excellent in hierarchical teams as long as the leader is at least minimally capable of doing his job. No inevitable disadvantages appear to result from the hierarchical arrangement, and, on the contrary, there appear to be some definite advantages when the model operates according to plan. That the overwhelming majority of experienced teachers have what amounts to a psychological block against it suggests that the hierarchical pattern will be slow in gaining acceptance. Ultimately, we tend to believe it will prevail.

Examples of Team Organization

A variety of formal and informal patterns fall under the general heading of cooperative teaching. The informal patterns, though we won't be directly concerned with them here, often provide clues to the readiness of a staff for the next, more formal arrangements.

They are, of course, easier to launch, but they are also more prone to abandonment if troubles are encountered. Each teacher risks less, and also receives less. The ease with which a member may withdraw makes decisions a little more risky and adventuresome enterprise less likely. Nevertheless, their informality makes them more accessible and attractive to the typical teacher who is considering team teaching, and it seems desirable that such teachers be encouraged to cooperate informally in the interest of their own growth and development.

The formal patterns toward which many schools are moving are of several possible types. Most of these have already been described in the literature, though other models undoubtedly will emerge in time.[21] A few examples may be useful here, not as exemplary models but to suggest some of the arrangements that are possible.

It might be well to reiterate that teams can vary greatly in size and composition. In the definition in Chapter 1, we stated simply that two or more teachers could constitute a team. Though two teachers can technically be called a team, in practice such a team would be less flexible and less well-endowed than a larger team whose members possess varying skills and interests. It therefore seems appropriate here to draw our examples from teams of three to seven members. It also seems fitting to select examples which reflect some of the different purposes of team organization.

LEXINGTON: HIERARCHICAL, MULTI-AGE, ELEMENTARY TEAMS. Perhaps the best known of all team enterprises is the one begun in the Franklin School in Lexington, Massachusetts, in 1957–1958. Because it was probably the first example of an entire school organized into teams and because it has been quite extensively discussed in the literature, the Lexington project has had a large influence upon the development of team structure and attendant theories of school organization. Therefore, a review of its brief history and its major features may be useful here.

In 1957–1958 the school was reorganized into four teams. Two of the teams were large, composed of five or six teachers; two were small, composed of three teachers. The titles of team leader and of

[21] A theoretical discussion of various team models can be found in John A. Brownell and Harris A. Taylor, "Theoretical Perspectives for Teaching Teams," *Phi Delta Kappan*, vol. XLIII, January, 1962, pp. 150–157.

senior teacher were used to designate teachers who had responsibility for leadership in the teams. Classwork in each team was planned jointly by all team members, and through various redeployment procedures the children were taught in groups that ranged in size from six to more than a hundred. The four teams were organized as follows:

Alpha: three first-grade teachers (senior teacher in charge)
Beta: six second- and third-grade teachers (team leader in charge
             assisted by two senior teachers)
Gamma: three fourth-grade teachers (senior teacher in charge)
Delta: five fifth- and sixth-grade teachers (team leader in charge assisted by a senior teacher)

Each team was assigned a part-time clerical aide, and the two larger teams were each assigned a quarter-time teaching assistant.

The original 1957–1958 model has been modified only slightly over the years. Since its inception it has been a formal, hierarchical scheme with three professional levels and a subprofessional level. Although in the beginning there were two teams at a single grade level, the original pattern also had two multigrade teams, and this has become the preferred, standard arrangement. There have, however, been some changes in structure and emphasis which are of interest. In 1958–1959, several changes resulted in the following arrangement:

Alpha: four first-grade teachers (team leader in charge)
Beta: six second- and third-grade teachers (team leader in charge assisted by a senior teacher)
Omega: Eight fourth-, fifth-, and sixth-grade teachers (team leader in charge assisted by two senior teachers)

Again clerical assistance was provided, as was part-time teaching assistance.

The organizational pattern for 1959–1960 was essentially the same as that for the preceding year. However, there were two major differences between the organization for 1958–1959 and for 1959–1960. One was a difference in structure; a new senior teacher position was created for a multipurpose specialist in art, music, and physical education (by 1961–1962 this concept was modified to call for three separate specialists, one in each area). The other change was one of emphasis. Whereas before 1959–1960 senior teachers were looked on essentially as grade-level chairmen or as assistant team leaders, in 1959–1960 team leaders and senior teachers alike were becoming specialists in a particular instructional area. The team leader, in addition, carried administrative responsibility for his team.

In 1960–1961 the Franklin School organization was again modified, this time to provide three teams of approximately equal size. Each team was responsible for the pupils of two grade levels, and each included two senior teachers, partly because an effort was being made to identify and train as many leaders as possible. Also, there were two building-wide specialists, one in art and music and the other in physical education. Part-time teachers were replaced by a new category of personnel, teacher aides, who had direct contact with children in noninstructional situations. Each team had approximately 33 hours of teacher-aide service per week.

In 1961–1962 and again in 1962–1963 the team structure remained essentially unchanged. However, in 1961 the Joseph Estabrook School, designed especially for team operations, opened its doors.[22]

Franklin and Estabrook schools being of similar size, they both employed the same multigrade model with three teams each. Full-time specialists in each of the fields of art, music, and physical education served the two team teaching schools jointly.

The present Lexington model, then, is depicted in Figure 3. A description of each of the roles illustrated in Figure 3 is provided below. It should be emphasized that more precise specifications of qualifications and functions are still to be written. However, the hierarchy is envisaged, ideally, as including these elements:

TEAM LEADER (TL)

An experienced, mature, master teacher of unusual talent, who has had extensive teaching experience, who possesses at least a master's degree, who has had training in supervision and human relations or educational sociology, and who is a specialist in an area of elementary education. Furthermore, this person would have demonstrated satisfactorily ability to

[22] See *Profiles of Significant Schools: Schools for Team Teaching*, New York, Educational Facilities Laboratories, 1961, pp. 36–42. See also Anderson and Mitchell, *op. cit.*, pp. 75–81.

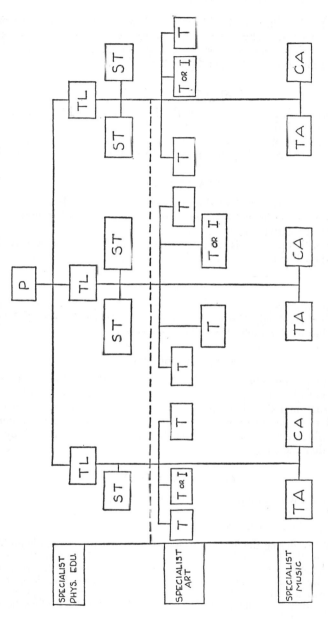

FIGURE 3. The Lexington Team Structure. P: Principal; TL: Team Leader; ST: Senior Teacher; T: Teacher; I: Intern; TA: Teacher Aide; CA: Clerical Aide.

work with teachers in a leadership role. It is anticipated that about one-third of this person's school day might be released for such purposes as observation and training of subordinates, planning, curriculum development, research and evaluation, and parent relations.[23]

SENIOR TEACHER (ST)

An experienced, mature person with above-average talent comparable to the well-regarded career teacher today. In addition, this person would have some degree of specialized competence in a particular area. This is seen as a terminal role, though it may lead to the position of team leader.

TEACHER (T)

This category is seen as including two types of personnel:
1. competent, experienced teachers of broad general training, and
2. teachers of relatively little experience.
The status of this position is regarded as equal to the status of the typical teacher today. For many teachers this represents a terminal role.

INTERN (I)

A trainee in a program of teacher education doing full-time supervised teaching in the school. The work of the intern is usually directed by a senior teacher working with the college supervisor.

TEACHER AIDE (TA)

A mature person who enjoys direct contact with children. A teacher aide does not qualify as a teacher but can supervise or work with pupils in noninstructional situations: e.g., supervise bus arrivals and departures, recess and lunch periods; operate mechanical aids to instruction; do housekeeping tasks; correct objective tests. Specific tasks are defined by the particular demands of each team.

CLERICAL AIDE (CA)

A person for whom no professional preparation is necessary. This person assists with the routine, nontechnical aspects of team operation: typing, duplicating, filing, and recording attendance.

[23] Experience during the first five years suggests that persons are more likely to succeed in the leader role if they possess these skills and qualities: (1) ability to initiate structure in the situation, as appropriate; (2) the quality of being considerate of others, as appropriate; (3) extraordinary knowledge of the learning process and educational goals; (4) artful talent in applying this knowledge and in selecting appropriate leadership behaviors for specific situations.

Because of their additional training and increased responsibilities, *senior teachers* receive a salary increment beyond the teachers' schedule, and *team leaders* receive an increment beyond that of senior teachers.

Since the more able and experienced members of the staff are elevated to newly created positions of greater influence, the *principal* of the school is accorded a position of enhanced prestige and responsibility. Freed from many routine administrative details (now assumed by team leaders and aides), it is theorized that the principal can give more effective leadership in curriculum development, in studies of resources, in instructional supervision, and in guidance. The principal may also become involved in the developmental and evaluative aspects of the program. By keeping abreast of current research, he is better able to provide staff members with information helpful in the improvement of the curriculum, of teaching methods, and of school practices in general.[24]

One of the advantages of the form of organization sketched above is the strength of leadership resources within the school. The principal and the team leaders, for example, are viewed in Lexington as the Administrative Cabinet and are responsible for the formulation of general school policy. This group plus the senior teachers constitute the Instructional Cabinet. By virtue of their specialized competencies the members of the Instructional Cabinet can hopefully be compared with the instructors in a teacher-training institution. This cabinet constitutes a mechanism for the constant reappraisal and upgrading of the curriculum and for the in-service training of the teaching staff.

While encouraging specialization and increased competence in comparatively narrow areas, the Lexington project does not advocate departmentalization as that term is commonly used in education. All teachers continue to teach all, or nearly all, subjects. On the other hand, though it is expected that each teacher will give instruction in language arts, arithmetic, social studies, science, art, and music, there are many opportunities for teachers to specialize. For example, one member of a team may assume a greater respon-

[24] For a more detailed discussion of the principal's changed role, see J. Lloyd Trump and Dorsey Baynham, *Focus on Change: Guide to Better Schools*, Chicago, Rand McNally, 1961, pp. 65–70.

sibility for that area of the curriculum in which he is more interested or more proficient than other members of the team. He may take the initiative in the planning stages of a new unit; he may prepare and conduct large-group sessions and suggest follow-up lessons; and, on occasions, he may provide in-service training for team colleagues. Perhaps another teacher may prefer to prepare transparencies and other visual materials for large-group instruction. Furthermore, to supplement its resources the team may use its part-time teachers and a wide variety of consultants and resource personnel from the community or from nearby institutions of higher education.

Although teams may consist of pupils of more than one age group (grade level), the team treats its entire pupil complement as a unit. The teachers of each team group and regroup their pupils for many different instructional purposes. Consequently, both group size and the basis of group composition usually vary for each class period. Using the remarks and recommendations of previous teachers and ignoring grade level designations, the teachers of each team group their pupils in language arts and arithmetic according to achievement. Although each of these groups represents a narrower range of achievement than is found in the typical self-contained classroom, team teachers generally find that they must also subdivide these groups for more individualized instruction.

Social studies and science groups may be determined in several different ways. They may be based on interest, special knowledge, or proficiency in a special skill such as reading, or these and other criteria may be used to create heterogeneous groups. At any time the whole team may be reorganized for specific purposes, or individuals may be reassigned to different groups. It is also possible for the pupils of one team to receive part of their instruction as members of groups of another team. This is referred to as cross-team grouping.

Multigrading, plus the frequent use of cross-team groupings to accommodate certain pupils, has given the school a high degree of nongradedness in its operations. Within teams the child's grade label is generally ignored. As the teachers gain more experience in pupil grouping and as they become more familiar with the curriculum sequences and materials now being developed, they may decide to discard the graded structure altogether. Then it is quite possible that the teams may overlap each other; one team with 6-, 7-, and 8-year-olds; another with 7-, 8-, and 9-year-olds; another with 8-, 9-, 10-, and 11-year-olds.

NORWALK: NEW CAREERS FOR SUPERIOR TEACHERS. In 1958–1959 another exploratory project was begun in Norwalk, Connecticut. Although it was very similar to the Lexington project in its basic structure and its underlying rationale, it had several unique characteristics. The Norwalk Plan, as it came to be known, has over the years undergone a series of changes, both additive and modifying, so that the present Norwalk situation is not necessarily reflected in the description that follows. However, certain features of the original model are of particular interest.

During the two year period 1958–1960, the Norwalk Plan involved three-member teams at a single grade level. Two of the team members were teachers, and the third member was a nonprofessional teacher aide. These three adults shared the total responsibilities of working with a group of children numbering about three times the usual size of a class (a total of 69 to 85 pupils) in classroom spaces equal to three regular rooms. Figure 4 shows this original team model.

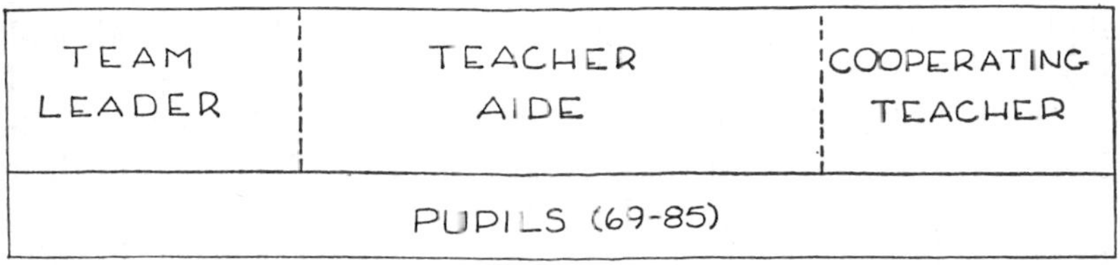

TEAM LEADER	TEACHER AIDE	COOPERATING TEACHER
PUPILS (69-85)		

FIGURE 4. The Original Team Model of the Norwalk Plan.

This model attempted to provide a more effective educational program, as well as to provide more prestige and status for the professional teachers involved without increasing or decreasing the cost of education to the community. The team leader received a salary supplement of approximately $500. The total amounts, including the salary paid to the teacher aide, came to approximately the same figure as the total salary that would have been paid to three regular teachers. Financially, therefore, the community was neither better nor worse off. The potential advantage to the community, it was argued, came from the fact that personnel, space, equipment, and money were being used more effectively.

The professional teachers selected for the Norwalk Plan were by intent fully qualified teachers. The team leader role called for a person of demonstrated superiority as an elementary school teacher and with evidence of leadership ability. The cooperating teacher role called for demonstrated superior promise for teaching and evidence of ability to function in a team.[25] Thus, one important limitation of the plan was that it depended for its success upon the availability of superior professional personnel.

The team leader, as the head of her team, provided leadership for the activities of the other members of the team. Other team members were directly responsible to her; she, in turn, was responsible to her principal. The cooperating teacher, at a lower level, worked cooperatively with the team leader in all of the areas of their instructional responsibilities. They planned schedules and teaching assignments cooperatively; they determined the kinds of groupings to be made; they developed new methods and materials; and they shared their observations concerning pupil growth and development.[26]

Teacher aides were expected to possess at least a high school diploma plus some training or experience with clerical work and with children. As it turned out, persons with very strong personal and technical qualifications proved to be available. Many were college graduates, and most were mature women with families of their own, who previously had worked with groups of children in summer camps or in church schools. Although they did not teach directly, these women assisted the teachers in several semi-instructional functions such as supervising seatwork, assisting with classroom control under teacher supervision, and operating electronic instruction equipment. Much of their time, of course, was allocated to record

---

[25] *The Norwalk Plan: An Attempt to Improve the Quality of Education Through a Team-Teaching Organization: A Two-Year Study Supported by the Fund for the Advancement of Education,* Norwalk, Conn., The Norwalk Plan, November 14, 1960, pp. 2–3.

[26] *Ibid.,* p. 2.

keeping, handling money, preparing typed materials and records, and so forth.

Freed of nearly all noninstructional functions, the two professional teachers conducted total-group (entire-team) lessons several times daily. In each case the teacher with the greatest competence in the subject matter involved took charge. Other lessons involved average-size classes (22 to 30), grouped either heterogeneously or homogeneously as circumstances warranted, and various smaller or larger groupings as desired. Independent work activities also were an important part of the child's school day.

In 1960–1961, the team approach in Norwalk was expanded to include teams of varying sizes (three-, four-, and five-member teams), dealing in some cases with pupils from adjacent grades (for example, Grades 5 and 6 in a multigraded arrangement). Team teaching was also extended to the secondary level. Furthermore, the team enterprises converged with other local school improvement activities in a comprehensive attack upon elementary and secondary school problems.

WISCONSIN: INTERNS IN TEAMS. Another pilot project of great interest is to be found in the state of Wisconsin. As a major component of the highly regarded Wisconsin Improvement Program, team teaching has taken several different forms in the eight cities that are affiliated with the University of Wisconsin. One of these patterns, as originally developed in five communities (Hales Corners, Janesville, Madison, Racine, and West Bend), involves graduate students who undergo an internship experience in the team setting.

The model for this program at the elementary level is quite similar to that in Norwalk; it calls for two experienced teachers with assistance to work with a group of pupils approximately three times the size of a typical class. Whereas in Norwalk the assistance is provided by a nonprofessional, in the Wisconsin model it is provided each semester by two interns-in-training, each on approximately half-salary. In most cases a part-time clerical aide is also available, and the total of the four interns' salaries plus the aide's is therefore virtually the same as the cost of a third full-time experienced teacher. Figure 5 shows the Wisconsin model.

The interns in their nonteaching semester carry on a full program of graduate study, and while teaching, they attend seminars on campus over the weekend. Also, in the summers preceding and following the academic year's work, the interns take additional course work. This 14-month program leads to a master's degree and a teaching certificate.

In the secondary schools of the 17 Wisconsin school systems with intern-in-team assignments, a wide variety of team patterns can be found. A team may consist of one teacher and one intern, or it may have several teachers and several interns. Whatever the pattern, the economics of these arrangements is essentially like that of the elementary teams.

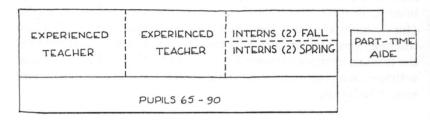

FIGURE 5. The Wisconsin Team Model.

Some of the elementary teams are organized on a simple hierarchical basis with one of the experienced teachers designated as team leader. In other cases the two experienced teachers share the leadership function equally. It is of interest to note that this team teaching pattern has been used in at least one instance at the kindergarten level with apparent success.

The Wisconsin models are of special significance because they have so effectively joined an internship program with a team teaching program. The combination creates an extraordinary opportunity to offer service and guidance to the aspiring young trainee and at the same time to enlist the local school staff in the business of teacher education. Like the Norwalk model, the Wisconsin models are subject to refinement and modification. Meanwhile, they have given direction and inspiration to an important segment of the educational enterprise.[27]

[27] For further information see *Making Teaching and Learning Better, op. cit.*

OTHER MODELS: BRIEF COMMENT. Reference is made in other chapters to some of the other types of team organizations which have been attempted in recent years. To report on all of them is impossible, and to select those of greatest salience or promise is risky and self-defeating. As the three previous descriptions have already pointed out, the projects themselves are changing. Furthermore, some of the most promising have not yet been reported in the literature, while others, though widely published, are still very vaguely understood because of highly generalized reporting (see Chapter 8). More than that, most of the pilot projects have not yet been developed to the point that they represent operationally the complete rationale on which they are based. For all these reasons, one must hesitate before cataloguing and appraising the programs known to be in existence. Nevertheless, it may be helpful for the reader to have a brief look at certain projects which follow lines somewhat different from those already mentioned.

One of the larger programs is under the auspices of the Claremont Graduate School in California. "In its essence, a Claremont Teaching Team is an instructional unit within a school. This unit is a combination of (1) a distinct student group, (2) a small faculty group with complementary talents responsible for teaching the student group, and (3) certain persons who assist the teachers and students (auxiliary personnel)."[28]

A secondary student team, to select one example, comprises 90 to 180 students in a similar program of courses. Each such team is assigned to a faculty team, three to six teachers who have the same daily conference period. Each teacher represents a certain academic discipline or subject area, and some of the members are expected to have such skills as remedial reading or counseling. The team takes responsibility over two years, if possible, for a substantial portion of the academic and counseling programs of the students.

Each Claremont team has an elected or appointed leader who receives a supplementary salary stipend plus an extra free period for planning and coordinating team activities. Auxiliary personnel

[28] John A. Brownell, ed., *Second Annual Report to the Ford Foundation by the Claremont Teaching Team Program for 1960–61*, Claremont, Calif., Claremont Graduate School, 1962, p. 3.

include a teacher aide on a part-time basis plus, on occasion, laymen with special talents.

Englewood, Florida, is the site of another well-known project which has included team teaching. Of special significance is the fact that the primary emphasis of this program is on nongradedness. The teams are usually multiage in make-up, and an unusually flexible building makes it possible for various classes and teams to merge and to separate with relative ease. Team organization is quite informal, and the bulk of subgroupings (across classes) ignores chronological age.[29]

For the reader who is interested in examining descriptions of both the projects noted above and the many projects not noted here, the bibliography and list of projects in the Appendix should be of help. A great many secondary school team teaching projects are associated with, or have received their initial stimulus from, the Commission on the Experimental Study of the Utilization of the Staff in the Secondary School. This agency of the National Association of Secondary-School Principals has reported through the *NASSP Bulletin* each January since 1958, and it has also produced a number of films and other materials which serve to explain and promulgate team teaching.

Some Considerations About Pupil Grouping

The topic of pupil grouping has perennial importance for educators. In determining the membership of a group, a teacher or staff invariably limits in some way or other the kinds of outcomes that may be expected from a given lesson. Many different criteria may be applied: commonality of background, similarity of need or potential, dissimilarity of background or potential, and so forth.[30] Almost always, however careful may be the planning of a group lesson, it nevertheless remains that each grouping decision represents a compromise of some sort.

Pupils are grouped, i.e. taught in aggregates, for at least two reasons: a constant one-to-one teacher pupil ratio is economically im-

[29] *Profiles of Significant Schools: Schools for Team Teaching, op. cit.,* pp. 14–19.

[30] Robert H. Anderson, "Organizing Groups for Instruction," in Nelson B. Henry, ed., *Individualizing Instruction, op. cit.,* pp. 239–264.

possible; and certain kinds of learning require, or are enhanced by, the presence and participation of other learners. One secret of successful grouping lies in understanding the background of pupils well enough to make sound predictions as to their potential contributions and reactions in the group situations that can be arranged. Another secret lies in knowing what the content of a lesson can contribute to the interest of widely varying pupils who confront that content together.

Obviously, the larger the group assembled, the more difficult it will be to make such predictions and to manipulate the content to suit each child's interests. Therefore, the use of large groups inevitably involves a certain degree of calculated risk.

That little is known to date of the merits and the faults of various possible patterns of grouping pupils for instruction is in large measure the result of the crudity of and the dubious motivations for the studies which have been done in the past. As Callahan notes with particular perception, most of the inquiry between approximately 1911 and 1951 into the class-size question was related to the efforts of administrators to cut costs and increase efficiency.[31] We may add that failure to be concerned with educational values, inadequate or faulty instruments and procedures for evaluation, and lack of resources for full-scale inquiry into the whole pattern has led most researchers and administrators into making colossal errors in their work and in the reports they have published in this area.

Because crudity in research techniques persists (see Chapter 10), more recent studies are often prone to similar errors. Sometimes, too, the researchers are less concerned with discovering truth than with justifying a value position (for instance, that large classes are inherently evil). At any rate, no studies known to the authors are of sufficient worth to warrant any definite conclusions about class size. It remains for appropriate theories to be developed, for appropriate research studies to be conducted, and for conclusions about class organization and instructional arrangements to be drawn.

Meanwhile, some tentative theories and some exploratory arrangements must be pursued. Projects, free of bad faith (e.g., cynical disregard of pupil welfare in the interest of some presumed economy)

[31] Raymond E. Callahan, *Education and the Cult of Efficiency*, Chicago, University of Chicago Press, 1962, pp. 232–240.

and careless practice, which examine the potentialities and the limitations of various sized class groupings are very much needed.

SMALL-GROUP INSTRUCTION. Perhaps the best place to begin our examination of class sizes is with the small group. Such a group is an aggregation of less than the 20–30 pupils generally accepted as a standard group in educational literature. The small group is usually a subgroup of a larger class, as in the case of high-middle-low groups to which pupils belong on a fairly permanent basis. At other times, the small group is highly informal or temporary, as in the case of a committee working on a brief project or a voluntary discussion group. The number of students involved may range from 3–4 to as many as 15–18.

The number to be involved in a given activity will of course vary in relationship to the nature of the activity and the needs of the persons who might be participating. Surprisingly, there is as yet rather little knowledge about the optimum size and composition of a small group. The growing evidence from related fields such as sociology and social psychology has been only partially translated into theories of schoolroom organization.

Of some interest is the conclusion reached by a group of scholars from various related disciplines who convened to discuss the changing American culture and its impact upon school practice, especially in the middle-school period.[32] Noting that the individual student (a group of one) is the key to all school arrangements, and stating as a criterion the amount of time the individual student should spend in each of his various activities, this group proposed that the total time spent by a child in the school might well be divided as is indicated in Table 1.

The conferees tended to agree with Goodwin Watson, who has postulated that "working, interacting groups seem to do best when composed of five to eight members. . . . Sizes now accepted for school classes are much too large for good cooperative work."[33]

---

[32] See "Middle School: A Report of Two Conferences in Mt. Kisco on the Definition of Its Purpose, Its Spirit, and Its Shape," report of meetings cosponsored by the Bedford Public Schools, Mt. Kisco, N.Y., and the Educational Facilities Laboratories, January, 1962.

[33] Goodwin Watson, *What Psychology Can We Trust?* New York, Bureau of Publications, Teachers College, Columbia University, 1961, p. 7.

TABLE 1. Proposed Class Groupings

Teachers to Students	1964	1974
0 to 1[a]	20–25%	increase
1 to 1[b]	5%	same
1 to 6[c]	25%	increase
1 to 12[d]	30%	decrease
1 to 120	15%	increase
1 to 400	1%	same

[a] Independent study on the child's own part in library, language laboratory, private study space, project areas, etc.
[b] Tutorial or counseling activity
[c] A working, interacting group
[d] Discussion and decision making
SOURCE: "Middle School: A Report of Two Conferences in Mt. Kisco on the Definition of Its Purpose, Its Spirit, and Its Shape," Mt. Kisco, N.Y., Bedford Public Schools and the Educational Facilities Laboratories, Inc., January, 1962; adapted from pp. 8–10.

They also felt that true discussion and valid decision making (as it relates to individual learning) is very difficult when the number of participants exceeds twelve. It was also the general conclusion of these scholars that the basic group of the future for many situations would comprise about six pupils.[34]

In the past, decisions to create smaller groups within a class have been influenced in large measure by the teacher's timetable and work load, by the physical and instructional resources available, and by the teacher's perceptions of each child's needs for companionship, personal attention, and the like. Surprisingly, there is virtually no respectable literature on class subgrouping or on the techniques and procedures which can and should be employed for small-group instruction. Apart from the obvious point that more personal involvement and intercommunication is possible when the numbers are small, little has been learned and promulgated over the years with respect to the actual advantages of small-group teaching and the means whereby such advantages can be realized. This is a rather shocking fact, and its discovery by the participants in pilot projects has been both unsettling and challenging.

[34] "Middle School," *op. cit.*, p. 9.

There is, therefore, considerable evidence to suggest that typical classroom teachers, when they confront a smaller (or, for that matter, a larger) group of pupils will tend to employ essentially the same teaching techniques as are used with the customary sized class. Though they may occasionally tend to engage in more direct conversation and to encourage more pupil initiated activity, the opportunity to engage in a basically different relationship or to promote learning through a consciously differentiated teaching strategy is usually forfeited.

According to the testimony and observations of university people associated with a number of team teaching projects, the teams have thus far failed to develop any unusual or promising techniques for instructing small groups. This may in part be the result of the preoccupation of the teams with other matters. However, it is greatly to be hoped that as teams stabilize and solve some of their more pressing problems they will turn their attention to small-group teaching as an exciting new field of inquiry and development.

CONVENTIONAL-SIZED GROUPS.   The reader may have observed in the preceding table of proposed class groupings that there is no mention whatever of class sizes between 12 and 120. Lest there be suspicion of an oversight, it needs to be stated that the omission was intentional.

Among school traditions the practice of assembling 20–30 pupils in fixed groups is one that has never been sufficiently examined. One of the authors once proposed, with tongue in cheek, that the original one-room school and later the multiteacher school may have assumed their shapes "because the available logs, other building materials, and engineering skills tended in the early colonial period to require a certain shape and size of classroom. The educator, bless his cooperative and adaptable heart, may then have developed the necessary social and technical arrangements . . . [to which he] developed such strong habits and loyalties that the pattern did not materially change."[35] Having failed to arouse indignant rebuttals and having reflected further, he would now offer the sincere observation that

[35] Robert H. Anderson, "The Junior High School," *Architectural Record,* vol. CXXIX, January, 1961, p. 127.

habit is probably the chief explanation for the profession's loyalty to class sizes in the 20–30 range.

There is of course another explanation, deriving from a common-sense view that a teacher-pupil ratio of less than 1 to 20 is financially unrealistic in the present American economic and social climate and that a teacher who divides his time and energy among 25 pupils can give better attention to each pupil than one who works with 30 or more. Thus we find that 20–30 represents a kind of practical compromise rather than an educationally derived concept.

Probably this concept deserves some defense as a policy to govern school budgeting and personnel arrangements since it serves to protect the interests of children against those who would cut costs no matter what the price. As a basis for planning class grouping within the framework of team teaching, however, it is of virtually no value. As the conferees at Mount Kisco pointed out, a group of 25–30 pupils is probably the least suitable means of serving individuals.[36] Putting it another way, a class of 25–30 pupils is best served by breaking it up frequently into subgroups of 6, subgroups of 12, and so forth. Whenever the teacher confronts as large a group as 25–30 pupils, the precise number involved becomes practically insignificant, and often there may as well be a much larger number present for all the effect it would have on procedures or outcomes.

In general, then, we are arguing that teaching teams ought to concentrate on small-group instruction as much as possible. Once given the flexibility a team arrangement can provide, continued use of the conventional 20–30 pupil grouping pattern is in no important way conducive to a superior learning-teaching situation.

LARGE-GROUP INSTRUCTION. This brings us full circle to the large group. Unfortunately, there is widespread misunderstanding about the relationship of large-group instruction to the theory and practice of teaching in teams. Further, the extreme dependence upon large-group arrangements in some team projects has led to justified criticism and has given team teaching a bad name in some quarters. It is therefore important to explain the proper place of such instruction in the theoretical model.

Probably it would be foolish not to enjoy the advantages that can

[36] "Middle School," *op. cit.*, p. 8.

accrue from appropriate use of large-group teaching, but at the outset let us make clear that there exists no mandate to do so. That teachers should have joint responsibility for a given group of students and that they should exchange criticisms and information in a true collaboration have been noted as the essential ingredients of a team operation. However, that there must be large-group, or for that matter small-group, instruction of a nonconventional nature is not set forth as a necessary condition. Therefore, a team could go about its work without ever assembling more than 30 pupils in the same place. Of course, it is doubtful if such an arrangement would be very advantageous.

It would seem that the use of large groups can be explained or defended in three possible ways. First, it is sometimes seen as *preferable* (i.e., more conducive to satisfactory learning outcomes) to conventional-size or small-group situations. Because the large-group lecturer must be responsible for a large number of students during a single period and because the large-group situation makes him more vulnerable to observation and criticism by his colleagues, he is apt to prepare his lessons with extreme care. The conditions for presenting a lesson to a large group may be relatively superior because of the availability of a wide range of audio-visual devices. Also, a mass audience may itself enhance the learning experience; the range of possible responses and the likelihood of contagion of responses are increased. Though it is recognized that improved preparation and increased use of audio-visual aids could (disregarding economic considerations) be provided in smaller groups, the potential virtue of a mass audience can be associated with large groups only.

Secondly, the large-group lesson sometimes seems capable of obtaining results (learning outcomes) *equivalent* to the results in less economical class groupings. As long as pupil audition, vision, and attention are maintained at an equivalent level, it may be that for some lessons (if they are appropriate to the needs and interests of all pupils concerned) it makes little difference whether the presentation (or other learning activity) involves 20, 50, or 100 or more pupils. In such cases, a central consideration is often one of economy (of time, personnel, or space).

Finally, there is the possibility of *deliberate compromise*. The large-group lesson may actually be somewhat inferior to alternative conventional (or other) arrangements that are possible, but sufficient or acceptable outcomes may be anticipated, and some other significant benefit (such as teacher time saved, or economy of resources) may be expected. Here there is a calculated risk involved, one minor loss being cancelled out by major (or minor) gains to the total enterprise.

Of course, if large groups are to be of maximum value, specific teaching methods must be developed for them. Progress in developing a technology for large-group instruction has not been quite as slow as it has been for small-group instruction. Many ideas and principles are emerging both from team teaching projects and particularly from certain projects that have devoted intensive effort to the subject of large-group instruction.

In the Harvard-Lexington Summer Program the following suggestions were prepared by several participants as a guide to teachers preparing for large-group lessons. Their intent was to clarify certain technical and mechanical details.

1. The seating pattern should be arranged to expedite the desired kind of interaction between teacher, pupils, and materials.

   A formal pattern seems appropriate when the flow of knowledge is from teacher, film, or machine toward the pupils.

   In large-group lessons it is essential that those in the fringe areas be able to hear and see at all times.

   When the roving microphone is used for audience participation, it is necessary to consider the aisle patterns.

   The seating pattern should provide for the orderly flow of pupils during entrance and departure.

2. Special provision should be made for efficient distribution and collection of materials.

   Materials may be distributed to each seat prior to the lesson.

   Materials may be handed to pupils upon entering and collected upon departure.

   Pupils can be trained to pick up materials on a table upon entrance and return same upon departure.

3. Special consideration should be given to the use and display of visual materials.

   Materials and equipment should be ready ahead of time.

   Visual materials, whether they be maps, pictures, flannelgraph figures, posters, or writing on a chalkboard, should be of sufficient size and so located that all pupils can see them.

Too many seemingly unrelated displays can at times be distracting to the pupils.

The moving around of displays and materials during the lesson should be avoided.

4. There are a few other minor technicalities to be considered.

Rhetorical questions should be avoided since pupils from habit will raise hands and expect to answer. An alternate approach is, "I know if asked this question, you would answer in this way. . . ."

Sharp focus is needed in lecturing or demonstrating to elementary school pupils. Organizing a presentation around clear, concise points—using a dramatic introduction, a thorough development, and a final summarization—seems a worthwhile procedure.

Teachers should avoid negative-type statements such as, "There are so many of you, I don't know whether you will be able to see or hear."

Adequate orientation before the large group and detailed specifications as to follow-up activities seem desirable.

It is hoped that these and other statements will undergo careful examination with a view to their refinement and supplementation so that eventually there will be available a rich literature in this aspect of instruction. Several notable beginnings have already been made.[37]

Teams in Action: A Summary

It is to be hoped that the previous portions of this chapter, along with discussions in other chapters, have provided a great many clues to the life and operations of a teaching team. It may, however, be helpful to select for further examination a few aspects of the team at work.

In general, the team will be comprised of persons with different talents and, therefore, with differing responsibilities. It will control, or have assured access to, a number of instructional spaces; it may also share or borrow other spaces for special or limited uses. It may control a given supply of instructional resources and may share still other resources. It may have exclusive responsibility for a given aggregate of pupils, or it may share responsibility with other adults.

[37] See, for example, Bryce Perkins, *et al.*, "Teamwork Produces Audio-Visual Techniques," *Grade Teacher*, vol. LXXVII, June, 1960, pp. 55–72.

It may enjoy the assistance of nonprofessional aides, or it may be forced to handle all school-related service functions. It may have sufficient supervisory and auxiliary services (such as remedial teachers and guidance workers) available to it, or it may be obliged to handle all problems on its own. It may function under an enlightened and reinforcing administration, or it may suffer under poor leadership. All these factors will of course bear upon the team's efficiency, morale, and accomplishments.

As a human organization, the team is subject to a great many stresses and strains. In general, its internal health will greatly affect its ability to cope with external pressures. Probably the greatest single factor in a team's success is the quality of the principal who is in charge of the school. The general climate created by the principal, his skill in providing direction and stimulation as needed, his ability to supervise and counsel the team leader, his organizational talent as schedules get jammed or as the physical plant proves inadequate, and his success in selection of personnel for assignment to teams will be of incalculable importance to each team's success.

The next most important factor will be the competence of the team leader. Earlier, the qualifications for leadership and the talents that predict success were briefly mentioned. The job calls for extraordinary people, to say the least. Yet it is of some interest that teams have appeared to be both productive and happy when the leader is somewhat less than superhuman and even when others in the team have (or appear to have) more talent for the role. Apparently this need cause no real problem as long as the role is being completely performed. Performance by the leader below an acceptable standard, on the other hand, can be disastrous.

Teams can be happy and yet unproductive. There is at least a degree of danger that a team could reach a comfortable plateau of performance beyond which progress is slow. Sometimes, of course, it is necessary to consolidate gains and breathe easily for awhile. In general, however, the team ought to have a fairly constant air of excitement and should work consistently at the challenging problems it faces. One way to achieve this is to compose teams of persons with just enough variety in backgrounds and philosophies to ensure a relatively high level of activity.

It is certainly not necessary for a team to be composed of socially similar people. The team members need only respect each other; it is not necessary that they be attracted to each other's personalities. Outright conflict in personality is probably dangerous, but a slight degree of social incompatibility is not necessarily injurious to a professional relationship. Common problems will tend to bind the team members together. Prominent among these will be the pressures of time, of work load, and of program coordination. No team ever has enough time available for planning because every arrangement is in effect an unsatisfactory compromise. Whether meetings are planned for early morning, for snatched moments at noon or during the day, for after-school hours, or for evenings and weekends, there will inevitably be discomfort for some. Each team must determine its own best rhythm and must learn how to accomplish good communication by maximum use of short cuts and how to defer the less urgent problems for later consideration. Stated in another way, a team must learn how to avoid wasting time and how to focus its energies on the problems most deserving of full team attention.

Problems of grouping have already been considered. No less important is the broad topic of curriculum reconstruction (see Chapter 5). Here the problem is not only that of helping teachers to recognize defects in the existing program, but also that of counseling patience and moderation so that the apparent need for wholesale reform does not literally overwhelm and exhaust them.

Teacher-pupil relationships and the reporting of pupil progress to parents pose further problems. In the beginning, elementary teachers in a team will tend to be alarmed by the fact that it takes much longer to become acquainted with the pupils than it did in the self-contained classroom. They need reassurance on this point, since the evidence from pilot teams very clearly shows that the problem is a temporary and soluble one. In fact, the data suggest that by approximately midyear the team members are in possession of much more information about each child than their counterparts in self-contained classrooms, even though the latter have only one-third to one-sixth as many pupils. Teams that remain with children over two or three years, of course, have an even greater advantage in the long run.

Reporting is usually a shared responsibility, each teacher serving as a clearing house and reporting agent for a certain number of the children. Usually this means the homeroom or attendance group for which that teacher takes regular responsibility, though sometimes the assignment may be based on some other criterion (such as special interest in the child). Quite frequently, and particularly in the case of parent conferences, more than one of the team members will become involved in the reporting procedure for a given child.

This very brief commentary on teams at work scarcely does justice to the whole range of problems to be encountered, but perhaps its essential optimism and its emphasis upon restraint in both ambitions and frustrations help to suggest the proper tone which ought to be established in a school venturing into the fray.

Chapter 7

The Organization of Space

CYRIL G. SARGENT
Educational Facilities Laboratories

Of the characteristics which have been identified as constituting the elements of team teaching, it is new personnel utilization and new groupings of pupils which have had the most marked effect on the design of school buildings. Yet just as team teaching is not discretely curriculum reorganization or new groupings of students or new technical aids or new personnel utilization, neither is the school designed for team teaching a response to merely one of these. Ideally it is the architectural expression of all of these elements in combination, or better, in effective relationship.

If for the moment, however, we consider it only as the provision of spaces of varied size or of spaces which can be enlarged or reduced, then team teaching schools have an interesting, if somewhat forgotten, past. In 1849 Henry Barnard described the plans of several schools which were designed for programs of instruction conducted by master teachers, each of whom would be responsible for the instruction of the entire student body, leaving to the assistants in smaller surrounding classrooms the task of hearing recitations and drilling the pupils in memorization of the lessons (see Figure 6).

Even with the development of the uniform graded school and the self-contained classroom, schools sought to achieve some flexibility of space for student groups of different size and for activities for which specialized teachers were provided. New York City had schools in the early 1900's which were equipped with moveable walls, consisting of a series of hinged wooden panels, in the upper half of which were large panels of glass. They were relatively ineffective because the panels would warp and bind and because technology simply was not up to the job of controlling sound (see Figure 7). Thus, until the end of World War II the schoolhouse became generally a series of equal-size classrooms lining each side of a long, narrow corridor.

Precursors of Team Teaching Schools

In the school building surge which followed World War II the word *flexibility* became increasingly used as a term to describe a need which reflected educational uncertainty, particularly on the secondary school level. The educator member of architect-educator teams felt unclear about the direction of the secondary school program and about the kinds of spaces that would be needed. But he felt certain of one thing—changes would be made. Therefore, he seized on the word flexibility and told the architect to design a flexible school. But flexibility is an illusive word, and many architects complained that the educators had merely shifted educational problems to them—unsolved. Without some central educational ideas or themes around which to plan and on which to build, architects could do little more than provide nonbearing interior walls, e.g., walls without conduits for heating or plumbing or lighting, walls which were not used to support the building structure itself.

As a result, schools which were, in one way or another, flexible were planned, designed, and built. They may have lacked legitimate educational fathering concepts, but they were conceived and born, and in some cases have grown or can grow into useful team teaching schools. At the same time they frequently lack some of the spaces that newly constructed team teaching schools are providing for teacher work areas or pupil resource and study centers.

Characteristics of Team Teaching Schools

Team teaching schools appear to have to satisfy four essential requirements if they are to function effectively.

First, they must accommodate groups of various sizes, for team teaching requires a reordering of teaching personnel relationships

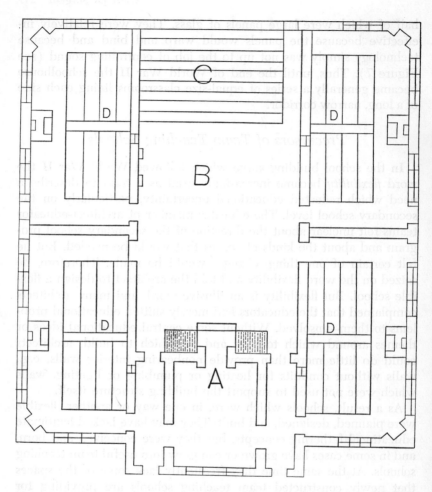

FIGURE 6. An Early Example of Varied Size Space. "The Hall B is 54 feet by 27, in which the infant school is taught and where the whole school is assembled for religious and other general exercises. Each of the four classrooms, D, . . . is divided into two rooms by a screen, both . . . under the supervision of an assistant teacher, who is aided in instruction by one pupil teacher." Henry Barnard, *School Architecture*, New York, Barnes, 1849, p. 261.

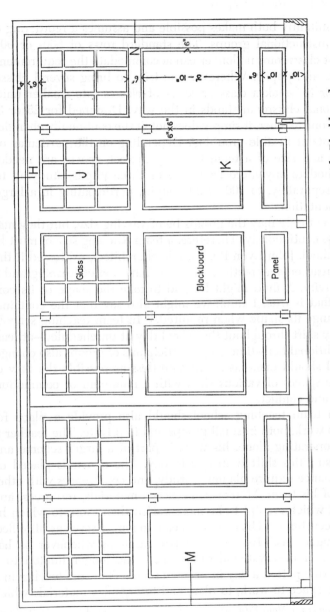

FIGURE 7. Elevation of Folding Partition between Classrooms, with Blackboard Panels and Glazed Top Panels. *The American Architect*, vol. CXV, May 7, 1919, p. 657. Reprinted by permission of *Architectural Record*.

and concomitantly both makes possible and assumes a reordering of the basic instructional groups. The standard rows of 800- or 900-square-foot classrooms no longer can accommodate the requirements of teachers and pupils. Wherever one tries to bring several classes together, or to break a class or series of classes into smaller units, the traditional classroom stands in the way. Designed for 25 or 30 pupils and one teacher, it simply does not fit the continually changing requirements of flexible grouping. Depending on the particular organization and size of a team teaching project, spaces are needed to accommodate anywhere from two or three pupils, studying together or separately, to 100 or 200 pupils, participating in a large-group presentation.

Second, not only may the groups be of varying size, but they may also change continuously. Therefore, a team teaching school must be a "fluid" school. John Lyon Reid, a school architect, expressed it this way: "Education is a creative, thoughtful method of learning and is a fluid activity. A fluid might be said to take the shape of its container. If that is true, I think we might also say that the container should change its shape when required."[1] In team teaching schools, groups may shift throughout the school day at unscheduled—at least by the traditional bell—times. The participants of groups also change. The school should make as nearly effortless as possible the flow of students to spaces of various sizes with a minimum of commotion, confusion, and conflict.

Third, a team teaching school should also provide a place for teachers to work, both in small groups and in private. The teacher is no longer operating alone; his work is part of a larger scheme and his responsibilities shift from day to day. The demands placed on his performance require planning, study, and conferences with other members of his team. Moreover, he needs materials, resources, and equipment which are apt to be more varied than those to which he has been accustomed. His classroom can no longer serve as his office. It is no longer "his." His planning is continuous whenever he has no teaching or observational duties; he is no longer limited to a traditional free period a day in his own room. Thus, the teacher in a team needs space to work, to plan, and to organize materials which

[1] *New Schools for New Education,* New York, Educational Facilities Laboratories, 1961, p. 31.

his greater specialization and released teaching time both require and enable him to prepare.

Fourth, team teaching schools tend also to alter the demands on pupils. More and more the pupils may be on their own, doing independent work, proceeding at their own best pace. Their homeroom may no longer be their base, their group no longer the same 25 or 30 pupils. And so, increasingly, team teaching demands schools which provide spaces for study, spaces where students can work on a paper or a laboratory project and where they can leave their work until they have finished their research. Libraries become busier; listening booths are used more frequently; laboratories are equipped with space for individual projects; and individual carrels, in libraries or placed in nooks and crannies or along a corridor wall of varying width, are emerging as necessary spaces.

The Concept of Flexibility

Since two of the characteristics of team teaching schools have been identified as the capacity to accommodate groups of various sizes and the capacity to provide for rapidly changing groups, it is natural that the concept of flexibility is regularly associated with such schools. But, as we have said, flexibility is a term the meaning of which is hard to pin down; around its definition rage many verbal storms. An example of this occurred at a recent conference of architects and educators at the University of Michigan. An exerpt from the report of that conference suggests the degree of disagreement.

Don Barthelme commented, "Flexibility is a myth, an expensive dream, a snare, a delusion, and only a word with which to fill the mouth. It's high time we architects spoke truthfully and advised our clients to save their money, and to save the damage done to good planning in its name." These remarks provoked equally spirited rejoinders. Douglas Haskell of the *Architectural Forum* observed that in his experience as an editor he had "watched a parade of certitudes come across the screen for many years," and that all of these had had to be modified in the course of time. John Lyon Reid announced that he had admired Barthelme's presentation greatly but that he was "in complete, unequivocal, and total disagreement with everything you said about flexibility." It should be noted that both Barthelme and Reid are outstanding designers who have done distinguished work in the school field and that Haskell is a widely respected editor.[2]

The resolution of these differences lies probably less in the realm of polemics than in a more careful definition of what we mean by flexibility. Caudill has abandoned the word itself in favor of four more precise and specific descriptions of the elements we usually think of in connection with it. They are:

expansible space—space that can allow for ordered growth
convertible space—space that can be economically adapted to
program changes
versatile space—space that serves many functions
malleable space—space that can be changed "at once and at will."

Each of the latter three kinds of flexibility possesses characteristics which are useful and in some ways necessary for team teaching schools. Of the three, convertible space is most commonly thought of and designed for in planning new schools. But, unless a school which is to be convertible is most carefully engineered for heating, lighting, and ventilating and unless the spaces when altered are efficient in shape and size with appropriate acoustics and exits, it may remain in effect only a dotted line on an architect's drafting board. Three classrooms may be converted into one by removing two walls, but the resulting long narrow room may be very inefficient for the new purposes for which it is to be used. Or a room when divided may lack its own ventilation units, lighting switches, or exits. Or an auditorium may be divisible on paper, but the resulting two "little theatres" may both have poor sight lines, acoustics, and storage facilities. All this is not to detract from the usefulness of the concept of convertibility, but rather to point out the care and detail in design and engineering which are required if a school is to be convertible or is to have a number of convertible spaces.

Three Architectural Approaches to Team Teaching Schools

Convertible space, versatile space, and malleable space all would seem to have their place in the planning and design of team teaching

[2] *Ibid.*, p. 13.

schools. Yet not all team teaching schools emphasize these conditions equally, nor are the architectural solutions similar. Indeed, there appear to be three quite different educational-architectural solutions in the design of these schools. These are the open plan, the loft plan, and the approach which has been designated as "planned variability."

The Open Plan

The open plan provides an area or series of areas without any interior walls and is found mainly in elementary schools. If one of the conditions of team teaching schools—especially when combined with the nongraded pattern of organization—is that there be as few barriers as possible to interfere with the free movement of students and teachers, then the open plan meets this criterion most successfully.

Usually in these solutions a group of three or more classrooms are "opened up" into one general instructional area with only such parts of the school as the library, administrative offices, and perhaps an all-purpose room or gymnasium being separate and distinct areas.

An elementary school in Carson City, Michigan, built in 1958, is one such school. It consists of a cluster of three open areas, two academic and one multipurpose. Each cluster is the equivalent of about four or five standard classrooms (see Figure 8). The pupils in such a school obviously have no room of their own, and each child's belongings are kept in a tote tray which he carries with him from group to group during the day and which he slides under his temporary desk where it fits like a drawer. In such a school the pupils and teachers may group in a variety of ways and change groupings whenever they wish. There is, of course, the problem of noise, but we shall leave that for later consideration.

A most unusual approach to the open-plan school is the experimental design of Caudill, Rowlett, and Scott. It consists of a dome under which there are no walls, and, except for the concrete stairway arches supporting the ceiling of the assembly area, the space inside the dome is completely free. Thus, the great virtue claimed for the dome is not only its apparent economy but its complete lack of supporting columns or load-bearing walls. Originally designed for Port Arthur, Texas, it was abandoned there upon the failure of a local

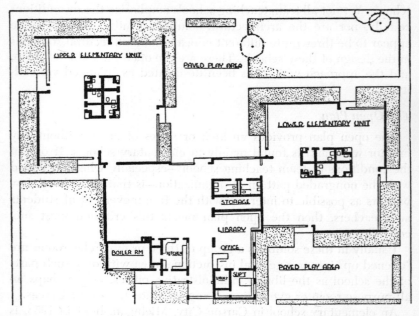

FIGURE 8. Carson City Elementary School, Carson City, Michigan. Louis C. Kingscott & Associates, Inc., Architects-Engineers.

bond issue but is now under construction in New York City as a satellite school adjacent to Queens College (see Figure 9).

The Loft Plan

Related to the open plan, but without its malleability, is the loft plan. This type of school, usually built on a basic module throughout, is, as its name suggests, a loft type of structure with interior partitions that can be taken down and reassembled to alter the size and shape and grouping of spaces. Costing about three to five times as much per linear foot, such moveable panels are substantially more expensive at present than nonbearing masonry and plaster walls. John Lyon Reid's Hillsdale High School in San Mateo, California, represents perhaps the extreme solution of this type (see Figure 10). While it was not designed originally as a team teaching school, Reid has shown how its later edition, the Mills High School, Millbrae,

California, can be revamped into a team teaching school or into a school for programs and methods of teaching quite different from those now developing under team teaching approaches. In Reid's schools the partitions are all modular steel panels which are locked in place at the base and ceiling and can be moved by the custodians over a weekend period. By extremely careful engineering of heating, lighting, and ventilating, a very wide choice and combination of spaces is possible.

Less flexible than the pure loft school is the RHAM Regional High School in Hebron, Connecticut, built in 1957 and planned to encourage the grouping of several teachers in the same subject for more efficient use of personnel as well as to foster relationships between complementary fields of knowledge. The academic units consist of four clusters, each containing the equivalent of four to six regular classrooms and each with its own central utility core, which is the only fixed element in each building. Around this core the spaces may be changed by altering the arrangement of the room dividers which consist of modular units of bookcases, storage cabinets, and coat racks. These cabinets are six feet tall, and, in the space between this height and the ceiling, a series of glass panels are inserted and held in place by spring clips. These clips are located in a grid pattern spaced at two foot intervals over the entire ceiling, which permits completely free change of areas along the lines of the grid.

Since the school relies almost completely on artificial illumination, there is little problem of lighting for the interior spaces when they are reordered (see Figure 11). Even the science unit was designed for future change by providing it with plastic waste traps and easily disconnected water and gas lines so that both laboratory benches and equipment can be moved. This is also an example of a school that was planned before its time. Designed for a new regional high school district, it was conceived as a school which would

. . . increasingly [recognize] the importance of the problem of *relating* knowledge. . . . Specialization and analysis means the tendency to isolate. In the future the emphasis may be on integration or synthesis. Boundary lines which have been drawn between knowledge specializations—artificial artifacts of the human mind—will be more and more broken down in an attempt to help the pupil form his own organization of knowl-

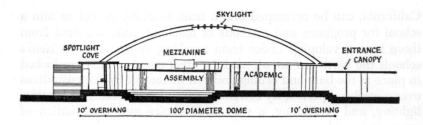

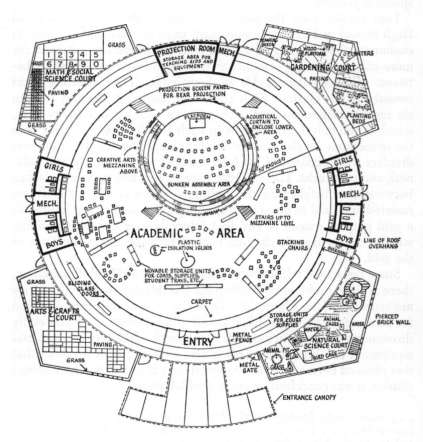

FIGURE 9. (*see legend on facing page*)

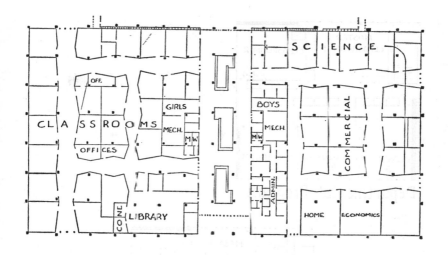

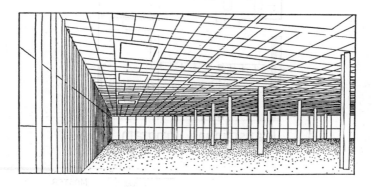

FIGURE 9 (opposite). Domed Elementary School Adjacent to Queens College. Caudill, Rowlett and Scott, Architects-Planners-Engineers, Houston; Oklahoma City; Stamford, Connecticut.

FIGURE 10 (above). Hillsdale High School, San Mateo, California. Classroom building, before partitioning, is a vast one-story space. John Lyon Reid, Architect. *Architectural Forum*, January, 1956, p. 134.

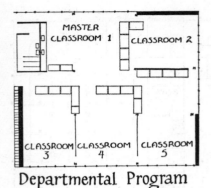

Departmental Program

Transitional Program

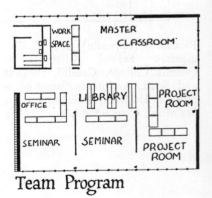

Team Program

FIGURE 11. RHAM Regional High School, Hebron, Connecticut. Louis J. Drakos & Associates, Architects, Farmington, Connecticut.

edge and his own understanding of himself. Subject matter specialization will be balanced by relational emphasis. This implies something other than one teacher in his or her isolated classroom cell. It implies a team of pupils and teachers working together in the future. Conceivably if such is the case, somewhat larger groups might break up into smaller work groups for certain activities which today are proscribed by the limitations of the one classroom—one teacher concept and design. Yet the pupils will still require the specialist and the more talented will wish to pursue their study . . . with teacher-specialists. . . .[3]

Subsequent administrative and teacher planning has not borne out this expectation, but the school plant itself remains capable of accommodating either the original intent or a variety of alternative modifications of the existing organizational relationships.

A modification of the loft plan which combines the moveable panel with the folding partition is found in the design of the Lessinger elementary school in Madison Heights, Michigan (see Figure 12). Here the basic physical structure is referred to as a "quad"—four classrooms, and a "centrum" consisting of a library, a planning center, and a central workroom. Some of the spaces may be divided at any time during the school day by moving folding partitions. The interior walls take longer to move but can be managed by the school custodian singlehanded. An interesting innovation in this school is the use of an inflatable rubber rim between the top of the panel and the ceiling, which when inflated both locks the panel in place and substantially increases the efficiency of the moveable wall as a sound barrier—an important requirement from the viewpoint of some teachers and administrators.

Planned Variability

In contrast to approaches which seek to provide convertible space or malleable space is the approach which attempts to build into the structure itself the basic spaces of different sizes and types. This approach, sometimes designated as planned variability, implies that enough is known about the reordering of student groups and teacher teams to permit the planning of spaces to fit the needs of groups of varying size and purpose. It further asumes that these spaces will be used regularly enough to insure their occupancy for a large per-

[3] Cyril G. Sargent, "Responsibility of School Design," *The School Executive,* vol. LXXVI, December, 1956, p. 52.

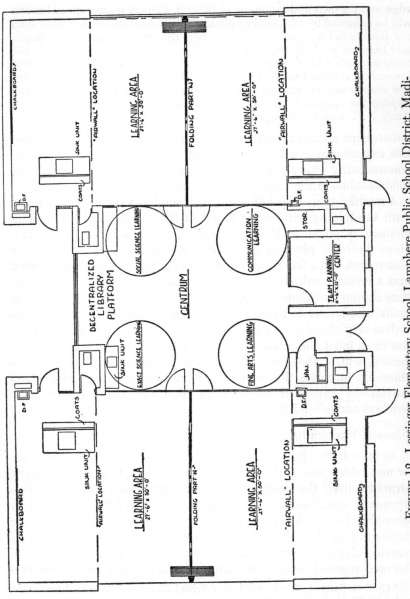

FIGURE 12. Lessinger Elementary School, Lamphere Public School District, Madison Heights, Michigan. H. E. Beyster & Associates, Architects, Detroit, Michigan.

centage of time in the course of a school day or week. This does not mean, however, that the program must fit into a rigid series of spaces of different size, for convertibility can be and sometimes is built in through the use of a limited number of moveable partitions or easily removable nonbearing walls.

This type of plan, in contrast to the loft plan or open plan, is based on the premise that spaces for different size groups and for different functions should be designed especially for them and should have properties peculiar to the type of instructional activity which each requires. The Wayland High School in Wayland, Massachusetts, and the Cold Spring Harbor Senior High School in Huntington/Oyster Bay, New York, are perhaps the two outstanding examples of secondary team teaching schools making use of this approach.

The educational program on which the architectural solution is based is first translated into time units for each of three sizes of instructional groups: seminar groups of 10 to 15 pupils, laboratory-classroom groups of 25 to 30 pupils, and large groups of 125 to 150. From these time equivalents the number of spaces for each size of group is determined. If the school happens to be one in which growth is expected, some convertibility can be built in by choosing a pattern of both school size and program requirements which is assumed to be a reasonably accurate forecast of directions and intent. Figure 13 gives the Cold Spring Harbor schematic analysis.

Table 2 shows the basic time distribution which was developed for Wayland. It indicates the number of instructional areas of various sizes for a variety of school enrollments and distribution of pupil times among seminar groups, laboratory-classroom groups, and large groups.

Thus, for a school of 1000 pupils where the students' time is assumed to follow the B time pattern (20 percent in large-group work, 60 percent in the laboratory-classroom, and 20 percent in seminar groups), two large instructional areas would be needed, along with 18 laboratory-classrooms and 17 seminar rooms.

Table 3 shows how such a school might be planned to move from a program emphasizing traditional groups of 25 to 30 to one with a greater emphasis on seminar and large-group work. As the school grows, the necessary transition can be achieved by moving through

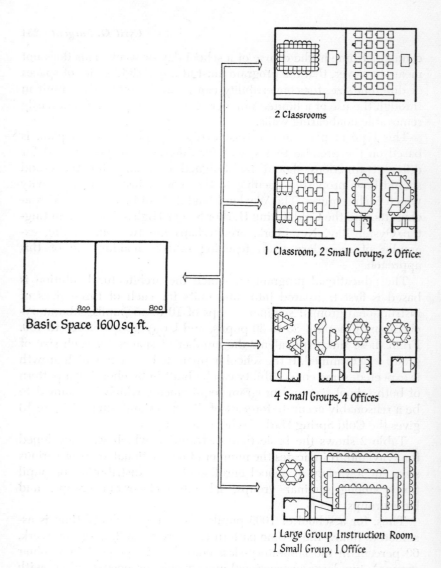

2 Classrooms

1 Classroom, 2 Small Groups, 2 Offices

Basic Space 1600 sq. ft.

4 Small Groups, 4 Offices

1 Large Group Instruction Room,
1 Small Group, 1 Office

FIGURE 13. Cold Spring Harbor Senior High School, Central School District No. 2, Huntington/Oyster Bay, New York. Analysis of "Planned Variability." The conventional classrooms at Cold Spring Harbor are designed to permit a wide variation of partition spacing and therefore a wide variation in use. Reprinted by permission of Educational Facilities Laboratories.

TABLE 2. Wayland High School Schedule of Academic Spaces Required at Various Stages of School Growth and Program Development

Stage	Total No. of Pupils in School	Large-Group Instruction			Laboratory-Classroom			Seminar		
		Type of Program[a]								
		A	B	C	A	B	C	A	B	C
V	1200	1	2	3	28	21	14	11	21	32
IV	1000	1	2	2	24	18	12	9	17	26
III	750	1	1	2	18	13	9	7	13	20
II	600	1	1	1	14	10	7	6	11	16
I	450	1	1	1	11	8	5	4	8	12

[a] Type of Educational Programs operate as follows:
A—(Time) = 10% in large groups, 80% in standard classrooms, 10% in seminars
B—(Time) = 20% in large groups, 60% in standard classrooms, 20% in seminars
C—(Time) = 30% in large groups, 40% in standard classrooms, 30% in seminars

a series of instructional stages while at the same time keeping excess nonutilized space to a minimum. Actually, Wayland was built initially for stage III. To accommodate the lower enrollment of 450 pupils, it was necessary to modify only two blocks of four seminar rooms so as to provide two areas for 30 pupils each instead of four areas for 15 pupils each. These spaces were so designed for access and utilities that they may be easily partitioned into eight seminar rooms when stage III of the program is actually reached.

TABLE 3. Academic Program Spaces Required at Wayland Senior High School

	Large Group	Laboratory-Classroom	Seminar
I-A			
450 students	1	11	4
10% large group			
II-B			
600 students	1	10	11
20% large group			
III-C			
750 students	2	9	20
30% large group			

The school was planned and built with a focus on academic centers. Each center has a study-resource area and space for individual offices for teachers. Figure 14 shows its mathematics and science center.

The Wayland approach is also reflected in the Estabrook elementary school in Lexington, Massachusetts. In both schools spaces were designed for specific functions, and the number of such spaces was determined by a careful program analysis. Lexington had some advantage over Wayland, for its participation with Harvard in the School and University Program for Research and Development (SUPRAD) helped to provide the necessary body of information on which to build the program.

In both schools two of the most carefully planned areas are the library resource centers and the large-group instructional rooms. In Wayland, in addition to the central library, which is viewed as the main repository of resource materials, there are in each academic unit decentralized resource-study areas where most of the currently needed books, magazines, and materials are available. Since the teachers have their offices here also, the center serves as a general workshop, study, and conference area. In the Estabrook School there is one school library, but it is large for most elementary schools and is flanked by individual study areas equipped both with space for reading and with booths for listening to tapes (see Figure 15).

The assembly-lecture halls in both schools are designed to accommodate the students in semicircular fashion behind rows of long tables, placed on raised tiers. These rooms are not conceived of or used solely as traditional lecture halls but are designed for all the various kinds of large-group instruction—demonstrations, audiovisual presentations, and certain kinds of discussion—which experiments in team teaching are showing to be most effective and most promising. These areas are fully equipped, specially lighted and ventilated, and entirely enclosed in order to use film projectors, overhead projectors, and closed-circuit television more efficiently.

The Estabrook School in Lexington is the first school of its size which was planned exclusively on the experience gained in team teaching experiments over the entire range of elementary school grades. Yet while it was planned and designed exclusively around the concept of team teaching, a condition—which some may view as

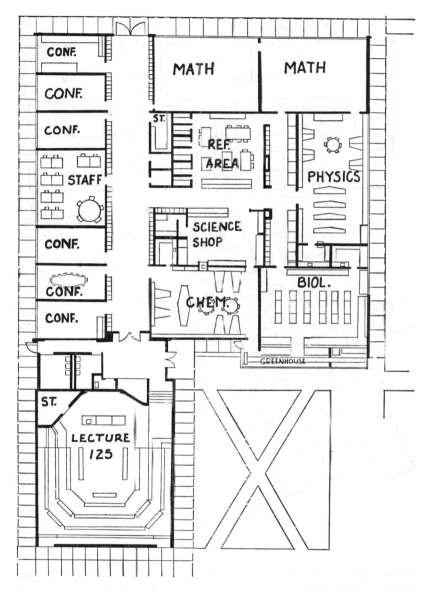

FIGURE 14. Wayland Mathematics-Science Center. Wayland High School, Wayland, Massachusetts. Reprinted by permission of Educational Facilities Laboratories.

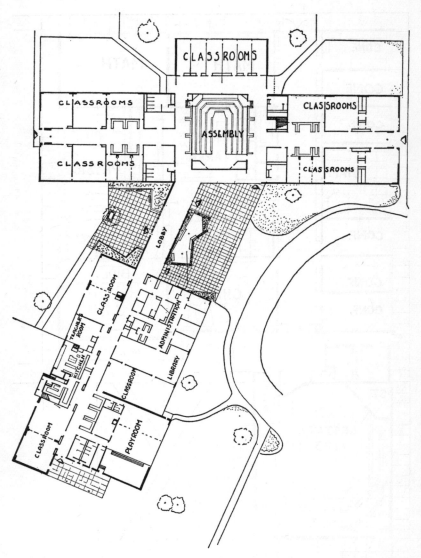

FIGURE 15. Estabrook Elementary School, Lexington, Massachusetts. Clinch, Crimp, Brown & Fisher, Architects, Boston, Massachusetts.

a restraint—was placed on both educators and architects in the course of its development. The school building committee felt impelled to insist that the school be so planned and designed that at any time it could be "reconverted" with a minimum of expenditure to a traditional school with a traditional program. For an estimated $18,000 Estabrook can be made to serve quite satisfactorily as a school of 23 classrooms for 621 pupils.[4]

Both Wayland and Lexington are cost-conscious towns. Both insisted that the plans be such that the cost per pupil approximate the state average cost. In this connection, one interesting fact is now emerging. In a school designed for team teaching, the standard measures of so many square feet per pupil or so many pupils per classroom area no longer hold. Some administrators are claiming that such schools can easily accommodate many more than the number for which they would be traditionally used. Perhaps a word of caution is in order here just as it was in the case of the claims that team teaching would reduce operating expenses. In all probability team teaching schools are not going to be less expensive if they provide the full range of necessary spaces and equipment needed to make this type of instruction most effective. They may be more efficient schools, they may make possible better learning conditions, but a by-product of lower construction cost per pupil is probably not to be expected. The measure of a team teaching school is in the provision of spaces, equipment, and a general quality of environment which makes possible a better program of instruction.

The Three Architectural Approaches and Acoustics

When the three approaches to team teaching schools—the open plan, the loft plan, and planned variability—are compared, some differences are fairly clear. The planned-variability approach adopts the position that special functions and different sizes of groups need special kinds of spaces. The others to a greater or lesser degree deny this. But beyond this there is another important difference which the three design types exhibit. This difference is in the approach to the problem of noise and its control. And it is the problem of acoustics which has been and continues to be the chief obstacle to

[4] It is estimated that under team teaching the capacity is 660.

what the Educational Facilities Laboratories has called "malleable space."

The control of sound is an intricate engineering problem. Sound bounces off hard surfaces, goes around corners and under doors, penetrates thin rigid partitions, and flows through duct work. It is the control of sound which is the central problem in the open-plan and even the loft-plan schools. Sound can be controlled. Walls can be sealed. There are patented "sandwich" panels which successfully block sound transmission. But one problem is cost, and another is to define just what noise means in a school and when and under what conditions it is disturbing. While it appears true that in the open-plan school pupils get used to the constant overtones of movement and noise, we know little, if anything, about the fatigue factor which may accompany the pupil's adjustment to the intrusion of noise on his concentration.

Some attempts have been made to reduce the noise level. Carpeting, rubber-tipped chairs and desks, and acoustical tile and heavy drapes are all being used to provide malleable spaces which will have reasonable acoustical tolerances. Most promising is the work of the Educational Facilities Laboratories, which has encouraged several national manufacturers to embark on research and pilot programs to develop and try out several types of acoustically effective moveable walls.[5] If these are successful, the firms can be expected to undertake full-scale production of them. At present their estimated cost is as much as five times that of the traditional cinderblock or frame and plaster wall. This was also true, however, no more than ten years ago of steel panel exterior walls, which now are competitive in price with the older brick masonry wall. If these present efforts are successful, then schools, and particularly team teaching schools, will within the next decade have spaces, convertible almost at will, which will be sound-controlled and which will have a cost that will make them acceptable to most school boards. When this becomes a reality, the school building will more effectively provide conditions for better study and learning.

[5] Educational Facilities Laboratories has also been responsible for publishing excellent reports on significant new schools and on new theories of school design. These reports are available without charge from Educational Facilities Laboratories, 477 Madison Avenue, New York 22, N.Y.

The Possibilities of Remodeling

It is not necessary to wait for new technical advances or even for new schools to introduce and develop programs of team teaching. The pioneering work at the Franklin School in Lexington, Massachusetts, was conducted in a conventional elementary school built in 1931. What is needed is imagination in using the existing spaces, in building portable space-dividers in the form of such things as bookcases and storage cabinets, and in making use of all too frequently wasted large areas.[6] The auditorium is obviously such a space, but even a basement space can be modernized with new lighting, flooring, and ventilation. Such arrangements are often adequate but generally far from ideal. It seems reasonably clear that teaching can be carried out in a wide variety of existing structures. And it is certainly true that for a time there may be some distinct advantage in working out arrangements and modifications of space in an older building before beginning to plan a new one, for the limiting characteristics of existing teaching areas may help to dictate the kinds and relationships of spaces which need to be included in a new school plan.

But experiences with remodeled spaces have shown that even minor inadequacies can place major limitations upon the over-all efficiency and effect of a team teaching program.

Environment and Learning

Whether schools are designed for team teaching or for traditional forms of instruction, whether they are open or loft construction or of variable size spaces, there remain intangible and subtle—or unfortunately, sometimes not too subtle—differences among them in terms of quality. How one responds to a building, to its form, its colors, its size, its warmth or austerity, can be summed up in a general judgment of the quality of the environment which has been created. Nor is this quality necessarily related to cost, although the types of finishes and the materials frequently do make a difference. Whether or not the quality of the environment which has been

[6] Many of the publications of the Educational Facilities Laboratories are of value in describing ways in which schools may be adapted for team teaching.

created has a direct effect on learning has not as yet been scientifically established.[7] But the belief that an environment which shows respect for students is one which will not only be satisfying to them but will also encourage better work and learning remains strong. Certainly the schools presented here include those which appear to value the children they serve and to surround them with an attractive, inviting, and friendly environment. Each new school provides the opportunity for a community to express in physical form its intent toward its children, and each new school can be as productive, as attractive, and as convenient as any other building in the community.[8]

[7] There is an exploratory study presently in progress at the University of Michigan concerning the effects of environment on learning.

[8] For a partial listing of publications dealing with new developments in school architecture, particularly with respect to team teaching, see the section on school buildings in the Appendix.

Chapter 8

Public Relations

ROBERT H. ANDERSON
Graduate School of Education, Harvard University

Even under stable conditions in school systems enjoying the confidence and respect of their patrons, the maintenance of good
public relations is a continuous challenge for school personnel. An
extensive literature on public relations, aimed at classroom teachers
as well as administrators and school board members, is testimony to
the seriousness of this problem. There is, furthermore, a keen awareness of the public-relations problems of the profession-at-large, as
attested by the activities and publications of the national and state
organizations which represent education.

Schools engaged in pilot projects of team teaching have, in addition to all the familiar and persistent public-relations problems of
other schools, a number of special problems. Some of these derive
from the fact that team teaching represents one form of change, and
the very mention of change in the schools is for some a signal for
alarm. Other problems derive from the probability that the new
arrangement will involve changes in the rate or amount of fiscal
expenditure, in architecture, in the patttern of school organization,
or in the personnel structure in the schools. Still other problems are
associated with the unfamiliar labels assigned to team members,
some of which have unusual implications for the teaching profession itself.

This chapter discusses some of the practical, legal, and strategic
questions and problems which the team teaching school is likely to
encounter as it faces its several publics.

Types of Authority to Be Satisfied

In every school situation there exist a number of separate authorities to be satisfied. Some of these are immediate and local, others are general to the profession, and others represent remote but ultimate authority.

Within the general framework of the state educational code or equivalent statutory regulations, each legally constituted school district has a great degree of local autonomy with respect to policies of operation and the program to be offered in the classrooms. Actually, the overwhelming majority of school districts tend to conduct their business along rather similar lines. Unfortunately, this is due less to state mandate than to the fact that teachers, publishers, and teacher-training institutions have tended over the years to reach a kind of consensus as to "best" procedure. The normative arrangement has therefore found its way into statute or into policy statements. The local community rarely elects to adopt unique curricula or policy, even though it enjoys rather broad latitude as a largely sovereign entity.

The limits of this sovereignty are usually to be found within state regulations governing accreditation (or its equivalent), certification of employed personnel, and qualification for state-provided financing. In general, the power to withhold monetary aid is the ultimate weapon of the state's education officers in dealing with local school district policies thought to be in conflict with the state's objectives. Certain minimum standards for the training of school workers, enforced through the process of licensing personnel for their various roles, are established in the interest of achieving these objectives.

Ultimately, of course, the state's purpose is to protect and enhance the educational welfare of its children. Coincidentally, its role is to protect the individual citizen from imprudent behavior on the part of school officials whose decisions involve tax levies and a certain degree of control over the activities and welfare of families with children.

It is within such a setting that we now consider the implications of team teaching, or equivalent unconventional practice, for school personnel who must deal with local, state, and national bodies, each with a stake in the nature of the child's education.

There is considerable variation in the effective quality of state departments of education. Some of them are quite small with limited budgets and limited powers. Others have substantial resources at their command and enjoy high reputation and prestige. Thus it is difficult to generalize about the role that is played by state officials in the activities of local school districts.

Although all state departments have some responsibility for the enforcement of standards and regulations, the policing function is essentially a secondary concern of most of them. Primary emphasis is given to the functions of servicing and assisting, and most state department personnel take the view that their role is to help local communities set high objectives, improve their practices, and acquire greater resources for the improvement of educational services. On the whole this same spirit also pervades the enforcement of those standards which prevent the adoption of unsatisfactory practices and resources. A notable example may be found in the resistance of state certification officers to pressures from harassed superintendents who in times of personnel crises may be tempted to employ substandard teachers.

Some state departments carry their attempt to improve the schools to its next logical step, that of facilitating experimentation and innovation. Often they disseminate information and recommend or encourage the trial use of promising practices. Sometimes they even manage to provide some degree of financial subsidization. For instance, the team teaching project in Auburn, Maine, owes much of its success to State Commissioner of Education Warren G. Hill, who managed to obtain for the project a grant from the Fund for the Advancement of Education. A project report clearly indicates the value of this aid: "This grant made possible the services of a clerical aide, professional travel, released time for planning by pilot team personnel, and valuable consultant services—all of which have proven vital to the life and growth of the project."[1]

Sometimes, too, the state will agree to waive certain regulations in the interest of legitimate research and development. The wording of

[1] "Team Teaching: A Report of the Pilot Team," Auburn, Me., Department of Education, September, 1960.

a certification law, for example, might conceivably restrain a school district from employing college-supervised interns or engaging in an equivalent training enterprise of promise. Literal enforcement of certain statutes, such as those governing the in-school supervision of pupils, might render it impossible to experiment with the use of non-professional assistants. The temporary relaxation of these rules under specified conditions can be a means whereby state officers contribute to the search for efficient and effective ways of utilizing personnel in the schools. In a number of places these and similar examples of state cooperation can be found.

On the other hand, one can find examples of state obstruction of research and development projects. One eastern seaboard state, not noted for the willingness of its state officers to countenance innovations, has made it almost impossible for a university within its own boundaries to carry out an apparently deserving project in the utilization of teacher aides.

Another area in which state authority bears upon potential innovation is in school architecture. Whether because of state financial subsidy, building code enforcement, or other policy-enforcement questions, virtually no public school buildings are constructed today without some form of approval by the state. Team teaching calls inevitably for buildings which will differ considerably from those to which existing codes and standards pertain (see Chapter 7). New problems of lighting, ventilation, traffic control, plumbing installation, acoustical protection, and adaptability of spaces are raised by the trend toward cooperative teaching. Numerous questions of sanitation, safety, and comfort come into focus as unconventional requirements are made by these programs, and often the existing code or regulation appears to prevent new arrangements from being attempted. Because of the understandable zeal with which state officials enforce rules which bear upon human safety, and also because some of the existing codes actually favor various powerful labor groups or manufacturing interests whose products and services might be affected, the innovating administrator sometimes comes to feel that approval of radically different architectural plans would be impossible to obtain.

Probably each state presents a somewhat different problem on such matters since some codes are more modern and legitimate than others, some states enjoy more enlightened leadership in building control than others, and some have a more satisfactory history of cooperation among the various departments whose interests are at stake. Also, in some states the superintendents of schools and school board members are themselves more effective in communicating (e.g., through their organizations) with state officials and in establishing a climate within which desirable regulatory and legislative changes can be made. In general, it is obvious that individual superintendents, seeking approval and assistance on unique building-planning arrangements, will fare better in those states where a superior climate exists.

Perhaps it should be noted in passing that the profession's recent history in this field offers grounds for optimism. Though some examples of stubborn and indefensible obstruction can be found, state officials have proved on the whole to be open minded and adaptable when confronted with unconventional plans. The fairly large number of interesting and flexible new schools already in use or under construction in many states is ample testimony on this point. That even more daring buildings will necessarily be proposed in the near future, however, prompts us to warn that the major battles on this front are yet to be fought. A well-developed program of public relations and liaison with state building authorities is therefore a necessary part of each local or state enterprise in organizational innovation.

Local Authority

Although most school boards are completely independent of local governmental authorities, quite a few are in some way controlled or influenced by such authority. A rather awkward and unusual situation occurs in Massachusetts with respect to the public supervision of school building programs. Instead of being merely another responsibility of the school board and its executive officer, the planning and supervision of new school construction is assigned to a separate School Planning Committee (or equivalent title). Although in actual practice these committees generally act as an arm of the school authority and in close cooperation with the superintendent and staff, it is at least theoretically possible for such a committee to plan and build a school which is very unlike what the school officials want. Though this may seem a rather bizarre illustration, the fact is that some of the first American schools designed and built for team teaching (e.g., Wayland High School in Wayland, Massachusetts, and Estabrook School in Lexington, Massachusetts) were created in the face of this arrangement. It should be obvious that the school officials in these communities necessarily devoted much effort to negotiations with the school building committees. It is equally obvious that these committees consisted of courageous and intelligent people.

Somewhat more universal is the problem of dealing with town and city officials whose interest is in the school operating budget. Since the education budget is generally the largest item in the local tax levy, school officials have long been accustomed to extensive negotiation about school expenditures of all sorts. Personnel costs being the largest part of every school budget, it is little wonder that teachers' salaries, the cost of secretarial and other supplementary services, and the costs of supervisory and consulting personnel are perennially the topic of much public discussion. Nor does any school worker need to be reminded how slowly and grudgingly most communities have responded to well-documented appeals for increases in the personnel budget. Therefore the pilot project which calls for, or appears to call for, a change in the level or kind of support in the personnel department is almost certain to arouse public interest and a certain amount of instinctive protest. The implications for a public-relations program in this area become immediately apparent.

Almost the same situation exists with respect to two related kinds of expense generally associated with the pilot projects. Educational supplies and equipment are usually provided too meagerly in the schools, and, although real improvement on this score is discernible across the nation, it remains almost a scandal that many teachers and pupils are denied the tools and materials necessary to do their job. Perhaps even more scandalous, though the public is virtually unaware of it, is the almost total disregard of research and development requirements in the school budget. Education may well be the only major segment of our national economy in which a significant fraction of the budget is not devoted to the development of new ideas, techniques, and resources. Even state and federal budgets have tended (until very recently) to omit research and development funds. As a result, the public long ago became accustomed to overlooking local research and development as a necesary aspect of operating good schools, and it seems almost certain that efforts to change the public's financial habits in this respect will proceed slowly and laboriously at best. Consequently, since pilot projects are most likely to require rather heavy support in supplies and equipment and in research and development, they will have to carry all the burden of the battle. It will be almost literally true that the projects, though basically innocent in terms of the total problem, will deserve the public complaint that they cost a lot more money.

Costs

What, then, is a reasonable position for school people to take on the cost problem? One theory states that team teaching might actually prove less expensive in the long run because resources of all kinds (personnel, supplies, school facilities) can be used more efficiently. Certainly there is some reason for optimism. School buildings designed for team use are inherently no more expensive than conventional structures. Even though such buildings may require special equipment or designing, their over-all capacity may be somewhat greater than conventional buildings of approximately the same dimensions. Similar arguments are sometimes offered with respect to personnel costs, which on a per-pupil basis may not exceed conventional arrangements, despite the salary supplements paid leaders and specialists and despite the use of teacher assistants or aides.

In general, however, it seems both imprudent and unethical to propose to a community that team teaching will do anything but raise the cost of education. Behind this statement are two assumptions: (1) the local educational situation is inevitably deficient in important respects, and (2) team teaching will tend to illuminate these deficiencies and create within the staff a greatly increased desire to do something about them. Both of these assumptions, especially the first, seem warranted on the basis of overwhelming evidence.

Unfortunately, such statements will in many communities come as a shock to the professional staff as well as to laymen, for the public-relations posture of school people has long been anaesthetic (relax and trust us, all is well) rather than a straightforward reporting of the school's strengths, weaknesses, and needs. In a sense, the patient has been either unwilling or unable to tell the doctor where it hurts, so that the cancer of poor educational practice has simply gone unchecked. Both the patient and the doctor are therefore likely to suffer untold dismay when the situation finally comes to light.

Many a sincere teacher and administator has unqualified confidence in the existing school program and in the general good health of the school system. Yet thoughtful and objective observers of the American educational scene are increasingly dismayed by the flabby structure of the curriculum, by the unhealthy persistence of superstition and factual error in what is taught, by the frequent unsuitability and occasional harmfulness of teachers' strategies of instruction and management, and by the apparent inability of the total school organism to modify its behavior in the face of dysfunction or crisis. To the extent that these observations are even partially valid, the schools and their staff are in very real trouble indeed.

Teachers in pilot projects are likely to discover this trouble sooner than their more traditionally oriented colleagues, and they will probably also be more inclined and better able to launch corrective measures. The extent to which their energies will permit them to carry out full-fledged reforms, however, will depend upon numerous factors influencing their work load and their morale.

Subtle Authority: Faith in the Status Quo

We have already indicated that state and local policies can either inhibit projects or facilitate them. Perhaps more subtle is the way written or unwritten policies and protocols can thwart a staff in its attack upon perceived problems.

Curriculum guides and courses of study, whether faithfully followed in the conventional setting or not, may suddenly become rather sacred to those out of sympathy with the divergent behavior of the reform group in a pilot school. Certain beliefs held widely within the teaching profession about the appropriate size of class groups or the emotional needs of children or the capacity of the child for enduring a variety of situations may become rallying points of indignation as the project members step further into the relatively unexplored territories through which the search for better practices leads them. These pressures will be felt not only locally but also nationally, as can easily be seen by looking at the content of national convention programs and the publications of national organizations (especially between 1958 and 1962). The authority of the established habits of a profession, whatever their justification, thus impresses itself upon those who would seek changes and creates a high level of anxiety within projects.

That the pilot projects are frequently under pressure to defend and justify themselves may be viewed as a good thing. The quality of thought and argument, the suitability and relevance of obtained data, and the general calibre of daily performance in the projects is likely to be higher because the pressures exist.

Yet, until rather recently there has been a large inequity in the prevailing climate since virtually all the pressure has been on the innovators. Believers in the *status quo* tended not to defend their own position with logical argument or firm and appropriate data. To them it seemed sufficient to assume the rightness (even the righteousness) of conventional practice, and their energies were directed not into analysis but into reflexive counter attack. Recently, the climate has changed at least enough so that a sober second look is being given the basic issues and arguments underlying innovations.

In passing, we may note with interest the contrast between the broader nature and improved quality of very recent discussions of prevailing methods of reading instruction in the elementary school and the predominantly nonconstructive and emotional response of the experts to such critics as Rudolf Flesch only a few short years ago. It seems quite possible that team teaching, which at first met with similarly nonconstructive and emotional responses, has already reached a stage where objective and dispassionate analysis is in order.

Public Relations Problems in Pilot Projects

In confronting the obstacles raised by various types of authority and in establishing its right to exist as an alternative pattern of school organization, the team teaching project will usually be required to deal with several rather special problems. Unlike the conventional or typical school, a reorganized school is expected to report its experience in great detail, to justify its operations within the rules of educational experimentation, to play the role of public change agent, and to deal with the discomfort which is often aroused in the minds of onlookers. Each of these problems, therefore, requires careful examination.

Frank and Complete Reporting

Because it is new and different, because it requires justification as an alternative or substitute arrangement, and because it represents a potential contribution to professional theory and knowledge, a pilot team teaching project ought to be evaluated and reported with special care. For a variety of reasons, however, this presents a rather challenging problem to the conscientious administrator or researcher.

Experience with research in team teaching and other forms of school reorganization over the past five or six years suggests that conventional research designs are generally inappropriate, standardized tests are frequently irrelevant, the profession's skill in phrasing questions for such research projects is limited, and the kinds of changes which can and should be measured are not well enough understood (see Chapter 10). This is in no sense an excuse for the inadequate research activities thus far conducted, but it does serve to warn the would-be experimenter that past history offers little helpful advice. At least until better techniques and instruments are developed, the kinds and amounts of data upon which evaluation and reporting will be based are essentially unsuitable.

Although broadside indictment of the measurement field would be unfair and unwarranted, the fact remains that most conventional schools are in much the same predicament with respect to the kinds and amounts of evaluative data upon which their planning and their public relations are based. Hence, too little is known about the true effectiveness of school programs and about the relative worth of this or that subdimension of the total school enterprise. What we have at best are global data, relevant in only a rough sense, plus thousands upon thousands of subjective impressions upon which tenuous conclusions are based.

This fact has sobering implications for team teaching. Though conventional teachers are probably no better able to explain, much less to justify, their own effectiveness in the classroom, the pressure for explanations and justifications is almost entirely upon the non-conventional teacher. Having little obvious recourse but to the usual inadequate procedures, this person finds himself confronted with two evaluation problems rather than one.

Added to this basically intellectual problem is an emotion-loaded problem that accompanies experimentation with human beings. Since so much emphasis is placed upon the presumed human values in conventional organization (e.g., the alleged emotional security a young child enjoys because he has only one teacher), the innovator finds himself at least implicitly accused of tampering with human welfare when he dares to try a contrary arrangement. Since it is uncomfortable and even threatening to be placed in this antichild category, the experimenter may tend to overreact in defense of his own scheme, whether or not he can muster actual data to support his position.

Sometimes such a reaction takes the form of offering theories as facts and hypotheses as data. Sometimes it takes the form of attacking the conventional pattern in order to justify the alternative. For reasons stated or implied earlier such argument is usually conducted with generalizations rather than with specific details. Occasional irrationality thus overtakes the earnest reformer who is frustrated by the difficulties of obtaining useful data, impatient with the unwillingness or inability of others to understand and believe the theories and plans to which he has a commitment, and irritated by the fact that his antagonists can demand tight and irrefutable research evidence from him though essentially barren of such evidence to support their own theoretical position.

Perhaps another factor in this situation is that many innovators have the passionate zeal of crusaders rather than the clean, cold eye of the research worker. Confronted by resistance and inertia, they tend to energize their passion as a means of making their ideas appear attractive. Sometimes, they make claims or promises in advance as part of the hard sale they perceive to be necessary. Then, committed to a particular predicated outcome, they find it emotionally and even intellectually difficult to recognize and accept contrary or unexpected evidence when and if it appears.

In view of the many pressures which beset the innovator, it is not surprising that he should wish to report as favorable results as possible. Sometimes this tempts him to rearrange and interpret the data in ways that support his theories. Other times it may tempt him to overlook, either deliberately or because of an intellectual blind spot, those data which appear to hurt his cause. Perhaps, as often as not, he fails to recognize the possible importance of data which are not obviously positive or negative but which could be of use to scholars who are asking questions different from his own. It is a fact that pilot projects often fail to make available to the profession at large a sufficient array of data upon which useful discussions can be based.

It therefore behooves the pilot projects to take special pains with complete and candid reporting. Though weighing and reporting of evidence that appears to be inconclusive may often seem to be a waste of time and resources, it nonetheless remains the obligation of experimental projects to place their experience and their data upon the record for the profession's use. Team teaching may profit only slightly from such actions, but the entire field of research in instruction and in school practices stands to gain in many ways.

Experimentation and the Scientific Myth

Another of the burdens borne by the participant in an exploratory or innovative project grows out of the profession's widespread naivete concerning experimentation. The conviction exists that educational problems lend themselves to relatively simple analysis, and assumptions are made about the scientfic validity of certain simple patterns of gathering and interpreting data. As is pointed out by Kaya in a most useful discussion of the reseach problem, the research model based upon comparisons of control groups and experimental groups is basically unsuitable in the situation confronting the team teaching researcher.[2] That scientific procedures of any type can be applied to the problem remains at least doubtful, yet the expectation of many is that experimental-control comparisons will be made and that such comparisons can serve as a valid basis for subsequent criticism and decision.

Another aspect of the scientific myth, well supported by the behavior of educational workers, is the belief that data once subjected to statistical analysis are immediately valuable and publishable. The quality and the usefulness of published research material

[2] Esin Kaya, "Problems in Evaluating Educational Plans in the School Setting," *The Journal of Educational Sociology*, vol. XXXIV, April, 1961, pp. 355–359.

in education is notoriously low, perhaps largely because editors and others have not learned to discriminate between studies that have something to say and studies that do not. If a sufficiently elaborate formula has been used and if the data are accompanied by Greek letters or other distinguishing signs, there are many who are inclined to accept the material as scientific and, therefore, good.

Thus, the researcher in a pilot project is expected to handle his data scientifically. Once he has some data in hand, it is often inconceivable to his friends that he may regard the data as inadequate or inconclusive. If he refuses to report, they immediately suspect that his data are injurious and negative. To avoid, then, the damaging implication that he is concealing unpleasant news, he may feel obliged to report what he has learned even though it may be of little value.

Public Attitudes Toward Change

In his attempts to inform interested parties about the status and needs of the schools, the educator faces many publics. Each specific school, of course, deals primarily with the parents of the children who attend the school and whose lives are affected directly by it. In the local community, however, there are numerous other persons whose lives (and pocketbooks) are influenced by the school in one way or another. Beyond the local citizenry there is a more general public whose membership includes both known friends and announced foes alike. It is to all these groups, to a greater or lesser extent, that the pilot school staff must address its public-relations activities.

In the present intellectual climate in the United States there is much ambivalence about the virtue and the proper direction of the public school system. Certainly it is true that public discussion of educational matters is extremely spirited and widespread, and on the whole this interest should have a healthy and desirable impact upon the welfare and the quality of tomorrow's schools. Yet the public is also quite restless on a number of policy questions, and they are frequently critical of the schools and the people who work in them.

Sometimes public criticism coincides with the criticisms that educators themselves are voicing about the schools. At other times the layman becomes aroused about things that are considered rather inconsequential or unrealistic by the educators. The proper role of phonics, the magic elixir, is a case in point. The virtues and limitations of phonics as an important aspect of reading instruction are reasonably well understood by teachers, and phonics plays an appropriately useful part in the instructional program of nearly all schools. Granted that there remain gaps in both research and practice in this field, it would seem that more is known about the proper place of phonics than about most other educational questions. Yet for over a decade phonics has dominated public discussion of school problems, and even men of distinguished reputation in their own fields have issued ridiculous statements to the effect that underemphasis upon phonics is at the root of all educational evil.

It would be unfair to imply that the bulk of school criticism is at this rather silly level, but it is discouraging that so little of the public debate leads to support for thorough curriculum reconstruction with attendant reforms in the ways schools are organized and supported. Widespread attention is given to phonics, to the evils of discussing the United Nations, and to the horrors of obscenity in *Huckleberry Finn,* while the overcrowded school, the outdated curriculum, and the overworked teacher remain undiscussed in public.

Though probably somewhat exaggerated, this situation serves as the setting for reform proposals in many schools. Compounding the problem is the historical virtue, proclaimed continuously by public-relations-minded schoolmen, of the conventional *modus operandi.* Having long been assured that the schools are healthy and that the self-contained classroom is the greatest invention since the wheel, the parent finds himself quite confused when the school people begin to talk about dramatically different arrangements and desperately urgent reforms. Almost instinctively he begins to resist; he worries about his youngster becoming a guinea pig in yet another departure from fundamentals, and he distrusts the apparent inconsistency of the educator. To the extent that increased tax cost is perceived or experienced as a concomitant effect, his resistance may become intensified.

It therefore behooves the schoolman to take special pains in the development of an intensive and well-conceived program of public relations. Gauging the nature and amount of public support for the schools, especially on the basis of their apparent understanding of the need for basic changes and reforms, he must estimate their readiness to support what the staff wants to do. A strategy must be developed for the presentation of public information, for public discussion of the issues involved, and for making the decisions needed to get the proposal underway.

Dealing with the Profession's Questions

Team teaching cuts across a number of very sensitive problems within the teaching profession. As an effective stimulant to basic reform, it becomes an irritant to those who feel either satisfied with the *status quo* or unwilling to expend the energies required to change it. More fundamentally, its very structure (both theoretical and operative) is abrasively opposed to certain other structures to which vast numbers of teachers are loyal. For these and related reasons the appearance of team teaching in various forms between approximately 1957 and 1961 led to considerable opposition at both local and national levels. By 1962 it appeared to some observers that the opposition literature had begun to change from an earlier tone of righteous indignation to a more objective though still doubting viewpoint. Nevertheless, it seems reasonable to postulate that the intraprofessional public-relations problem will remain a very important and delicate one for many years to come.

Doubtless the vigor, and occasional irrationality, of the earlier critical reaction was prompted by the audacity of the new arrangements and the hucksterish behavior of some of the crusaders, or their friends. Newspapers and other media were almost immediately attracted to team teaching, perhaps in part because their writers caught the spirit of the bold new enerprises and perhaps more because these enterprises were sure-fire controversial news material. Foundations' representatives, the directors of projects, school authorities, and various apostles of the new faith surprised and sometimes offended their listeners by overclaiming, by overselling, by careless or implausible explanations, or by otherwise succumbing to their own enthusiasms. As a result considerable damage was done to the ideas represented in the team teaching movement.

Among the most regrettable consequences of this early evangelism was that the general public and the profession were encouraged

to believe that a quick and easy solution to time-honored problems was in sight. In part to persuade communities that team teaching was worth trying at all, in part as a reaction to counterattacks,
and in part because of their own naive faith, the proponents made
cheerful predictions of the outcomes to be expected. By the time
these predictions, however prudently they might in some cases have
been worded, had been translated by journalists and other listeners
(whether friendly or not), the record had become splashed with
sanguine overoptimism.

There is at this writing no body of evidence, nor any perceived
trend in the accumulating data, to show that an optimistic view is
unwarranted. Rather, the basic problem has been that of moderating
expectations on a longitudinal scale and clarifying the fact that the
potential advantages of team teaching will take much longer to
realize than was predicted. On the whole the argument for patience
seems now to have been distributed widely enough so that pro-
tagonists and antagonists alike appear willing to wait for the data
to emerge. If this is true and if the more restrained tone of recent
literature on team teaching has made it more informative, it could
well be that the profession has been spared an internecine battle
which would have been both unpleasant and unnecessary.

It may be well, however, to keep in mind the fundamental issues
around which lively discussion is certain to continue. One of these
is the apparent threat to the academic freedom and the professional
autonomy so long and rightly cherished by teachers. Another is the
clash between the traditional egalitarian attitudes of teachers and
the provision for differential status and rewards in the hierarchical
patterns of certain team teaching proposals. A third is the alleged
invasion of the professional domain by the subprofessional and paraprofessional personnel incorporated into some team arrangements.
A fourth, pertaining chiefly to the elementary school, is the introduction of specialist personnel into a setting intentionally hospitable to
the generalist. The fifth is the increased emphasis within teaching
teams of the supervisory function and related forms of critical exchange among professionals.

THREAT TO AUTONOMY. Autonomy is a concept often misunder-
stood by teachers, and the influence of team membership upon a

teacher's rights of independent professional decision is frequently assumed to be detrimental. It has not been proposed that teachers should surrender these rights to a group nor that teams should develop uniform and consistent patterns of professional thought and action. On the contrary, a diversity of talents will strengthen a team by increasing its flexibility of response to the enormous range of problems it is expected to solve. To be sure, a certain degree of agreement on fundamental issues (especially concerning goals, it might be emphasized) is necessary among the members. Also, it seems reasonable to expect that teachers will implement team decisions in a manner that is rationally and strategically defensible. These requirements do influence the degrees of freedom a teacher may exercise, but their chief effect should be an extremely beneficial one; it should reduce, if not eliminate, the eccentric or idiosyncratic elements in a teacher's behavior and should substitute for them, over time and with the assistance of colleagues, a professional repertoire that may be confidently defended.

SALARY DIFFERENTIALS. Not all team teaching projects are hierarchical in structure, and only a small number have as yet provided for the designated leaders to be paid higher (or supplementary) salaries. Nevertheless, one of the most widely discussed justifications of team teaching is that it may aid the profession in its efforts to attract higher quality individuals into teaching. This clearly implies, and it is usually so stated, than an economic incentive will be attached to the incentive of leadership opportunity. Thus another lively issue is the clash between the standard policy of equal-pay-for-equal-people and any arrangement which pays more to some than to others.

Merit pay, in simple terms, is a system intended to award more generous salaries to the more competent and influential teachers in a school system. Though it is a generally acceptable and even popular idea among segments of the general public whose own economic lives are largely governed by the merit pay principle, merit pay has not enjoyed the confidence and support of teachers themselves. Because they believe that no valid criteria exist for judging teaching performance, they lack confidence in the ability of supervisors and administrators to make evaluative judgments of their work.

Some have suggested that teaching, for various economic and sociological reasons, tends to attract the relatively less ambitious, venturesome, or spirited persons among college graduates. This factor, in conjunction with the culturally approved view of teachers as selfless servants of the commonweal, seems to orient teachers away from the more general culturally approved view of human beings as people who want to get ahead in the world. Whether or not these explanations are valid, it remains that economic incentives appear to be much les strong in the teacher force than in other skilled occupations, and, in the few places where militant behavior is exhibited in salary negotiations (e.g., the unionized effort in larger cities), the notion of a uniform salary policy appears to be dominant.

It is extremely important to realize that team teaching proposes another kind of differential pay. Several different teaching roles are envisioned, some of them involving different and presumably more challenging responsibilities. Differentiation in function is therefore related to differentation in reward. As long as there exists no disagreement concerning the greater difficulty in performing the more rewarded role, there is unlikely to be a charge of discrimination or injustice if such a system is followed. Attention will then be centered not upon an artificially induced problem of inequity but upon the more manageable question of whether or not the incumbent is carrying out his unique role with the necessary skill.

ENTER THE NONPROFESSIONAL.   Our third problem is concerned with the legitimacy of using noncertified adults to work in the schools with children. Although this sensitive matter, a subject of bitter and irrational wrangling from 1955 to 1960, appears to be less hotly disputed at present, it is nevertheless worthy of our consideration.

Various studies of the teacher's work load have helped to point out that trivial, routine, and nonteaching functions absorb a large fraction of the teacher's time and energy. Although it remains for someone to demonstrate that many of these functions might well be eliminated from the school altogether, much progress has been made in finding ways of reassigning them to persons who have had less than full-fledged professional training and who wish to play a lesser role in the work life of the school.

It seems scarcely necessary to document or summarize the history and the literature of nonprofessionals in the schools (see Chapter 2). Though the profession's initial reaction to pioneer projects in the use of teacher aides (especially the Bay City project, circa 1955, and the Norwalk Plan, circa 1958) was very largely negative, in the intervening years there has developed a growing appreciation of the rationale for using aides. There is less angry outcry about "turning the job over to amateurs." Debate tends now to center upon the proper limits of the aide's work with children, a variety of legalistic questions about the child-supervisory responsibilities of certified professionals, and the extent to which such responsibility can or should be reassigned.

As Chauncey has suggested, a general objective for staff utilization might well be the creation of arrangements that will enable the teacher to function, during the largest part of his working day, at the level of skill, ability, and insight for which his background and preparation have, hopefully, prepared him.[3] Although a teacher needs in some way to keep in touch with the more routine aspects of school life, especially in terms of the child's responses, it is frightfully wasteful to enslave the teacher with complete responsibility for these things at the expense of higher priority functions.

The profession seems increasingly ready to accept several assumptions that can serve as a basis for personnel utilization:

1. Each job draws on a hierarchy of skills.
2. A job can be differentiated on the basis of the level of skill required for the performance of its components.
3. The various components of a job can be assigned to different classes of personnel with different training and different kinds of skills (and, probably, different sorts of commitments).
4. Personnel should make maximal use of their most valuable skills and abilities.
5. If highly trained personnel are to spend a sufficient portion of their time and energies upon tasks requiring their most valuable skills, it will be necessary to delegate the related but less skilled functions to other personnel (or even to machines).
6. Presently, in most schools teachers regularly perform a number of

[3] Henry Chauncey, "More Effective Utilization of Teachers," in National Manpower Council, *The Utilization of Scientific and Professional Manpower*, New York, Columbia University Press, 1954.

functions (clerical, monitorial, and housekeeping chores, for example) that can be assigned to other persons.

7. Elementary school pupils are capable of relating satisfactorily to more than one adult figure in the school.

8. Teachers can acquire necessary knowledge about "the whole child" through various means; it is not necessary that teachers be directly involved with all noninstructional or routine situations involving the pupils in order for such knowledge to be acquired.[4]

On the basis of these assumptions and with the necessary precautions against abdication of true teaching functions on the part of certified teachers, it therefore seems justifiable to reorganize schools in such a way that the noninstructional and routine jobs are taken over by teacher assistants of various kinds.

Of some interest here is the apparent size and quality of the manpower pool in this field. Several pilot projects have found that a large number of applicants are available for the aide positions, that many of these are persons of attractive background and personality, and that some have training and experience in such job-related skills as typing, record keeping, and materials preparation. Experience also suggests that these people find their work enjoyable, that there is relatively low turnover among them, and that they are well accepted as working colleagues by teachers.

The presence of aides within teams is unquestionably a welcome relief for team teachers. They seem to feel that their own role becomes a more prestigeful one since they have been relieved of some onerous (and relatively degrading) chores in favor of more difficult and important work and since they now have a degree of supervisory control over another kind of worker.

Unfortunately, most teachers in conventional classrooms are deprived of these services and satisfactions. Understandably, therefore, they are envious of their colleagues in the teaching teams. "It is unfair," they have been heard to say. "Just give to us regular teachers the same kind of assistance and we'll show 'em a thing or two!" There is no suitable answer to this complaint, for in fact the aide-supported teams have frequently enjoyed the advantage at least in this one respect.

[4] This list is adapted from an unpublished paper by Ellis A. Hagstrom, "Toward a Definition of the Role of Teacher Aide," Harvard University, May, 1960.

However, there is a point of view that holds out some promise to the deprived professional community. The very existence of teacher aides in some team teaching projects is providing an important lesson for the profession as well as the public. A precedent is being established for the potential expansion of this practice to other teachers and other schools. If the aides prove to be useful, as indeed seems to be the case, then it should eventually be apparent that all teaching would profit from nonprofessional support. It would therefore seem appropriate for other teachers to voice not their indignation at the present situation but rather their interest in the opportunities that may come to all teachers in the future.

SPECIALIZATION. The fourth problem around which we may expect lively professional discussion has to do with specialization in the elementary school. Like many of the other topics considered here, such as the use of nonprofessional assistants, this is an issue which exists quite apart from team teaching as a specific pattern of organization. For a long time there has been much confusion in practice and in the literature about the generalist role of the so-called self-contained-classroom teacher. In many schools an impressive number and array of specialists (music, art, special education, physical education, library, remedial reading, and so forth) have supplemented the work of the regular teacher. Sometimes these people have literally replaced the regular teacher, whose contact with the specialist is often limited to a social greeting at the moment the pupils are surrendered or retrieved. In other instances the two professionals have worked in very close cooperation. It suffices here to note that self-containment has rarely been literally achieved, and pupils have frequently had to deal with numerous professional personalities in the course of their schooling.

Stated another way, the profession has for many years recognized that there are limits to the competencies that may be expected of a single individual and that a number of teaching functions call for a high degree of special knowledge and training. As knowledge has increased, as children have become interested and knowledgeable in a widening complex of topics, and as professional technology becomes more precise, it becomes more obviously impossible for any individual to handle the total job. Of sheer necessity teachers seek ways to escape the frightening weight of such a global responsibility.

Until arrangements such as team teaching began to emerge, the only apparent alternative to the self-contained pattern was departmentalization. One of the advantages of this arrangement was that it limited each teacher's responsibility to that content area in which he presumably possessed strong interest and competency. Among its weaknesses or disadvantages, on the other hand, were two that have long concerned educators. The absence of continuous communication between the several teachers responsible for a given child made his school experiences fragmented, and the tendency of class schedules to become fixed and arbitrary reduced the freedom of teachers to curtail or lengthen a particular class experience.

One of the most important differences between team teaching and most departmental arrangements is that there is a built-in obligation (with facilitating machinery) for intrastaff communication. In fact, one of the best tests of a team teaching project is to examine the ways communication is carried on. If the various specialists are permitted to remain out of touch with the work and decisions of their colleagues and if specific instructional problems are not regularly the focal point of staff discussions, then it is not a legitimate team operation. As for the tyranny of fixed schedules, it remains a problem to some degree in team situations. However, it is clear that a team with some foresight can build into its program a degree of flexibility not possible in a departmentalized program.

In the belief that team organization is relatively free of the severe limitations of departmentalization and in recognition of the need for highly competent instruction in the several branches of the curriculum, most team teaching models call for specialization in function. Elsewhere the authors have discussed the rationale for such models and the expectations that may reasonably be held for the specialists representing various disciplines. Our purpose here has been primarily to examine the aspects of specialization which have implications for public relations with the profession. It seems reasonable to state that the objections most likely to be raised by conventionally oriented teachers appear to be answerable in terms of the very values to which the questioners are loyal.

NEW ASPECTS OF SUPERVISION. Supervision, as a label for the acts of one person designed to influence and improve the decisions and performance of another person, is built into the very fabric of a teaching team. Because all of its members are certified professionals, rarely so self-assured or sensitive that constructive suggestions and criticisms will offend, there may be considerable peer supervision in a team. Certainly it need not be limited to superordinate-subordinate communication, which is the most prevalent supervisory pattern in conventional schools. Perhaps supervision by peers would be a fairly acceptable concept to most teachers, but their lives as presently organized are generally devoid of opportunities for observing each other at work. In general, hardly any real exchange is possible unless two or more parties have been involved, in one way or another, in the same teaching episode.

In hierarchical teams, where a designated leader receives a differential salary, there is a strong implication that the leader has certain supervisory authority over his colleagues in lesser roles. The actual limits of this authority, especially as it may relate to major evaluative decisions (such as approving the teacher's election to tenure, or advancement in rank and salary), are unclear in definitions of the role and hence in the minds of many teachers.

The team leader may play various kinds of leadership roles, and he is indeed charged with some responsibilities that may require authoritarian behavior. It is expected that he will make decisions, and it is further expected that he will be capable of exerting strong influence upon the behavior of team members. Since team members may be in need of counseling or guidance in the planning and management of their work, it is to be hoped that the team leader's talents plus the quality of his relationship with the teacher would combine to allow him to step in. However, the team leader role is best seen as a position of *leadership within teaching*, and hence the foregoing applies primarily to those problems that have to do with teaching as such. There is not, nor should there be, any implication that the team leader has ultimate supervisory authority over the team teacher. This is a function reserved for the principal, upon whose shoulders the decisions of hiring, firing, assigning, disciplining, and rewarding must rest. The team leader may play a minor or indirect role in such matters, but it is much more accurate to define him as the teacher's colleague than as his boss.

In this rather long digression we have concerned ourselves with five fundamental issues with which members of the teaching profession engaged in team teaching will have to be concerned in order to answer to their professional colleagues. We shall now proceed to discuss two further relationships in which many teaching team projects find themselves involved.

The School-University Relationship

One of the more interesting and important trends in American public education today is the tendency for school systems and universities to join forces in the search for better practices. Many pilot team teaching projects have involved some form of liaison between public school workers and people in the universities who have taken responsibility for various aspects of research and development. Usually the liaison is temporary and minor in scale, although in some cases there is a very close clinical relationship over an extended period of time.

One partnership of this sort has existed in New England since 1957 in the form of the School and University Program for Research and Development (SUPRAD).[5] The pilot team teaching project in Lexington, Massachusetts, has from its inception been supported by SUPRAD, and a number of Harvard faculty members have been closely associated with Lexington personnel. In this project, as presumably in all other projects which merge the interests and identities of school practitioners and research-oriented consultants, a number of problems have arisen which require resolution.

Without clearly defined areas of authority, confusion may arise with respect to a decision about which tests to use or which teaching strategy to employ. Competition for the loyalty of workers may develop if the two allied agencies become entangled over policy or procedural questions. The sharing of both credit and responsibility,

[5] See all of the following: Francis Keppel and Paul A. Perry, "School and University: Partners in Progress," *Phi Delta Kappan*, vol. XLII, January, 1961, pp. 174–180. Paul A. Perry, "A Question of Quality," *Harvard Graduate School of Education Association Bulletin*, vol. VII, Summer, 1962, pp. 2–24. *SUPRAD: An Interim Report on the School and University Program for Research and Development 1957–1962*, Cambridge, Mass., SUPRAD, 1962.

in terms of the contractual intentions of the two parties, must also be watched carefully. These are but a few examples of problems which could become troublesome as the two groups attempt to work together.[6]

Lest it be inferred that school-university relationships are inevitably problematical, attention should be called to the remarkable success of shared enterprises in many parts of the country. It may be said that some of the most exciting and useful educational research in this century has come about at least in part because of the trend toward clinical partnership. Moreover, the people in the schools and in the universities have found that they have much to give to each other, and both profit in the exchange. While independent action in the two separate settings may continue as the predominant arrangement, it now seems safe to say that joint action will emerge as a much used and much valued alternative.

We may at least be certain that the school-university relationship will develop along various lines and that it will excite some interesting studies by sociologists as well as educators. Doubtless these analysts will discover that an extraordinary kind and amount of communication is characteristic of the relationship. Considering the relative insularity of the typical teacher and university worker and further considering the increasing complexity of teaching and research functions, it would seem that an arrangement which quickens the tempo of professional discussion is potentially a good thing.

The School-Foundation Relationship

One of the inescapable things about educational change, and probably most other forms of change, is that it costs a great deal of money. Earlier we have discussed the deplorable lack of financial support for educational research and development at all levels of tax-supported government. The American economy has characteristically depended heavily upon private philanthropy for the support of such research. Preposterous though it may seem, this has meant that many school systems have therefore received the bulk of their

---

[6] For a more detailed discussion see Robert H. Anderson, "School-University Cooperation and the Lexington Project," *The Journal of Educational Sociology,* vol. XXXIV, April, 1961, pp. 382–386.

support for school studies, for the stimulation of new ideas, or for the purchase of nonstandard equipment from such impoverished groups as the PTA. That a number of major philanthropic foundations, notably the Ford Foundation and the Carnegie Foundation have chosen to contribute vast portions of their resources to the support of educational innovation has therefoe been a blessing of considerable importance.

It is certainly no secret that nearly the whole development of team teaching in America can be traced in one way or another to the generosity of the Ford Foundation and its several affiliated agencies (especially the Fund for the Advancement of Education). This has often created an awkward situation, probably as much so for the foundation as for the people in the profession.

For a variety of reasons, ranging from sincere concern over the policy power wielded by the foundations to the disgruntled outbursts of disappointed grant seekers, it is frequently pointed out that grant money is not an unmixed blessing. There is suspicion in some quarters that the foundation people favor only those projects which fit into their own notion of good practice. At the same time the complaint is often heard that foundation personnel and the attractive publications of the foundations tend to disseminate and sell innovations even before they have been adequately tested. Probably there are seeds of truth in these suspicions, yet at the same time it seems very unlikely that an organization composed of diverse and imaginative people could ever reach full agreement on a particular program or methodology to advance as a party line. It also seems unlikely that they would wittingly be guilty of unethical, irrational, or frivolous behavior in view of the trust which has been placed in them by the profession and by the agencies of government to which they are ultimately accountable.

In his interesting study of educational change in New York State, Brickell comments upon the role of the foundations (among a number of outside institutions and organizations) in facilitating change.[7] He notes that the Fund for the Advancement of Education follows a policy of sponsoring demonstrations, which it submits to the judg-

[7] Henry M. Brickell, *Organizing New York State for Educational Change,* Albany, New York State Department of Education, December, 1961, p. 107. Also see pp. 59–60.

ment of the profession. He notes further that the profession is suspicious of new approaches in education, and, therefore, it is difficult for foundations to promote the spread of such approaches (as opposed to demonstrations thereof). For example, critics frequently charge that the apparent success of a demonstration is due not to the validity of the arrangement but to the advantages purchased by the foundation's funds.

One undeniable contribution made by the foundations, also noted by Brickell, is that their support has made it possible for a great number of able people in education, whose customary fate is to be immersed in great responsibilities, to "be freed to concentrate at least temporarily on limited functions."[8] Certainly the professional literature and its underlying scholarship has been stimulated and enriched by the thinking such grants have made possible, and, in turn, the lives of many thousands of educators have been touched in ways that could well make a difference in the future.

The foundations have probably made their share of mistakes, but on the whole it seems their influence has been of magnificent dimensions. Further, the writers of this volume, admittedly the beneficiaries of substantial grants, have never felt that their own freedom of thought or action was even minutely limited by the behavior and expectations of the foundation personnel with whom they have dealt. In other words, the integrity of the foundations in their relationship to educators has not seemed questionable.

What may be a real problem is the integrity of some educators. Many a schoolman has probably found himself hungering after the same dollars and fame to which certain of his friends have fallen heir, and cynically he may have been tempted to announce his conversion to the same religion. If team teaching (or television teaching, or foreign language laboratories, or what have you) seems to be attracting the foundation fish these days, he cheerfully baits his hook with it. Quite likely such behavior, reprehensible though it be, is among the chief reasons for the feeling that the foundations cause educators to sell their souls. Sometimes it appears there is a seller's market!

This amounts to a cruel statement, and it should not be inferred

[8] *Ibid.*, p. 59.

that such behavior is widespread. Yet there has always been a certain amount of bandwagon jumping and opportunism among persons of both good intention and bad. The generous support given to team teaching by foundations has proved an attraction to these kinds of people. However, it has also attracted and encouraged persons of sound personal motivation and high professional commitment, persons to whom the underlying philosophy and potential of team teaching has appealed as something worth testing. That many of these deserving people have been among those selected by the foundations for grant support is the authors' fervent hope.

This chapter has attempted to examine an array of public-relations problems with which the participants of team teaching projects are likely to be confronted. Some of these problems are related to the urgent matter of launching and first-stage survival. The necessity for satisfying various types of authority, as described in the opening section of the chapter, was later related to the understanding, approval, and support which must ultimately be gained for team teaching from the general and local public and the profession. Ways in which established attitudes and beliefs are threatened by team teaching and its attributes and certain plausible arguments which may offset these threats have been discussed. Several rather special problems, such as the relations between school people and research workers and the rather touchy matter of foundation support, were also examined within the broad frame of public relations.

One implication of this chapter is that team teaching has various kinds of surface validity which may make it easier, once understood, for the public and the profession to accept it. Perhaps it should also be acknowledged that, whatever the effort to avoid it, an aura of glamour has surrounded the idea ever since it first broke into the news. Therefore, we find ourselves wondering how long it will take before realistic and objective appraisals will be possible.

It would seem that taxpayers and others with a direct financial stake will not long be content to pay extra for glamour and bright promises. Moreover, the profession itself will not tolerate team teaching if it appears to be failing in its purposes. Hopefully this volume will have proved helpful in defining these purposes more explicitly, and in providing a clearer view of the numerous professional objectives, besides the obvious goals of enhanced pupil achievement and adjustment, toward which team teaching may tend to steer the profession. In other words, there is now a pressing need to understand the ways in which team teaching may bring about a general improvement in the quality of public education.

Chapter 9

The Teacher and Team Teaching:
Suggestions for Long-Range Research

DAN C. LORTIE

School of Education, University of Chicago

Americans who govern complicated organizations today have little choice—they are forced, more and more, to commit themselves to rationally designed and closely controlled programs of innovation. Schoolmen, where the public demands quality in education, cannot claim exemption from this trend; excellence is not found in schools which bog down in unreflective conservatism or in those which vacillate from fad to fad. But large-scale development guided by research is very difficult, and we find no surplus of able administrators eager to initiate and lead it. We must supplement our scarce resources of imaginative administration with persons interested in the application of social science; we must develop an effective division of labor which combines the commitment, persuasive talents, and capacity for shrewd, immediate decision found in the competent administrator with the detachment, conceptual skill, and ability to suspend judgment that mark the capable social researcher.

This chapter relates the work of the sociologist to that of creative administrators currently wrestling with an important large-scale innovation, team teaching. How can the sociologist, carefully trained to avoid commitments to specific social solutions, assist those who are forming specific solutions to educational problems? I believe he can be of real assistance if his role is properly understood and provided he is willing to commit himself to using social science in furthering the general goal of rational adaptation among educational institutions. We can find similar roles in our society where persons with a general commitment assist others whose commitments are specific. The certified public accountant, for example, holds a general commitment to the rules of modern business, but he is not bound by the specific decisions of clients. His controlling function is, in fact, jeopardized if serious doubt is cast on the dispassionate quality of his analysis or the impartiality and thoroughness of his reports.

The sociologist can, in my opinion, serve best in a somewhat analogous way. Without prior commitment to a given solution (such as team teaching), he can show his interest in rational planning and rational assessment by assisting in the formulation of research plans for observing a given innovation. Such plans can be made without *a priori* evaluation and gain both scientific validity and professional repute where the fewest assumptions are made on the desirability or undesirability of a specific program of action. Research plans should incorporate the prior thinking which enables study of the change *as it occurs* and thus provide those who will make assessments with explicit evidence. For without careful thought before the event, much of import will happen which will go unobserved and unrecorded; without a frame of reference to guide their observations, the most sensitive men can focus on phenomena which later prove unimportant. Team teaching is a major innovation, and the principal assumption here is that it would be most serious if, ten years from now, we lacked the data to know why it did or did not succeed.

The author of this chapter will try to show, in some detail, how such prior thought and planning can serve those interested in any final assessment of team teaching. In doing this, we shall focus on how team teaching might influence the teacher at work, and shall use the method (we can call it "functional extrapolation") of comparing what we know about schools today with how they might change under team teaching. This will be done under three major headings: (1) The Teacher and the Authority System, (2) The Teacher and the Reward System, and (3) The Teacher and the Career System. In each instance a description and analysis of the conventional situation will be followed by a tentative prediction of the likely effects of team teaching. The purpose, we wish to make very clear, is not to assess team teaching now but to point towards those research questions which will permit the gathering of data that will have value in making a final assessment. Nor is the purpose to delineate final hypotheses since every astute researcher knows that hypotheses change with increased understanding of the phenomena under scrutiny. But if we start to raise questions now, it is likely that our later hypotheses will be truly relevant and that we shall build a useful record of how empirical study has refined our thinking.

A word is necessary on the method of "functional extrapolation." In beginning with the current situation, we seek first to understand the consequences of a given pattern of behavior in the public schools.[1] Such analysis is based on the unearthing of as many interconnections as we can find—it does not end with the formal or stated purposes attributed to a given behavior pattern. Noting the differences between the proposed innovation and our understanding of the current reality, we can postulate, one at a time, likely effects from the differences. We may continue by asking whether the proposed innovation has other features which might offset the initially expected effects. The process of thought is obviously speculative and selective and suffers from the many gaps in our knowledge of the present situation. It does, however, show certain virtues: it generates hypotheses and guides for research observation, it relates to current sociological theory and research, and it builds a record which can be reviewed and compared with the unfolding reality. Through time it connects theory and research with action and acts to strengthen both.

The Teacher and the Authority System

Every formal organization must find a way to distribute socially approved power (authority) within its ranks if it is to accomplish its purposes effectively, but the specifics of such authority distribution are more complex than is frequently perceived. Our knowledge of the situation in public schools, for example, is still scant. Although there are numerous statements on how authority should be handled in such organizations, we have few studies which describe and

[1] Robert K. Merton, *Social Theory and Social Structure*, New York, Free Press, 1949, chap. I.

analyze what actually occurs. Throughout this chapter we shall notice how our lack of knowledge of existing conditions hampers planning for change.

The American public schools can be described as partially bureaucratic in the technical sense of that term.[2] Public accountability is attained through lay, policy-making boards, coupled with a hierarchy of administrative offices occupied by personnel selected on technical grounds and trained for their functions. Legal authority is vested in the lay board and its chief administrative official, the superintendent. Theoretically, all other authority is delegated by those at the apex of the system, and subordinates possess no separate legal authority for their activities. In the formal sense, teachers are employees of the school board and superintendent; the law does not recognize them as "independent professionals."

The bureaucratic model, in emphasizing the formal distribution of authority, does not prepare us for many of the events that actually occur in public schools. Teachers, for example, lay claim to and get, informally, certain types of authority despite lack of formal support for it in either law or school system constitutions. We can see the outcropping of these claims in the emphasis on "democratic administration" taught in schools of education and in the adaptations made to faculty opinion by administrators. School officials will assert that no principal can survive long in a school where the faculty is determined to see his resignation. Wise administrators urge that curricula be developed by faculty groups rather than handed down in line decisions. Schoolmen make a sharp distinction between the formal curriculum and what teachers actually do in classrooms and thus implicitly assert the likelihood that the two are different. Several policies favored by administrators have not been implemented because of teacher opposition—one thinks of resistance to administrative discretion in salary payment (merit pay) and to attempts to introduce more hierarchy within faculties. The bureacratic map of public schools, then, leaves out certain parts of the territory, notably those which point to powers held by teachers (and, of course, students) which are nowhere given formal sanction.

Sociologists have encountered similar situations elsewhere, par-

[2] Peter M. Blau, *Bureaucracy in Modern Society*, New York, Random House, 1956.

ticularly in those organizations where members of high-prestige professions work under general administrative control. But there are interesting differences between teachers and members of these other professions. Doctors, for example, have economic power in their control over patients' selection of hospitals, and this power is supplemented by political power in the form of potent professional associations and in the executive committee of the hospital medical staff.[3] They possess another type of authority which Smith terms "charismatic" and which is symbolized by their capacity to define a situation as a medical emergency. Engineers and professors may have less economic or political power than doctors as groups, but they possess more individual bargaining power because they can participate in career circuits independent of a single employer. It is easier for engineers and professors than it is for public school teachers to build the independent reputations that facilitate work mobility. Lawyers work either independently as self-employed professionals or, according to research conducted by one sociologist, in firms where the independent nature of their decision making is respected.[4] Teachers possess few of the power resources found in other professions. Lieberman points out the passivity of their occupational associations.[5] They also lack the economic sanctions found in fee professions, their career circuits are relatively undeveloped, and, as we have noted, their formal and legal status within school systems is weak.

How do teachers get the authority which observers state they possess? What mechanisms grant them some ability to act in ways consistent with their work values? It is our hypothesis that the authority teachers possess stems from the spatial work arrangements found in most schools and from informal rules that are connected with those arrangements. The self-contained classroom, in this view, is more than a physical reality, for it refers as well to a social system, a set of recurrent and more or less permanent social relationships. Under this arrangement the teacher is separated from immediate supervision, and intrusion into his private domain is prevented

[3] Harvey Smith, "Two Lines of Authority: The Hospital's Dilemma," in E. Hartly Jaco, ed., *Physicians, Patients, and Illness*, New York, Free Press, 1958.
[4] Personal communication from Erwin O. Smigel.
[5] Myron Lieberman, *Education as a Profession*, Englewood Cliffs, N.J., Prentice-Hall, 1956.

by a set of understandings subscribed to by administrative officers and teacher colleagues. A set of norms exist which act to buttress the ecological separation: (1) the teacher should be free from the interference of other adults while teaching, (2) teachers should be considered and treated as equals, and (3) teachers should act in a nonintervening but friendly manner toward one another. Since these rules apparently reinforce one another, they can be considered a pattern—a pattern which we call "the autonomy-equality pattern." This pattern, it must be emphasized, is not a formally accepted one and probably breaks down in crisis situations involving a teacher and the public. In the usual course of events, however, it seems to summarize how teachers strive to relate to each other and to administrative officials.

If the preceding line of analysis is correct, the type of authority which teachers hold is not the kind we associate with the prestige term *professional,* for it is not the possession of the teacher *by right* but emerges in an informally supported, ecologically enhanced set of work arrangements. It is authority based on isolation since, unlike professional authority, it is not generally given effective support by a guild or an association. The lack of strong occupational associations, in fact, suggests that teachers are protected against each other as well as against administrators and members of the community. It must be emphasized that this type of authority is fragile, and, confronted with the full formal authority of a school board or an agitated community, it is likely to crumble. There will be variations, as well, in the amount and type of authority teachers possess in different kinds of systems. Small systems continue a pattern which Solomon terms "paternalistic," while in the largest city systems the trend seems to be to a type of unionism which seeks in a variety of ways to create collective authority for classroom teachers.[6] But the general situation appears to be one where teachers get whatever work authority they possess through the informal pattern of autonomy-equality.

The work of the public school teacher is almost inseparable from the arrangements we have described, and we have no appreciable experience with teaching under alternative structural arrangements.

[6] Benjamin Solomon, "A Profession Taken for Granted," *The School Review,* vol. LXIX, Autumn, 1961, pp. 286–299.

Consequently, we face analytic difficulties in discerning what aspects of teaching stem specifically from these structural arrangements. In advancing hypotheses as to what might happen with team teaching, we can only estimate what the likely effects will be since the influence of the authority factor is not open to precise measurement. But we can begin the necessary if imprecise task we have set ourselves by identifying some of the apparent consequences of the autonomy-equality pattern.

Although the autonomy-equality pattern contradicts the concept of special rewards for special effort, it does *allow teachers to differ in their level of effort*. Administrators who complain that some teachers try to get away with the least possible effort will give credit to some whose dedication is unlimited. There is, of course, a minimal level of effort built into the school schedule, and there are other controls which decree what effort is minimally acceptable from a public school teacher. But the absence of close observation in conventional self-contained classroom arrangements means that teachers can differ in how hard they work both in the classroom and without. There are, presumably, norms among faculties that define a reasonable week's work, but autonomy-equality makes it very difficult for those who seek to enforce such norms. It is possible for teachers who take their work seriously to put in many extra hours outside the classroom without making a point of it to their colleagues, and, although reliable data are unsurprisingly scarce, our own researches suggest that there are some teachers who work extremely long hours. There is a somewhat boundless quality about teaching which can carry the conscientious teacher into a heavy work schedule. After all, at what point can such a teacher feel that his classes cannot be improved by more preparation or that extra time with students would not teach them more? External controls, then, work to insure minimal effort and fail to inhibit maximum effort under autonomy-equality. A levelling-off can occur only where teachers internalize a common standard of what constitutes appropriate work levels. Some teachers, feeling that additional effort on their part would be self-exploitation, probably hold back. Others, apparently, continue to work extremely hard despite the less vigorous exertions of their colleagues.

Variations in teaching style and content are also favored by the autonomy-equality pattern, for teachers, solving teaching problems in isolation from each other, are likely to select different solutions. The teacher's style—his or her particular way of solving problems—will, over time, reflect unique personality configurations. For some will find that discussion works best for them while others will prefer to use lectures and demonstrations. The content of any curriculum never exhausts the possibilities for treating the materials, and teachers exercise considerable editorial judgment in applying even the most carefully delineated curriculum plans. Differences in teacher values will find expression in the various ways in which they exercise this judgment. Such possibilities for variation have important consequences for the teacher role and who can occupy it. Since considerable variation is possible, a broad range of personality types and a broad range of personal values can be expressed in the role. This means that teaching as an occupation can and probably does recruit persons who are quite diverse in personal make-up and conviction.

Autonomy-equality is associated with *variation in the definition of what constitutes good or bad teaching.* There is considerable evidence that no clear consensus exists among public school personnel as to what criteria should be applied to evaluate teaching performance. Where clear criteria are lacking, it seems reasonable to expect that people will answer the question of adequacy of performance in ways which satisfy them personally, and indications are that teachers do differ in how they answer these questions for themselves. Autonomy-equality is permissive in this regard, for the teacher who works alone can develop his own answers. He is free, on the other hand, to join associations (such as the once highly influential Progressive Education Association) and to seek to persuade colleagues that his answers are worth general acceptance. Autonomy-equality, then, is associated either with laissez-faire or persuasion, but in general it weakens attempts to impose any single definition of "good teaching" and thus enhances variety. Criteria for good teaching being variable, different conceptions of desirable educational goals can exist simultaneously in a school or school system.

The fourth area where autonomy-equality can be examined is in its *consequences for the teacher-class relationship.* The frequently heard statement that teaching is an art implies that the decisions made by teachers cannot always be made explicit or formulated in terms of general rules. Supporting evidence for this position is found in those instances where everyone agrees that a given teacher is outstanding, yet all find it difficult to verbalize the reasons for his achievement. The work of the teacher involves a level of intuitive judgment where artistry can be effective without being communicable. Autonomy-equality, inasmuch as it leaves the teacher free to work spontaneously, encourages expression at this intuitive level. Not forced to justify his decisions, the teacher feels free to play his hunches. Such hunches may be based on accurate assessments of student needs, but to make these assessments explicit may be beyond the analytic capacity of the teacher.

A very elusive aspect of the teacher-class relationship, class rapport, seems to be related to the autonomy-equality pattern. Teachers associate effective teaching with a subtle quality of rapport with students, and analysis of their descriptions of high rapport reveals mechanisms studied in a field sociologists call "collective behavior." The tone which teachers ascribe to such moments of high rapport is reminiscent of certain types of controlled crowd situations: there is the same focusing of attention on a common object, the same quick mutual reactions, and the same loss of personal awareness.[7] What we do not yet know is whether such states of high rapport can arise where more than one adult is teaching in a single classroom. Under autonomy-equality the teacher unself-consciously relates directly to the class and need not concern himself with the possibly different reactions emanating from other adults. Can adults work together in a way which permits them the same free-wheeling emotional freedom and which results in an equally intense relationship?

There is another question which arises when we ask how autonomy-equality relates to the teacher-class relationship. To what degree is that condition known as satisfactory discipline a function of control by one rather than several adults? Discipline involves many quick judgments and quick actions, and, as any parent knows, such judgments are difficult to make and act on where two parents have not worked out a common stance. Under autonomy-equality,

[7] H. Blumer, "Collective Behavior," in A. M. Lee, ed., *Principles of Sociology,* New York, Barnes & Noble, 1957.

the individual teacher selects the level of discipline he desires. Students cannot, where one teacher is clearly in charge, employ the tactics of *divide et impera*.

In summary, then, we hypothesize that the pattern of autonomy-equality is associated with teaching in several ways. It enhances variation among teachers in the amount of effort they put into their work, the styles they employ, what they teach, and their definitions of what constitutes good teaching and desirable outcomes. We have noted that teaching as an unverbalized art, in teacher-class rapport and in order-maintenance, is adapted to autonomy-equality. If these observations are valid, the autonomy-equality pattern acts to enhance variation among teachers which might otherwise be asserted as prerogatives of the individual professional. There are indications that the teaching craft, as we have developed it, depends upon an isolated work pattern. In short, autonomy-equality supplies teachers with the personal and spontaneous choice which they would have if they possessed the privileges granted those in high-prestige, fee-taking professions. In sociological parlance, autonomy-equality based on isolation is the functional equivalent of the clearly delineated privileges of the doctor, architect, or successful artist. It acts to limit the influence of the formal and bureaucratic order which, on paper, is the structure of the American public school system.

Before we speculate on how team teaching might influence the teaching craft by changing the authority structure, we must consider the alternative forms that authority might take under team teaching. The writer believes that two polar possibilities exist. Team teaching might strengthen the formal authority structure so greatly that schools will become essentially *vertical-bureaucratic* in their authority arrangements. It is also possible that team teaching will diffuse authority into the hands of small colleague groups and take the *horizontal-collegial* form. Since both alternatives are possible from the essential characteristics of team teaching, emphasis on one set of characteristics rather than another would be the determining factor.

There are two features of most team teaching projects that are of enormous sociological importance. First, team teaching insists that teachers work closely together, and it suggests that teachers will often work simultaneously with the same group of students.

Thus, the isolation found under autonomy-equality disappears. Secondly, teaching teams frequently contain a hierarchy of authority positions, formally designated by such titles as team leader, senior teacher, and so forth (earlier in this book it is suggested that such a hierarchy is virtually essential for the effective functioning of a teaching team). Thus, the norm of teacher equality is displaced. Two difficult questions arise. Since team teaching seeks to combine elements which, according to our previous discussion, seem to be unstable in mixture (close working relationships and hierarchical rank), which of the two elements is likely to dominate? And, where one rather than another dominates, what are the likely effects on teaching and learning?

What is certainly clear is that the widespread adoption of team teaching will bring about significant changes in the status of the American public school teacher. Individualism, previously supported by the autonomy-equality pattern, will be weakened by pressures either from administrative officials or close colleagues, and teachers who rejoice in their working autonomy must face difficult, important questions in taking their stand on the issue of team teaching. Perhaps the most important query they must answer is whether they can find other sources of autonomy once the isolation of autonomy-equality is gone. It is possible that they might find a more powerful type of protection than the tentative and uncertain power based on informal understandings which they now possess.

Authority: The Vertical-Bureacratic Outcome

In conventional school situations, administrators find it impossible to supervise teachers closely. The span of control is generally too broad and their tasks too numerous to allow full-time involvement in supervisory duties. Team teaching, however, offers a solution to the problem of control by segmenting faculties into small units. Even the largest school, with teams each under a leader, could be brought under effective administrative control. It is conceivable that under some circumstances this possibility for holding a tight rein on the teacher's activities would be seized and used. The structure of the school could feature a lengthened line of authority stretching from the top administration, through principals and team leaders, to classroom teachers. Where team leaders identify themselves with management, they might see themselves not as spokesmen for a group of teachers but as local admnistrators responsible for implementing school and school system policies. If there were a system where the team leaders generally did assume this stance, few classroom teachers could escape the minute control found in tight administrative structures.

It is difficult to predict the circumstances under which this extreme type of vertical authority would emerge, for it would call for considerable change in the work values of public school personnel. There are some school boards, one suspects, which would welcome the chance to run the show, but how many superintendents would go along with that ambition? Would administrators emerge who see themselves as strong line officers eager and ready to issue multiple orders over detailed matters? One also notes that the possibilities for gaps in the line of authority are numerous and that these gaps are accompanied by the likelihood of role conflicts at several levels in the hierarchy. (Even where the concept of line authority is strong, as in industry, foremen are men in the middle and must choose between identifying up with management or identifying down with the workers.) One can also visualize several variations from the extreme case of clear-cut line authority, and research must be planned to study these varieties when and if they emerge. It is distinctly possible that teaching and learning will differ according to the dominant mode of authority distribution and organization.

The consequences of this type of authority system are manifold, and discussion of them would take more space than is available here. As far as the classroom teacher is concerned, however, it probably would result in routinization of task and subordination of status, especially where team leaders were closely coordinated throughout the school system. Levels of output could be more closely controlled than under current arangements since the amount of effort expended by individual teachers would be readily apparent and would influence administrators' attitudes and actions toward them. Teaching style and content could come under the control of a dominant leader since he would possess powerful sanctions. Educational objectives would become more specific and standard throughout the system, whether explicitly stated or not. Team leaders would serve as the focal point in the teacher-class relationship, for it is likely that where vertical authority is paramount, students would recognize the higher status and greater authority of the team leader. The range of choices made by the classroom teacher would contract, and the locus of professional decision would be concentrated above him in a formal stucture. The possibilities for close coordination of system activities make it likely that a greater degree of curriculum specification would be found throughout all grades and schools. The position of the nonleader teacher would call for less personal initiative and require fewer complex decisions because decisions of any difficulty would, presumably, be made at the team leader level or above. The process involved would be one which industrial sociologists call "de-skilling" in the working ranks.

To examine the desirability or undesirability of the close supervision of teachers could involve us in exceedingly long, complicated, and even heated deliberations, but research can, we believe, be planned to resolve some of the issues. One argument for increased centralization is that it brings about greater standardization among different teachers and schools, and that standardization, paced by better qualified teachers, will result in a higher level of student learning. The implicit assumption is, of course, that the quality of teaching varies directly with the amount of supervision. Providing a clear-cut definition of student learning is accepted, such an assumption is testable by standard research techniques, and the variety of outcomes likely with team teaching means that comparative situations will be available for study. Another argument for centralized control rests in the success of the armed services in teaching certain specific skills (e.g., jet plane flying) and communicating set bodies of information (the navigation taught novice naval officers). Research could, using a variety of educational outcomes with relevant tests, inquire into whether the vertical authority system results in more effective teaching in some specific areas. Conversely, it might be found that such a structure is less effective in teaching nonmilitary types of capacity such as initiative, a questioning attitude, and respect for equalitarian values. Sociologists would be interested to see if vertical-authority school systems tend toward a single set of values in all classrooms and thus act to counter pluralism in our society. Close observation of the content and values expressed in the classroom could permit analysis based on firsthand data. The argument that centralization means quicker adoption of innovations can also be tested by comparing the receptivity to change of vertical-bureaucratic systems with that of other authority distributions.

The lines of inquiry suggested, then, are several. Observations should begin on the organizational realities that occur with team teaching, and close attention should be paid to the degree to which school boards eager for close control are able to attain it. The role of the classroom teacher should be watched carefully to see whether it comes to require less personal ability and imagination, and the stances taken by team leaders toward their superordinates and subordinates should be the subject of intense research effort. The mechanisms of supervision should be studied closely, and the levels of effort, styles, emphases, and techniques of teachers should be recorded in a variety of situations. Instructional outcomes should be examined and data gathered in terms of a wide range of things learned, from mechanical skills to abstract values. The task of those who will assess team teaching in the future will require great philosophical insight. It should not be hampered by ignorance of what vertical-bureaucratic authority means for teaching and learning but should begin with results and assess those results in terms of several value positions. With knowledge, there is a much greater likelihood that the debate and discussion that takes place will reach rational levels of discourse.

Authority: The Horizontal-Collegial Outcome

By initiating close working relationships among small groups of teachers, team teaching might result in a form of authority now rare in public schools—the "collegium," where equals rule their affairs by internal democratic procedures.[8] Although such structures are not common in our society, we do find them in some universities, churches, and artistic groups. The sociological theory devoted to this form of authority is less well developed than that dealing with bureaucratic organization. We should expect, however, that where there is a strong emphasis on internal equality and close, harmonious relationships, such groups will tend to resist formal and lasting status differences. The members will have an interest in granting

[8] Everett C. Hughes, "Institutions," in Lee, *ibid.*

leadership according to the needs of the immediate group. Leadership in a collegial team will reflect the sentiments and norms of the small group. As noted previously in this book, even the most informal of groups will feature leadership of some kind. However, attempts by outsiders, such as bureaucratic superiors, to impose a rigid hierarchy are likely to encounter resistance.

Small groups having stability through time tend to develop common ways and common expectations which bind members into a miniature society.[9] The group, in short, develops a culture which may encompass a wide variety of concerns. In work groups it may define the nature of high performance, the amount of effort involved in a fair day's work, and the appropiate relationships that should obtain among members and between members and outsiders.

Our analysis of the conventional school situation suggests that teachers in teams will confront many problems requiring solution in the group context. Who will handle discipline when several teachers observe an infraction? How will teachers cope with students who show deference to one team member and none to another? Will team members display disagreements over facts or interpretations in front of their students, or will they stoutly maintain a united front? These questions can, of course, be answered in several ways. But we cannot predict *a priori* how a given team will answer the questions or whether a group of teams will select similar answers. Our knowledge of small groups and the processes whereby they build cultures permits us to say only that they will come up with collective answers to many of these questions. We cannot say which will be dealt with by the group and which will be left to individual choice, and we cannot predict the specific solutions which will be selected in those areas where collective rules are developed. It seems likely, however, that teams will develop norms to cover both the appropriate level of effort and the style and content of member teaching, and that teacher-student relationships will be a critical area for team concern. We can illustrate the complications by considering the question of effort levels.

It is reasonable to predict that teams will define a normal amount of effort, and that they will develop techniques for controlling both the slacker and the eager beaver. But what will that level of effort

[9] George Homans, *The Human Group*, New York, Harcourt, Brace, 1950.

be? Will joint teaching, with its attendant visibility of individual work, result in higher standards of presentation and preparation? (We do know that the best law, medicine, and architecture is practiced where professionals face the criticism of colleagues and get assistance as well.) Will teams enforce effort levels equal to those of the dedicated teacher today or less demanding levels? If they choose the latter, how will the average effort of teachers compare with the average found in conventional situations? It is obvious that only carefully conducted research can answer a question such as this.

What of the teacher's craft and instructional outcomes, where teams bring about horizontal, collegial authority? Would a tendency toward conformity in presentation of materials, for example, reduce teacher satisfactions or lower student interest and achievement? Or would emulation of the best teacher raise performance levels and student effectiveness? Would content become more exciting when team members chose to argue in front of students, or would students find themselves unable to cope with the intellectual and emotional complexities introduced by open disagreement among people they consider to be authorities? Or will team members, necessarily concerned with maintaining smooth relationships within their group, choose to avoid open disagreement and thereby present students with less variety of thought than they would find in going from one teacher to another in conventional schools?

Should the team come to play a central part in the teacher's work orientation, problems of integration would assuredly arise within schools and school systems. Perhaps one development would be competition between teams, and, if this occurred, researchers would have to watch, most specifically, what rules were used to judge winning or losing in such rivalries. Where winning is defined in ways consistent with system objectives, such competition could enhance the achievement of organizational goals. Where the rules are selected for institutionally irrelevant purposes (e.g., ease of measuring output and victory), such competition could, however, retard achievement of the system's aims.

One possible outcome from collegial teams could have important repercussions for the "art of teaching." Under autonomy-equality individual teachers can work at their own teaching and develop highly effective techniques which are not communicated to others. Under vertical-bureaucratic structures, teaching is likely to become formalized into organizational procedures, and, where lay control is heavy, the craft may tend to be ignored or lost if the distinction between teachers and nonteachers is weakened. Collegial teams call for close cooperation, and this may, initially, inhibit the spontaneous improvisation of the isolated teacher and require "scripts" for the teachers. In time, however, this could move teaching into a more recorded form, and improvements might accumulate in a context of conscious choice and refinement. This could lead to a greater emphasis on scientific values (communicability, accumulative experience) coupled with clinical practice, and such an outcome could do much to advance the state of the art.

The hypotheses put forth point to a variety of research possibilities and suggest a variety of techniques. It is clear that we shall need detailed observational reports which cover the subtle interactions involved in the development of team cultures. Close watch should be kept on how each team defines its norms and how individual members react to those norms. Records of conferences will necessarily be supplemented by observations of classroom behavior and running accounts of the attitudes of teachers as individuals. Not to begin early would be serious since turnover among teams may be highly significant. It may represent, for example, the screening out of particular personality types and the selection of others. Such researches can profit from the experience of social scientists in a variety of settings, particularly the studies of industrial work groups. It is clear that research cannot be of the hit-and-run variety, but that research personnel will have to be in steady, regular contact with teams as this new organization of teaching develops.

The Teacher and the Reward System

Organizations are more than systems of authority; they can also be viewed as systems of inducements or rewards for participation in the activities of the organization and adherence to its objectives. Our specific task here is to inquire briefly into the current situation and to raise questions on how team teaching might change the system of rewards for teachers. We shall classify rewards into two groups for purposes of this discussion. (1) *Extrinsic* rewards are those which are attached to a given role and are, in the main, transferable from one occupant to another: money income, power, and prestige. (2) *Intrinsic* rewards, or gratifications, are available to persons occupying a given role but will differ depending on what occupants value in that situation. Here personal predilections will play a considerable part. Most discussions of the teacher's role center almost entirely on extrinsic rewards, but this discussion will deal largely with intrinsic ones. That the discussion must be tentative in the current state of our knowledge is obvious, but such discussion may stimulate the work needed to fill the enormous gaps in our research literature.

Perhaps the most interesting feature of the system of extrinsic rewards facing American public school teachers is the absence of sharp differentiation. A teacher may spend a lifetime in the field without more than doubling annual income. As Benson points out, the teacher can be replaced, on retirement, by a junior beginning teacher.[10] Power and prestige differentials among teachers are relatively insignificant under the rules of autonomy-equality. Promotion is very limited and usually involves increased administrative responsibility even where the higher status roles are primarily instructional in nature (e.g., department head, supervisor). Whatever informal differentiation a principal may choose to make in allocating students or rooms or schedules must not arouse the ire of teachers who are quick to spot favoritism and to cry "foul." This lack of differentiation reinforces the concept of equality at the expense of quality; for the outstanding and mediocre, by any definition, receive approximately equal extrinsic rewards.

We should expect that intrinsic rewards differ among teachers according to their personalities and their view of their work, but preliminary research suggests that some intrinsic rewards occur frequently even among persons who otherwise seem different. One of the most interesting is craft pride—the satisfaction that comes when a teacher sees definite results from his work. The specific results sought for and obtained differ, of course (one teacher might refer to test scores where another will cite a student whose self-confidence

---

[10] Charles Benson, *The Economics of Public Education*, Boston, Houghton Mifflin, 1961.

blooms), but indications that one's efforts made a difference are extremely important to teachers working, as they do, in an intangible and indeterminate craft. Even with autonomy-equality and the self-contained classroom, teachers do not find it easy to identify the specific contribution they have made to an individual student or group of students (in fact, we suspect that teachers sometimes define the desirable outcomes of their work in ways which simplify self-assessment and make it possible to enjoy the gratification of getting results). Under autonomy-equality a teacher is relatively free to emphasize a given facet of his role (e.g., counsellor of troubled students or raiser of perplexing questions) and to spend additional time and effort on it. Thus can intrinsic rewards be magnified and the total role made more gratifying.

There can be little doubt that affective responses from students are of great importance to classroom teachers, but they differ in how they cope with such responses. Some teachers feel little inhibition in seeking student popularity and consider students excellent judges of teacher ability, while others profess enormous skepticism on the reactions of students until they have left school. With the live-and-let-live arrangements of autonomy-equality, teachers are free to opt which stance they will take. Perhaps of greater importance, however, is that the separation of classes and teachers found in conventional situations limits competition among teachers for student approbation and protects those who receive relatively little. They are spared the shame of direct comparison and may, in fact, perceive themselves to be considerably more popular than they are. Autonomy-equality acts to maximize gratifications that derive from student responses by permitting teachers to choose their modes of relating to it.

Teachers talking about the good things in their work are likely, especially at the elementary level, to mention the sociable intercourse they have with other teachers, and their talk reminds one of the "pure sociability" described by Simmel, where people enjoy interaction per se.[11] The work of teachers places them under two unusual strains. First, teachers, to be effective, must be able to think and talk at the level of their students. Continued day after day, this can result in a kind of infantilization which teachers seem to fear, for it

[11] Georg Simmel, "The Sociology of Sociability," in Talcott Parsons, *et al.*, *Theories of Society*, New York, Free Press, 1961, vol. I, p. 157.

threatens their hold on adulthood and their self-esteem as mature persons. Furthermore, teaching is a controlled activity where spontaneity in the classroom must be inhibited. Therefore, teachers probably need both adult sociability and relatively relaxed, unguarded interaction with others. Although teachers at leisure often do talk shop, autonomy-equality means that each teacher is talking about his unique experiences. Where his colleagues are equals, he can do so in a comfortable, off-guard way without too much fear of consequence for himself and his career.

Teachers, it has been said, are particularly fond of "whodunits" and other adventure stories. If that is so, I suspect that it stems largely from the relative lack of adventure in their work. Their interactions are scheduled and repetitive, their work content is frequently routinized, and their contact with a variety of adults is scarce in the insulated social world of the public school. The pattern of autonomy-equality, inasmuch as it permits the teacher leverage in content and approach, permits a self-directed variety to offset the danger of boredom which can undermine the precious quality of enthusiasm, which most observers consider a necessity of effective teaching.

There are undoubtedly other gratifications of a recurrent nature in teaching (autonomy per se is one—teachers will tell how they failed to perceive its importance on entering the field but have come to appreciate working as one's own boss). But the major point is that the sheer institutionalization of teaching in the self-contained classroom has created, over the years, a set of vested intrinsic gratifications. Those who have entered teaching and stayed in it are presumably those who have found intrinsic gratifications sufficient to offset the undoubtedly limited extrinsic rewards in the role. Team teaching will certainly expand our understanding of this area since it makes changes in both extrinsic and intrinsic rewards for public school teachers. Will new rewards arise which will make teaching attractive in completely different ways?

Rewards: The Vertical-Bureaucratic Outcome

Where team teaching takes a vertical emphasis, the position of team leader will provide an important amount of differentiation in extrinsic rewards. Presumably pay, authority, and prestige gains will be greatest for team leaders where hierarchical facets receive the greatest encouragement. Schools, as organizations, will augment their resources of incentives with this position and will have more leeway in rewarding those whose services are found to be most valuable. This aspect of team teaching has already received considerable attention, and so it need not delay us here. There is, however, a possible side effect of this new step which is of interest to those who would augment the total extrinsic rewards available to teachers.

It is quite possible that the prestige gains made by team leaders will result in prestige losses for teachers who do not occupy that role. One is tempted, in seeking to label these teachers, to call them ordinary teachers to differentiate them from their senior colleagues. We encounter here a somewhat mysterious property of prestige systems—they are at times quite finite in that deference paid to some results in deference lost to others. Where the status "teacher" is undifferentiated, the status of an individual teacher stems primarily from the status of the group. Where some teachers are accorded special recognition, however, the position of those who do not receive such recognition is weakened, for other teachers may ask, overtly or covertly, why they have not attained the more honored post. Should students consider the difference between leaders and nonleaders important, the authority of nonleaders might well wane, and this could lead to an increase in disciplinary problems. In short, two types of extrinsic rewards—prestige and authority—could show a net decrease when we consider *all* teachers under vertically oriented team teaching. Such an outcome is potentially one of enormous gravity, for few persons today wish to reduce the status of the teaching profession. Research should be conducted to examine such changes and to watch for any countervailing trends such as the possibility that vertical team teaching, by establishing higher standards of performance, could raise public evaluation of teachers generally.

It appears certain that intrinsic rewards will change when team teaching results in a heavy emphasis on vertical-bureaucratic authority. Team leaders, where the extreme vertical form prevails, are not likely to gain much over the teacher working under autonomy-equality today. For if team teaching is used as a vehicle for increasing the rigidity of line authority, team leaders may find themselves unable to exercise free choices. When team leaders exercise authority over their subordinates but are not in turn regulated closely by their superiors, they will, of course, obtain whatever gratifications are associated with leading a group of subordinates.

The majority of classroom teachers, however, will have to shift the loci of their intrinsic rewards. For example, close supervision will make it difficult for a teacher to feel that any given outcome is clearly his own achievement. All achievements, and possibly failures, must be shared with the supervisor. Here again, personality differences must clearly be taken into account, for some teachers, more passive or dependent than others, may feel pleasure in meeting the expectations of an immediate superior. On the other hand, the more independent and aggressive teachers would undoubtedly find their satisfactions decreased. The psychic income obtained from student responses would undergo similar changes in situations where teachers of unequal rank worked with the same students. We would expect that where ranking is taken seriously by teachers, students will also be expected to respect it (students who failed to support the status distinctions would, afer all, create tensions among faculty members adjusted to these distinctions). But developing such mechanisms will not be easy, and some junior teachers may compensate by identifying closely with students and thereby challenging faculty solidarity. This problem of aligning student response with faculty hierachy may prove too difficult, and it could be a strong pressure countering rank and favoring collegial equality. But even if successful mechanisms can be developed, most teachers will still have to accept a lower level of affective response from students than occurs with autonomy-equality.

Emphasis on rank differences would decrease the pure sociability possible among teachers, at least in the presence of superordinates possessing genuine authority. The tendency for persons in stratified groups to choose equals for social purposes is well known and can be seen in the army's provisions for recreational facilities that are separated according to rank. The net cost of this change, however, may not be high if team relationships are internally cordial or if teachers find close, relaxed associations outside their work. But where ordinary teachers fear their superiors' judgments in class, it is unlikely that they will find it easy to mix with them outside. Research observers should watch these phenomena very carefully. Specifically, free period and lunch groups should be observed for tendencies toward grouping according to rank. In larger schools leaders may sort themselves out socially while nonleaders may similarly prefer the company of others of like status, but awkward situations may arise where the school staff is too small to support separate sociability groupings.

It is difficult to foresee the effect of vertical orientation on the opportunities for variety among teachers. Certainly the freedom to follow one's own mood will be lost where group planning replaces individual planning, but the leader's attitude toward specialization is probably more crucial. Leaders favoring regular assignments and specialization may inhibit opportunities for change while those who prefer rotation and generality may enhance it. The team situation opens up, in theory, a larger number of potential roles and activities for the individual teacher.

Despite the lack of data we have on current teacher gratifications and the speculative nature of this discussion, future research might hypothesize that there will be a net decrease in rewards of both types for *most* teachers if team teaching follows the vertical-bureaucratic line of development (the comparatively few teachers who have special status in the teams will, of course, receive increased extrinsic rewards). If the findings surprised the researchers, they would be forced to discover whether substitute gratifications have arisen. Or they might find that teachers develop ways to guarantee the persistence of prized rewards by developing new and subtle informal arrangements within the changed formal organization.

Rewards: The Horizontal-Collegial Outcome

Predicting the effect of collegially oriented teams on the system of extrinsic rewards (money income, prestige, and authority) available to teachers is almost impossible at the present time. First, the ways in which these rewards are distributed will have enormous effect on their legitimacy and psychological meaning as far as teachers are concerned. They could become empty formalities in the eyes of both those who do and those who do not receive them as currently occurs in some schools where the rank of department head is almost meaningless. Secondly, collegial teams which persist will develop a stake in the extrinsic reward system, for they will want to align rewards with their own norms and judgments in the interests of team cohesiveness. Yet central administration will also care about such distributions of rewards since they mobilize efforts to achieve system-wide goals and interests. One would expect, therefore, that there will be a significant and continuing struggle between teams and the central administration for control over the allocation of meaningful rewards. When teams do not subscribe to the means used by top administrators or the specific decisions they make, they will probably depreciate formal differentiation and supplement it with a prestige and authority system of their own. They may never be able to control money rewards (unless teams are given the right to elect leaders), but they could weaken the significance of money differentials for team members.

One situation which would augment the total extrinsic rewards available for all team teachers would be where there is close agreement between administrative and peer judgments on the proper allocation of differential income, prestige, and authority, for in this instance team leaders would receive increments which do not detract from the rewards of other teachers. Other teachers would probably regard such additional rewards as just payment for valuable services rendered. To bring about this high level of consensus will not be easy, and, where it is lacking, it is doubtful that team teaching will add any appreciable set of extrinsic rewards to the total currently available to public school teachers. Those who see the addition of rewards as a basic feature of team teaching should concern themselves, if this reasoning be accurate, with finding ways to ensure consensus among team members and administrative officers. Research efforts could assist in discovering what situations enhance such consensus and what situations militate against it.

The question of what will happen to intrinsic rewards under collegially-oriented team teaching is fascinating. As noted before, the type of craft pride found among teachers working under autonomy-equality is essentially individualistic with delight accompanying recogniton of one's personal effectiveness with students. But can this type of craft pride be replaced by one which is collective in form? Can teachers come to feel equal pride in the accomplishment of their teams? Commentators have felt for years that the division of labor found in factories results in the alienation of the worker from his product. Dubin, however, in a most suggestive article, points to the possibility that workers obtain alternative forms of gratification from participation in a complex system of specialization.[12] We know little of this phenomenon and are therefore ill equipped to predict under what conditions team identifications can replace individualistic ones. This issue is central, however, if team teaching is to give its participants a sense of pride and accomplishment linked to work effort. It is here that the personality psychologist's researches will be especially valuable, for it seems most likely that some teachers will find team-centered achievement gratifying while others will not. For team teaching to succeed, it will be necessary to identify such personality differences and to recruit those who obtain personal gratification in small-group settings. Without a predisposition of this type of reward, it seems unlikely that team members will put forth their best energies.

The role of affective response from students is also a crucial question when we anticipate collegial teams working with a common group of students. Differential student response could, after all, threaten the solidarity of the team, and members would eventually have to resolve emotionally complex issues of jealousy and pride. One solution lies in heavy controls on competition (professional ethics) which specify just how the individual practitioner may seek to obtain clients, or more appropriately in this case, impress them. If teams find it necessary to employ such controls, teachers will be less free to seek popularity with students and to win their cooperation. This could result in less affective response and a consequent deprivation for team teachers generally. However, an alternative source of gratification, which will probably become a prized reward, will be found in the approbation of colleagues. The instructional consequences of this change could be most interesting since it raises age-old issues of pedagogy. Who teaches most and best, the teacher who seeks to win students to his side or the teacher who lays down rigorous demands? Freed from the quest for popularity, will teachers increase the work loads they give students, and will this result in an increase or decrease in total learning? It is possible that team teachers may select other ways of coping with differences in student

---

[12] Robert Dubin, "Industrial Workers' Worlds: A Study of the 'Central Life Interests' of Industrial Workers," *Social Problems*, vol. IV, 1956, pp. 131–142.

response and may reinforce team members who manage to receive it. If so, what alternative gratifications will occur for those sterner teachers who are either unable or unwilling to win student approval? The questions here are important ones, and working on them as they arise in team teaching should prove informative to educational knowledge and practice in general.

The gratifications associated with colleague interactions are likely to take a different form in collegial-team situations, for close working relationships, long hours at a time, will probably make spontaneous, nonwork intercourse less frequent. Teammates will find it harder in outside interaction to avoid work content and the inevitable tensions associated with it. For some teachers (notably those with rich social lives outside of school), this will probably be a minimal loss since the dangers of infantilization are reduced where adults work together. But the problem of finding free and uncontrolled interactions will be aggravated for some teachers, and this may prove fateful for those whose nonwork lives are lonely. Perhaps such needs will impel teachers to find associations among members of other teams and will thereby act to reduce competition between teams. But researchers observing team teaching would be wise to consider the total needs of people at work, for we have considerable evidence that work interactions fulfill many general needs for people.

Depending on the specific handling of task assignments, horizontally organized team teaching could increase or decrease possibilities for variety. If some team members are highly motivated and prepare carefully, the remaining members of the team may find the intellectual content of their day more interesting and variegated. If assignments are rotated, the individual teacher's work round may be more varied than where autonomy-equality makes repetitive demands. On the other hand, decisions by teams to move toward separate classes and fixed, specialized assignments could result in less variety for individual teachers. For under autonomy-equality a teacher can make changes from one presentation to the next without worrying much about the reactions of other teachers or about an over-all plan. It will be interesting to see whether teams opt the more flexible or more rigid handling of assignments and to discover the circumstances which affect the choice.

It seems likely that team teaching with a horizontal-collegial emphasis will introduce considerable change in the intrinsic rewards received by teachers. If this be so, the consequences are of great importance, for a change in these selective mechanisms which attract people to and keep people in teaching will ultimately produce a change in the composition of the teaching force. And this could easily set off a chain reaction of further changes. If we are to understand what directions such change is likely to take, we shall need a constant inventory on the make-up of teachers as team teaching spreads. Close cooperation is indicated, then, between psychologists interested in personality and sociologists interested in the group phenomena involved in team teaching.

The Teacher and the Career System

One of the major objectives of team teaching is to introduce a career line for public school teachers to increase the attractiveness of the field for able male graduates of better quality colleges and universities. The aim is to create positions (such as team leader) which combine greater rewards with a broader scope of influence and thereby make more rational use of limited numbers of highly qualified personnel. The research sociologist can assist in this phase of team teaching both by indicating potential and unanticipated consequences which could undermine the objective of higher quality teaching, and by suggesting research approaches to monitor the unfolding of intended and unintended processes. Here research has an infrequent ally—time—for team teaching, even if it spread rapidly, will have its greatest effect on teacher careers several years from now. The self-contained classroom model is what potential recruits to teaching now visualize, and it will be some time before potential teachers think in terms of the team form. It will also take several years for us to learn how teachers react to the career possibilities inherent in team teaching.

We can examine the possible effects of team teaching on teaching careers by isolating three key career points: (1) how team teaching will influence the image of teaching held by young people considering education as a career alternative, (2) how team teaching will affect the trial years of the beginning teacher, and (3) what the likely effect of team teaching is on opportunities for advancement for teachers. We shall consider each of these questions in turn and speculate on how the two polar types of team teaching might differ from current career realities.

The Image of Teaching and Potential Candidates

When today's teachers are questioned about their reasons for going into teaching, they are likely to emphasize that teaching afforded the opportunity to work with children, offered them the chance to express a personal predilection (e.g., love of a given subject), and promised a secure if modest future. These specific reasons (oversimplifications of a complex set of career decisions) align neatly with the teacher's role under autonomy-equality. Teachers working under conventional arrangements spend the vast proportion of their working time with children, have relative freedom in stressing their interests, indulge in limited interpersonal competition, and face few risks. Young people who are considering teaching as a career and who have been taught in schools with teaching teams will possess a different image of the role than those entering the profession today. They will note the importance of teacher-teacher relations, the necessity for joint planning (with its consequent reductions in personal choices), and the differences between teachers in extrinsic rewards received. How might this different image held by potential members of the field influence the kinds of persons attracted into teaching?

Where students perceive team teaching as heavily stratified (vertical-bureaucratic), it seems probable that two quite different kinds of persons might be interested. The first would be those who fancy themselves in the role of team leader and have the ambition and confidence to try for it. These young persons will be those for whom external signs of prestige, authority, and income are important. But a second group will also be attracted, those who note the lesser responsibilities of the ordinary teachers of the team and feel that they could achieve the more limited objective. It is the latter possibility which has not, to my knowledge, been discussed. The self-contained classroom, although it does place a ceiling on aspiration, also provides a floor under it. No teacher can avoid the ultimate responsibility for a given group of students. But vertical-bureaucratic team teaching will impress some young people as providing comfortable, low-responsibility niches. If team leaders are firm in their bureaucratic role, some potential teachers will not fail to note the discrepancy in decision-making power and responsibility. We can all too readily forget that not everyone is attracted to positions of authority and responsibility. Armies are staffed primarily by men content to stay in the ranks and, as Hughes points out, managers who complain about unambitious employees might find things intolerable if all decided to seek greater glory.[13] Inasmuch as this latter group is attracted to teaching and not weeded out in the training process (a possibility where those selecting teachers might be tempted to say that they are all right for ordinary teaching), one would still hear the complaints that too many teachers have a marginal commitment to their work.

Verical-bureaucratic outcomes, as we have noted, would also attract the ambitious youngster. But again a difficult question arises. Would such persons want to stop at the position of team leader, or might they not be pressed to attain positions which offer greater honorifics, namely high *administrative* positions? Where hierarchical values are emphasized, such an ambition seems rational in terms of the social system, for to be merely a teacher is to link oneself with those unable or unwilling to climb the ladder of bureaucratic prestige. Thus would vertical-bureaucratic teams tend to undermine the objective of creating attractive posts *in teaching*, and a possible result would be an aggravation of problems rather than a solution. If teaching posts are staffed by persons low in ambition and self-confidence and by ambitious persons using teaching as a stepping-stone, the role of the classroom teacher is depreciated rather than enhanced.

Collegial-horizontal teams will probably create a different impression on students considering teaching as a career. Young people will note, we trust, that some teams work together harmoniously and critically. Such teams should attract youngsters who enjoy association with equals and who fear neither the limelight nor the possibility of criticism. However, whether or not they will be able to express their personal predilections is a somewhat more complex question. Teams which allow members free rein and tolerate diverse opinions before students should attract new teachers with strong

[13] Everett C. Hughes, *Where Peoples Meet*, New York, Free Press, 1952.

personal interests and convictions, but those teams which handle internal tensions by blandness and a united front will probably repel creative persons.

The role of the team leader will not be dramatic in teams which emphasize collegial relationships, and the status of the nonleader teacher will not suffer by comparison. Prospective teachers, therefore, will be impressed less by rank differences among teachers and more by their equal and close working relationships. Where the image of team teaching is horizontal-collegial, the person considering teaching as a career will face less psychological risk. Under vertical-bureaucratic conditions a new teacher faces an all-or-nothing situation—one either achieves the status team leader or not. But the prospective teacher thinking in terms of horizontal-collegial teams may consider it more worthwhile to *plan* on becoming an ordinary teacher and to *hope* for leadership status. Most young persons will probably assess teaching in terms of its minimum and maximum possibilities for them. If the minimum is a desirable objective per se, it seems likely that more persons will express an interest.

The research implications of these comments are clear enough. Those studying the effects of team teaching should observe how it influences students in their atitudes toward teaching as a career for themselves. Such studies should pay special attention to which students are attracted by which types of teams and should compare them both amongst themselves and with those attracted to teaching where autonomy-equality prevails.

The Trial Period: The Beginning Years

Although there is no intensive research on the subject, it appears that the initial teaching period is currently one of rather severe testing for the neophyte. No matter how carefully he has been prepared for the teaching role, there is the inevitable moment when he must take over a class, establish leadership, and maintain it over a period of time. Not all make it, and the fact that some wouldbe teachers are either chased out by rebelling students or find the experience more draining than rewarding has important consequences for schools. Schools screen out, in this somewhat harsh fashion, those who cannot meet the minimum demands of the role. We cannot know whether this result is a desirable outcome or not without close research on the process and clear indices of desirability. We can say, however, that the screening procedures of sink or swim are closely related to classroom arrangements which make each teacher responsible for a given group of students. Furthermore, it grants to students and to administrators considerable sway in determining who persists in teaching and who does not. Students, in cooperating or failing to cooperate, have a critical effect on the beginning teacher's career; and administrators, in deciding to rehire or not or in writing a favorable or lukewarm recommendation, also play a crucial role.

Without foreknowledge of the specific mechanisms that teams will develop to recruit and test new members, it is difficult to make any specific predictions of what will happen to the screening process. It seems likely, however, that the judgments of fellow educators will increase in importance and the role of students decline. It is unlikely that teachers working with a new member of the profession will stand by while classes get out of control or will create other situations calculated to disenchant the neophyte. It is likely, in short, that the rigors of sink or swim will be seriously modified.

Strongly hierarchical (vertical-bureaucratic) teams will probably feature the gradual induction of the new teacher, assignment by assignment, for a strong team leader, invested in maintaining the standing and effectiveness of his team, will be loathe to permit dangerous mistakes by beginners. Intervention by the leader will limit the influence of students. The leader and the principal will, where hierarchy reigns, make the key decisions which encourage or discourage the beginning teacher, and their standards will be critical for the composition of the staff. Such standards might vary from those which reject where the slightest signs of weakness are revealed to those which require a monumental patience with ineptitude. For good or for ill, the corrective mechanism supplied by student judgments would be weakened, and administrative judgment made paramount. Those who argue that students are perceptive judges of good teaching will consider this change a loss while those who disagree will not. But those conducting research would be in a position to provide information by observing differences that occur where students play a large role and where students play a small role in selecting teachers. It may turn out, of course, that students have rebelled most effectively against those teachers who wish to raise work output levels, and that, when students are stripped of their power, they work much harder!

Horizontal-collegial teams will feature a different situation. Here other teachers, as a group, will play a large role in the induction or rejection of a new teacher. For where members have a large investment in the over-all performance of their team, the capacity of a new member is of vital importance. Teams, like team leaders under vertical-bureaucratic arrangements, could decide to carry a slow beginner, and the limits of their tolerance would be crucial for the beginning teacher. Principals and superintendents might well be loathe to overrule judgments made by team members who could accurately claim greater familiarity with the beginner's performance and capabilities. Teams would, we should expect, struggle to get rid of an undesired new member and fight to retain a valued one. The decision to retain a new teacher would, in short, be a public rather than private matter, and the successful teacher would be one who made a favorable impression on colleagues as well as on students and administrators. This alone would be a great source of strength for teams in their relationships with the central administration, for the ability to accept or reject new members could, under some circumstances, be a weapon in struggles over autonomy or control. A further consequence would be to strengthen the persistence of norms developed within the teams, for inasmuch as they exercise selective power, they will do so using the norms where they judge themselves. The role of those placing new teachers in schools with divergent, collegially oriented teams will become important, for the judgment of what team should receive what applicant will have widespread repercussions.

Promotion and Advancement

There are two ways in which teachers can be upwardly mobile. They can leave teaching and move into administrative posts, or they can move geographically into schools which offer students of higher status and other attractions.[14] Under autonomy-equality, the controls on promotion to administration seem to be somewhat ascriptive since men, compared to women, seem to obtain these positions earlier and

[14] Howard S. Becker, "Role and Career Problems of the Chicago Public School Teacher," unpublished Ph.D. dissertation, University of Chicago, 1951.

more frequently than strict probability would decree. Geographical mobility, however, is relatively simple under autonomy-equality since teachers can leave a position and take on a new one without creating organizational problems at either end. But changes are taking place in this system as teaching and administration become more professionalized and as post-graduate work becomes more instrumental in sorting out candidates for promotion.

Schools emphasizing the bureaucratic features of team teaching will, we expect, place the power of appointment to team leader positions in the hands of principals and superintendents. The creation of this post means that for teachers wishing advancement as teachers, relationships with administrators will become crucial. It is also likely that horizontal mobility will decrease among team teaching schools since many will promote from within. The instructional effects of this shift in power cannot be easily predicted but will probably vary according to the values of line administrators. Where these officials emphasize school-wide activities (committee work, extra administrative duties, public relations) as the basis for promotion, the classroom work of the teacher may be depreciated. But where these officials are willing to emphasize and assess classroom teaching, promotion may go to those with strong teaching records. Of course, unless sharp advances are made in methods of assessing teacher performance, there will be more problems introduced by these promotions. What, for example, of positions held by men versus women? Will male principals (the everincreasing trend is toward line officers of the male sex) place women as leaders over men as frequently as the opposite? And will principals be able to disregard completely the habitual criteria of age and seniority in making their decisions? Administrators may find that although the added position of team leader creates a new incentive to advance system obligations, it also creates a series of somewhat costly side effects. When team members have little influence on who leads their teams, one might expect that resentment at a mistake will be greater than under current arrangements. Today, a disappointed teacher is at least free to go back to his room and do his own work his own way. With a bad leader he will face problems in doing what he considers a good job.

Where teams operate with collegial authority, the team leadership position will probably come to be valued by teachers and administrators alike, and it will be valued because of its peculiar demands; the talent necesary to play this mediating role will not be plentiful Corson describes the crucial role of the department head in a university, and the position of a team leader in collegially organized teams will have much in common with that difficult role.[15] One can predict that much time and effort will be spent on how to select a new team leader, for, as we have mentioned, this choice will concern all teachers. Promotion to team leader involves more than the distribution of a scarce and potentially valued reward. It presents a number of teachers with a leader who will either advance or hinder the quality of their work and the outcome of their future careers. Many administrators will want to solve the problem as objectively as possible, and the press for such objectivity may result in new attempts to define and measure teacher effectiveness.

The creation of the team leader position will mean that some teachers will develop an ambition to fill the post yet fail in impressing others with their suitability. The development of such inappropriate ambitions means that a disposal problem is created; schools will have to find ways to deal with persons who believe that they deserve the position but do not get it. To retain such persons in small teams could, where their bitterness is strong, prove highly disruptive to team effectiveness. Law firms can solve the problem in part by finding high-paying positions for men they cannot promote to partner status. High-status universities, the most inclined to reject young academics for tenure positions, assist them in finding positions in lower status colleges. They can do this because a status order is openly recognized in higher education. But schools, in the main, are not openly graded and have little power to find nonschool employment for the disappointed employee. This problem, unless solved, could be potentially dangerous to team teaching, for if any considerable number of established teachers become disenchanted, the probability that it will succeed is sharply reduced.

One could list other questions about how the introduction of a teaching post of high prestige will influence teacher careers. Will it act to slow down geographical mobility by holding teachers in systems on the expectation of promotion? How will it affect the balance

[15] John Jay Corson, *Governance of Colleges and Universities*, New York, McGraw-Hill, 1960.

of influence in schools of married versus single women? Will enough married women invest themselves in team efforts to earn promotion, or will single women come to dominate through undivided commitment to their work? Will men stabilize their careers at the team leader position, and, if they do, how will principals and superintendents be recruited? These questions indicate that in the career area as well as elsewhere, considerable research will be needed to support an informed judgment on how team teaching affects schools, teachers, and students. The research needed, as is obvious, will have to include intensive studies of the selection system, the orientation system, and the promotion system for teachers. But we shall also need extensive studies which follow the careers of teachers through time, from one position or system to another. And, as is generally the case, we shall require inquiries into the conventional situation if we are to understand how team teaching changes the general shape of teaching and administrative careers.

It is obvious that this chapter is not a modest proposal. The logistics implied by the research suggestions are those of large-scale, expensive social inquiry. It cannot be undertaken by making a few observational forays into schools with team teaching but will require a somewhat elaborate structure of its own. A mechanism must be developed specifically for long-range research and assessment, and such a mechanism must provide both for the independence of the researchers and their complete access to schools. Those developing team teaching (teachers, administrators, applied researchers, etc.) will have neither the time nor the energy to address themselves to the broader questions raised in this chapter. Nor should the effectiveness of these creative persons be reduced by requiring them to divert attention from the manifold and pressing problems they must solve if team teaching is to work at all. It is easy to overlook the fact that the hundreds and thousands of small adjustments made by such persons in our schools actually amounts to the construction of a complex new social organization. The study of this organization and the longer range research program involved is a job for professional researchers who have neither a stake in nor a responsibility for the solution of the manifold operating problems.

But if our proposal is not modest, neither is team teaching. It is no minor technical change in schools, and we cannot conceal its potential ramifications by such innocuous phrases as "staff utilization" or "personnel policies." To spell out its potential influence on our society would require another chapter, but, since schools are crucial agencies in the socialization of successive generations, it seems obvious that basic changes in them are potentially basic changes in our way of life. Surely we ought not to make casual assessments of such innovations; our policy makers in education and the community at large should be provided with every shred of evidence we can assemble to ease their task. In short, the time to begin intensive research on team teaching is now.

Chapter 10

Research on Team Teaching

GLEN HEATHERS

School of Education, New York University

The development of team teaching, in common with the development of any other innovation in educational practice, should proceed through four interrelated phases: design, implementation, evaluation, and dissemination. The purposes of the design and implementation phases are to devise the plan and to engineer it to the point where it is ready for formal evaluation. The evaluation phase should determine outcomes of the plan in various types of school settings. If the results of the evaluation of the plan are favorable, the task of the dissemination phase is to foster the widespread adoption of the plan.

Currently, the development of team teaching is not following this four-phase progression. In many projects the design, implementation, and evaluation phases are being telescoped into one. The dissemination of team teaching is proceeding at a rapid pace even though the plans being employed are incompletely designed, have never been successfully implemented, and have not been properly evaluated.

To date, almost all of the research on team teaching has focused on its evaluation. But research is important in designing and implementing a new plan. Also, research can be of great value in planning and conducting programs to disseminate a plan. It is our contention that the development of team teaching is being impeded by a general failure to apply appropriate research strategies within each of the four phases.

The Place of Research in Designing Team Teaching Plans

Designing a new team teaching plan is a process of devising a model that interrelates features of the plan, aspects of the instructional situations where it is to be employed, and anticipated outcomes of the plan. The originators of a plan ordinarily begin by specifying certain purposes they hope the plan to achieve and then identify certain organizational arrangements that they believe may accomplish these purposes.

To make the position of teacher more attractive, some team teaching plans have been designed primarily to induce highly qualified teachers to remain in teaching and not to move into administrative positions in the schools or leave the educational profession. Teachers may like their jobs better if they are relieved of nonprofessional chores, or given salaries above the usual scale, or permitted to specialize in the curricular areas they most enjoy teaching, or provided with more time for study and lesson planning, or offered opportunities for teamwork in planning and conducting instruction, or given special status such as that of team leader. Other team teaching plans have been designed to improve the quality of instruction. In these plans, it is implied that instruction will be improved through such features as team planning, supervision of less experienced teachers by master teachers, flexible grouping, television instruction, and provisions for independent study.

Theory and research in psychology, sociology, cultural anthropology, and education can help designers decide on the features of a team teaching plan that may be expected to lead to desired outcomes. For this reason, a careful review of relevant theory and research should be undertaken, and a systematic effort should be made to apply the findings of this review to the design of the plan. Ideally, the plan's designers would find in the research literature established relationships between the variables employed in team teaching plans and various outcomes that are of concern to educators.

In point of fact, social science theory and research on such topics as motivation, interpersonal relations, group processes, and institutional behavior are in early stages of development and offer mainly general guidelines for the educational planner (see Chapter 3). Likewise, educational theory and research are not advanced to the point where there are more than a few tested relationships between organizational arrangements or instructional procedures and educational outcomes. Despite these limitations, the design of a team teaching plan should take account of related theory and research because research studies offer help in identifying relevant variables, because research literature offers ways of defining and measuring numerous variables that are involved in team teaching, and because research studies report some relationships that have been found among variables that are involved in any teaching-learning situation.

Market research would be of value in designing a team teaching plan. Any educational innovation is developed to serve practical ends. It is a product that is intended to be used. Should not the designers of team teaching plans conduct surveys of the potential market for such plans? A survey could give valuable information on educators' concerns about various outcomes that team teaching might accomplish, on attitudes of schoolmen toward team teaching or present conditions in the schools—space, equipment, personnel, etc.—that would be relevant to introducing team teaching, and on the willingness of school systems to make the various changes that would be needed to implement team teaching (see Chapter 8).

An example of a market survey in education is one conducted in 1959 by the Experimental Teaching Center at New York University to determine attitudes of school superintendents in the New York Metropolitan Area concerning various educational innovations.[1] One finding was that 25 percent of the respondents reported that they would be interested in adopting a team teaching plan. Among these, several indicated that they would need teachers having special qualifications before they would consider introducing team teaching.

The findings of a market survey on team teaching would not necessarily be binding on the designers of new plans. They might elect to design plans that were not intended primarily for today's market. In this case, there would remain the obligation of changing the market to win acceptance of the plans that were developed. This obligation

---

[1] Glen Heathers and Lou Kleinman, *School Superintendents' Views on Elementary Teachers Who Are Prepared to Specialize in One Curricular Area,* New York, Experimental Teaching Center, New York University, July 8, 1960.

might be held in abeyance until a plan had been designed, implemented, and evaluated and was ready for widespread dissemination.

Once the initial version of a team teaching plan has been developed, exploratory research should be undertaken as a basis for improving it. This critical part of the design phase is seldom neglected in industry or the military, where "tooling in" or "wind tunnel research" is standard practice. Educators, however, very often take an innovation directly from the drawing board into a full-scale attempt to implement and evaluate it. This is a very wasteful practice since a preliminary tryout of a new plan always exposes gaps or errors in it.

In the case of team teaching, it is perhaps fortunate that today's designers of plans can take advantage of previous experience with such plans either by reading the literature or by visiting various projects that are underway. It would be somewhat revolutionary, but perhaps wise, if the hundreds of persons currently engaged in projects were to take the position that almost everything accomplished thus far belongs in the design phase. We now have accumulated a considerable body of information about relevant plan variables, situational variables, and outcome variables. We have some tentative evidence as to relations among these variables. We know some things about what specifications a plan must include if its features are to be implemented effectively. In short, much exploratory research on team teaching has been accomplished, and it should now be possible for designers of plans to develop a few fairly sophisticated and detailed models.

What should the design of a team teaching plan contain? At the minimum it should state the outcomes the plan is intended to achieve, the plan's essential features, the school settings in which it is meant to be used, and a rationale linking features of the plan with its anticipated outcomes. Designing the plan in very general terms is not sufficient. Each of the above should be stated in detail.

Educators are interested in a great many outcomes that might result from team teaching plans. It is the obligation of the designers of a plan to specify what particular outcomes the plan is intended to achieve. Likewise the features of the plan should be carefully delineated. In some plans, for example, there is a hierarchical team structure. In these plans it is essential not only to describe the various team roles, but also to specify the formal working relationships that team members should have with one another. Some plans make provisions for teacher specialization and flexible grouping. The design of these plans should be specific as to what sorts of specializations are required and what grouping patterns are to be used. Many descriptions of team teaching plans do not indicate the types of school situations for which the particular plan was designed. Is the plan meant for students in the primary years of schooling, in the intermediate years of the elementary school, in junior high school, in senior high school, or in college? Is the plan suitable for small schools as well as large?

The statement of rationale is an area of weakness in most published reports on team teaching plans. The reader continually encounters unsupported assertions that a given feature of a team teaching plan will improve the quality of instruction. The hazards of this sort of reasoning have been pointed out by Drummond.[2] If one follows his assumption that high-quality learning requires high interaction between teacher and student or among students, it may not follow that large-group instruction under highly qualified teachers will improve learning. The instructor may indeed have a carefully prepared lesson and may have great skill in lecturing. However, the large group session may work to the disadvantage of the individual student because the material has not been adapted to his particular learning needs and because he has only limited opportunities to discuss the material with the teacher or with other students. Drummond offers a number of other valuable illustrations of problems encountered when one assumes that some feature of a plan will lead to a particular outcome.

The design of a plan sets the stage for implementing and evaluating it. For this reason it is important to consider how detailed the specifications for each feature of the plan should be. If the requirements of the plan are made highly specific, the plan probably cannot be implemented in many school situations. Because of differences from one school to another, it may be essential that the design of the plan allow for a certain amount of variability in the way each of its features is placed into operation. This sort of variation applies to size of team, areas of teacher specialization, and specific patterns of

[2] Harold D. Drummond, "Team Teaching: An Assessment," *Educaional Leadership*, vol. XIX, December, 1961, pp. 160–165.

grouping for instruction. However, for purposes of research on team teaching, it seems clear that the design of the plan should be as detailed as practicable, and school systems should be given as few options as possible with regard to implementing its feature. Thus the critical projects on implementing and evaluating the plan should be conducted in school systems that provide situations that come as close as possible to meeting the ideal requirements of the plan. Normally these will be school systems having a high level of readiness to adapt their programs to suit the requirements of the plan. It may prove desirable to take account of certain differences in school settings by designing two or more versions of the team teaching plan.

Another question about the design of a plan is to what extent it should include strategies for implementing it. It does seem desirable that these procedures be spelled out in detail prior to formal efforts to implement and evaluate the plan. Otherwise, there is the likelihood that some features of the plan either will not be fully implemented or will be implemented in different ways in different schools that are involved in research projects. If this reasoning is correct, the design of the plan should include strategies for setting up teaching teams, conducting team planning, reorganizing curricular materials and testing programs, and conducting instruction with flexible grouping (see Chapter 5).

An examination of published reports of designs for team teaching plans reveals that few of these satisfy the requirements that have been stated above for describing the plan or for outlining procedures to be used in implementing it. One of the most detailed designs is that offered in a report on the Norwalk Plan of Team Teaching.[3] This design, entitled "Models for Team Teaching," is 19 pages in length. It lists the essential characteristics of the plan, states its general purposes, specifies the team structure and the roles of team members, describes the interrelationships among team members, and outlines the steps to be taken in planning and implementing the instructional program. The model says little about how the program is to be placed in operation. It lacks a clear statement of rationale linking the plan's features with its intended outcomes. Indeed, the

[3] *The Norwalk Plan of Team Teaching, Third Report*, Norwalk, Conn., The Norwalk Board of Education, 1961, pp. 15–33.

intended outcomes that have to do with the quality of instruction are stated in highly general terms. Despite these limitations, the Norwalk report comes closer to giving a full design statement than any other report that has come to the writer's attention.

Research Needed on Implementing Team Teaching Plans

In his analysis of educational change programs, Brickell identified just three phases: design, evaluation, and dissemination.[4] He did not consider implementation to be a distinct phase and evidently considered it to be a part of the design or the evaluation phase. Our reason for treating implementation as a phase in its own right is that a plan cannot be evaluated until the problems of implementing it have been solved. A good case can be made for the position that none of the organizational plans currently being tested in America's schools has yet been fully implemented in any locality. This applies to nongraded schools, to the Stoddard dual progress plan, and to the several team teaching plans. True, the basic organizational structures of these plans frequently have been placed in effect, though even in this respect there are many variations in the actual organizational arrangements that have been made when introducing a given plan within different local settings. Often the plan has been modified to fit the school, rather than the school being modified to fit the plan.

In implementing a plan, research is needed to develop instruments and procedures that measure the extent to which each feature of the plan has been placed in effect. Such measures constitute the operational definition of the plan. They are needed from the outset of the implementation study in order to give it direction. These measures should cover both structural and functional components of the plan—qualifications, positions, and role definitions of team members; methods of communicating information about students; procedures in lesson planning, scheduling, and grouping; utilization of space and equipment; and so on. Research skills in testing, inter-

[4] Henry M. Brickell, *Organizing New York State for Educational Change*, Albany, The University of the State of New York, The State Education Department, December, 1961.

viewing, rating, and observing are required to develop these measures.

The choice of schools where the plan is to be implemented should be made with great care. If different versions of the plan or different approaches to its implementation are to be compared, it is essential that the schools assigned to the different treatments be as nearly similar as possible. If the purpose of the implementation study is to determine how effectively the plan can be implemented in different types of settings, schools should be selected to represent the types of setting desired. Since the personnel and funds for conducting an implementation study are always limited, it usually is desirable to concentrate on one or two settings to insure a thorough study.

A careful field survey should be conducted as a basis for selecting the school to be included in the implementation study and as an aid in planning the study. The survey should provide answers to such questions as these: Is the school setting appropriate for trying the plan? What students and staff would be involved? What changes in personnel, scheduling, grouping, space, equipment, curriculum, and tests are required? Is there resistance to making the changes needed? In conducting such a field survey, observations, interviews, and questionnaires are appropriate. Katz gives a useful list of variables to take into account in studying a social organization and offers a list of ten procedures that should be employed in scouting the local situation.[5]

The major task during the implementation phase is that of conducting the change process that places the plan in operation. This process of installing an organizational plan takes years to complete. It begins with the decision to implement the plan in a given school system. It includes forming the project staff, preparing a general plan for conducting the local change program, preparing needed materials, establishing and training the teaching teams, installing the organizational features of the new plan, and solving the many problems that are involved in teamwork in the conduct of instruction.

Research in group dynamics, particularly action research in community or institutional settings, offers valuable guidelines for con-

[5] Daniel Katz, "Field Studies," in Leon Festinger and Daniel Katz, eds., *Research Methods in the Behavioral Sciences*, New York, Dryden, 1953.

ducting change programs.[6] Research in these areas shows the desirability of having voluntary participation in change programs and of involving participants as fully as practicable in all phases of the program from initial planning through final evaluation. Also, research in group dynamics offers numerous valuable findings with respect to the role and behavior of effective leaders of change programs.

Unfortunately, research on small teams has not advanced to the point where it offers much guidance for establishing teaching teams or conducting team teaching. Bray, in an illuminating survey of theory and research in relation to team functions with special reference to the military, points out that there is a dearth of sound research on "the analysis and measurement of team performance, team composition and organization, and team training."[7] He points out that measures of team effectiveness, based on an adequate classification of team tasks, are urgently needed. Also, he notes that the research evidence at hand does not clarify to what extent team effectiveness depends on the individual competencies of team members and to what extent on the combination of persons making up the team or on the structure of the team.

Bray warns that research on team functioning must also take into account the special nature of the conditions under which the team performs. "It may also be necessary, if prediction of team performance in real situations is the ultimate goal, to conduct basic research under the usual conditions of 'noise' in the system and usual variability of incentives for effective teamwork."[8] In other words, much of the research needed must be performed with teaching teams at work in the schools, since findings of studies with other types of teams in other types of situations may not be fully applicable to teaching teams.

[6] Dorwin Cartwright and Alvin Zander, eds., *Group Dynamics Research and Theory*, 2nd ed., Evanston, Ill., Harper & Row, 1960. Marie Jahoda, Morton Deutsch, and Stuart W. Cook, *Research Methods in Social Relations*, 2 vols., New York, Holt, 1951. Ronald Lippitt, *et al.*, *The Dynamics of Planned Change*, New York, Harcourt, Brace & World, 1958. Herbert A. Thelen, *Dynamics of Groups at Work*, Chicago, University of Chicago Press, 1954.

[7] Charles W. Bray, "Toward a Technology of Human Behavior for Defense Use," *American Psychologist*, vol. XVII, August, 1962, pp. 534–536.

[8] *Ibid.*, p. 536.

Research on the process of implementing a team teaching plan will normally employ case-study methods that call for gathering data continuously on each aspect of the process, taking stock of progress made in implementing features of the plan, diagnosing problems encountered, devising ways of solving problems, and gathering data on the effectiveness of solutions that are tried. The outcome of this research process should be a set of guidelines or principles for implementing the plan. These guidelines, often tentative and subject to change on the basis of further experiences with implementing the plan, would cover the general strategies for enlisting the cooperation of the school's personnel, organizing teacher teams, establishing team processes, training teacher teams, utilizing learning materials and equipment, and articulating teacher teams with the over-all program of the school or the school district.

The assessment of implementation calls for employing the measures based on operationalized definitions of the plan's features that were referred to earlier. It is difficult to measure the degree to which certain features of a plan have been placed in effect. Organizational features such as size of team, assignment of team members, frequency of team conferences, grouping of students, and use of space and equipment are relatively easy to measure. But accurate measurements of team functioning in planning and conducting instruction are difficult to obtain. Reports by team members are apt to be incomplete and unreliable. Quantitative aspects of teamwork that are readily measured are apt to be less significant than qualitative aspects that are hard to measure.

The final task in the implementation phase of developing a team teaching plan is to utilize what was learned in the formal field tryout as a basis for improving the statement of the plan's design. The implementation study might lead to modifying some features of the design of the plan. The major contribution of the implementation study would be in revealing the specific procedures that are needed to accomplish full implementation of the plan.

Requirements for Evaluating a Team Teaching Plan

Five bases for evaluating a team teaching plan have been employed at one time or another by educators. Two of these do not require measuring outcomes of the plan, and a third measures certain side effects that may occur when a plan is introduced rather than outcomes directly related to features of the plan.

1. A team teaching plan may be evaluated simply by deciding that it introduces certain desired features into the school's program. Many educators appear to believe that a sufficient reason for adopting a team teaching plan is that it provides for increased cooperation among teachers, or frees teachers from nonprofessional chores, or provides for flexible grouping. Accepting a plan at face value rests on the faith that its features will lead to desirable outcomes. Logically, educators should demand evidence that this faith is justified. In fact, many do not wait for such evidence before adopting a plan.

2. An important basis for evaluating a plan is whether or not it is workable in given types of school situations. Regardless of its merits in theory, a plan that cannot be implemented successfully, or that is excessively difficult to implement, is not a good plan. Often educators decide whether or not to adopt an organizational plan on the basis of how difficult or costly it is to install and operate, without waiting for evidence as to whether its outcomes justify the burdens of implementing it. Determining a plan's workability is a purpose of the implementation phase as discussed in the previous section of this chapter. If its designers retain their faith in a plan they have been unable to implement fully, they may elect to develop new approaches to its implementation with the hope that they will prove to be successful.

3. Some leaders of educational reform evaluate organizational plans by the extent to which they stimulate a climate of change in the schools. This may seem to be a trivial basis for evaluating a plan, but it has been advocated by educators who believe that it is important for America's schools to break out of established ways and to try new approaches to instruction. "Focus on change" is indeed a slogan of today's reform movement in education. Team teaching, in common with other new plans for organizing instruction, does seem to satisfy the criterion of inducing many changes in a school's program. School systems that introduce team teaching usually find themselves re-examining almost every aspect of the educational program and at least contemplating changes in educational goals, cur-

ricula, grouping procedures, uses of space and equipment, and teacher education.

4. Almost everyone would agree that a definitive evaluation of a team teaching plan requires meauring its outcomes. Most of the formal evaluation studies have compared outcomes of team teaching with outcomes of traditional organizational plans, usually the self-contained classroom in the elementary school or the conventional departmentalized plan in the junior and senior high schools. The majority of these studies have used as criteria of outcome the attitudes of students, parents, and teachers toward the plans, measures of sudents' achievements in the plans being compared, and measures of students' personal-social adjustment in the two plans. Other criteria of outcome that are used less frequently are instructional costs, turnover of personnel, and in-service education of teachers.

5. There is a major weakness in evaluating a team teaching plan by comparing its outcomes with those obtained in another organizational plan; a comparative study does not tell how *well* team teaching accomplishes any given outcome. Educators should not be satisfied to learn that team teaching accomplishes a given outcome as well as a traditional plan, or even that it accomplishes that outcome somewhat better. Many educational outcomes are accomplished poorly at present. The critical question is: How well does team teaching accomplish the essential objectives of the educational program? In order to answer this question, standards must be set, and the outcomes of team teaching judged against these standards. It is remarkable how seldom educators employ well-defined standards in evaluating educational innovations. If team teaching is to have a place in school programs that have been designed specifically to achieve excellence in education, evaluations of team teaching must be made in terms of standards of excellence.

There are several fundamental requirements that should be satisfied in any studies that evaluate team teaching plans in terms of their outcomes, whether these studies use comparative or absolute standards. These requirements have been outlined by Kaya in her analysis of problems in evaluating educational plans.[9] Two require-

[9] Esin Kaya, "Problems in Evaluating Educational Plans in the School Setting," *The Journal of Educational Sociology*, vol. XXXIV, April, 1961, pp. 355–359.

ments are that all variables involved in the study be operationally defined and that appropriate measures of each of these variables be selected or developed. As Kaya points out, educators often fail to define variables operationally. For example, they may speak of a team teaching plan or of the self-contained classroom plan as though it were an entity rather than specifying its features in ways that can lead to accurate measurement. Also, they often do not give operational definitons of outcome variables. Creative thinking, critical thinking, and self-instruction often are not included in lists of learning outcomes and seldom are measured in today's achievement tests. In his recent review of the progress of educational testing, Chester Harris noted that achievement-test development was not giving attention to defining achievement "except in the obvious manner of labeling content."[10] He called attention especially to a failure to develop tests of students' problem-solving strategies.

The research design for an evaluative study must satisfy a number of requirements. The list of outcome variables selected for measurement should include not only those outcomes the plan was especially designed to achieve. Numerous outcomes that are of concern to educators may be affected by the plan—costs, teacher turnover, student adjustment, etc. One value of survey studies during the design or implementation phases is that they call attention to certain outcome variables that should be included in evaluation studies.

The study design should include an explicit and detailed statement of the rationale that relates features of the plan to various potential outcomes. The rationale must take into account certain variables in the school situation that are likely to interact with features of the plan in determining outcomes. A well-formulated rationale does more than offer a theoretical justification for predicted outcomes. Also, developing such a rationale always strengthens the design of a study by calling attention to situational or outcome variables that had not been thought of previously and that must be considered in the study design.

One requirement for an evaluative study that is often ignored is that it include measures of the actual implementation of each feature

---

[10] Chester W. Harris, "Review of This Issue," *Review of Educational Research*, vol. XXXII, February, 1962, p. 105.

of the plan or plans being evaluated. Many evaluative studies in education fail to include such measures. Instead, reports of these studies merely describe the general features of the plan and proceed on the asumption that they have all been fully implemented. In actuality, any feature of a team teaching plan, or of a self-contained-classroom plan, is seldom implemented to the same degree and in the same way in different schools. Differences in outcomes obtained in various tests of a plan may very well be due to differences in its implementation.

Numerous evaluative studies of team teaching employ a control group design in comparing a team teaching plan with another organizational plan. As Kaya points out, there are serious difficulties that must be surmounted in designing an evaluation using a control group.[11] Matching two schools or two school systems is exceedingly difficult because of the many variables involved. It is not enough that the schools be comparable in such variables as mean IQ of students, per-pupil costs, socioeconomic and educational levels of parents, or teachers' education and experience. One school may have superior facilities, a principal with superior administrative skills, or better morale in its professional staff. If the curricular materials and instructional methods in the two schools differ markedly, it may be impossible to obtain a meaningful comparison of students' achievements in the two settings. When a control group is used, it is necessary to include a large number of schools or school systems in both experimental and control groups. Otherwise adequate control of situational variables cannot be achieved. It is unfortunate that many evaluative studies in education ignore these difficulties in establishing a control group and, therefore, yield comparative data that cannot be interpreted.

Often a pretest-posttest study design should be employed in comparing a new organizational plan with the plan that was previously employed. This type of design has the advantage of controlling many situational variables that are very hard to take into account in a control group. A pretest-posttest study requires that all of the variables involved be measured prior to the introduction of the new plan and then measured again under the new plan. If it is desired, periodic measurements may be taken during the course of the study

[11] Kaya, *op. cit.*, pp. 357–358.

to obtain evidence on the process of implementing the new plan. During the course of a pretest-posttest study it is important that measures be obtained of changes in situational variables that might account for some of the outcomes obtained under the new plan. For example, if new curricular materials are introduced, or if greater use is made of television and programed learning than under the previous organizational plan, these changes might be responsible for differences in learning outcomes under the two plans that are being compared.

In evaluating any educational innovation, the halo effect must be considered. Perhaps the outcomes obtained in a test of the innovation result from its being different from established practice and from the fact that it attracts special attention. It is probable that the strength of the halo effect associated with team teaching declines during the several-year duration of an evaluative study. Also, as team teaching becomes a more familiar practice in American schools, the halo effect should weaken. When evaluative studies compare team teaching with some other organizational plan, every effort should be made to equate the amounts of attention paid to the plans being compared. It must be recognized that the influence of the halo effect on the outcomes of a plan cannot be measured accurately. In interpreting results from comparisons of the old and the new in education, one must always hold in mind the possibility that the halo effect is partially responsible for those results.

Research Needed on Disseminating Team Teaching Plans

In his study of educational change in New York State, Brickell conducted a survey of the process of change in local schools.[12] His findings may be summarized as follows: pressures for change normally come from outside the educational profession; local administrators usually are the ones who introduce new instructional programs; an administrator's decision to adopt a new program is influenced most directly by observing a program in successful operation in a school very similar to his own; and the judgment that a program is successful usually is based mainly on whether students "react with interest or enthusiasm" to the program.

[12] Brickell, *op. cit.*, pp. 11–62.

If Brickell's findings give a fair picture of the present bases for adopting new programs, there is serious need for improving the process of disseminating educational innovations. Research is needed to develop and test dissemination procedures. One important area for research is on training local school personnel in ways of evaluating educational programs. If schools continue to judge programs largely on the basis of whether students enjoy them, sophisticated evaluative studies that measure such outcomes as students' achievement of operationally defined learning goals will have little influence on educational change.

Perhaps the reason that school administrators tend to judge the success of programs chiefly on students' reactions is that research has not provided the information needed to evaluate them on other bases. Surveys might reveal that administrators fail to take cognizance of research findings mainly because those findings are not presented to them in usable form. If this were found to be true, various methods of communicating research information to school leaders should be tried.

Many times a program is adopted widely before it has been properly developed and tested. Certainly this has been the case with team teaching plans. Research is needed to determine how often such adoptions are due to urgent pressures to copy changes made elsewhere, the conviction that the program has proven its worth, or the belief that the best way to judge a program's values for one's school is through a local tryout. Studies also are needed of the consequences of adopting partially developed programs. A desirable consequence would be that a school's experience with a program prepared it to incorporate improvements as research made them available. An undesirable consequence would be that difficulties in implementing the program led a school to abandon it before the needed research had been completed.

Brickell has proposed that the New York State Education Department conduct the dissemination of tested innovations on a statewide basis.[13] He has recommended that the dissemination process should be delayed until an innovation has been fully evaluated in a variety of school settings. At this point, all school districts in a region would be required to participate in a School Development

[13] *Ibid.*, pp. 67–68, 85–89.

Unit that they would finance and administer. Units would demonstrate the innovation "with all the types of students and in all the types of school settings" where it had proven to be effective. Further, each unit would train teachers throughout the region in employing the innovation until such time as nearby colleges and universities could take over the training function. This dissemination program would require local school districts to surrender considerable autonomy. Also it would require the state education department both to conduct large-scale evaluations of any innovations that held promise of improving education and to take leadership in massive dissemination programs. It appears very unlikely that these requirements could be met at this time.

The usual approaches to disseminating educational innovations are much more informal and much less massive than Brickell's proposal. The most common approach is for local school leaders to adopt an innovation after reading about it and after visting schools where it is in operation. Another approach is for the agencies that develop and evaluate an innovation to help local schools install it. Still another approach is for these agencies to conduct special training programs at a central location and invite representatives from different school districts to take part. Since team teaching is being disseminated in all of these ways, studies of these various approaches should be undertaken to determine their relative advantages and disadvantages.

Research Findings on Team Teaching

The preceding sections of this chapter have outlined research problems and approaches in relation to four phases in developing a team teaching plan—design, implementation, evaluation, and dissemination. The purpose of this section is to present a review of research studies of team teaching as reported in publications. What are representative findings in these studies? How much reliance can be placed on these findings in view of the research methodologies employed? What significance have these findings for making policy decisions in regard to local adoptions of team teaching plans?

Reviewing published reports on team teaching projects is a frustrating experience. Only a few reports present specific findings, and these do not give sufficient details about research methods to permit an adequate appraisal of the studies. Previous reviews of research on team teaching have been confined to listing major findings without evaluating the research methods employed. Trump offers on one page a list of 17 tentative findings of the Experimental Study of the Utilization of the Staff in the Secondary School.[14] The summaries of findings in the reviews by Cunningham and by Drummond each occupies less than a page.[15] The writer has not located any published reports of research studies on the design, implementation, or dissemination phases. True, the literature contains reported findings on numerous aspects of implementing team teaching, but these usually are summary statements without supporting data. The only research reports worthy of the name are accounts of evaluation studies dealing with certain outcomes of team teaching.

Findings Related to Implementing Team Teaching

Doubtless much has been learned about implementing team teaching in the hundreds of projects that are underway across the country. Unfortunately, very little of this knowledge has yet appeared in published reports. The reviewer is limited to culling from the literature various statements about progress and problems in the implementation process and to pointing out the sorts of findings that educators are awaiting.

Are team teaching plans workable in today's schools? In other words, can the features of these plans be implemented successfully? Certainly the general framework of team teaching plans can be placed in operation. Otherwise projects involving these plans would not survive year after year, and the team pattern would not spread throughout a school system as is happening at Norwalk, Connecticut, and in other localities. There are viable teams ranging in size from two to as many as a dozen members. Various forms of teacher specialization and flexible grouping are in operation. Many teams employ non professional aides, teacher interns, or part-time teachers. Hierarchical structures involving team leaders and several categories

[14] J. Lloyd Trump, "Summary and Some Findings," *NASSP Bulletin,* vol. XLIII, January, 1959, p. 285.
[15] Luvern L. Cunningham, "Team Teaching: Where Do We Stand?" *Administrator's Notebook,* vol. VIII, April, 1960. Drummond, *op. cit.,* p. 162.

of teachers and aides have been implemented. Some teams have salary schedules that offer special increments to high-status members.

Aside from reporting operational features of plans, the literature has little to say about how successfully those features have been implemented. In his review of early findings of projects in secondary schools, Trump claimed that flexible scheduling and the use of carefully selected and trained subprofessional persons had been successful.[16] Also he claimed that class size had been shown to bear little relationship to student achievement. This last claim must be received with healthy skepticism. When the lecture method is used, and when students are grouped on the same bases in large and small classes, it is reasonable that class size would bear little relation to the students' achievement. However, small classes should clearly be advantageous when the learning goals call for differentiating students' learning experiences, for class discussion, or for individual work that is guided by the teacher. The finding Trump reports probably results from comparing superior large-group instruction with faulty small-group instruction and from using standardized achievement tests that do a poor job of measuring important aspects of learning.

A number of problems encountered in implementing team teaching plans have been mentioned in the literature. Numerous reports point out that some teachers are unsuited for team teaching but do not specify what makes them so. Other reports note difficulties in identifying effective team leaders. In one project at least it was found that team teaching greatly increased the time required for planning and coordination.[17] This may be a desirable thing, but it does raise a problem requiring solution. A common finding is that teachers work harder in team teaching plans than in conventional plans. Whether this should be attributed to team teaching or to the process of changing from one plan to another has not been determined.

What effects has team teaching on the conduct of administrative and instructional functions that are not specifically part of the plan

[16] Trump, *op. cit.*, p. 285.

[17] Robert O. Hahn, Jack Nelson, and Getrude Robinson, "Team Teaching: A Second Look," *Journal of Teacher Education*, vol. XII, December, 1961, pp. 508–510.

being implemented? A useful list of such functions may be found in an article by Brownell and Taylor under the heading of hypothetical advantages of team teaching.[18] Almost all of these functions actually can be performed better with team teaching—if the claims made in various reports of team teaching projects are to be trusted. It is claimed that team teaching gives teachers more time for planning, makes better provisions for curriculum development, makes it easier to regroup students frequently, makes it easier for principals to communicate with teachers, and makes better provisions for substitute teaching. Also it is claimed that team teaching strengthens in-service teacher education and facilitates supervision of student teachers.

A number of improvements in instructional procedures have been said to result from teamwork and flexible grouping. Conducting field trips is easier. Sequencing the student's program from year to year is more manageable. Some reports claim that improved correlation of subject matter results from team teaching and that guidance functions are conducted better because of more sharing of information about students. However, other reports claim that the correlation of subject matter and the conduct of guidance functions are performed better in the self-contained classroom. Evidently, more and better research is needed to resolve these conflicting claims.

In a previous section of this chapter it was stated that one basis for evaluating a new organizational plan is the extent to which it stimulates various associated changes in a school's program. Numerous reports on team teaching projects point out that such changes have occurred, particularly in curricular sequences and in the uses of new instructional materials and devices. For example, a report on the Norwalk Plan claims that team teaching has been a catalytic agent for improvements in curricula, audio-visual materials, instructional techniques, and teacher cooperation.[19] These improvements have been system-wide, extending beyond the boundaries of the team teaching program. Obviously, it is not possible to determine to what extent such changes should be attributed to team teaching,

[18] John A. Brownell and Harris A. Taylor, "Theoretical Perspectives for Teaching Teams," *Phi Delta Kappan,* vol. XVIII, January, 1962, pp. 150–157.
[19] *The Norwalk Plan of Team Teaching, Third Report, op. cit.,* p. 7.

as such, rather than to the fact that the school system has become engaged in systematic efforts to improve instruction.

This brief review of what has been reported about implementing team teaching has been more a survey of research needs than of research findings. The literature gives no indication that the types of implementation studies listed by the Commission on the Experimental Study of the Utilization of the Staff in the Secondary School have been conducted.[20] The school administrator who seeks guidance in implementing team teaching will receive little help from the research findings reported thus far. He still must rely mainly on his own judgment, supported by observations of team teaching in action and by advice from leaders of projects. He can turn, with some profit, to a few published reports offering suggestions on implementation that digest the experience of project leaders. One example is the report of the summer-school project at Concord, California, that contains a chapter entitled "Suggested Guidelines for Establishing a Team Teaching Program."[21] Another example is the model for team teaching in the Norwalk Plan that was referred to earlier.[22] This model was developed in part from data in teachers' diaries.

Student Achievement with Team Teaching

One major purpose of most team teaching projects is to improve the quality of instruction. It appears that this purpose has not yet been achieved, judging from published reports. The conclusion Drummond reached in 1961 still holds true: "Students do as well or perhaps a little better on standardized tests when taught by teaching teams of the various types described."[23] Drummond points out that differences found between team teaching and a conventional plan of organization usually are not statistically significant. It also is important to note that the studies reported usually have lacked adequate controls.

A representative report is provided by the project in Jefferson

---

[20] Trump, *op. cit.*, pp. 285–290.
[21] Harvey R. Wall and Robert W. Reasoner, *Team Teaching*, Concord, Calif., Mt. Diablo Unified School District, 1962, pp. 118–123.
[22] *The Norwalk Plan of Team Teaching, Third Report, op. cit.*, pp. 15–33.
[23] Drummond, *op. cit.*, p. 162.

County, Colorado.[24] During 1959–1960, about 1500 students in seven high schools were taught by three-teacher teams, with flexible grouping, in the areas of English, mathematics, science, history, and typing. Appropriate subtests from the Iowa Tests of Educational Development were used to compare achievement of experimental and control groups. The control groups were formed by taking students from the same grade in the same district and by attempting to control school size and the training and experience of teachers. Using the analysis of covariance, no statistically significant differences in achievement between experimental and control groups were found in any subject except English. With English III, team teaching proved superior at the .05 level of confidence. With English II, on the other hand, the conventional plan of organization proved superior at the .05 level of confidence. How can this rather startling reversal be explained? It is highly unlikely that it can be due to differences in the nature of English II and English III. One possibility is that team teaching was exceptionally well conducted with English III and poorly conducted with English II. The fact that the report does not tell how the two plans being compared were implemented prevents checking on this interpretation. Another likely interpretation is that controls for such factors as age, IQ, socioeconomic background, and teacher competencies were not adequate. The report does not present data on how well these or other factors were controlled.

A study of student achievement in the Norwalk Plan provides representative findings on the outcomes of team teaching in the elementary school. The report for the second year of the plan at Norwalk, 1959–1960, involves seven three-teacher teams, each having a group of 75–90 students from one of Grades 2 to 6.[25] Four of the seven teams taught the same groups as in 1958–1959 but at the next higher grade level. For these groups, progress was reported for the two-year span. No control groups were employed in the data analysis. Grade equivalent gains in Stanford Achievement Tests

[24] Robert H. Johnson, M. Delbert Lobb, and Lloyd G. Swenson, "An Extensive Study of Team Teaching and Schedule Modification in Jefferson County, Colorado, School District R-1." *NASSP Bulletin,* vol. XLIV, January, 1960, pp. 79–93.

[25] *The Norwalk Plan: A Two-Year Study,* Norwalk, Conn., The Norwalk Board of Education, September, 1960.

were computed for each team and were compared with gains according to national norms for comparable periods of schooling. Out of 48 instances of comparing team teaching results with national norms, gains with team teaching equaled or exceeded the norms in 39 instances. The fault with this analysis is that it is not based on Norwalk norms for the self-contained classroom. It is to be expected that Norwalk would exceed the national norms under any plan of organization because this community is well above the national average in socioeconomic level, education of parents, and provisions for schooling. We learn very little about the merits of team teaching when we are told that with team teaching Norwalk still exceeds the national norms in learning progress.

In a report on the third year of the Norwalk Plan (1960–1961), achievement-test results are evaluated with the use of control groups.[26] Control groups were set up by the matched-pairs technique on the basis of grade level and IQ. No consistent superiority was found for either team teaching or the self-contained classroom. Out of 194 comparisons involving different subtests and different groups of students, 90 favored team teaching while 114 favored the self-contained classroom. Few of the comparisons yielded statistically significant differences. Team teaching showed to advantage particularly in the areas of reading and spelling. The self-contained classroom held the advantage in language and in arithmetic skills and problem solving. In a special spelling test, team teaching groups held a marked advantage in Grade 5, while groups in the self-contained classroom did at least as well as team teaching groups in Grade 6. These divergent results suggest that the implementation of team teaching was uneven from subject to subject and from grade to grade. The absence of data on how the plans under comparison were implemented from group to group prevents determining the correctness of such an interpretation. While it appears that the control groups in this study were carefully drawn, it would have been desirable for the report to include tabular data on how well the experimental and control groups were matched in age, IQ, socioeconomic level, and teacher competencies.

The Jefferson County and Norwalk project reports were selected as examples because they provide more data on student achieve-

[26] *The Norwalk Plan of Team Teaching, Third Report, op. cit.*, pp. 8–10.

ment than other reports and because they illustrate some recurrent problems of research design and data interpretation. Rather than cite other reports, the writer offers his general observations about the approaches that have been used in evaluating student achievement in team teaching.

1. Data on student achievement are limited to what is measured by standardized achievement tests. Such tests stress tool skills, vocabulary, and information, and slight or ignore numerous important learning outcomes including those related to "the process goals of education" that are described in Chapter 11. In consequence, the research reports give no evidence on whether or not team teaching produces gains with respect to learning critical thinking, creativity, competencies in inquiry, or self-instruction.

2. The studies reported in the literature fail to examine whether team teaching has different effects on the achievement of students of different ability levels. One plausible result would be for team teaching to be most effective with high-ability students because these students are best equipped for learning in a variety of settings. It also is plausible that team teaching would be most effective with low-ability students on the assumption that it offers these students special opporunities for learning in small-group and tutorial settings.

3. None of the project reports gives data on the features of team teaching, or of the plan with which it is compared, *as implemented.* The plans are treated as entities, and the reader is expected to assume that their features have been placed in operation fully rather than being implemented to different degrees and in different ways in particular school settings. This failure to measure the independent variables in a study is a fundamental error in research. How can one relate measures of student achievement (the dependent variables) to features of team teaching (the independent variables) if no measures are taken of how team teaching is implemented?

4. None of the research reports gives satisfactory evidence that situational variables were controlled. Frequently, the reports state which variables were placed under control, but rarely do they contain any data that would help the reader judge how well these controls were accomplished.

5. The lack of data on the implementation of plan variables and

on the adequacy of controls prevents determining why, in a given study, team teaching may appear to be advantageous with certain subjects or certain grade levels and not with others.

6. None of the research studies reported in the literature has been designed to answer questions about the contributions that separate features of team teaching plans make toward learning outcomes. What is required is systematic variation of the major features of plans to determine the extent to which specialist teaching, flexible grouping, nongraded advancement, the use of nonprofessional aides, or teamwork is responsible for whatever results are obtained. Also, studies are needed that systematically vary such features as team size and team organization.

7. Not one of the research studies that have been reported has evaluated team teaching with the use of standards of student achievement related to excellence. In every study, achievement was measured either in relation to national norms or to local norms based on a conventional plan of organization for instruction. This is less a criticism of these research studies than of the educational profession in general since, at this time, well-formulated standards of educational excellence do not exist.

What guidance can the school administrator receive from published reports of student achievement with team teaching? The reports offer assurance that team teaching does at least as well as conventional plans with respect to the learning outcomes measured by standardized tests. This assurance may make the administrator feel free to experiment with team teaching. Also, if an administrator is interested in finding a way of dealing with a teacher shortage and discovers that team teaching has value in this regard, he may decide to adopt this plan with the assurance that the gains made in relation to teaching personnel are not offset by losses in student achievement. However, if the administrator is concerned about learning goals that are not measured by standardized tests, he may demand further evidence before judging that team teaching has no deleterious effects on students' learning.

If the administrator desires to improve the quality of education, he will probably interpret the research findings as demonstrating that merely installing the organizational features of team teaching is not sufficient to increase student achievement. Associated changes in curriculum, learning materials and equipment, and teacher education probably are essential if team teaching is to foster student learning.

Perhaps the school administrator will elect to suspend judgment because team teaching is not sufficiently developed to permit determining what effects it will have on learning. Doubtless it is true that a great many valuable findings of current research projects have not yet reached publication. Certainly this is the case with the project in Lexington, Massachusetts. Informal reports of this project contain important findings both on the implementation of the Lexington Plan and on its learning outcomes. It is evident that it takes a school system several years to develop a team teaching program to the point where its potential outcomes can be realized. Five years is a short time for this process to be accomplished, and only a few projects, as of 1963, have been in operation that long.

Student Adjustment under Team Teaching

Educators who are concerned about the effects of team teaching on students' personal-social adjustment may be reassured by the fact that research studies have in no instance found evidence that team teaching harms students in this respect. In fact, some studies have found that, with some indicators of adjustment, team teaching holds a distinct advantage over conventional organizational plans. Nearly all of the published data on student adjustment are from elementary schools. This is understandable since educators are most concerned about the effects on student adjustment that may result if elementary schools depart from the self-contained classroom.

The published reports on student adjustment are limited in value because they depend on student responses to standardized adjustment inventories and to questionnaires on attitudes about team teaching. Also, it is unfortunate that the data in the reports are not broken down by ability group, and only one report was found that gives attention to students with special problems of adjustment.

Two reports give results with the California Test of Personality. The project at Oceano, California, employed teams of two or three teachers in second, fourth, and sixth grades.[27] Teacher specialization

[27] Andrew S. Adams, "Operation Co-Teaching. Dateline: Oceano, California," *The Elementary School Journal*, vol. LXII, January, 1962, pp. 203–212.

and flexible grouping were used. No major changes in adjustment scores were found at any of the three grade levels when fall and spring testings were compared. A weakness of the Oceano study was that no control groups were used. The project at San Jose, California, employed two-teacher teams in Grades 4, 5, and 6.[28] Teacher specialization and flexible grouping were practiced. At each of the three grade levels, a control group was set up that was equated in IQ with the experimental group. Changes in adjustment scores between fall and spring testings were slight, and no significant differences were found between experimental and control groups. The differences favored the experimental groups in Grades 4 and 5, while the scores of the control group were slightly more favorable in Grade 6.

A report on the Norwalk Plan compares scores on the California Aspects of Personality test for students under team teaching who were tested in the spring of 1960 and the spring of 1961.[29] Statistically significant gains (Chi-square test) were found with both boys and girls in Personal Adjustment and in Total Adjustment, but not in Social Adjustment. Gains for the boys were significant at the .05 level while those for the girls were significant at the .01 level. A weakness of this study was that no control groups were used, and it is not possible to be sure that the gains were not a function of age changes in adjustment scores. Also, different forms of the test were used in the two testings and the differences found may have been a function of differences in the two forms (A and B).

A report on the first two years of the project at Norwalk summarizes students' attitudes toward team teaching.[30] This is one approach to measuring student adjustment if one assumes that positive or negative attitudes toward a plan are indicators of adjustment. Over-all, approximately four students out of five expressed a favorable attitude toward having more than one teacher, studying in more than one room, and being a member of a group that was larger than a regular class. About four out of five felt that they had gotten to know one teacher as well as in a regular class. Nearly nine

[28] *An Experimental Team Teaching Approach in the 4th, 5th and 6th Grades in the Union School District,* San Jose, Calif., Union School District, September, 1961.

[29] *The Norwalk Plan of Team Teaching, Third Report, op. cit.,* pp. 11–12.

[30] *The Norwalk Plan, A Two-Year Study, op. cit.,* pp. 16–18, 22.

out of ten felt that they made as many or more friends under team teaching as when they were in a regular class. Expressed attitudes of students showed no systematic differences from one grade to another over the range of Grades 2–6.

In this same report are data on the adjustment of students with special problems. The approach was to select students scoring below the twenty-fifth percentile of the California Test of Personality and from these to select for further study those who were identified by teachers as having special adjustment problems under team teaching. At the same time, teachers listed students whom they judged to be very well adjusted under team teaching. An analysis was made of reports for the previous year when these students were in the self-contained classroom. Of 20 students judged to be extremely shy or withdrawn under team teaching, all but three had been reported to have special problems the previous year. Of 38 students identified as extremely aggressive, 34 had been classified the same the year before, three had had learning or behavior problems, and only one had been rated as well adjusted. Out of 51 students rated as very well adjusted under team teaching, 12 had been reported as having some type of adjustment problem the previous year. This method of studying adjustment has some obvious limitations. However, the findings suggest rather strongly that team teaching is at least as apt to contribute to the adjustment of withdrawn or aggressive children as is the self-contained classroom.

Some findings of the Norwalk project that are of particular interest come from a comparative study of initial adjustment in junior high school on the part of students who had experienced team teaching in the elementary school and students who had not.[31] There were 118 Norwalk Plan students in the experimental group and 108 non-Norwalk Plan students in the control group. There was no significant difference between the groups in the percents of students who reported that they liked junior high school, though 82 percent of the Norwalk Plan students said so against 73 percent of the non-Norwalk Plan students. Significant differences (.01 level of confidence) favored the Norwalk Plan students with respect to not being bothered by the large number of students at school, by the large number of teachers, or by the numerous rooms in which

[31] *The Norwalk Plan of Team Teaching, Third Report, op. cit.*, pp. 12–13.

they studied. It appears that experience with team teaching in the elementary school prepares students to adjust to junior high school. One might reason that the job of the elementary school is to adjust students to elementary school, not to junior high school. However, if it is shown that team teaching does not harm students' adjustment in the elementary school and, at the same time, prepares them for junior high school, an advantage has been gained. Unfortunately, the study report does not provide data on how well the Norwalk Plan and non-Norwalk Plan groups were equated in terms of such control variables as IQ and parents' socioeconomic levels.

The research approaches that have been used in evaluating student adjustment have most of the same weaknesses that are true of research on student achievement. There is a lack of operational definitions of adjustment and a failure to use appropriate instruments and procedures for measuring adjustment. Not enough attention is paid to studying the adjustment of different subgroups of students. The fact that no specific data are given on the implementation of team teaching and of the self-contained classroom seriously limits the interpretation of findings. Also, when experimental and control groups were used, controls usually were not satisfactory.

School administrators will find in the research studies no indications that team teaching is apt to create more adjustment problems than it solves. Probably team teaching, or any other plan of organization, improves the adjustment of some students and lessens the adjustment of others. In theory, at least, team teaching has certain advantages over the self-contained classroom with respect to student adjustment. A student who might fail to get along with his teacher in the self-contained classroom can select an identification figure from among several members of a team. If personal-social development requires learning to adjust to various adults and peers in various settings, team teaching appears to offer richer learning contexts than the self-contained classroom. The question is whether the variety of adjustment situations in a team teaching situation confuses or overwhelms the student. The answer to this question doubtless depends on how team teaching is implemented with respect to meeting students' personal-social needs. Once again, in theory, team teaching offers a solution since a variety of possibilities can be worked out by virtue of the great flexibility permissible in this sort of plan. A valuable discussion of this aspect of team teaching will be found in the report from Concord, California.[32]

It should be noted that the findings on student adjustment under team teaching are highly similar to findings with other plans for the elementary school that provide specialist teaching, frequent room changes, and flexible grouping. The reader is referred to reports on the Stoddard dual progress plan and the semidepartmentalized plan being employed in Tulsa, Oklahoma.[33] Also, the reader will find Carbone's study of children's mental health in nongraded and graded plans of value.[34]

Parents' Attitudes about Team Teaching

The majority of parents having children in team teaching projects are in favor of the team approach if one can rely on the few studies of parents' attitudes that have been reported in the literature. At Oceano, California, 78 percent of the parents of fourth graders who returned anonymous questionnaires indicated that they would prefer team teaching for their children the following year, 10 percent were uncertain, and 12 percent were opposed.[35] Numerous parents reported that their children were more interested in school, had learned more, and had made more friends than under the self-contained classroom.

At the end of the first year of the project in Grades 4 to 6 at San Jose, California, 83 percent of the parents returned an attitude questionnaire on their children's participation in the team teaching program.[36] Sixty-seven percent of the respondents said they would like their children to continue in the plan, 20 percent were uncertain, and 13 percent preferred the self-contained classroom. Three out of four were satisfied with their children's academic progress. Four out of ten felt that their children's attitudes toward school

[32] Wall and Reasoner, *op. cit.*, pp. 70–72.

[33] *Three-Year Report of the Experimental Teaching Center, 1958–1961,* New York, Experimental Teaching Center, New York University, November 1, 1961, pp. 14–20. A. Hugh Livingstone, "Does Departmental Organization Affect Children's Adjustment?" *The Elementary School Journal,* vol. LXI, January, 1961, pp. 217–220.

[34] Robert F. Carbone, "The Non-Graded School: An Appraisal," *Administrator's Notebook,* vol. X, September, 1961.

[35] Adams, *op. cit.*, pp. 210–211.

[36] *An Experimental Team Teaching Approach* . . . , *op. cit.*

were better, while about one in ten felt these attitudes were not as good.

After one year of team teaching at Norwalk, Connectitcut, 90 percent of the parents of children in Grades 2 and 5 in the plan responded to an attitude questionnaire.[37] Favorable attitudes toward the team approach were expressed by 78 percent of the parents of the second graders and by 72 percent of the parents of fifth graders. Over-all, 63 percent favored having their children under team teaching the following year, 19 percent were uncertain, and 18 percent were opposed. Sixty percent felt that their children had made more acquaintances or friends under team teaching, and only 4 percent felt they had made fewer.

The findings reported are not sufficiently specific or detailed to indicate what features of team teaching were chiefly responsible for the parents' attitudes. Findings from a project on the semi-departmentalized dual progress plan in the elementary school suggest that parents respond to a new organizational plan as a totality rather than having differential attitudes about its major features.[38] Thus, the proportion of favorable attitudes toward this plan in general was about the same as toward each of its features (specialist teaching, ability grouping, and nongraded advancement). Such results are not surprising, for since most parents have only occasional and brief contacts with the schools, most of their attitudes toward the school program are based on limited information.

The high percentage of returns at San Jose and Norwalk and the similarity of attitudes expressed by parents in all three projects cited above lend credibility to the findings reported. It is uncertain to what extent the parents' attitudes reflect such halo factors as cooperation with the school administration or gratification with having children in a new program. At any rate, these findings are encouraging to administrators who are concerned about community support for team teaching. The fact that a third or more of the parents expressed uncertain or unfavorable attitudes toward team teaching poses problems of program improvement and parent education.

[37] *The Norwalk Plan, First Report,* Norwalk, Conn., The Norwalk Board of Education, July, 1959, pp. 24–25.
[38] *Three Year Report of the Experimental Teaching Center, op. cit.,* p. 21.

Teachers' Attitudes about Team Plans

The literature contains very little information about teachers' attitudes concerning team teaching. Numerous articles report that most team members are favorable toward team teaching after experience with it. This is not surprising in view of the fact that most teachers in today's projects are volunteers. Results from three projects are cited below to indicate the sorts of attitudes teachers have expressed and to pose certain problems of study design and the interpretation of findings.

At the end of the first year of the Oceano, California, elementary school project, recorded interview protocols were obtained on the attitudes of the seven teachers in three teams.[39] These teachers were volunteers who were chosen for their personal-social characteristics and for the curricular areas in which they wished to specialize. Four of the seven were reported as fully in favor of continuing in the project, while three wanted to try again if certain changes were made in flexible grouping and if soundproof movable walls were provided.

A report from the project at San Jose, California, gives attitudes of ten members of two-teacher teams in Grades 4 and 6.[40] In response to an attitude questionnaire given after the first year of the project, six teachers reported that they were much happier in team teaching, and none reported having difficulties in adjusting to other team members. Eight felt they were working much harder than they had worked in the self-contained classroom. In response to a question about the effect of team teaching on their freedom to take initiative in making decisions, three felt they had more freedom, five felt there was no change in this respect, and two felt they had less freedom. Seven felt that their students were learning more than in the self-contained classroom. All ten felt they were meeting students' psychological needs as well or better than they had met these needs in the self-contained classroom, despite the fact that four felt they didn't know their students as well. Students' classroom behavior, according to nine teachers, was about the same as

[39] Adams, *op. cit.*, p. 211.
[40] *An Experimental Team Teaching Approach* . . . , *op. cit.*

before. Seven teachers felt that communication with parents was as good as before, and three felt it was better.

A report on the Norwalk Plan after two years summarizes attitudes of the 14 volunteer team teachers without giving specific findings.[41] The most attractive feature of team teaching, in the views of these teachers, was escaping from clerical and other routine duties that were being performed by nonprofessional aides. Salary increments were considered desirable but less important. At least one-third of the teachers said they would have joined the project without salary increases. Most of the teachers favored the specialization feature. Most felt they could adjust to losses of autonomy and could accommodate themselves to differences among team members in teaching methods or methods of classroom management.

The Norwalk report includes findings of a questionnaire study comparing attitudes of teachers in the system who were "close" to the project with those of teachers who were not. Closeness referred either to being in a school having some team teaching or to having visited and studied team teaching. In the spring of 1959, when four teams were in operation in the district's elementary schools, 50 percent of the teachers in the system who were close to the project favored team teaching, while 24 percent of those not close favored it. In the spring of 1960, 44 percent of those close to the project were favorable, while 28 percent of those not close were favorable. Each year, about one-fourth of the teachers close to the project were not in favor of team teaching, as compared with one-third of those teachers who were not close. The popularity of team teaching at Norwalk, after three years of the project, reached the point where 140 teachers wished to enter the program. During the fourth year, two entire elementary schools were organized for team teaching, partly because many teachers were willing to enter the program.

Considering the importance that team teaching plans assign to teachers' roles and working relationships, it is remarkable how few studies of teachers' attitudes have been reported. Equally remarkable is the superficial nature of these studies. They do not describe the teachers whose attitudes are reported in terms of such characteristics as their age, length of service, educational background, area of specialization, roles in teacher teams, or in-service prepara-

[41] *The Norwalk Plan, A Two-Year Study, op. cit.*, pp. 11–15.

tion for their roles. Also, they do not relate teachers' attitudes to information about the implementation of the plans. Obviously, teachers' attitudes are a function of their experiences in a plan as implemented more than they are a function of the plan as set down on paper. Further, the reports are silent with respect to the attitudes of nonprofessional members of teams. What gratifications and frustrations do they experience in their roles as teachers' helpers?

A school administrator will find little help in establishing or conducting team teaching from published reports of teachers' attitudes. These studies provide few clues that can help him decide upon the size or structure of teams, upon the choice of team members, or upon procedures for implementing a plan. Perhaps the most valuable finding for his purposes is one reported from Norwalk: teachers considered the most important feature of team teaching to be the relief from nonprofessional chores. Other findings that have value for administrative decision making are that teachers respond favorably to provisions for specialist teaching and do not object in principle to special salary increments. On this latter point, it should be noted that teachers frequently question the fairness of salary differentials for team leaders and other professional members of the team. Evidently, the responsiblities of leadership often are shared about equally by two or more teachers even when a team leader has been designated.

Team Teaching and the Teacher Shortage

Many projects employ nonprofessional aides, teacher interns, or part-time teachers. One result of using nonprofessional aides and teacher interns is that the ratio of fully qualified teachers to students is reduced. The use of part-time teachers provides a way of bringing onto the staff qualified persons who otherwise would not resume teaching. In view of the critical shortage of qualified teachers, these features of team teaching may be of great importance. Unfortunately, reports of projects employing personnel in the above categories do not offer detailed information on the extent to which they are contributing to the relief of the teacher shortage. The reader must draw his own inferences on this important matter.

Another way in which team teaching may help relieve the teacher shortage is by providing working conditions and special inducements of status and salary that keep teachers from moving into administrative posts or from leaving the profession. The published literature tells almost nothing about the extent to which team teaching plans have been effective in reducing teacher turnover. A report from Norwalk illustrates the sort of data on teacher retention that is needed from every team teaching project.[42] After two years of the Norwalk Plan, not one of fourteen team teachers had left the project. Three or four teachers, cooperating teachers during the first year of the project became team leaders during its second year. After two nonprofessional aides left the project early in the first year, none has left the project as of the end of the second year. These findings involve too few individuals and too short a time span to be of much significance. Also, comparative data on teacher turnover under other plans of organization are needed. It would be relatively easy and inexpensive to conduct a national survey of personnel turnover with team teaching, as compared with the self-contained classroom in the elementary school or the usual departmentalized program of the secondary school. At the same time, survey data could be obtained on the extent to which nonprofessional aides, interns, and part-time teachers were contributing to the relief of the teacher shortage.

Team Teaching and the Cost of Instruction

The cost of instruction is an important reality of education as well as a highly sensitive one. In a time of great expansion in educational facilities and equipment, it is vital to determine the cost of an organizational plan in relation to its educational products. Can team teaching do the job of instructing students as well or better than conventional plans of organization without increasing costs? Drummond estimates that team teaching costs a little more than conventional plans but admits that the increased outlays of money may be due not to team teaching as such but to the purchase of equipment and materials that are found to be necessary.[43] Perhaps these additional purchases would be found necessary whether or not team teaching were introduced. Another point to note is that increased costs are to be expected during the period when a

[42] *Ibid.*, p. 3.
[43] Drummond, *op. cit.*, p. 162.

new plan is being developed and tested. Team teaching is still in this period.

The costs of team personnel for a given group of students need not be higher than in the self-contained classroom even when salary increments are offered to high-status members of the team. This is shown in a report on the Norwalk Plan that presents a table giving a plan for salary payments to team members in teams of different sizes.[44] The table shows that if a nonprofessional aide is employed in place of a qualified teacher, the difference between the salaries of an aide and a qualified teacher can be used for salary increments. With this scheme the salary budget for instruction of a group of students is not increased. If the aide relieves teachers of routine duties in an amount totaling the full-time services of one teacher, the instructional program is assumed not to suffer.

Improving the Strategy of Research on Team Teaching

The foregoing review of published reports shows that research on team teaching has scarcely moved beyond the stage of preliminary exploration. Only a few tentative findings on the implementation and evaluation of team teaching have been reported thus far. Virtually no research studies have been reported that focus on the design, implementation, or dissemination of team plans. The studies evaluating outcomes have usually been superficial and poorly designed. Doubtless the volume of published research will increase rapidly during the next few years as reports on a number of major projects reach publication. However, there is no assurance that the scope or quality of these research studies will improve markedly over the studies already reported. The over-all strategy of research must be strengthened greatly to place the development of team teaching on a sound basis.

Major guidelines for conducting research on each phase of the development of team teaching were outlined in the early sections of this chapter. The weaknesses of the research studies that have been reviewed can be attributed largely to not following these guidelines. The requirement for operational definitions of plan variables, situational variables, and outcome variables has not been

[44] *The Norwalk Plan of Team Teaching, Third Report, op. cit.,* p. 36.

met and, in consequence, the studies have not employed adequate procedures and instruments to measure these variables. Also, the studies reviewed have failed to meet the requirement for an explicit rationale that hypothesizes certain interrelationships among plan, situational, and outcome variables. A well-formulated rationale is necessary if the researcher is to make effective use of principles drawn from previous research in psychology, sociology, and education and if he is to have an adequate basis for drawing conclusions about relationships between features of a plan and its outcomes.

One great fault in the strategy currently being employed with research on team teaching is the failure to develop plans through the design and implementation phases before attempting to evaluate them. Fattu has called attention to the fact that "applied research and development" in government, industry, and medicine have been found to require great expenditures of time and resources before yielding a useful product or process.[45] Educational researchers have much to learn from the study of research and development procedures in these fields. Fattu, in the same article, proposes that educational research probably can benefit greatly from utilizing the methods of operations research that have been developed in the social sciences to achieve optimal solutions to organizational problems that involve many interacting functions.

One lesson that researchers on team plans should have learned is that it is not possible to implement a plan effectively until a large number of interrelated changes have been made with respect to scheduling, grouping, staff utilization, staff training, curriculum, tests, grading and reporting, facilities and equipment, learning materials, and so on. A great deal of applied research and development is needed to accomplish these changes. In most projects it has been assumed that these changes can be accomplished by the project staff while conducting team teaching. This has proven not to be the case. The proper strategy would be to make the design and implementation phases the focus of major projects whose purpose is to bring team teaching plans to a level of development that makes them ready for full-scale evaluation.

[45] Nicholas A. Fattu, "The Role of Research in Education—Present and Future," *Review of Educational Research*, vol. XXX, December, 1960, pp. 409–421.

Attempts to evaluate team teaching at this time are premature unless the purpose is to obtain very general and tentative information about the workability cf plans and about their outcomes. Results of the evaluations reported in the literature might lead a reasonable man to conclude that team teaching does no harm and little good. Such a conclusion would be unfortunate since team teaching plans have not yet been developed and implemented to a point where one can even estimate their potential contributions to education.

Several major faults in the design of previous evaluative studies of team teaching must be ccrrected. A critical fault has been the failure to relate measures of plan features as implemented to measures of outcomes. Another fault has been a failure to take adequate account of variables in the school situation that could reasonably have a bearing on outcomes. Most of the evaluative studies have been so small in scope that they could not possibly achieve control of important situational variables such as socioeconomic level or staff competencies. This criticism applies to all studies that have compared team teaching plans with conventional organizational plans. Still another fault in evaluative studies has been their failure to employ effective measures of important outcome variables. In particular, measures of student achievement and of student adjustment have been inadequate because of their reliance on standardized achievement tests and personality inventories.

The strategy of educational research depends greatly on the number and quality of educational researchers. Presently there is a crippling shortage of such persons, as may be seen in the plight of university centers that are engaged in educational change projects. In almost every educational research center, the one or two or three staff members who are competent to provide leadership in developing and evaluating educational innovations are called upon to serve so many projects that they are unable to do a good job of serving any. Unless this situation is corrected, the result is apt to continue to be a proliferation of inadequately developed and inadequately tested instructional changes in the nation's schools. This surely is not the way to accomplish a revolution in instruction.

The writer has proposed several approaches to remedying the

critical shortage of educational research personnel.[46] One approach would be to require that everyone obtaining a doctorate in education receive training in the conduct of developmental and evaluative research on educational materials, procedures, or programs. Another approach is to attract researchers from the graduate departments of psychology, sociology, and cultural anthropology into research in education. Also, school administrators should be given an introduction to the nature and procedures of educational research in order that they can make sound decisions with respect to local change programs. Further, it is desirable for every school system to employ one or more educational research specialists to take leadership in designing and conducting change programs.

A sound strategy of research on team teaching cannot be employed without institutional support. Financial support for major research undertakings is essential. The unwillingness of granting agencies to provide sufficient funds for applied research and development on new organizational plans has been a stumbling block. Ordinarily, funds have been granted for demonstration-tests of plans rather than for bringing plans to the level of development where they are ready to be tested or demonstrated. This has been true with team teaching plans, nongraded plans, and the dual progress plan. In consequence, the research projects on these plans have largely short-circuited the design and implementation phases. The major curriculum projects in science and mathematics and projects on programed instruction have not been hampered by the lack of funds for development. With these projects, large funds have been made available both for developing materials and for evaluating and disseminating them. The future of research on organizational plans, including team teaching plans, depends greatly on whether sufficient funds are provided to support research on the design and implementation of these plans.

[46] Glen Heathers, "Field Research on Elementary School Organization and Instruction," *The Journal of Educational Sociology,* vol. XXXIV, April, 1961, pp. 338–343.

Chapter 11

Team Teaching and
The Educational Reform Movement

GLEN HEATHERS

School of Education, New York University

Today's educational reform movement is bringing forward a bold redefinition of the nature and purposes of education and a multiplicity of innovations in materials, media, and organizational arrangements that are intended to accomplish a revolution in instruction. It is remarkable how seldom these two aspects of the reform movement have been brought into direct relation. On the one hand, there are speeches, articles, and books that offer exciting conceptions of education for excellence; of education for the space age; and of instruction that fosters in each student the full development of his capabilities for acquiring, evaluating, and using knowledge. On the other hand, there are various new plans for organizing instruction, new teacher education programs, new technological aids such as television and programed instruction, new projects to upgrade and update the curriculum, and new programs for the gifted and the culturally deprived. The theorists of reform say little about how their visions of the new education can be realized, and the engineers of reform rarely have much to say about how the changes in instruction they are developing and testing will foster the realization of any basic educational goals.

A second characteristic of the reform movement is that the many approaches to change in instruction are developing in relative isolation from each other, even though they are in fact closely interdependent. The movement today consists of a dozen or more

345

relatively independent submovements—team teaching, nongraded schools, programed instruction, educational TV, new curricula in mathematics, new curricula in science, and so on. The lack of agreement among educators on an explicit statement of educational goals is one reason for this situation. The lack of a theory of the instructional process that would provide a sound basis for organizing and conducting an educational *system* is a second reason for these piecemeal approaches to educational change. A third reason for the fragmentary character of the reform movement is, of course, to be found in the intellectual and emotional commitments of the innovators to their particular programs.

Another major characteristic of the reform movement is the hasty, often superficial way in which the various innovations are being developed, implemented, and evaluated. Most of the thousands of change programs under way in research centers or schools across the country suffer from the lack of adequate planning, adequate facilities, or adequate personnel. Unless this situation is changed by giving proper attention to the requirements for sound educational engineering, America's instructional revolution is likely to accomplish mainly changes in the forms of instruction with few major changes in its substance or quality.

Team teaching, in five short years, has won a prominent place within the reform movement. It has gained widespread support from America's educators and is under test in hundreds of school systems and colleges. This vigorous growth should not delude anyone into believing that team teaching has escaped the weaknesses that characterize other types of change projects. Clearly it is the face validity of team teaching that is chiefly responsible for its rapid dissemination, since the implementation and evaluation of this type of organizational plan are still in the beginning stages. Faith in this approach to school organization is invited by its provisions for new patterns of specialization in teaching, for greater cooperation among teachers in planning and conducting instruction, for aides to relieve teachers of nonprofessional duties, and for greater flexibility in the conduct of the student's instructional program. Also, school administrators are encouraged to join the team by the generally favorable attitudes of students, parents, and teachers in schools that are trying team teaching.

Team teaching projects partake of the same shortcomings that are characteristic of the reform movement generally. Judged by published reports, most projects have been planned without particular attention to basic educational goals. Also, these reports say very little about the processes of team teaching. The emphasis, instead, is placed on the organization of the team, on descriptions of the roles of team members, and on ways of grouping for instruction. How the team actually functions in planning and conducting instruction is usually left for the reader to surmise. Further, most accounts of team teaching give scant attention to the sorts of changes in curriculum, testing, guidance procedures, teacher education, and the education of school administrators that are required for effective implementation of the team organization. Finally, most projects have been set up as demonstration-tests that lack the provisions required for adequate evaluation.

In theory, there are good reasons to expect that team teaching can make important contributions to improving the quality of instruction. Preliminary tryouts have been, in the main, encouraging. Currently there is sufficient interest on the part of school leaders and teachers, university researchers, and foundations to provide team teaching with the sorts of development and testing that are needed to determine its potential contributions to education. The important question is whether the proponents of team teaching will now address themselves to understanding and remedying the shortcomings that have been found in the early tryouts of this promising approach to school improvement.

Basic Educational Goals and Team Teaching

If team teaching is to improve the quality of instruction, it will do so by helping students attain the basic goals of education. It is reasonable to expect that all team teaching projects would be planned with this fact in mind and would make explicit how teamwork can foster the attainment of certain educational aims. In point of fact, most projects have lacked this feature. True, the literature of team teaching is replete with claims that this type of plan will improve the quality of instruction. But the reasons offered in support of these claims may be summed up in the assertion that team teaching will provide better instruction to more students more of the time. The implication is that whatever the educational goal one has in mind, team teaching will contribute toward its attainment. This implication merits examination. The logical approach is to begin with a listing of basic educational goals and then to consider how the features of team teaching may be related to their attainment.

Of course, educators often disagree among themselves with respect to the essential goals of education. Some are devotees of child-centered education with its emphases on life adjustment and personal-social development. Others are devoted to basic education with its emphasis on a thorough grounding in the major intellectual disciplines. Some educators place the emphasis on general liberal arts programs. Others favor early specialization in preparation for a trade or profession. In view of such disagreements, it might seem a waste of time to try to develop a list of basic educational aims. However, it is highly probable that the great majority of American educators—traditionalists, progressives, and reformers—do agree fairly well about which general educational goals merit a place in the school's program. Their disagreements, it is held, lie mainly in their precise definitions of these goals, in the relative emphases they assign to them, and in the methods they favor for attaining them. With these assumptions in mind, a list of generic educational goals that apply to almost any curricular area can be offered.

Almost all of the commonly accepted basic educational aims can be grouped into three categories—content goals, process goals, and personal-social goals. Content goals have to do with learning things about any field of human knowledge, whether it be a physical science, a social science, one of the humanities, one of the arts, or any subject whatever. Process goals have to do with learning those competencies, interests, and habits that are needed in acquiring, evaluating, or using knowledge in any subject-matter area. Personal-social goals have to do with developing the sorts of characteristics that are related to one's style of life, personal well-being, and social effectiveness. In the paragraphs that follow, sixteen generic educational goals are grouped in terms of these three categories. Obviously, this list is arbitrary, and the goals listed overlap considerably. The reader is reminded that this list of goals is offered simply for the purpose of examining how team teaching relates to achieving various sorts of educational outcomes.

CONTENT GOALS. In any area of knowledge, the major content goals have to do with learning (1) terminology, (2) classification, (3) information, (4) explanatory theory, and (5) technological applications of information and theory. Of these five goals, American education has tended to emphasize the first three, particularly the teaching of information (facts). Leading spokesmen of the reform movement have raised objections to the stress on teaching information and are urging that the stress be placed instead on teaching the theory of a discipline. They reason that a student cannot acquire more than a small fraction of the factual knowledge in a field and that his time would be better used in learning the general structure of ideas that orders knowledge of the field and provides the basis for understanding that knowledge and for employing it to serve practical ends.[1] This is not a new idea. John Dewey believed it, but his followers did not do a good job of practicing it.

PROCESS GOALS. Some spokesmen of reform have proposed that the schools should make a fundamental shift in emphasis from content to process goals.[2] Instead of stressing the acquisition of particular bodies of knowledge, the reformers would place the stress on teaching students how to acquire, interpret, evaluate, and communicate knowledge. They argue that our rapidly changing scientific-technological society places a premium on adaptability to novel and unpredictable situations and that educators can best prepare students to live in such a society by teaching in terms of the process goals. What are these process goals? There is no generally accepted list, but the following list of eight will serve. These are: (1) tool skills, (2) critical thinking, (3) creative thinking, (4) inquiry, (5) self-instruction, (6) self-evaluation, (7) interests, and (8) study habits.

Only one of these goals—tool skills—now receives systematic atten-

[1] Jerome S. Bruner, The Process of Education, Cambridge, Mass., Harvard University Press, 1961.
[2] Glen Heathers, Notes on the Strategy of Educational Reform, unpublished manuscript, dittoed, November, 1961. Joseph J. Schwab, "The Teaching of Science as Enquiry," in Joseph J. Schwab and Paul F. Brandwein, The Teaching of Science, Cambridge, Mass., Harvard University Press, 1961, pp. 1–103.

tion in most American schools and colleges. Tool skills include reading, writing, speaking, counting, computing, and using various instruments for observing, manipulating, and measuring things. The reform movement is giving particular attention to improving the teaching of critical and creative thinking, the methods of inquiry, and self-instruction. Major research programs on thinking, inquiry, and creativity are underway and already are making contributions to educational practice.[3] Self-instruction is emphasized in a number of educational programs that are being tested, notably in tests of the Trump plan for the secondary schools,[4] in projects that employ learning programs or other individual technological aids, and in various honors programs. America's schools are still a long way from giving the process goals the central place in education, but it now appears that the reformers will move strongly in that direction.

PERSONAL-SOCIAL GOALS. Recent controversies about educational goals have been concerned with the extent to which the schools should assume responsibility for developing the student's personal-social characteristics. The personal-social goals under consideration include (1) values—social, esthetic, theoretical, etc., (2) personality make-up—emotional security, positive self-concept, self-assertion, etc., and (3) social behavior patterns—self-control, cooperation, tolerance, etc. The progressive educators have given strong emphasis to such goals, while many of the reformers have claimed that the schools should focus on developing the student's intellectual powers and leave to home and community the primary responsibilities for developing his personality and his social behavior. The latter position obviously requires qualification inasmuch as the schools must continue to be concerned about the student's adjustment and comportment at school and about those personal-social characteristics that affect his readinesses for learning. Also, it seems clear that citizenship education, with its stresses on democratic values and prac-

---

[3] Jerome S. Bruner, Jacqueline J. Goodnow, and George A. Austin, A Study of Thinking, New York, Wiley, 1956. J. Richard Suchman, "Inquiry Training in the Elementary School," The Science Teacher, vol. XXVII, November, 1960, pp. 42–48. E. Paul Torrance, Guiding Creative Talent, Englewood Cliffs, N.J., Prentice-Hall, 1962.

[4] J. Lloyd Trump, Images of the Future: A New Approach to the Secondary School, Commission on the Experimental Study of the Utilization of the Staff in the Secondary School, 1959.

tices, will continue to be an important aspect of American public schooling.

ACCOMPLISHING GOALS. Before we look at team teaching in relation to the three sets of educational goals listed above, we should note two trends of the educational reform movement that can contribute greatly toward accomplishing these goals. One is the growing emphasis on having the student master any given learning task before proceeding to a new task. This calls for establishing clear and reasonable standards of accomplishment and for seeing to it that the student is assigned what he is prepared to learn, that he studies with appropriate methods, and that he continues studying the assignment until he has gained command of it. The second trend is toward providing each student with an individualized program of studies that is suited to his needs and to his learning rate. Two major types of changes in educational practices are being developed to foster individualization: nongrading the schools so that students can proceed along the curricular sequences at different rates in accordance with their rates of learning, and using learning materials and devices that enable the student to study independently and proceed at his own pace.

Now what has team teaching to do with accomplishing the generic goals of education within any curricular area? It was claimed earlier that only a few of the team teaching projects that have been established to date were planned with such objectives in mind. It also is our contention that team teaching, per se, can have only secondary relationships to the accomplishment of basic educational goals. This is not to say that team teaching cannot improve the quality of education in relation to its basic aims. Rather, it is to say that a genuine instructional revolution calls for putting first things first and that team teaching is not one of these first things. In support of this contention, we may examine each major feature of team teaching in its relation to fostering the accomplishment of educational goals. The features to be examined are those that are incorporated in the more complex team teaching projects.

New patterns of teacher specialization, a feature of many team teaching projects, have been put forward as an important way of improving the quality of instruction. As noted in previous chapters, increased teacher specialization is a feature of several new organizational plans, including the Stoddard dual progress plan and some versions of the nongraded school. Here we are concerned with specialization as it is practiced in teaching teams. In the elementary school some team teaching projects introduce subject matter specialization in areas such as reading, mathematics, or science. In the secondary school team members may specialize in particular aspects of a subject. Thus English teachers may specialize in grammar or literature.

It seems clear that subject matter specialization can lead to improved teaching if the specialist teacher has more knowledge of his subject, more enthusiasm for it, and more skill in teaching it than was, on the average, true of the teacher previously assigned to teach it. However, specialization offers no guarantee whatsoever that teaching of a subject will improve with respect to such goals as critical thinking, inquiry, self-instruction, or command of theory. Whether or not these goals are achieved depends essentially on the teacher's basic preparation, not on specialization. Thus the elementary science specialist, like the common branches teacher, can teach facts in preference to theory and can focus instruction on readings and demonstrations rather than on observations and experiments.

In teaching teams, members may specialize in method as well as in subject matter. They may specialize in large-group, small-group, or individual instruction or in the use of such technological aids as TV, tapes, or learning programs. Again, these varieties of specialization have no essential relation to accomplishing any one of the basic educational goals. Large-group instruction and educational television have been defended as permitting many students to study under a thoroughly prepared and inspiring teacher. Doubtless interest in the subject can be aroused, and values inculcated, in these ways. Also, it is possible in large groups or on TV to present dramatic models of theorizing or of inquiry. However, these situations have severe limitations with respect to any learning goals where effective instruction depends upon recognizing initial differences in achievement level and differences in learning rate. There are great differences among students with respect to learning most of the generic goals, and whole-class teaching in large groups is a poor way of taking account of such differences. Clearly, inquiry, critical thinking, creative thinking, and self-instruction can be accomplished best in small-group or individual settings. Because team teaching can provide such settings, it can open the way to teachers who know how to organize and conduct instruction in relation to these goals, but, once again, whether or not these goals are realized depends mainly on the teacher.

Teacher aides simply free trained teachers to devote a greater share of their time than formerly to instruction. They bear no direct relationship to the attainment of any given educational goal.

Technological aids such as learning programs, tapes, or language laboratories sometimes are used by teaching teams. It would seem that these aids promote the goal of self-directed learning. The difficulty is that the materials studied with the use of these devices usually are highly structured and actually minimize self-instruction aside from the aspect of self-pacing. Learning programs stress mastery but at the expense of not teaching the student to evaluate his performance, since evaluation is built into the program. Learning progams, by their very nature, are ill suited for teaching creative thinking and inquiry.

The key feature of team teaching—teacher cooperation—can foster any given educational goal only if the team members know how to direct their efforts toward that goal. There is nothing about teacher cooperation by itself that guarantees improved instruction in relation to any learning goal. Teamwork simply provides opportunities for improving the training and supervision of instructional personnel and opportunities for planning and conducting better prepared instructional programs. If the team leader or other experienced members of the team are well versed in teaching in terms of a given educational goal, the team situation provides a good setting for showing a novice teacher how to work toward that goal. This assumes that both the experienced teacher and the novice are familiar with the curricular area in question. Otherwise their communication will be on so general a level that it will probably be ineffective.

Presumably, the greatest value of the team conference is in planning the instructional programs of all the students assigned to the team. This calls for a highly complex and time-consuming set of intercommunications, particularly if the attempt is made to take into account each student's progress and learning needs in each curricular area and in relation to different learning goals within that area. Even though the team might include as few as 75 students, it is doubtful that it ever could complete such a task of planning for each student in team conferences. Because of time limitations, this planning task calls either for dividing the task among team members or for utilizing efficient methods of handling masses of information such as those employing electronic computers.

It has been claimed that the team conference provides an excellent setting for sharing information about children's adjustment and personal-social development and for taking this information into account in planning and conducting instruction. This assumes that teachers are skilled in appraising a student's status and problems in these areas and that they know how to create situations that are favorable for the adjustment and personal-social growth of different students. This is a large order when one considers teachers' very limited training in guidance. It is probable that the team would need to include a well-qualified guidance specialist on a full-time basis in order to make substantial achievements in relation to the personal-social goals of education.

If the analysis we have made of team teaching in relation to basic educational goals is correct, we should not expect team teaching by itself to lead to any major changes in the quality of instruction. At best, team teaching offers improved ways of utilizing existing materials, facilities, methods, and personnel. The most fundamental weaknesses in American education are not faults in organization for instruction. Instead, they are faults in curricula, tests, instructional facilities and equipment, teaching methods, and the training of school leaders and teachers. None of these bases for instruction has been soundly developed in terms of the generic goals listed earlier or in terms of individualized education.

During the coming years we may expect significant improvements in each of these foundations for instruction. Curriculum projects in mathematics are developing sequences beginning at the primary level that stress mathematical reasoning and the discovery method of learning. The science curriculum is in process of thorough revision to bring materials up to date and to place much greater emphasis on theory and scientists' methods of inquiry. There are indications that curricula in the social sciences will be revised to reduce the present emphasis on teaching information and to place increased emphasis on theory, critical thinking, and inquiry.

The development of adequate achievement tests must await the completion of the new curricula. Today's tests tend strongly to emphasize terms, tool skills, and information. In every curricular area there is a lack of tests to measure the student's competencies in the process goals of creative thinking, inquiry, self-instruction, and self-evaluation. Furthermore, today's standardized tests are not geared to any one curricular sequence and offer the teacher little help, therefore, in determining the student's level of advancement in terms of the sequence.

New designs for school buildings are providing flexible learning space to permit instruction with groups of any size desired and to provide semiprivate carrels for independent study. Because of construction costs it will be many years before most schools can adopt these new designs. With many new intructional devices developed and in quantity production, any school system that desires and can afford such devices can have TV and overhead projectors for large-group instruction, as well as language laboratories, magnetic tapes, and learning programs for individualized, self-paced study.

It looks as though these developments in curricula and learning equipment are outrunning the parallel developments that are needed in instructional methods and in the preparation of school leaders and teachers. It is remarkable how little established knowledge we have of the teaching-learning processes in relation to achieving any designated learning goal. This becomes clear when one examines texts on child development, educational psychology, or educational guidance, or texts on methods of teaching in any subject matter area. One finds discussions of general principles of teaching and learning and many tips to teachers, but one does not find a well-developed theory of teaching; nor does one find systematic accounts of how a teacher may go about diagnosing students' learning readinesses, planning lessons to achieve particular learning goals, organizing and conducting instruction in terms of those goals, or evaluating students' progress toward them.

Fortunately, research on learning, thinking, and teaching is in a period of rapid development; and before the end of the present decade, we may expect to know a great deal about the teaching-learning process.[5] A thorough treatment of research methods in this area is now available in the *Handbook of Research on Teaching* edited by Nathan L. Gage.[6]

Considering that curricula, tests, and teaching methods are poorly developed in relation to the generic educational goals, it is not surprising that the schools of education are not doing an adequate job of preparing school leaders and teachers to plan and conduct instruction that leads students toward realizing those goals in the various curricular areas. However, improvements in the education of school personnel can occur at the same time that curricula, tests, and teaching methods are being developed. The training of all school personnel must be anchored in clearly formulated behavioral definitions of the generic educational goals. Presently, America's schools of education, with few exceptions, make no attempt to develop their programs around operational definitions of learning goals. Consequently, most school administrators, curriculum specialists, school psychologists, guidance specialists, and teachers undertake their assignments with vague notions about what such goals as critical thinking, creative thinking, inquiry, or self-instruction amount to in terms of students' behavior. Without operational definitions of basic educational goals, school personnel cannot hope to do a good job of planning, conducting, and evaluating instruction.

Professors of education bear the chief responsibility for remedying this shortcoming in the training of educational personnel. It is up to them to develop the best working definitions of the generic goals that can now be formulated and to organize their programs of professional education in terms of those definitions. Educational theorists and researchers can perform a much needed service by focusing their efforts on helping instructors of education courses make this critical transformation in the preparation of school personnel. Liberal arts departments can aid greatly in speeding this process, particularly if they go beyond conducting basic research on matters related to education, and work actively with education professors on the job of improving the definitions of educational objectives and of trans-

---

[5] Paul R. Klohr, "Studies of the Teaching Act: What Progress?" *Educational Leadership,* vol. XX, November, 1962, pp. 93–96.

[6] Nathan L. Gage, ed., *Handbook of Research on Teaching,* Chicago, Rand McNally, 1963.

lating them into programs for the preparation of school leaders and teachers. Thus far, liberal arts professors have been making their greatest contributions in the area of curriculum improvement, particularly in mathematics and science. They have equally important contributions to make to the substance of teacher education. This is true of psychologists, sociologists, and anthropologists, all of whom can aid greatly in defining the generic goals and in designing basic professional education courses focused on these goals. It is also true of professors of the subject-matter disciplines, who, in teaching their disciplines, can help translate the generic goals in terms of the content of education courses.

We have seen, then, that team teaching is not a fundamental approach to improving the quality of instruction and that the potential contributions of team teaching cannot be determined until major developments have occurred in the form of imbedding the generic educational goals into curricula, tests, instructional methods, and the training of school personnel. This position is not intended to discourage faith in team teaching but only to locate the position that team teaching can occupy in the context of fundamental educational reform. Given its proper place in this context, the contributions of team teaching to the improvement of instruction may well be of great importance.

The Processes of Team Teaching

The organizational features of team teaching plans—specialization, use of aides, flexibile grouping, etc.—are given detailed attention in reports on team projects. Unfortunately, these reports are almost silent with respect to the processes of team teaching that bring its organizational structure to life. This fact cannot mean that the proponents of team teaching consider it unnecessary to spell out the processes of teamwork. What it probably represents is a lack of definite notions about what these processes should be. Clearly, future developments in team teaching depend in large measure on developing and testing specific procedures for team functioning.

The heart of teamwork within any team teaching plan consists of intercommunication among team members in planning and evaluating instruction and cooperation among them in carrying out the specific instructional assignments that are decided upon in team planning. The more critical of these probably is intercommunication. The key to effective communication among members of a team is speaking a common language with respect to educational goals and with respect to methods of achieving them. If this common language is to prove adequate for planning and evaluating instruction, it must be sufficiently explicit to provide a basis for locating points of agreement and disagreement about educational goals and to enable team members to decide upon specific instructional procedures that are intended to accomplish specific learning outcomes with students.

We have every reason to doubt that today's teachers speak this sort of common educational language. They do not agree on the essential purposes of education. Many believe that the essence of education is to be found in teaching tool skills, vocabulary, and information. Some are mainly concerned about the student's personal-social development. A few would focus education on achieving the process goals of critical thinking, inquiry, and self-instruction. Such basic differences in educational philosophy are hard to reconcile and, when they exist within a team, are bound to affect intercommunication of team members. The writer has been told by members of two-teacher teams in elementary schools that agreement on educational philosophy is often the deciding factor in the ability of two teachers to work together.

An equally important limitation on intercommunication within the team is teachers who lack a common set of operational definitions of the generic educational goals that were listed in the preceding section of this chapter. Anyone who doubts that this is true should ask any group of teachers he chooses to define such goals as creative thinking, inquiry, or self-instruction in terms of specific student behaviors that indicate their attainment. Or, instead, he might ask the group of teachers to select from among a set of test items those that are relevant to each of a number of generic educational goals. The answers he obtained would almost certainly be characterized by vagueness and by great disagreements from teacher to teacher. This is not an indictment of teachers, since similar results would be found if these tasks were presented to public school administrators or specialist consultants, or to professors of education. The inability of teachers to agree on the behavioral definitions of educational goals simply reflects the failure of educational leaders to develop and teach such definitions. Recently, serious efforts have been made to develop explicit definitions of educational goals, and we now have Bloom's taxonomy of goals in the cognitive area, and Kearney's book on elementary school objectives.[7] However, these taxonomies give incomplete coverage of the generic goals and are not in a form that enables teachers to use them effectively in planning and conducting instruction. Further, such taxonomies are seldom made a systematic part of teacher education programs.

Since teachers lack good working definitions of the basic educational goals, it is not surprising that they lack a clear understanding of the methodology of teaching in terms of these goals. Given this situation, the team's planning and evaluation of instruction will probably be characterized either by vague decisions reached in team conferences, by decisions made independently by team members, or by decisions made by one team member for another without the latter's full understanding.

In analyzing the processes and problems of teacher teamwork, it would be very helpful if detailed case studies of team functioning were available. These case studies would reveal a geat deal about current practices in team planning and cooperative instruction. In the absence of such reports of actual team functioning, we may speculate that members of today's teacher teams spend a high proportion of the time given to team conferences on discussing a few students, particularly those students with emotional or conduct problems. Other students likely to receive a large share of attention are those with reading difficulties and those with outstanding gifts. A corollary speculation is that the great majority of students in the team receive very little attention in the team conferences. One bit of evidence about today's teachers that lends credibility to these speculations is the fact that a high proportion of reports on students' classroom learning problems that have been given to the writer by elementary and secondary teachers have dealt with emotional and conduct problems. Observations of teacher conferences, or of conversations in teachers' rooms, also reveal teachers' predilections for

[7] Benjamin S. Bloom, *Taxonomy of Educational Objectives, Handbook I: Cognitive Domain*, New York, Longmans, 1956. Nolan C. Kearney, *Elementary School Objectives*, New York, Russell Sage Foundation, 1953.

talking about a few students of high visibility and not talking about students who do not stand out from the group.

Ideally, team planning would provide the sort of educational guidance that involves diagnosing each student's accomplishments and learning readinesses in the different curricular areas, planning a specific program of studies suited to his learning needs, evaluating his progress periodically, identifying his learning problems, and making special provisions for resolving those problems. In accomplishing effective educational guidance, it is especially important that information about the student as a person be taken fully into account and that proper attention be paid to the integration of learning experiences from one curricular area to another. In order to deal with these matters of guidance, team members must have such information available to them at all times and must take it into account without delay in planning and conducting instruction.

Considering the complexity and the time demands of planning the total educational programs of a large number of students, it is important to determine how much of this planning requires direct intercommunication among team members. Thus, when different members of a team are responsible for different curricular areas, to what extent is it desirable and practicable for team planning to encompass the choice of curricular materials and tests and the specific lesson planning for that area? Very often the team member responsible for the given area will be most competent in these matters and will gain little from having other team members involved in making the needed decisions. Perhaps team planning should be almost entirely restricted to matters concerned with the integration of learning experiences in the different curricular areas, the consideration of personal-social factors, the grouping of pupils, the uses to be made of space and equipment, and the special competencies of team members.

Face-to-face communication has much to recommend it, but it is extremely time consuming. Since no teaching team will have more than a few hours per week for team conferences, it is of great importance that ways be found of communicating and organizing information aside from team conferences. One approach is to concentrate the communication functions in the team leader or in a guidance specialist on the team such as the "facilitator" being em-

ployed at the University of Chicago Laboratory School.[8] Another
appoach—and this seems to hold more promise—is to employ an information system that uses electronic computers for storing, integrating, and disseminating the many bits of evidence that should be
taken into account in planning and evaluating instruction.

Flexible grouping in team teaching plans is intended to foster the
individualization of instruction through making exceptional provisions for small-group or individual study. Teachers are made available for instructing small groups of students either by having other
students taught in large-group sessions or by having students work
at tasks they can perform by themselves under the supervision of a
teaching intern or a teacher aide. The processes of team planning
that are required to make flexible grouping serve its purposes are
highly complex. If the needs of each individual student in the team
are to be served in the special groupings, a multitude of interlocking
decisions must be made. The team must decide for each student in
each curricular area what his learning needs are and then set up a
system of groupings that represent the best practicable solution to
serving the needs of all students taken together. The groupings must
be changed frequently as students' needs change.

How does the team decide that *these* students are the ones who
now require small group instruction, while *those* students can properly be assigned to large group sessions or to work with programed
materials? How does the team decide that this small group of students should devote extra time this week to reading, while this small
group should spend extra time on mathematics, and these gifted
students should be given special opportunities for project work in
science or art or creative writing? The literature of team teaching
does not describe the procedures that teams have developed to
answer such questions as these. Considering the complexity of the
problems raised by flexible grouping, it is safe to guess that no team
has developed adequate solutions to these problems and that most
teams offer the benefits of small-group and individual work mainly
to students with remedial problems and to gifted students.

[8] Roy A. Larmee and Robert Ohm, "University of Chicago Laboratory
School Freshman Project Involves Team Teaching, New Faculty Positions,
and Regrouping of Students," *NASSP Bulletin*, vol. XLV, January, 1960, pp.
275–289.

The method of obtaining individualized instruction is not flexible grouping, especially not the sort that uses many large-group sessions. Rather, the method is to increase the proportion of time that all students can engage in independent, self-directed study. When this result is achieved, the teacher is freed of the necessity for whole-group teaching and can devote the bulk of his time to guiding the individual learner. Programed materials foster individualization by enabling the student to work alone and at his own pace. A more fundamental approach to individualization is to teach each student those competencies in self-instruction that enable him to program his own learning tasks and to perform them independently.

Teamwork has been discussed thus far in terms of intercommunication among team members. Other major determinants of team functioning are team structure and team membership. The literature has much to say about team structure, but mainly on the descriptive level. Many questions about the organization of teaching teams have yet to be answered. For example, what should be the size of a team? The larger the team, the greater the possibilities for specialization and for flexible grouping. But, also, the larger the team, the more complex and time consuming are the problems of intercommunication and supervision. A hierarchical structure headed by a team leader has theoretical advantages for integration of functions and for the morale of favored members. However, as is noted in Chapter 9, breaking from established patterns of equality among teachers can pose serious problems of cooperation and of morale. Much research evidence is needed that relates variables of team structure to measures of team effectiveness and to staff recruitment and retention. Also, as was pointed out in Chapter 10, research on team membership is needed to determine the extent to which effective teamwork depends upon members' possessing certain personal-social characteristics, upon the nature and clarity of team tasks, upon team structure, upon members' task involvement, or upon whether members speak a common language.

The Education of Personnel for Teacher Teams

Taking "new directions in teacher education," to use Woodring's expression, is one of the outstanding aspects of today's educational reform movement.[9] The developments in teacher education during the past decade have been focused on several major themes. One theme concerns the shortage of teachers and has involved programs to recruit teachers from new sources such as past and present liberal arts graduates and ways of utilizing today's teachers more efficiently through educational television, the use of teacher aides, etc. Another theme has been the improving of the liberal arts background of teachers through increasing the amount of course work in the basic subject matter disciplines, with special attention to the teacher's area of specialization. Fifth- and sixth-year programs have been developed to attain these objectives. Yet another theme has been the increased use of the teaching internship. Finally, there has been a raising of standards for admission to teacher education programs and for teacher certification. One will find accounts of these approaches in Woodring's book; in the February 1960 issue of *The High School Journal;* in Hodenfield and Stinnett's *The Education of Teachers;* and in a recent pamphlet, *The New Teacher,* that describes teacher education projects supported by the Ford Foundation.[10]

What "new directions" are needed to prepare personnel for team teaching? The previous sections of this chapter have pointed out a number of major requirements for effective membership in a teacher team. According to the analysis that was offered, the most important requirement is that each professional member of the team have a thorough grounding in the fundamentals of instruction. He must have a specific understanding of the generic educational goals and of the basic processes of instruction that can accomplish these goals with the students he is called upon to teach. Further, it is evident the preparation for team teaching must include training in the processes of teamwork and training for certain specialist roles within the team—team leader, specialist in programed instruction, specialist in large-group instruction, etc.

It is our contention that members of teaching teams, in common with teachers generally, need a fundamentally different program of teacher education than is presently being offered. Currently, teacher

[9] Paul Woodring, *New Directions in Teacher Education,* New York, The Fund for the Advancement of Education, 1957.
[10] *Ibid. The High School Journal,* vol. XLIII, February, 1960. G. K. Hodenfield and T. M. Stinnett, *The Education of Teachers,* Englewood Cliffs, N.J., Prentice-Hall, 1961. *The New Teacher,* New York, The Ford Foundation, 1962.

education can be characterized as providing, on the one hand, a very general orientation to educational foundations through course work in educational history and philosophy, educational sociology, and educational psychology, and, on the other hand, an introduction to specific materials and techniques of instruction in one or more curricular areas. What is lacking is course work that provides operational definitions of the generic educational goals delineated here and systematic training in the ways of achieving each of these goals. The latter calls for learning how to plan and conduct instruction toward these goals within a given curricular area by utilizing various curricular materials, diagnostic and evaluative instruments, and grouping procedures.

Clearly, there is need for a radical transformation in the substance of professional course work in education in order to provide each teacher with generalizable competencies in the basic processes of instruction. The new teacher education program would be based in part on recent research on curriculum, teacher-student interaction, and methods of teaching toward such generic goals as critical thinking and inquiry. Some guidelines for the development of new professional education programs may be found in Sarason, Davidson, and Blatt's *The Preparation of Teachers: An Unstudied Problem in Education,* and in *Teacher Education: A Reappraisal,* edited by Elmer R. Smith.[11]

The sort of program that is proposed would consist of course work and internship experiences organized in terms of a number of basic themes such as the following:

1. Operational definitions of the generic educational goals.
2. Principles of building curricula that emphasize the generic educational goals and that give proper attention to determinants of sequence.
3. Instruments and procedures of educational evaluation.
4. Methods of diagnosing students' learning readinesses.
5. Methods of grouping students for instruction, with emphasis on individualization.

[11] Seymour B. Sarason, Kenneth S. Davidson, and Burton Blatt, *The Preparation of Teachers: An Unstudied Problem in Education,* New York, Wiley, 1962. Elmer R. Smith, ed., *Teacher Education: A Reappraisal,* New York, Harper & Row, 1962.

6. Lessons that are directed toward the accomplishment of given generic goals.
7. Learning materials and equipment for conducting individualized programs of study.
8. Special methods and materials for teaching students to achieve the process goals of critical thinking, inquiry, creativity, self-instruction, and self-evaluation.
9. Methods of pupil-team learning.
10. Processes of teamwork in planning and conducting instruction.

This program of professional course work on the fundamentals of instruction would need to be supported with intensive and continuous internship experiences in order to accomplish the translation of principles into practices within school settings. Obviously, such a program would require that the student already be well grounded in the liberal arts and that he already have acquired a sound academic background in the curricular areas he planned to teach.

Preparation for team teaching must satisfy a number of requirements that, while not necessarily peculiar to team teaching, are especially important within this type of plan. These requirements involve small-group processes, flexible grouping of students, and specialist roles within the team. Course work in group processes or group dynamics is needed, with use of role playing. Ideally, the future team member would learn about group processes as a member of a team. This approach is illustrated by a course at Los Angeles State College where 100 students in secondary education studied under three instructors, who employed specialization and flexible grouping in conducting the course.[12] Each student studied under each instructor in groups ranging in size from 100 to 2 and also received individual tutoring. Training in group processes may also occur through teaching internships in schools that employ team teaching.

The best preparation for employing flexible grouping is training in what we have called educational guidance. Such training calls for a focus on the individual learner. The student teacher needs to learn how to build a program of studies for the individual within one or more curricular areas. This requires that he understand how to integrate information about the learner's aptitudes, achievements,

[12] Jack Nelson, Robert O. Hahn, and Gertrude A. Robinson, "Team Teaching for Teacher Education: The New Approach," *Journal of Teacher Education,* vol. XII, September, 1961, pp. 380–382.

interests, and personal-social characteristics that is derived from tests, observations of the learner's behavior, and reports from his teachers and other school personnel. Once he has accomplished this, the student teacher is in a position to study how the team may set up groups of different sizes that bring together learners who are ready to study together. Obviously, internship experiences within teacher teams is the best setting for learning how to apply competencies in educational guidance within the context of flexible grouping.

It is questionable whether training for specialist roles within the teacher team should, at this time, be a part of preservice teacher education. Certainly, if time permits, every teacher should receive at least an introduction to principles of group leadership and to the utilization of such instructional aids as television and learning programs. However, it seems preferable that training programs for team leaders and for specialists in programed learning, large-group instruction, etc. should be given to experienced teachers who have been selected on the basis of their performance in teacher teams.

In-service education for team teaching is necessary for two reasons. First, preservice education cannot fully prepare the teacher to participate in the team teaching program of the school system where he finds employment. Also, today's team teaching programs usually are staffed with teachers who have had no previous preparation for this type of plan.

Most school systems must conduct in-service teacher education programs under conditions that seriously limit their effectiveness. Budgetary restrictions often prevent the team from undergoing an intensive training program before it undertakes instruction. Under these conditions, on-the-job training must be resorted to after starting team teaching, and that training is apt to be restricted to urgent problems of instruction rather than to be devoted to a systematic program for developing team competencies. Furthermore, most school systems suffer from a shortage of experts who are competent to organize and lead training programs in team teaching.

Solutions to these local problems of training teaching teams call for funds that enable the school system to free team members for an extended period of training and to obtain the active participation of university professors in the training process. Some universities now offer summer workshops in team teaching. The Harvard-Lexington Summer Program is an example. It is to be hoped that universities soon will establish special training programs for team leaders and other team specialists. Another way of bringing help from the universities is for school systems to employ professors as part-time consultants to aid in conducting their in-service programs.

The universities should correct some of the weaknesses in team members' preparation for teaching in the interest of enabling them to make significant improvements in the quality of their teaching within the team structure. For example, a team member may need to take additional courses in his field of specialization. Also, the university-sponsored program of training for teamwork might include instruction in how to teach students to achieve the various generic educational goals. An illustration of this approach is the 1962 Harvard-Lexington Summer Program in which the training of team teachers was built around teaching the process goals of tool skills, inquiry, initiative (self-instruction), and self-evaluation.

Problems of Implementing Team Teaching Plans

Attempting to implement a new organizational plan within a school system is apt to be at once highly frustrating and highly instructive. Those who are responsible for establishing and testing any organizational plan—whether it be a team teaching plan, a nongraded plan, the Stoddard dual progress plan, or any other—agree on two basic and closely related conclusions: (1) it is much easier to accomplish the organizational changes called for in implementing the structural features of a plan than it is to make the plan's organizational structure function effectively in accomplishing its purposes; and (2) any major new organizational plan involves demands for change in virtually every component of the instructional program—curriculum, tests, grading and reporting, use of space and equipment, teacher training and utilization, use of specialist consultants, functions of administrators, and school-community relations. In grappling with these facts of life of instructional reorganization, a project staff is apt to find itself involved in asking these questions: What, precisely, are our educational aims? How can we do a better job of accomplishing these aims through team teaching? What other changes must we undertake if we are to do a good job of instruction with team teaching?

The extent to which these matters come to attention depends, of course, on the magnitude of the organizational changes that are introduced, as well as on the degree to which a project staff is concerned about accomplishing changes in the basic quality of instruction rather than merely changes in its formal properties. In many local team teaching projects, only two or three teachers are involved, the main changes instituted have to do with subject-matter specialization, flexible grouping is not employed, and relatively little team planning occurs. Often such projects are initiated on an informal basis because school administrators or teachers think team teaching is a good idea and want to give it a try. In such projects, problems of implementation are minimal and are apt to involve mainly questions of whether the team members get along with one another.

In team teaching programs the most serious problems of implementation arise in the more complex projects, incorporating such features as large teams with a hierarchical structure, new patterns of specialization, and flexible grouping, and, in schools that introduce instructional changes, with the chief purpose of improving the quality of instruction.

Obviously, the more complex the team teaching project becomes, the more difficult it is to place it in operation. The larger the team, the more difficult and time consuming become the problems of coordinating the functions of team members. The potential gains from increased specialization of role in larger teams may be offset by intensified problems of interpersonal relations among team members and by the more complex patterns of intercommunication in team planning conferences.

The use of flexible grouping in team teaching can foster greater individualization of instruction and can make time available for individual or group planning by team members. However, the implementation of flexible grouping, if it is to accomplish these purposes, makes severe demands on a team. Decisions must be reached by the team leader, or in team conferences, on such questions as these: What materials are to be taught in large-group sessions, and by whom? What small groups should be formed in each curricular area, with what learning goals, according to what time schedule, and under which team members? What uses should be made of individual tutoring? How is the instruction a student receives in different groups and under different teachers to be correlated to provide the student with a program suited to his individual needs? It should be noted that the use of flexible grouping calls for such decisions on a week-to-week, even a day-to-day, basis.

It is clear that the team must reach a high level of professional competence to accomplish the purposes of specialization and flexible grouping. Also, it is clear that these functions call for well-defined curricular sequences, appropriate learning materials and equipment, adequate tests for diagnosing students' learning readinesses and achievements, and smooth procedures for efficient intercommunication among team members. As was indicated earlier in this chapter, some of these requirements go beyond the present level of educational development and can be met only through innovations.

Today, any school system, college, or university that is interested in improving the quality of instruction will not be satisfied with mere changes in the organization of instruction. Its leaders almost certainly will be sensitive to the reform movement's call for achieving excellence in education and will be eager to take advantage of any promising new developments in curriculum, tests, or instructional equipment. Most school systems that are testing team teaching are at the same time adopting the newly developed curricular materials in mathematics and science at both elementary and secondary levels. Many are employing educational TV and language laboratories. Certainly, in September, 1963, a great many school systems will be making some use of programed instruction.

A school system that is committed to improving the quality of instruction will wish to incorporate these various instructional innovations as part of the implementation of a new organizational plan such as team teaching. In one sense, this makes the implementation of team teaching easier because most innovations in curriculum, tests, and instructional aids can help the teaching team realize its objectives of high-quality individualized instruction. In another sense, these other innovations complicate the implementation of team teaching by requiring team members to develop new procedures for incorporating the various innovations within their new organizational plan.

The problems of implementing a team teaching plan become clearer when a systematic program of evaluation is included in the project. Adequate evaluation of any new plan requires specific measures of the various features of the plan as well as specific measures of various possible outcomes. A superficial, impressionistic evaluation of a plan is likely to settle for evidence on the extent to which the general structure of the plan was placed in effect, without probing to determine the extent to which the purposes of the structural changes were realized in the processes of instruction.

An illustration drawn from a field test of the Stoddard dual progress plan will help clarify the point we are making. The school system in question gave evidence that it had implemented those features of this plan that were intended to accomplish nongrade-level advancement in mathematics and science in the intermediate years of elementary school. Students were grouped for instruction in each of these areas on the bases of achievement and ability without respect to grade level. The specialist teachers of these subjects were given in-service course work on ways of conducting nongraded advancement with their groups. It would seem, on the surface, that this aspect of the dual progress plan had been implemented. However, careful analysis of the actual instructional process revealed that the teachers were not advancing different groups at different rates along the curricular sequences. They were teaching in the new plan in the same way they had taught under the familiar grade-level system. The formal structure of the plan had been partially implemented, but the changes in instruction the plan called for were not taking place. The lesson of our illustration, generalized to encompass any organizational plan, is that a careful evaluation of the implementation of any plan is desirable because it tends to make the test of the plan honest by revealing requirements for its full implementation that otherwise might be passed over.

It is hard to overestimate the importance of adequate planning and of adequate personnel for the successful implementation of any team teaching program. After five years of experience with various team teaching programs, the leaders of the team teaching movement have gained a considerable understanding of the factors involved in the implementation of team teaching and of the approaches that are needed for taking these factors into account in installing a team teaching program. Any new project that is instituted should enlist the services of directors of previous projects from the universities or from other school systems to aid them in developing adequate plans for their project. Clearly, these plans should take into account not only matters of team organization and personnel but also changes needed in curriculum, tests, learning materials and equipment, and the training of team members. It is reasonable to assume that this period of planning and training should require a year or two before a new program is actually launched.

There is an acute shortage of personnel both in the universities and in local school systems for taking leadership in developing and conducting programs of educational change. Richard C. Anderson has proposed that "there is a need for a new role in education, that of educational engineer."[13] He points out that the tasks of program development in education call for devising practical applications of behavioral science principles. For this reason, educational engineers should be well versed in behavioral science theory and research methods. In addition, they must have a practical turn of mind and be both willing and able to apply their research training to the problems of developing and implementing educational materials, procedures, and programs. The educational engineer needs more than skills in applied research. Also he needs to be capable of taking leadership in his work with school administrators and teachers. Anderson suggests that school systems should employ educational engineers on a full-time basis to provide effective local leadership in educational change. He holds such a position in the public schools in East Brunswick, New Jersey.

What is the Future of Team Teaching?

Team teaching can refer simply to injecting the theme of team-work into the conduct of instruction, or it can refer to an approach to organizing the total instructional program. It is not clear at present whether the school of the future will be described as having a team teaching plan of organization, or whether it will be described

[13] Richard C. Anderson, "The Role of Educational Engineer," *The Journal of Educational Sociology,* vol. XXXIV, April, 1961, pp. 377–381.

as employing the theme of teacher teamwork within an organizational plan that bears some other name. What seems clear is that team teaching is one of the foremost themes of the educational reform movement and, unless present trends change sharply, will hold a prominent place in the new education that is taking shape. It is significant that teacher teamwork is an important feature of two major approaches to organizing instruction that are developing alongside team teaching. These are the nongraded-school plans and the semidepartmentalized dual progress plan designed by George D. Stoddard.

One can see several good reasons for expecting team teaching to become widely practiced in America's schools and to remain so. The sanctum of the autonomous teacher, the self-contained classroom, is being destroyed by insistent pressures toward greater teacher specialization and toward greater diversity in the instructional arrangements made available to the individual student. New patterns of teacher cooperation are essential for maintaining the integrity of the school's total program as it impinges upon staff members and upon individual students. Thus teacher teamwork of some form is becoming a necessity. Furthermore, team teaching probably will survive and grow because it provides a partial solution to the teacher shortage through offering special status and financial incentive to teachers and through utilizing teacher aides to relieve teachers of nonprofessional tasks.

In the long run, perhaps the strongest reason for believing that team teaching will have a prominent place in tomorrow's instructional programs is that it provides a system for incorporating and integrating most of the major themes, or lines of development, in the reform movement. A hierarchical organizational scheme such as the Lexington Plan, in theory at least, can accommodate any sort of staff specialization that develops. This includes any type of subject matter specialist, specialists in educational guidance, specialists in instruction using educational media such as television or learning programs, teaching interns, or teacher aides. Such a plan, through provisions for flexibility in grouping and other instructional arrangements, also can accommodate developments such as nongrading and independent study that are intended to increase the individualization of instruction. Further, team teaching plans are well suited for making use of new designs for school buildings that permit great flexibility in the use of learning space.

It will not be easy for team teaching to establish a place in American education. Any of its sponsors who look for easy victories should recall that many promising organizational plans have been developed during the past half-century, have been received with enthusiasm by forward-looking educators, have been adopted widely, and yet have faded from the educational scene. One might reason that the platoon plan, the Winnetka Plan, and other plans failed because they were educationally faulty or because they became out of date. But one also might reason that these plans never were implemented well enough to realize their potential and that they were given up because they did not achieve sufficient improvements in instruction to justify the burdens of maintaining them.

A hierarchical team teaching plan is highly complex, and for this reason is difficult to install and difficult to maintain in operation. Judging by the history of other organizational plans of comparable complexity, this sort of plan will establish a secure place in American education only through being implemented well enough to approach its potential contributions both to staff satisfaction and to the improvement of instruction.

The future of team teaching is not assured by the approaches to its development and evaluation that have been employed during its first five years on the educational frontier. Many of the projects under way across the country reflect a premature emphasis on disseminating team teaching, rather than an emphasis on developing and testing this sort of a plan. In many instances pressures for the immediate adoption of new plans come from local sources, either from within the school administration or from the community. This is a time of change in education, and almost every school system feels an urgent need to try team teaching along with other sorts of innovations. Important pressures for speeding the dissemination of team teaching also come from foundations and other granting agencies. The policy of these organizations often places more emphasis on the quantitative aspects of educational change than on the qualitative aspects. Such a policy has the advantage of stimulating widespread educational innovations, but it has the disadvantage of fostering changes that in many cases will fail to achieve their purposes because of faulty design and inadequate implementation.

It should not be forgotten that development and research are never ending processes. New plans for team teaching will continue to appear, new methods of implementing teamwork will be developed, and new findings will be forthcoming from research evaluations. Policy makers who are interested in team teaching will, each succeeding year, have a sounder basis for making judgments about the advantages and disadvantages of this sort of organizational plan. It is important for them to recognize that team teaching is still in its pilot phase and that they should not expect more than tentative evidence as to its effectiveness at this time.

If one accepts that the pilot phase of bringing about an educational reform should mainly have the purposes of stimulating interest, exploring possibilities, and gaining insights into the dimensions of the change processes that are involved, one may conclude that the first five years of the team teaching movement have been fruitful. Interest in team teaching is at a high level among school administrators and teachers. Numerous plans for team teaching have been designed and placed on trial. Early tryouts of these plans have exposed and clarified a host of problems that must be solved if team teaching is to be effectively implemented and soundly evaluated.

Probably another five years are needed to develop team teaching plans to the point where they are ready for full-scale evaluation. What is accomplished during this next phase of development will depend greatly on whether it is decided to focus on efforts to achieve major improvements in the quality of education through team teaching, or whether the objectives are mainly to provide new organizational arrangements without particular regard to the educational product. Since team teaching is part of the educational reform movement, it is to be hoped that new projects will be planned specifically to foster the accomplishment of such generic goals as theory, critical thinking, inquiry, and self-instruction and that they will place a strong emphasis on improving the individualization of instruction. Hierarchical team teaching plans seem well suited as media for advancing these purposes of the reform movement, and it would indeed be unfortunate if projects involving these plans were not specifically designed to foster excellence in instruction.

It is clear that the dissemination of team teaching will continue to outrun its development and evaluation. This probably does more good than harm since it produces a widespread receptiveness to improvements in team teaching as they become available. However, the most critical need at this time is for a small number of major developmental projects that focus on the key problems of design and implementation. To be effective, these projects must be well staffed with "educational engineers" who are competent to work out and implement solutions that take the themes of team teaching from the drawing board into the conduct of systematic programs of instruction. When such developmental projects have been completed, major evaluative studies can be undertaken to determine whether or not the faith that many educators place in team teaching is justified.

Bibliography
and
List of Team Teaching
Projects

Appendix

Note

Though the following bibliography and list of team teaching projects is extensive, the editors of this text do not consider it to be complete. There are imporant writings that have undoubtedly been overlooked. Furthermore, the editors are confident that the list of projects is merely a sampling of the team teaching activity now in progress. This appendix is presented in the hopes that it will be of help to those wishing to do further reading about team teaching and to those wishing to locate team teaching projects near them.

I. General: Books and Pamphlets

And No Bells Ring, Film on Team Teaching, Parts I & II, Commision for the Experimental Study of the Utilization of the Staff in the Secondary Schools.
   A visual presentation of many of the principles of team teaching. An attempt to encourage experimentation in this field.
Bennis, W. G., K. Benne, and R. Chin, *The Planning of Change,* New York, Holt, 1961.
Brickell, Henry M., *Commissioner's 1961 Catalog of Educational Change,* Albany, N.Y., The University of the State of New York, The State Education Department, October, 1961.
   Notes and describes team teaching projects in New York State.
Brickell, Henry M., *Organizing New York State for Educational Change,* Albany, N.Y., New York State Department of Education, December, 1961.
Brubacher, John S., *A History of the Problems of Education,* New York, McGraw-Hill, 1947.
   Contains a brief description of the monitorial systems of Bell and Lancaster.

Comenious, John Amos, *The Great Didactic* (trans. by M. W. Kestige), London, A. & C. Black, 1896.

Davis, Harold S., *The Effect of Team Teaching on Teachers,* Detroit, Mich., Wayne State University, November, 1962.
This dissertation on team teaching includes a comprehensive bibliography.

Dean, Stuart E., *Elementary School Administration and Organization: A National Survey of Practices and Policies,* Bulletin No. 11, United States Department of Health, Education and Welfare, Office of Education, 1960, pp. 84–86.
Interesting findings on the use of teacher aides.

Decade of Experiment, New York, The Fund for the Advancement of Education, 1961.

Duval, Frank H. and Edgar H. Mueller, *Promising Elementary School Practices,* University City, Mo., Public School District, 1960.

"Exploring Improved Teaching Patterns," *The Bulletin of the National Association of Secondary-School Principals,* vol. XLIII, January, 1959.
All articles dealing with specific projects are listed separately.

The Flexible School, Washington, D.C., National Education Association, Department of Elementary School Principals, 1957.

Goffman, Erving, *The Presentation of Self in Everyday Life,* New York, Doubleday, 1959.

Goodlad, John I. and Robert H. Anderson, rev. ed., *The Nongraded Elementary School,* New York, Harcourt Brace, 1963.
Major treatment of the history and nature of elementary school organization, and reasons for current trends toward elimination of graded school structure.

Heathers, Glen, ed., *The Journal of Educational Sociology,* vol. XXXIV, April, 1961.
Special Issue edited by Glen Heathers on "Conducting Field Research in Elementary Education." The whole issue is of particular interest to people experimenting with team teaching on both elementary and secondary levels. Most articles are listed separately.

Heinemann, Arnold H., ed., *Froebel Letters,* Boston, Lee & Shepherd, 1893.

Henry, Nelson B., ed., *Individualizing Instruction,* The Sixty-first Yearbook of the National Society for the Study of Education, pt. I, Chicago, University of Chicago Press, 1962.

Howell, John J., Constance M. Burns, and Clyde M. Hill, *Teacher Assistants,* New Haven, Conn., Yale-Fairfield Study of Elementary Teaching, 1958.

Huxley, Thomas H., *Science and Education,* New York, Appleton, 1895.

Klaus, David J. and Robert Glaser, *Increasing Team Proficiency Through Training: A Program of Research,* Pittsburgh, Pa., American Institute for Research, December, 1960.

Lambertsen, Eleanor C., *Nursing Team Organization and Functioning*, New York, Teachers College, Columbia University, 1958.

Lancaster, Joseph, *Improvements in Education*, New York, Collins and Perkins, 1807.

McGaughy, J. R., *An Evaluation of the Elementary School*, New York, Bobbs-Merrill, 1937.
  Contains among other things a description of the Hosic Plan of cooperative teaching.

Morse, Arthur D., *Schools of Tomorrow—Today*, Albany, University of the State of New York, The State Education Department, 1960.
  Describes many of the new forms of educational organization. Includes team teaching, nongrading, teaching aides, television teaching, tape teaching, etc.

Newcomb, Dorothy Perkins, *The Team Plan: A Manual for Nursing Service Administrators*, New York, 1953.

"New Horizons in Staff Utilization," *The Bulletin of the National Association of Secondary-School Principals*, vol. XLII, January, 1958.
  All articles dealing with specific projects are listed separately.

Pestalozzi, Johann H., *Leonard and Gertrude* (translated by Eva Channing), Boston, Ginn, Heath, 1885.

"Progressing Toward Better Schools," *The Bulletin of the National Association of Secondary-School Principals*, vol. XLIV, January, 1960.
  All articles dealing with specific projects are listed separately.

The Pursuit of Excellence: Education and the Future of America, Special studies project Report V of the Rockefeller Brothers Fund, America at Mid-Century Series, Garden City, N.Y., Doubleday, 1958.

Rashdall, Hastings, *The Universities of Europe in the Middle Ages*, London, Clarendon Press, 1936.

Salmon, David, ed., *The Practical Parts of Lancaster's Improvements and Bell's Experiment*, London, Cambridge University Press, 1932.

"Seeking Improved Learning Opportunities," *The Bulletin of the National Association of Secondary-School Principals*, vol. XLV, January, 1961.
  All articles dealing with specific projects are listed separately.

Shayon, Robert L., FM Radio Program on Team Teaching, *Everybody's Mountain Series*, Urbana, Ill., National Association of Educational Broadcasters.
  Tape available on rental basis.

Simon, Herbert A., *Administrative Behavior*, 2nd ed., New York, Macmillan, 1960.

Smith, Elmer R., *Teacher Education*, New York, Harper & Row, 1962.
  Includes chapters by Ralph W. Tyler, Paul Woodring, Robert N. Bush, Judson T. Shaplin, John I. Goodlad, and Alvin C. Eurich.

Snyder, Edith Roach, ed., *The Self-Contained Classroom*, Washington, D.C., Association for Supervision and Curriculum Development, 1960.

Stoddard, Alexander J., *Schools for Tomorrow: An Educator's Blueprint,* New York, The Fund for the Advancement of Education, 1957.
Teachers for Tomorrow, Bulletin No. 2, New York, The Fund for the Advancement of Education, 1955.
Teaching by Television, New York, The Fund for the Advancement of Education, 1957.
Time Allocation in the Elementary School, Cambridge, Mass., New England School Development Council, 1959.
> Discusses the time allotment problem in general, and relates it to new projects in team teaching, etc.
Time, Talent and Teachers, New York, The Ford Foundation, 1960.
Trump, J. Lloyd, *Images of the Future,* Commission on the Experimental Study of the Utilization of the Staff in the Secondary School, 1959.
> Attempts to give a picture of what the secondary school of tomorrow might be like by combining many of the significant trends that are observable today.
Trump, J. Lloyd, *New Directions to Quality Education: The Secondary School Tomorrow,* Commission on the Experimental Study of the Utilization of the Staff in the Secondary School, 1960.
> A brief outline of most of the major directions that improvements have been taking in the secondary schools today.
Trump, J. Lloyd, *New Horizons for Secondary School Teachers,* Commission on the Experimental Study of the Utilization of the Staff in the Secondary School, 1957.
> An introduction to and discussion of various aspects of the problem of staff utilization in the secondary school with possible experimental studies listed.
Trump, J. Lloyd and Dorsey Baynham, *Focus on Change: Guide to Better Schools,* Chicago, Rand McNally, 1961.
Ulich, Robert, *Three Thousand Years of Educational Wisdom,* Cambridge, Mass., Harvard University Press, 1947.
Woodring, Paul, *New Directions in Teacher Education,* New York, The Fund for the Advancement of Education, 1957.
> This book deals with teacher traning, and the last chapter discusses how team teaching may fit into a training program.
Wrightstone, J. Wayne, "Class Organization for Instruction," *What Research Says to the Teacher,* No. 13, Washington, D.C., National Education Association, 1957.

II. General: Articles

Ackerlund, George, "Some Teacher Views on the Self-Contained Classroom," *Phi Delta Kappan,* vol. XL, April, 1959, pp. 283–285.
"Aides and Secretaries," *School Management,* vol. LX, May, 1958, pp. 36–37, 74–75.

Anderson, Robert H., "Team Teaching," *CAPCI Bibliography*, No. 4, Association for Supervision and Curriculum Development in Cooperation with NEA Research Division, November, 1960.

Anderson, Robert H., "Team Teaching," *NEA Journal*, vol. L, March, 1961, pp. 52–54.
Treats team teaching as a significant development of ideas both old and new.

Anderson, Robert H., "Team Teaching—Backgrounds and Issues," Cambridge, Mass., Advanced Administrative Institute, 1959.
A discussion of the whole area of team teaching with an attempt to present background information and raise questions about team teaching. It uses as an example the project in Lexington, Massachusetts.

Anderson, Robert H., "Team Teaching in Action," *The Nation's Schools*, vol. LXV, May, 1960, pp. 62 ff.
Gives a general description of team teaching and describes briefly how it works in Lexington, Massachusetts; Norwalk, Connecticut; and Englewood, Florida.

Anderson, Robert H., "Team Teaching in the Elementary School," *The Education Digest*, vol. XXV, November, 1959, pp. 26–28.
Describes team teaching in general using project in Lexington, Massachusetts as an example.

Anderson, Robert H., "Time Allotment: A View on Priorities," *Educational Horizons*, vol. XXXVII, Winter, 1958, pp. 34–39.
Reviews the crisis in the schools, including misplaced emphasis and the problem of time allocation, and goes on to indicate how schools can redefine priorities and establish more efficient procedures.

Anderson, Robert H. and Donald P. Mitchell, "Three Examples of Team Teaching in Action," *The Nation's Schools*, vol. LXV, May, 1960, pp. 62–65.

Andree, Robert G., "How to Improve Instruction with Teaching Teams," *School Management*, vol. IV, November, 1960, pp. 51–54, 114.

Bray, Charles W., "Toward a Technology of Human Behavior for Defense Use," *American Psychologist*, vol. XVII, August, 1962, pp. 527–541.

Broadhead, Fred C., "Pupil Adjustment in the Semi-Departmental Elementary School," *The Elementary School Journal*, vol. LX, April, 1960, pp. 385–390.

Brown, Alma, "Learning about Individualized Teaching," *Educational Leadership*, vol. XVI, March, 1959, pp. 346–350.

Brown, Giles T., "Wired for Teaching," *Overview*, vol. I, July, 1960, pp. 40–41.

Brownell, John A. and Harris A. Taylor, "Theoretical Perspectives for Teaching Teams," *Phi Delta Kappan*, vol. XLIII, January, 1962, pp. 150–157.

A presentation of some models for teaching teams.

Brubaker, Charles W. and Lawrence B. Perkins, "Space for Individual Learning," *The School Executive,* vol. XVIII, February, 1959, pp. 43–58.

Bruntz, George C., "The Team Approach to Social Science Teaching," *The High School Journal,* vol. XLIII, April, 1960, pp. 370–374.

Bush, George P. and Lowell H. Hattery, "Teamwork and Creativity in Research," *Administrative Science Quarterly,* vol. I, December, 1956, pp. 361–372.

Bush, Robert N., "The Problem of a Flexible Schedule in High School," *Educational Leadership,* vol. XVIII, June, 1961, pp. 207–208.

Bush, Robert N., "The Team Teaching Bandwagon," *California Journal of Secondary Education,* vol. XXXV, April, 1960, pp. 207–208.

Calhoun, Mary, "The Teaching Team," *Child Guidance in Christian Living,* Methodist Publishing House, April, 1960.
Discusses cooperative teaching as carried on in certain church schools.

Chase, Francis S., "More and Better Teachers," *The Saturday Review,* vol. XXXVI, September, 1953, pp. 16–17.

Chase, Francis S., "New Conditions Confront Education," *The School Review,* vol. LXV, Spring, 1957, pp. 3–11.

Chase, Francis S., "The Schools I Hope to See," *NEA Journal,* vol. XLVI, March, 1957, pp. 164–166.

Chauncey, Henry, "More Effective Utilization of Teachers," *The Utilization of Scientific and Professional Manpower* (a publication of the National Manpower Council), New York, Columbia University Press, 1954.
Argues that it should become possible for the teacher to function at a higher level of skill, ability, and insight for a larger portion of the working day.

Cleland, George L., "Interest of State Departments of Education in Staff Utilization Studies," *NASSP Bulletin,* vol. XLII, January, 1958, pp. 181–184.
A plea that state departments of education, if they are to play a strong role in modern education, must be flexible in their standards with regard to experimentation of the staff utilization type.

Cocking, Walter D., "Basic Organization of Schools," *The School Executive,* vol. LXXVIII, October, 1958, p. 7.

Cocking, Walter D., "Proposals on Structure," *The School Executive,* vol. LXXVIII, December, 1958, p. 6.

Cunningham, Luvern L., "Keys to Team Teaching," *Overview,* vol. I, October, 1960, pp. 54–55.

Cunningham, Luvern L., "The Teacher and Change," *The Elementary School Journal,* vol. LXII, December, 1961, pp. 119–129.

Cunningham, Luvern L., "Team Teaching: Where Do We Stand," *Administrator's Notebook*, vol. VIII, April, 1960.
A brief attempt to explain and categorize team teaching.
Cunningham, Luvern L., "Viewing Change in School Organizations," *Administrator's Notebook*, vol. XI, September, 1962.
Dean, Stuart E., "Team Teaching: A Review," *School Life*, vol. XLIV, September, 1961, pp. 5–8.
Dean, Stuart E. and Clinette F. Witherspoon, "Team Teaching in the Elementary School," *Education Briefs*, No. 38, Washington, D.C., United States Department of Health, Education and Welfare, Office of Education, January, 1962.
Deason, J. P., "What They Say about Teacher-Aides," *The School Executive*, vol. LXXVII, December, 1957, pp. 59–60.
Diederich, Paul B., "Independent Reading: Lowest Cost Relief of High School Congestion," Princeton, N.J., Educational Testing Service.
Another approach to school reorganization.
Dillman, Beryl R., "An Appraisal of NASSP's Staff Utilization Study at the Close of Its First Two Years," *NASSP Bulletin*, vol. XLIV, January, 1960, pp. 13–18.
An attempt to reach some conclusions about what has been accomplished in general during the first two years of this study.
Downey, Lawrence W., "Secondary Education: A Model for Improvement," *The School Review*, vol. LXVIII, Autumn, 1960, pp. 251–265.
Drummond, Harold D., "Team Teaching: An Assessment," *Educational Leadership*, vol. XIX, December, 1961, pp. 160–165.
Eckelberry, R. H., "A Timely Report on an Urgent Problem," *The Journal of Higher Education*, vol. XXX, October, 1959, pp. 401–402.
Falk, Philip H., "The Improvement of Instruction," *The Bulletin*, Madison Education Association, Madison, Wis., vol. XXX, April, 1960.
A very short article which warns of the dangers of leaping on a bandwagon of team teaching before it has been thoroughly tried and tested.
Fischler, Abraham S., "Use of Team Teaching in the Elementary School," *School Science and Mathematics*, vol. LXII, April, 1962, pp. 281–288.
Fritz, John, "Educational Technology—Boon or Bane?" *The School Review*, vol. LXVIII, Autumn, 1960, pp. 294–307.
Fullerton, Bill, J., "Team Teaching Activities," *The Outlook in Student Teaching*, Forty-first Yearbook, Cedar Falls, Iowa, The Association for Student Teaching, 1962, pp. 80–93.
Gaffney, Matthew P., "Higher Education's Relationship to Staff Utilization Studies," *NASSP Bulletin*, vol. XLII, January, 1958, pp. 188–192.
An attempt to show that the goals and purposes of the NASSP are similar to the goals and purposes of various schools of education throughout the country.

Gilbert, Edward H., "A Design for School Improvement," *Administrator's Notebook*, vol. VII, May, 1959.

Gilchrist, Robert S., "Promising Practices in Education," *Phi Delta Kappan*, vol. XLI, February and March, 1960, pt. I, pp. 208–211; pt. II, pp. 269–274.

    Mr. Gilchrist suggests questions the answers to which will determine if new practices are really "promising." He gives examples of practices in several curricular areas.

Gilchrist, Robert S., *et al.*, "Curriculum News," *Educational Leadership*, vol. XVII, May, 1960, pp. 517–520.

Ginther, John R. and William A. Shroyer, "Team Teaching in English and History at the Eleventh-Grade Level," *The School Review*, vol. LXX, Autumn, 1962, pp. 303–313.

Goodlad, John I., "News and Comment," *The Elementary School Journal*, vol. LIX, October, 1958, pp. 1–17.

    Discusses the need for new practices in the schools and looks briefly at projects in Englewood, Florida; Flint, Michigan; Fort Wayne, Indiana; and University City, Missouri.

Goodlad, John I. and K. Rehage, "Unscrambling the Vocabulary of School Organization," *NEA Journal*, vol. LI, November, 1962, pp. 34–36.

Gray, Harold F. and Carl T. Fynboe, "Teaching Assistants," *California Journal of Secondary Education*, vol. XXV, April, 1960, pp. 246–247.

Hager, Phil E., "Nineteenth Century Experiments with Monitorial Teaching," *Phi Delta Kappan*, vol. XL, January, 1959, pp. 164–167.

    A description of the rise and fall of the monitorial system.

Hagstrom, Ellis A., "New Opportunity for Outstanding Teachers," *Grade Teacher*, vol. LXXVIII, January, 1961, pp. 13, 104.

Hamalainen, Arthur E., "Some Current Proposals and Their Meaning," *Educational Leadership*, vol. XVI, February, 1959, pp. 271 ff.

Hanson, Earl H., "Teacher Utilization," *American School Board Journal*, vol. CXXXVIII, April, 1959, p. 12.

Harris, Ben M. and J. G. Umstattd, "The American High School, 1960–Revisited in 1970," *Texas Looks at Staff Utilization*, The University of Texas, January, 1960.

Heathers, Glen, "Field Research on Elementary School Organization and Instruction," *The Journal of Educational Sociology*, vol. XXIV, April, 1961, pp. 338–343.

Hechinger, Fred M., "Defensive Move: N.E.A. Unit Seeks to Protect the 'Self-Contained Classroom,' " *The New York Times*, October 30, 1960.

    This article reviews the material covered in E. R. Snyder, *The Self-Contained Classroom*.

Hechinger, Fred M., "No Magic Formula: Utopia, An Innovator Warns, Is Not Just Around the Corner," *The New York Times*, February 12, 1961.

Hills, R. J., "A New Concept of Staff Relations," *Administrator's Notebook,* vol. VIII, March, 1960.

Hoban, Charles F., Jr., "Research in New Media in Education," *Three Conference Working Papers for the National Conference on Teacher Education and New Media,* The American Association of Colleges for Teacher Education, January, 1961.

Hoppock, Ann, "An Opposing View—Team Teaching: Form without Substance," *NEA Journal,* vol. L, April, 1961.

Howe, Harold, II, "Needed: A Radical Change," *The Saturday Review,* vol. XLIII, September, 1960, pp. 73–74.

Kaya, Esin, "Problems in Evaluating Educational Plans in the School Setting," *The Journal of Educational Sociology,* vol. XXXIV, April, 1961, pp. 355–359.

Kidd, J. W., "Question of Class Size," *The Journal of Higher Education,* vol. XXIII, November, 1952, pp. 440–444.

Lambert, Philip, "Team Teaching for the Elementary School," *Educational Leadership,* vol. XVIII, November, 1960, pp. 85–88, 128.

McAuley, J. D., "Elementary Education—Five Straws in the Wind," *Phi Delta Kappan,* vol. XLI, June, 1960, pp. 394–396.
    The five trends in elementary education discussed are: science, downward pressure of content material, homogeneous grouping, departmentalization, and "business."

Mead, Margaret, "Thinking Ahead: Why is Education Obsolete?" *Harvard Business Review,* vol. XXXVI, November–December, 1958, pp. 23–30.
    Raises some questions about provisions for secondary school pupils in particular.

Michael, Lloyd S., "New Directions to Quality Education in Secondary Schools," *NASSP Bulletin,* vol. XLV, January, 1961, pp. 11–18.

Michael, Lloyd S., "What are We Trying to Accomplish in the Staff Utilization Studies?" *NASSP Bulletin,* vol. XLIII, January, 1959, pp. 5–10.
    An outline of all the purposes the Commission has evolved since its appointment in May, 1956.

Michael, Lloyd S. and J. Lloyd Trump, "Ideas Directing Education," *The School Executive,* vol. LXXVIII, June, 1959, pp. 23–25.

Miel, Alice, "The Self-Contained Classroom: An Assessment," *Teachers College Record,* vol. LIX, February, 1958, pp. 282–291.
    Miel advocates a modified self-contained classroom in which one teacher acts as a home-base leader with the regular classroom facilities supplemented by other people, materials, and machines.

Morse, Arthur D., "Open Minds and Flexible Schools," *The Saturday Revew,* vol. XLIII, September, 1960, pp. 67–68.

Nelson, Lester W., "The Fund for the Advancement of Education Helps

Schools Plow New Ground," *NASSP Bulletin,* vol. XLII, January, 1958, pp. 177–180.
   A description of the fund, its purposes, and its relation to the NASSP in providing funds for staff utilization studies.

Nelson, Lester W., "The High School of the Future: Implications as Viewed by an Administrator," *California Journal of Secondary Education,* vol. XXXIV, October, 1959, pp. 383–384.

Nelson, Lester W., "New Ideas in Education," *Harvard Graduate School of Education Association Bulletin,* vol. IV, September, 1959, pp. 11–16.

Ohm, Robert E., "Toward a Rationale for Team Teaching," *Administrator's Notebook,* vol. IX, March, 1961.

Park, Charles B., "Better Utilization of Teacher Competencies," *The Journal of Teacher Education,* vol. VII, June, 1956, pp. 101–110.

Park, Charles B., "The Teacher Aide Plan," *The Nation's Schools,* vol. LVI, July, 1955, pp. 45–55.

Partridge, Arthur R., "Staff Utilization in Senior High School," *Educational Leadership,* vol. XVIII, January, 1961, pp. 217–221.

Prescott, George A. and Bryce Perkins, "New Careers for Teachers," *Connecticut Teacher,* April, 1959.

"Recent Experimentation," *National Education Association Research Bulletin,* vol. XXXVII, October, 1959, pp. 93–94.

Reid, Chandos, "Children Learn Through Many Media," *Childhood Education,* vol. XXXVI, February, 1960, pp. 248–254.
   Reid suggests that children learn best when they have the freedom to explore their interests.

Shane, Harold G., "Elementary Schools Changed Only a Little During Fabulous Fifties," *The Nation's Schools,* vol. LXV, April, 1960, pp. 71–73 ff.

Shaplin, Judson T., "Team Teaching," *The Saturday Review,* vol. XLIV, May 20, 1961, pp. 54–55, 70.

Shumsky, A. and R. Mukerji, "From Research Idea to Classroom Practice," *The Elementary School Journal,* vol. LXIII, November, 1962, pp. 83–86.

Singer, Ira J., "Team Teaching and the School Librarian," *School Libraries,* vol. II, October, 1961, pp. 21–23, 38.

Stiles, Lindley J., "Individual and Team Teaching," *Wisconsin Journal of Education,* January, 1960.
   A review of the educational situation as it exists today and an attempt to place team teaching within the educational framework.

"Teacher-Aides: Current Practices and Experiments," *Educational Research Service Circular,* No. 5, July, 1960.

"Team Teaching," *Professional Growth Program,* vol. VII, New London, Conn., Croft Educational Services, October, 1961.
   Includes guides for teachers, administrators, and principals.

"Team Teaching—A Definition," *Massachusetts Teacher*, vol. XL, December, 1960, pp. 17–18.

Thelen, Herbert A., "Classroom Grouping of Students," *The School Review*, vol. LXVII, Spring, 1959, pp. 60–78.

Travers, B. H., "The Teaching Team in Australian Education," *The Australian Journal of Education*, vol. V, November, 1961, pp. 145–152.

Trump, J. Lloyd, "Brief History and Recommendations of the Commission on the Experimental Study of the Utilization of the Staff in the Secondary School," *NASSP Bulletin*, vol. XLV, January, 1961, pp. 275–281.

Trump, J. Lloyd, "Flexible Class Schedules," *California Journal of Secondary Education*, vol. XXXV, February, 1960, pp. 94–95.

Trump, J. Lloyd, "Image of the Future Secondary School Principal," *California Journal of Secondary Education*, vol. XXXV, December, 1960, pp. 517–523.

Trump, J. Lloyd, "A Look Ahead in Secondary Education," *NASSP Bulletin*, vol. XLII, January, 1958, pp. 5–15.

An attempt to give a picture of what the secondary school of tomorrow might be like by combining many of the significant trends that are observable today.

Trump, J. Lloyd, "More Staff Utilization Experimentation Is Needed," *NASSP Bulletin*, vol. XLII, January, 1958, pp. 209–213.

Presents outline of experimental studies that might be made in staff utilization.

Trump, J. Lloyd, "Others Are Also Extending Horizons in Staff Utilization," *NASSP Bulletin*, vol. XLII, January, 1958, pp. 197–208.

A listing of various staff-utilization projects about which information was available at this time.

Trump, J. Lloyd, "Some Questions and Answers about Suggestions for Improving Staff Utilization," *NASSP Bulletin*, vol. XLV, January, 1961, pp. 19–28.

Trump, J. Lloyd, Virgil W. Gillenwater, and Charles D. Rowley, "Summer Workshops on Staff Utilization," *NASSP Bulletin*, vol. XLIV, January, 1960, pp. 316–322.

Contains reports of discussions, some of which deal with team teaching.

Umstattd, J. G., "Staff Utilization Studies Reviewed by a Secondary Education Specialist," *NASSP Bulletin*, vol. XLII, January, 1958, pp. 193–196.

Brief comments and observations.

Weiss, Thomas M. and Mary Scott Morris, "A Critique of the 'Team Approach,'" *The Educational Forum*, vol. XXIV, January, 1960, pp. 207–208.

"What Teachers Say about Better Use of Their Time," *School Management*, vol. IV, May, 1960, pp. 63–66.

Wigderson, Harry I., "Team Teaching," Visalia, Calif., Tulare County Superintendent of Schools Office, June, 1962.

Contains extensive bibliography.

Wilson, Raymond G., "Accreditation Standards and Staff Utilization," *NASSP Bulletin*, vol. XLII, January, 1958, pp. 185–187.

This article encourages state accreditation agencies to continue to maintain an open-minded attitude toward projects dealing with staff utilization.

III.   School Buildings

"A & M Consolidated Senior High School, College Station, Texas," *Profiles of Significant Schools*, New York, Educational Facilities Laboratories, May, 1960.

Anderson, Edward and John C. Harkness, "Planned Variability," *The Nation's Schools*, vol. LXV, April, 1960, pp. 83–91.

Wayland High School, Wayland, Massachusetts.

Anderson, Robert H. and Donald P. Mitchell, "Team Teaching: New Learning Concepts Demand Changes in School Plant Design," *The Nation's Schools*, vol. LXV, June, 1960, pp. 75 ff.

Points out how space requirements in future schools will differ greatly from conventional requirements in order to accommodate such innovations as mechanical aids and team teaching. Discusses the matter of flexibility and its various uses.

Andree, Robert G., "An Image of the Future Arises in Olympia Fields," *The Nation's Schools*, vol. LXV, July, 1960.

Description of a new high school designed for team teaching in Park Forest, Rich Township, Illinois.

"Belaire Elementary School, San Angelo, Texas," *Profiles of Significant Schools*, New York, Educational Facilities Laboratories, September, 1960.

Campbell, Edward A., "New Spaces and Places for Learning," *The School Review*, vol. LXVIII, Autumn, 1960, pp. 346–352.

The Cost of a Schoolhouse, New York, Educational Facilities Laboratories, 1960.

This volume on school building costs and considerations, especially pp. 126–239, is closely related to questions of school personnel organization.

"Flexible Classrooms for a Flexible Curriculum," *School Management*, vol. III, November, 1959, pp. 45–47.

Lamphere Public Schools, Madison Heights, Michigan.

"Heathcote Elementary School, Scarsdale, New York," *Profiles of Signifi-*

cant Schools, New York, Educational Facilities Laboratories, September, 1960.

"Hillsdale High School, San Mateo, California," *Profiles of Significant Schools,* New York, Educational Facilities Laboratories, June, 1960.

"Holland High School, Holland, Michigan," *Profiles of Significant Schools,* New York, Educational Facilities Laboratories, September, 1962.

"Montrose Elementary School, Laredo, Texas," *Profiles of Significant Schools,* New York, Educational Facilities Laboratories, June, 1960.

"The New High School," *Overview,* Design Project Number Six, March, 1962.

New Schools for New Education, New York, Educational Facilities Laboratories, 1961.

The architectural implications of *Images of the Future,* by J. Lloyd Trump. Based on the architectural workshop conducted by the University of Michigan, October 19–20, 1959.

"Newton South High School, Newton, Massachusets," *Profiles of Significant Schools,* New York, Educational Facilities Laboratories, February, 1960.

"North Hagerstown High School, Hagerstown, Maryland," *Profiles of Significant Schools,* New York, Educational Facilities Laboratories, February, 1960.

Pino, Edward C., "The Lamphere Quad—A New Dimension in School Design," *Michigan School Board Journal,* vol. VI, September, 1960.

Profiles of Significant Schools: High Schools 1962, New York, Educational Facilities Laboratories, 1961.

Contains excellent material on new types of high school construction for a variety of different programs. Team teaching schools considered at length are: Ridgewood High School, Norridge, Illinois; Wayland High School, Wayland, Massachusetts; Lamphere Senior High School, Madison Heights, Michigan; and Cold Spring Harbor Senior High School, Huntington, New York.

Profiles of Significant Schools: Schools for Team Teaching, New York, Educational Facilities Laboratories, 1961.

Specific references listed separately. Has a general introduction about Team Teaching and then explores various significant architectural answers to the demands of such organization.

"Public School No. 9, Borough of Queens, New York City," *Profiles of Significant Schools,* New York, Educational Facilities Laboratories, September, 1960.

Rice, Arthur H., "Here Are Some Factors That Affect Future Schoolhouse Planning," *The Nation's Schools,* vol. LXV, April, 1960, pp. 74–77.

"Rich Township High School, Olympia Fields Campus, Rich Township, Illinois," *Profiles of Significant Schools,* New York, Educational Facilities Laboratories, May, 1960.

School Building Conference, Challenges of the Immediate Future—A Sum-

mary, Cleveland, Ohio, The Educational Research Council of Greater Cleveland, 1960.

"Two Saginaw Middle Schools, Saginaw Township, Michigan," *Profiles of Significant Schools,* New York, Educational Facilities Laboratories, 1960.

"Wayland Senior High School, Wayland, Massachusetts," *Profiles of Significant Schools,* New York, Educational Facilities Laboratories, January, 1960.

IV. *Projects*

A. Elementary Schools

ARIZONA, TUCSON

Profiles of Significant Schools: Schools for Team Teaching, New York: Educational Facilities Laboratories, 1961, pp. 60–62.

CALIFORNIA, CONCORD

Wall, Harvey R. and Robert W. Reasoner, *Team Teaching: A Descriptive and Evaluative Study of a Program for the Primary Grades,* Concord, Calif., Mt. Diablo Unified School District, 1962.

CALIFORNIA, COTATI

Project begun Fall, 1961.

CALIFORNIA, COVINA

Profiles of Significant Schools: Schools for Team Teaching, New York, Educational Facilities Laboratories, 1961, pp. 50–54.

CALIFORNIA, FREEDOM

Project begun September, 1960.

CALIFORNIA, MARTINEZ

Montgomery, Charles D., "Bibliography: Staff Utilization Studies," Martinez, Calif., Contra Costa County Schools, October, 1960.

CALIFORNIA, OCEANO

Adams, Andrew S., "Operation 'Co-Teaching' dateline: Oceano, California," Oceano, Calif., Freedom Union School District.

CALIFORNIA, SAN JOSE

"An Experimental Team Teaching Approach in the 4th, 5th, and 6th Grades in the Union School District, San Jose, California," San Jose, Calif., Union School District, September, 1961.

"Mid-Year Evaluation of an Experimental Team Teaching Approach in the 4th, 5th, and 6th Grades, Union School District, San Jose, California," San Jose, Calif., Union School District, January, 1961.

CONNECTICUT, GREENWICH

Buder, Leonard, "Teaching by Team Due in Greenwich," *The New York Times*, May 16, 1961.

Profiles of Significant Schools: Schools for Team Teaching, New York, Educational Facilities Laboratories, 1961, pp. 44–49.

"Team Teaching: An Approach to Elementary School Instruction," Greenwich, Conn., Greenwich Public Schools, January, 1960.

CONNECTICUT, NORWALK

The Norwalk Plan: An Attempt to Improve the Quality of Education Through a Team-Teaching Organization: A Two-Year Study Supported by the Fund for the Advancement of Education, Norwalk, Conn., The Norwalk Plan, November 14, 1960.

The Norwalk Plan: A Study Designed to Establish New Careers for Teachers, First Report, Norwalk, Conn., Board of Education, July, 1959.

Perkins, Bryce, *et al.,* "Teamwork Produces Audio-Visual Techniques," *Grade Teacher,* vol. LXXVII, June, 1960, pp. 55–72.

Descriptions and illustrations of the ways audio-visual and other materials are being used in the Norwalk Plan.

Team Teaching at the Fox Run Elementary School, Norwalk, Conn., Fox Run Elementary School, 1961.

A parents' report from the PTA.

Wilson, Liz, "150 Mittens," *Mark,* April 23, 1960, pp. 5–8.

Description of the Norwalk Plan in operation.

FLORIDA, CORAL GABLES

Indication of team teaching in progress.

FLORIDA, ENGLEWOOD

Bahner, John M., "Grouping Within a School," *Childhood Education,* vol. XXVI, April, 1960, pp. 354–356.

Bahner, John M., "Reading Instruction in Various Patterns of Groupings in Grades Four Through Six," Conference on Reading, University of Chicago, 1959, pp. 95–98.

Bahner, John M., "Team Teaching at Englewood School," Englewood, Fla., Englewood Elementary School, October, 1960.

Profiles of Significant Schools: Schools for Team Teaching, New York, Educational Facilities Laboratories, 1961, pp. 14–19.

FLORIDA, TITUSVILLE

New Horizons in Learning, Titusville, Fla., Brevard County Board of Public Instruction, December 12, 1960.

GEORGIA, DEKALB

Carmichael, Bennie, "Others Also Study Staff Utilization: Effecting Better Use of Educational Manpower and Resources," *NASSP Bulletin,* vol. XLIII, January, 1959, pp. 274–282.
    Describes a school and university cooperative program.
Drummond, Harold D. and William Benjamin, "Using Superior Teachers for Instructional Leaders," *Research Bulletin No. 2,* DeKalb, Ga., Peabody-Public School Cooperative Program, September, 1958.
    See also university section for further material on the Peabody-Public School Cooperative Program.
Fulford, Bert W., "Report of the Skyland Elementary School," DeKalb, Ga., Skyland Elementary School, December 16, 1959.

ILLINOIS, CHICAGO

Alice, Sister Mary, R. S. M., "Administration of the Nongraded School," *The Elementary School Journal, vol. LXI,* December, 1960, pp. 148–152.
Linklater, Irene and Ernelle Geyler, "Monthly Progress Report," Chicago, Oriole Park Elementary School, April, 1960.

ILLINOIS, LAGRANGE

Indication of team teaching in progress.

ILLINOIS, WOODSTOCK

Indication of team teaching in progress.

INDIANA, FORT WAYNE

"Teamwork for Teachers," Fort Wayne, Ind., Francis M. Price School.

IOWA, CEDAR FALLS

"The Experimental Team Teaching Project in the Lincoln Elementary School, Cedar Falls, Iowa," Cedar Falls, Iowa, Lincoln Elementary School, October 27, 1960.

MAINE, AUBURN

"Questions and Answers about Team Teaching," *Elementary School News,* vol. V, Auburn, Me., Department of Education, November 13, 1959.

Shedd, Mark R., "Team Teaching," *Maine Teacher,* May, 1960.
Report of the Auburn, Maine Project.
Shedd, Mark R., "Team Teaching and Its Impact Upon the Role of the
Elementary School Principal," *Maine Elementary School Principals
Newsletter,* April, 1960.
Written by the person who initiated a team teaching plan in Auburn,
Maine.
"Team Teaching: A Report of the Pilot Team," Auburn, Me., Department
of Education, Sepember, 1960.
Webber, Lewis E., Richard E. Babb, and Claire Chasse, "Brief Report,
Evaluation and Projection of the Pilot Project in Team Teaching,"
Auburn, Me., Auburn Team Teaching Project, June, 1960.

"Report on the Experiment in Team Teaching in the Elementary Schools,"
Baltimore, Baltimore Public Schools, June 30, 1960.
"Team Teaching Being Tried in Five Schools," *Staff Newsletter,* Balti-
more, Baltimore Public Schools, February 12, 1960.

Team teaching in the beginning stages.

Anderson, Robert H., "Report to the Administrative Board of the School
and University Program for Research and Development on the Franklin
School Project in Lexington, Massachusets during the Academic Year,
1957–58," Cambridge, Mass., SUPRAD, 1958.
Anderson, Robert H., "Report to the Administrative Board of the School
and University Program for Research and Development of the Franklin
School Project in Lexington, Massachusetts during the Acadamic Year,
1958–59," Cambridge, Mass., SUPRAD, 1959.
Anderson, Robert H., "School-University Cooperation and the Lexington
Project," *The Journal of Educational Sociology,* vol. XXXIV, April,
1961, pp. 382–386.
Anderson, Robert H., Ellis A. Hagstrom, and Wade M. Robinson, "Team
Teaching in an Elementary School," *The School Review,* vol. LXVIII,
Spring, 1960, pp. 71–84.
Hagstrom, Ellis A., "The Teaching Teams Project, Franklin School, Lex-
ington, Massachusetts: A Brief Description," Cambridge, Mass.,
SUPRAD, November 10, 1959.
A background paper used for distribution to project visitors and
others upon request. See more recent publication by Stone and
Bahner.

Hagstrom, Ellis A., and Beverly S. Stone, "The Teaching Teams Project, Franklin School, Lexington, Massachusetts: A Brief Description," Cambridge, Mass., SUPRAD, November 1, 1960.
    See more recent version by Stone and Bahner.
Levensohn, Alan, "Team Teaching for Elementary Schools," *School Management*, vol. II, December, 1958, pp. 45–48.
Morse, Arthur D., *Schools of Tomorrow—Today*, Albany, University of the State of New York, The State Education Department, 1960, pp. 9–25.
Profiles of Significant Schools: Schools for Team Teaching, New York, Educational Facilities Laboratories, 1961, pp. 36–42.
Stone, Beverly S. and John M. Bahner, "The Teaching Teams Project, Lexington, Massachusetts," Cambridge, Mass., SUPRAD, April, 1962.
Thomas, John, "Large-Group Instruction," *Massachusetts Teacher*, vol. XL, May, 1961, pp. 11–13.

MASSACHUSETTS, NORTON

Mahoney, William M., "Try Co-ordinate Teaching," *American School Board Journal*, vol. CXXXIX, November, 1959, pp. 13–14.

MASSACHUSETTS, WAYLAND

Team teaching in progress. See high school section.

MICHIGAN, ANN ARBOR

Indication of the beginning of a project.

MICHIGAN, BIRMINGHAM

Crandall, Edwin and Walter Piel, "The Birmingham Plan for Coordinate Team Teaching: A First Report on One Type of Team Teaching," Birmingham, Mich., Birmingham Public Schools, November, 1960.

MICHIGAN, CARSON CITY

"Flexible Classrooms for a Flexible Curriculum," *School Management*, vol. III, November, 1959, pp. 45–47.
    Architectural planning.
Hough, Jim, "School Without Partitions Stimulates 'Space Age' Education," *Lansing State Journal*, March 6, 1960.
Profiles of Significant Schools: Schools for Team Teaching, New York, Educational Facilities Laboratories, 1961, pp. 20–24.
"A Team Approach to Teaching at the Carson City Community School," Carson City, Mich., Carson City Community School, January 30, 1959.

MICHIGAN, FLINT

Indication of team teaching in progress.

MICHIGAN, MADISON HEIGHTS

"Overview: Lamphere Educational Action Project," Madison Heights, Mich., Lamphere Public Schools, August 2, 1960.
Pino, Edward C., "The Lamphere Quad—A New Dimension in School Design," *Michigan School Board Journal*, vol. VI, September, 1960.
Profiles of Significant Schools: Schools for Team Teaching, New York, Educational Facilities Laboratories, 1961, pp. 26–30.

NEW MEXICO, FARMINGTON

Indication of team teaching in progress.

NEW YORK, GLEN COVE

"Team Teaching," Glen Cove, N.Y., The Glen Cove Public Schools, Office of the Principal, Landing School.

NEW YORK, LONG BEACH AND OSSINING

Anderson, "Summary of Ossining Teachers' Reactions to the Dual Progress Plan: June, 1959," New York, New York University School of Education, Experimental Teaching Center, September 9, 1959.
Anderson and Beilin, "Long Beach Parents' Reactions to the Dual Progress Plan: June, 1959," New York, New York University School of Education, Experimental Teaching Center, October 8, 1959.
"Annual Report of the Experimental Teaching Center: July 1, 1958-June 30, 1959," New York, New York University School of Education, Experimental Teaching Center, October, 1959.
Report of first year of operation.
"Annual Report of the Experimental Teaching Center: July 1, 1959-May 31, 1960," New York, New York University School of Education, Experimental Teaching Center, June, 1960.
Report of second year of operation.
"Answers to Basic Questions on the Cooperative Study of the Dual Progress Plan," New York, New York University School of Education, Experimental Teaching Center, September 2, 1958.
Beilin, "A Comparison of Attitudes of Long Beach Pupils Toward the Dual Progress Plan in June 1959 and in June 1960," New York, New York University School of Education, Experimental Teaching Center, September 28, 1960.
Beilin and Anderson, "Attitudes of Ossining Pupils toward the Dual Progress Plan: June 1959," New York, New York University School of Education, Experimental Teaching Center, September 17, 1959.
Bishop, David W., "The Role of the Local Administrator in Reorganizing Elementary Schools to Test a Semi-Departmentalized Plan," *The*

Journal of Educational Sociology, vol. XXXIV, April, 1961, pp. 344–348.
"Long Beach Progress Report, July 1, 1958 to June 30, 1959," Long Beach, N.Y., Long Beach Public Schools.
Describes the first year of the project at Long Beach.
"The Meaning of Nongraded Advancement in the Dual Progress Plan," *ETC Notes,* No. 1, New York, New York University School of Education, Experimental Teaching Center, February 16, 1959.
Describes the nongraded part of the project.
"Provisions for Language Arts–Social Studies in the Dual Progress Plan," *ETC Notes,* No. 2, New York, New York University School of Education, Experimental Teaching Center, February 16, 1959.
Describes the traditional part of the project.
Radomisli, "Long Beach Parents' Reactions to the Dual Progress Plan: June, 1960," New York, New York University School of Education, Experimental Teaching Center, August 16, 1960.
Radomisli, "Long Beach Teachers' Reactions to the Dual Progress Plan: June, 1960," New York, New York University School of Education, Experimental Teaching Center, June 29, 1960.
Radomisli, "Ossining Parents' Reactions to the Dual Progress Plan: June, 1960," New York, New York University School of Education, Experimental Teaching Center, August 23, 1960.
"The Dual Progress Plan," Ossining, N.Y., Union Free School District No. 1.
Heathers, Glen, "The Dual Progress Plan," *Educational Leadership,* vol. XVIII, November, 1960, pp. 89–91.
Heathers, Glen, "The Dual Progress Plan and Departmentalization in the Elementary School," New York, New York University School of Education, Experimental Teaching Center, December 15, 1958.
Heathers, Glen, "Proposal for Organizing Instruction in a K-6 Elementary School," New York, New York University School of Education, Experimental Teaching Center, November 16, 1959.
Heathers, Glen, "Report of Reactions of Ossining Parents to the Dual Progress Plan: June 1959," New York, New York University School of Education, Experimental Teaching Center, September 1, 1959.
Heathers, Glen and Morris Pincus, "The Dual Progress Plan in the Elementary School," *The Arithmetic Teacher,* vol. VI, December, 1959, pp. 302–305.
Hechinger, Fred M., "The New Dual Progress Plan for Grade Schools," *Parents' Magazine,* vol. XXXV, February, 1960, pp. 35, 123, 124.
A good general statement of and introduction to the ideas and purposes embodied in the Dual Progress Plan.
Radomisli, "Ossining Teachers' Reactions to the Dual Progress Plan: June, 1960," New York, New York University School of Education, Experimental Teaching Center, July 5, 1960.

'Report of Union Free School District No. 1, Town of Ossining, New York, July 1, 1958-June 30, 1959," Ossining, N.Y., Ossining Public Schools.
Stoddard, George D., *The Dual Progress Plan*, New York, Harper & Row, 1961.
Stoddard, George D., "The Dual Progress Plan," *School and Society*, vol. LXXXVI, October 11, 1958, pp. 351–352.
Trachtman, Gilbert M., "The Role of an In-Service Program in Establishing a New Plan of Elementary School Organization," *The Journal of Educational Sociology*, vol. XXIV, April, 1961, pp. 349–354.

NEW YORK, NEW YORK

Team teaching in progress in several elementary schools.

NEW YORK, PATCHOGUE

Indication of team teaching in progress.

NEW YORK, SCHENECTADY

Indication of team teaching in progress.

PENNSYLVANIA, ALLENTOWN

Indication of team teaching in progress.

PENNSYLVANIA, BERWYN

Boyer, Randall R., "Minutes of Education Committee Meetings: Tredyffrin-Easttown Elementary Schools," February 27, 1961.

PENNSYLVANIA, PITTSBURGH

"Pittsburgh Schools Get Ford Grant for Teacher Team Construction Plan," *School Boards*, vol. V, July, 1960.
　　An indication that team teaching is beginning in five elementary schools in Pittsburgh.
Pupils, Patterns, and Possibilities, Pittsburgh, Pa., Board of Public Education, 1961.
　　An extensive report on the very large Pittsburgh team teaching project.

TENNESSEE, CHATTANOOGA

Indication of the beginning of a project.

TENNESSEE, DAVIDSON COUNTY

Basler, Roosevelt and David Turney, "Secretarial Help for Classroom Teachers," *Research Bulletin No. 1*, Nashville, Tenn., Peabody-Public

School Cooperative Program, September, 1958.
Extensive experiment in use of clerical aides.
Turney, David T., "The Instructional Secretary as Used by Classroom
Teachers. Number One of a Series of Studies on Effecting Better Uses
of Educational Manpower and Resources," Nashville, Tenn., Peabody
Research and Development Program, 1959.
See also university section for further material on the Peabody-Public
School Cooperative Program.
Turney, David T., "A Study of the Classroom Use of Secretarial Help in
the Public Schools of Davidson County, Tennessee," *NASSP Bulletin*,
vol. XLIV, January, 1960, pp. 335–340.

WISCONSIN, JANESVILLE

"Team Teaching in Janesville," Janesville, Wis., Janesville Public Schools,
May, 1961.

WISCONSIN, MADISON

Lambert, Philip, "Report to the Administrative Committee of the Madison
Schools and the University of Wisconsin on the Washington School
Project in Madison, Wisconsin, During the Academic Year 1959–1960,"
Madison, Wis., Wisconsin Improvement Program, 1960.
Making Teaching and Learning Better: The Wisconsin Improvement Program, 1959–1961, Madison, Wis., Wisconsin Improvement Program,
1962.
Rehage, Kenneth J., "News and Comment," *The Elementary School Journal*, vol. LXI, October, 1960, pp. 1–3.

B. Junior High Schools

CALIFORNIA, PALO ALTO

Indication of the beginning of a project.

CALIFORNIA, SAN DIEGO

Bloomenshine, L. L., "San Diego Uses the Teaching Team Approach to
Staff Utilization," *NASSP Bulletin*, vol. XLIII, January, 1959, pp.
217–219.
A brief description of team teaching projects in four or five schools.
Bloomenshine, L. L., "Team Teaching in San Diego—The First Year,"
NASSP Bulletin, vol. XLIV, January, 1960, pp. 181–196.
A review of the first year and an attempt at subjective evaluation.
Bloomenshine, L. L. and T. Malcomb Brown, "San Diego, California,
Conducts Two-Year Experiment with Team Teaching," *NASSP Bulletin*, vol. XLV, January, 1961, pp. 147–156.

"Report on the Two-Year Experimental Project in Staff Utilization, 1958–1960," San Dego, Calif., San Diego City Schools, June, 1960.

COLORADO, LAKEWOOD

Profiles of Significant Schools: Schools for Team Teaching, New York, Educational Facilities Laboratories, 1961, pp. 32–35.

FLORIDA, SARASOTA

"Large-Class Experimental Program at Brookside Junior High School, Sarasota, Florida," Sarasota, Fla., Board of Public Instruction, 1961.

ILLINOIS, DECATUR

Beggs, Davd W., "Lakeview Junior-Senior High School, Decatur, Illinois, Faculty Studies and Develops a Variety of Staff Utilization Projects," *NASSP Bulletin*, vol. XLV, January, 1961, pp. 85–91.
Beggs, David W., "Summer Staff-Utilization Workshop Enables Lakeview Junior-Senior High School Teachers to Plan Studies," *NASSP Bulletin*, vol. XLIV, January, 1960, pp. 254–256.
"The Road to Progress: The Decatur-Lakeview Plan," Decatur, Ill., Decatur Public Schools, September, 1960.

KANSAS, SALINA

Indication of team teaching in progress.

KANSAS, SHAWNEE MISSION

Team teaching used but discontinued.

MASSACHUSETTS, LEXINGTON

Hendrick, Fannie A., "Teacher Teams at the Muzzey Junior High School, Lexington, Massachusetts," Lexington, Mass., Lexington Public Schools, January 10, 1961.

MICHIGAN, SAGINAW

"Two Saginaw Middle Schools, Saginaw Township, Michigan," *Profiles of Significant Schools*, New York, Educational Facilities Laboratories, 1960.

MINNESOTA, WHITE BEAR LAKE

Indication of team teaching in progress.

NEW YORK, HICKSVILLE

Indication of team teaching in progress.

NEW YORK, HUNTINGTON

Team teaching in progress.

OHIO, WILLOUGHBY

Indication of team teaching in progress.

PENNSYLVANIA, COATESVILLE

McDonald, Samuel E. and John J. McKenna, "Team Teaching at William T. Gordon Junior High School, Coatesville, Pennsylvania," Coatesville, Pa., Coatesville Area Schools, 1959–1960.
"Project Pyramid: Phase II," Coatesville, Pa., Coatesville Area Schools, 1960.

PENNSYLVANIA, PITTSBURGH

Pupils, Patterns, and Possibilities, Pittsburgh, Pa., Board of Public Education, 1961.

PENNSYLVANIA, WEST CHESTER

Stetson, G. Arthur and James P. Harrison, "A Junior High School Designed for Team Teaching," *American School Board Journal,* vol. CXL, May, 1960, pp. 39–42.

UTAH, DUCHESNE

"An Experiment in the Utilization of Teacher Time Through the Use of a Teaching Team in the Roosevelt Junior High School, Duchesne County School District," Salt Lake City, Utah, Utah Central Research Committee, March 31, 1959.
Noall, Matthew F. and Lawrall Jensen, "Team Teaching at Roosevelt Junior High School, Duchesne County, Utah," *NASSP Bulletin,* vol. XLIV, January, 1960, pp. 156–163.
    Description of a small, closely supervised project in a combined English-Social Studies program at eighth-grade level.
"Report of the Utilization of the Teaching Team Project at the Roosevelt Junior High School, Duchesne County School District, Utah," Salt Lake City, Utah, Utah Central Research Committee, August, 1959.
Riggle, Wanda, Lawrall Jensen, and Matthew F. Noall, "Team Teaching Project, Roosevelt Junior High School, Duchesne County School District, Utah," in Matthew F. Noall, "Utah Schools Conduct Variety of Studies under Statewide Organization," *NASSP Bulletin,* vol. XLV, January, 1961, pp. 234–238.

UTAH, OGDEN

"An Integrated Course of Study in United States History and Language Arts," Salt Lake City, Utah, Utah Central Research Committee, 1960.
Noall, Matthew F. and Gale Rose, "Team Teaching at the Wahlquist Junior High School, Weber County, Utah," *NASSP Bulletin*, vol. XLIV, January, 1960, pp. 164–171.
  Description of team teaching in an eighth-grade English-Social Studies program. Hypotheses listed, and some support for hypotheses offered.
Wyatt, Sidney L. and Matthew F. Noal, "The Wahlquist Teacher Team Project," in Matthew F. Noall, "Utah Schools Conduct Variety of Studies under Statewide Organization," *NASSP Bulletin*, vol. XLV, January, 1961, pp. 229–232.

WASHINGTON, SEATTLE

Indication of team teaching in progress.

WASHINGTON, SELAH

Indication of team teaching in progress.

WISCONSIN, JANESVILLE

Making Teaching and Learning Better: The Wisconsin Improvement Program, 1959–1961, Madison, Wis., Wisconsin Improvement Program, 1962.

WISCONSIN, RACINE

Making Teaching and Learning Better: The Wisconsin Improvement Program, 1959–1961, Madison, Wis., Wisconsin Improvement Program, 1962.
Stoltenberg, James C., "Team Teaching in Junior High School," *Educational Leadership*, vol. XVIII, December, 1960, pp. 153–155.

C. High Schools

CALIFORNIA, CARMEL

Indication of team teaching in progress.

CALIFORNIA, LAFAYETTE

Nelson, James, "Lecture Classes and Team Teaching at Acalanes High School," Lafayette, Calif., Acalanes High School, January, 1961.

CALIFORNIA, PALO ALTO

"Cubberly to Become Laboratory for Tests," *Palo Alto Times*, August 16, 1960.
Laurits, James D., Joseph M. Cronin, Hamlin D. Smith, and Shirley Ann Turner, "Description: Team Teaching Project, Senior Social Studies," Palo Alto, Calif., Cubberly Senior High School, 1961.

CALIFORNIA, SAN DIEGO

Bloomenshine, L. L., "San Diego Uses the Teaching Team Approach in Staff Utilization," *NASSP Bulletin*, vol. XLIII, January, 1959, pp. 217–219.
A brief description of team teaching projects in four or five schools.
Bloomenshine, L. L., "Team Teaching in San Diego—The First Year," *NASSP Bulletin*, vol. XLIV, January, 1960, pp. 181–196.
A review of the first year and an attempt at subjective evaluation.
Bloomenshine, L. L. and T. Malcomb Brown, "San Diego, California Conducts Two-Year Experiment with Team Teaching," *NASSP Bulletin*, vol. XLV, January, 1961, pp. 147–166.
Paullin, Charlene, "Team Teaching in General Music Classes in San Diego," *California Journal of Secondary Education*, vol. XXXVI, March, 1961.
"Report on the Two-Year Experimental Project in Staff Utilization, 1958–1960," San Diego, Calif., San Diego City Schools, June, 1960.

CALIFORNIA, SAN JOSE

"Team Teaching Goes Over Big with Freemont Students," *Palo Alto Times*, August 16, 1960.

CALIFORNIA, SANTA CLARA

Indication of team teaching in progress.

CALIFORNIA, STOCKTON

"First-Year Report Team Teaching," Stockton, Calif., Franklin Senior High School, July, 1961.

CALIFORNIA, SUNNYVALE

"Team Teaching Report—1959–60," Sunnyvale, Calif., Freemont High School, 1960.

COLORADO, DENVER

Indication of team teaching in progress.

COLORADO, LAKEWOOD

Johnson, Robert H. and M. Delbert Lobb, "Jefferson County, Colorado, Completes Three-Year Study of Staffing, Changing Class Size, Programming, and Scheduling," *NASSP Bulletin*, vol. XLV, January, 1960, pp. 57–77.

Johnson, Robert H. and M. Delbert Lobb, "The Transformation of the Sacred Secondary-School Schedule," *California Journal of Secondary Education*, vol. XXXV, February, 1960, pp. 96–105.
    Along with reviewing material covered more fully elsewhere, this article discusses developments for 1960.

Johnson, Robert H., M. Delbert Lobb, and Gordon Patterson, "Continued Study of Class Size, Team Teaching and Scheduling in Eight High Schools in Jefferson County, Colorado," *NASSP Bulletin*, vol. XLIII, January, 1959, pp. 99–103.
    Covers much the same material in shorter form as the 1960 article.

Johnson, Robert H., M. Delbert Lobb, and Lloyd G. Swenson, "An Extensive Study of Team Teaching and Schedule Modification in Jefferson County, Colorado, School District R-1," *NASSP Bulletin*, vol. XLIV, January, 1960, pp. 79–93.
    Notes past problems and findings and indicates hypotheses and assumptions which form the basis for future study.

Lobb, M. Delbert, "A Description of a Continued Experimental Study of Means of Improving the Utilization of the Staff in Education 1959–60," Lakewood, Colo., Jefferson County, Colorado School District R-1, September, 1959.
    A more detailed account of this project. Hypotheses listed.

Lobb, M. Delbert, "An Experimental Study of Means of Improving the Utilization of the Staff in the Secondary Schools," Lakewood, Colo., Jefferson County, Colorado School District R-1, July, 1959.
    Basis for 1960 *NASSP* Article. Has more details on evaluation.

Patterson, Gordon, Lloyd G. Swenson, and Robert H. Johnson, "Classes of 10, 20, 35, and 70 under Varied Conditions are Taught in Jefferson County, Colorado, to Discover Effects on Students and Teachers," *NASSP Bulletin*, vol. XLII, January 19, 1958, pp. 165–167.
    This original article presents the early intentions of the project along with the hypotheses that were tested. Results of this year's work given in later articles.

Smith, Vernon N., "Team Teaching Has Advantages," *The English Journal*, April, 1960.
    A discussion of team teaching and its advantages for the teaching of English.

CONNECTICUT, BRANFORD

"Team Teaching in Branford High School," Branford, Conn., Branford Public Schools.

FLORIDA, SARASOTA

Indication of the beginning of a project.

FLORIDA, TITUSVILLE

New Horizons in Learning, Titusville, Fla., Brevard County Board of Public Instruction, 1961.

ILLINOIS, ARLINGTON HEIGHTS

Cashen, Valjean, E. Eugene Oliver, Harold Slichenmyer, and Alvin L. Kulieke, "Fourteen Staff Utilization Studies in Township High School District 214, Arlington Heights," *NASSP Bulletin,* vol. XLIV, January, 1960, pp. 211–232.
    Team approaches to core curriculum, world affairs, and general math. Part of a large experimental program.
Slichenmyer, H. L., "Arlington Heights, Illinois, Studies Curriculum and Testing, Instruction Assistants, Team Teaching and Modern Technology in Fourteen Projects," *NASSP Bulletin,* vol. XLV, January, 1961, pp. 41–49.
Slichenmyer, H. L., "Eleven Studies Are Started in the Arlington and Prospect High Schools, Arlington Heights," *NASSP Bulletin,* vol. XLIII, January, 1959, pp. 242–244.
    An early article which merely indicates team teaching is in progress.

ILLINOIS, CHICAGO

Hanvey, Robert and Morton S. Tenenberg, "University of Chicago Laboratory School, Chicago, Illinois, Evaluates Team Teaching," *NASSP Bulletin,* vol. XLV, January, 1961, pp. 189–197.
"An Informal Report on the Freshman Project 1961–1962," Chicago, The Laboratory Schools, The University of Chicago, February, 1962.
Larmee, Roy A. and Robert Ohm, "University of Chicago Laboratory School Freshman Project Involves Team Teaching, New Faculty Position and Regrouping of Students," *NASSP Bulletin,* vol. XLIV, January, 1960, pp. 275–289.
    A fairly complete description of a project in which team members come from different subject areas.
Ohm, Robert E. and Roy A. Larmee, "The Role of Coordinator of Instruction in the More Effective Utilization of the Teaching Staff," Chicago, Laboratory School of the University of Chicago, February 6, 1958.
    Discussion of the rationale behind and the purposes of a coordinator

of instruction as a member of a team which cuts across subject matter lines.

Ohm, Robert and Morton Tenenberg, "Staff Reorganization Through Differentiation of Teaching Functions," *NASSP Bulletin*, vol. XLIII, January, 1959, pp. 263–265.

Outline of the project with description of the role of team coordinator.

Ohm, Robert, *et al.*, "A Proposal Submitted to the School Improvement Program for the Continuation of the Unified Arts Project of the Laboratory School," Chicago, Laboratory School of the University of Chicago, August 11, 1958.

Tenenberg, Morton S., "University of Chicago Laboratory School Freshman Staff Utilization Project: Final Report, 1959–60," Chicago, Ill., Laboratory School of the University of Chicago.

ILLINOIS, CHICAGO HEIGHTS

Indication of team teaching in progress.

ILLINOIS, CICERO

Antal, John, Elizabeth Dixon, Joseph Wintering, and Homer Young, "Illinois Staff Utilization Study: Team Teaching," Cicero, Ill., Cicero Public Schools.

A fairly complete description of the project. Project limited to combined American History-American Literature.

Cooper, Walter L., "J. Sterling Morton High School and Junior College, Cicero, Illinois, Uses Tapes, Language Laboratories, and Team Teaching," *NASSP Bulletin*, vol. XLV, January, 1961, pp. 79–84.

Cooper, Walter L., "Staff Utilization Studies in J. Sterling Morton High School and Junior College, Cicero, Illinois," *NASSP Bulletin*, vol. XLIII, January, 1959, pp. 247–249.

Cooper, Walter L., "Uses of Tapes, Language Laboratory, and Teaching Teams at the J. Sterling Morton High School and Junior College," *NASSP Bulletin*, vol. XLIV, January, 1960, pp. 233–243.

ILLINOIS, DECATUR

Beggs, David W., "Lakeview Junior-Senior High School, Decatur, Illinois, Faculty Studies and Develops a Variety of Staff Utilization Projects," *NASSP Bulletin*, vol. XLV, January, 1961, pp. 85–91.

Beggs, David W., "Summer Staff-Utilization Workshop Enables Lakeview Junior-Senior High School Teachers to Plan Studies," *NASSP Bulletin*, vol. XLIV, January, 1960, pp. 254–256.

"The Road to Progress: The Decatur-Lakeview Plan," Decatur, Ill., Decatur Public Schools, September, 1960.

ILLINOIS, EVANSTON

Carpenter, William G., Jean E. Fair, James E. Heald, and Wanda B. Mitchell, "Closed-Circuit Television is Used at Evanston Township High School," *NASSP Bulletin*, vol. XLII, January, 1958, pp. 19–54.
Use of closed-circuit television and cadet teachers seems to lead to team teaching.

Mitchell, Wanda B., "Evanston, Illinois, Township High School Expands Use of Closed-Circuit Television in 1957–58," *NASSP Bulletin*, vol. XLIII, January, 1959, pp. 75–78.
First two attempts at team teaching described. Progress in other areas noted.

Pannwitt, Barbara S., "Evanston, Illinois, Township High School Reports on Five Years of Projects, Including Television, Team Teaching, and Large and Small Group Instruction," *NASSP Bulletin*, vol. XLV, January, 1961, pp. 245–248.

ILLINOIS, MATTOON

Clawson, H. A., "English and Science Studies in Mattoon Senior High School," *NASSP Bulletin*, vol. XLIV, January, 1960, pp. 257–263.
Team Teaching in sophomore English. Students regrouped for each new unit of material.

Clawson, H. A., "Mattoon, Illinois, High School Tries Team Teaching and Science Orientation," *NASSP Bulletin*, vol. XLV, January, 1961, pp. 93–99.

Clawson, H. A., "Science Lecture and Team Approaches in English are Tried in Mattoon High School," *NASSP Bulletin*, vol. XLIII, January, 1959, pp. 245–247.

ILLINOIS, NORRIDGE

Heller, Melvin P. and Elizabeth Belford, "Team Teaching and Staff Utilization in Ridgewood High School," *NASSP Bulletin*, vol. XLVI, January, 1962.

Heller, Melvin P. and Eugene R. Howard, "A New High School Organized for Quality Instruction," *NASSP Bulletin*, vol. XLV, January, 1961, pp. 273–274.

Profiles of Significant Schools: High Schools 1962, New York, Educational Facilities Laboratories, 1961, pp. 23 ff.

ILLINOIS, NORTHBROOK

Bovinet, Wesley G., "Glenbrook Reports on Four Experiments on Utilization of Staff," *NASSP Bulletin*, vol. XLIV, January, 1960, pp. 244–253.
Team teaching in mathematics and science.

Bovinet, Wesley G., "Intern Program, Team Teaching and Language Laboratory at Glenbrook High School," *NASSP Bulletin,* vol. XLIII, January, 1959, pp. 249–254.
    Includes description of in-service training of new teachers.
Watson, N. E., "Glenbrook High School, Northbrook, Illinois, Projects on Internship, Large Classes, Team Teaching, Teacher Aides, and Language Laboratory," *NASSP Bulletin,* vol. XLV, January, 1961, pp. 51–56.

ILLINOIS, PARK FOREST

Andree, Robert G., "An Image of the Future Arises in Olympia Fields," *The Nation's Schools,* vol. LXV, July, 1960.
    Description of a new high school designed for team teaching.
Andree, Robert G., "Large Classes and Effective Teaching," *The Clearing House,* vol. XXXIII, February, 1959, pp. 334–336.
Hemeyer, Will and Jean B. McGrew, "Big Ideas for Big Classes," *The School Review,* vol. LXVIII, Autumn, 1960, pp. 308–317.
"How to Improve Instruction with Teaching Teams," *School Management,* vol. IV, November, 1960, pp. 50–54, 114.
"Rich Township High School, Olympia Fields Campus, Rich Township, Illinois," *Profiles of Significant Schools,* New York: Educational Facilities Laboratories, May, 1960.
"Teachers Tell Secret of Big Class Success," *Park Forest Reporter,* March 8, 1961.

ILLINOIS, RIVERSIDE

Branson, G., and F. T. Dombrowski, "Team Teaching in American History: Grade II," Riverside, Ill., Riverside-Brookfield Township High School, 1960.
Briggs, David H., William G. Mohrusen, and B. Glenn Richardson, "English II—Coordinated Group (Team Teaching)," Riverside, Ill., Riverside-Brookfield Township High School, 1960.

ILLINOIS, SKOKIE

Team teaching in progress.

ILLINOIS, TAYLORVILLE

Dillon, Carl L., "Taylorville, Illinois, Senior High School Uses Tape Recorders, Team Teaching, and Large-Group Instruction to Improve Staff Utilization," *NASSP Bulletin,* vol. XLV, January, 1961, pp. 179–188.
Drake, Jackson M., "Group Guidance, Administrative Patterns, Driver Training and Tape Recordings Are Studies in the Taylorville Senior

High School," *NASSP Bulletin*, vol. XLIV, January, 1960, pp. 268–274. General article which indicates some team teaching.

Hurley, William, *et al.*, "Team Teaching and Use of Recorders in Taylorville Senior High School," *NASSP Bulletin*, vol. XLIV, January, 1960, pp. 268–274.
Team Teaching in Sophomore English.

ILLINOIS, WINNETKA

Burdine, F. J., W. P. Gregory, L. C. Irwin, and J. F. MARRAN, "English-Science, History Program in Coordinated Skills," Winnetka, Ill., New Trier High School, March, 1958.

IOWA, CEDAR FALLS

Picht, Merle and Robert Kemp, "Comments on the Proposed Team Teaching Experiment in Speech," Cedar Falls, Iowa, Cedar Falls Community Schools, November 2, 1960.

Ziesmer, Marvin W., "High School Team Teaching Experiment," Cedar Falls, Iowa, Cedar Falls Community Schools, 1961.

KANSAS, SHAWNEE MISSION

Team teaching used but discontinued.

MASSACHUSETTS, CONCORD

Indication of team teaching in progress.

MASSACHUSETTS, NEWTON

Bissex, Henry S., "Newton Plan Challenges Traditions of Class Size," *The Nation's Schools*, vol. LXV, March, 1960, pp. 60–64.

Bissex, Henry, "Second Stage: Revision, Extension of Newton Plan Studies," *NASSP Bulletin*, vol. XLIII, January, 1959, pp. 106–119.
Second article on Newton's large-group lecture project.

Carroll, John B., *et al.*, "Final Report of the Committee on Newton Plan Evaluation for the School and University Program for Research and Development," Cambridge, Mass., SUPRAD, April, 1960.

Howe, Harold, II, "The High School Principal in Newton, Massachusetts Reacts to Redeployment," *NASSP Bulletin*, vol. XLIV, January, 1960, pp. 122–138.
Third article on Newton's large-group lecture project.

Levensohn, Alan, ed., *Newton Plan Studies*, Newton, Mass., Council on Newton Plan Studies, Newton High School, 1958.

"Newton South High School, Newton, Massachusetts," *Profiles of Significant Schools*, New York, Educational Facilities Laboratories, February, 1960.

Rinker, Floyd, "Subject Matter, Students, Teachers, Methods of Teaching and Space are Redeployed in the Newton, Massachusetts, High School," *NASSP Bulletin*, vol. XLII, January, 1958, pp. 69–80.
First article on Newton's large-group lecture project.

MASSACHUSETTS, WAYLAND

Anderson, Edward and John C. Harkness, "Planned Variability," *The Nation's Schools*, vol. LXV, April, 1960, pp. 83–91.
New Schools for New Education, New York, Educational Facilities Laboratories, 1961, pp. 34–37.
Profiles of Significant Schools: High Schools 1962, New York, Educational Facilities Laboratories, 1961, pp. 23 ff.
"Wayland Senior High School, Wayland, Massachusetts," *Profiles of Significant Schools*, New York, Educational Facilities Laboratories, January, 1960.

MASSACHUSETTS, WESTON

The Accordian Plan, Cambridge, Mass., The New England School Development Council, 1960.
This report of a study of a committee in Weston, Massachusetts, advocates a new pattern of school and class organization.

MICHIGAN, HOLLAND

"Holland High School, Holland, Michigan," *Profiles of Significant Schools*, New York, Educational Facilities Laboratories, September, 1962.

MICHIGAN, LIVONIA

Wilson, Richard W., William R. Young, and Fred A. McGlone, "A New Frontier in Education: An Experimental Application of the Technique of Team Teaching Instruction in American Government for the School Year 1960–61," Livonia, Mich., Livonia Public Schools, August 31, 1960.

MICHIGAN, MADISON HEIGHTS

"Overview: Lamphere Educational Action Project," Madison Heights, Mich., Lamphere Public Schools, August 2, 1960.
Pino, Edward C., "The Lamphere Quad—A New Dimension in School Design," *Michigan School Board Journal*, vol. VI, September, 1960.
Profiles of Significant Schools: High Schools 1962, New York, Educational Facilities Laboratories, 1961, pp. 25 ff.

MICHIGAN, SAGINAW

"Two Saginaw Middle Schools, Saginaw Township, Michigan," *Profiles of Significant Schools,* New York, Educational Facilities Laboratories, 1960.

MINNESOTA, ST. PAUL

Doane, Kenneth R., ed., "A Study in the Team-Teaching of Twelfth Grade Social Studies and Eleventh Grade American History," St. Paul, Minn., John A. Johnson Senior High School, 1960.

MINNESOTA, WHITE BEAR LAKE

Some indication of team teaching in progress.

NEBRASKA, OMAHA

Gibson, Mrs. R. E., "Final Report on the Westside High School Teaching by Tape Project," *NASSP Bulletin,* vol. XLIV, January, 1960, pp. 56–62.
    This project involves cooperation effort but is not primarily concerned with team teaching.
Gibson, Mrs. R. E., "The Tape Recordings Experiment Is Expanded in Westside Junior and Senior High Schools, Omaha, Nebraska," *NASSP Bulletin,* vol. XLIII, January, 1959.
Pickrel, Glenn, Charles Neidt, and Romain Gibson, "Tape Recordings Are Used to Teach Seventh Grade Students in Westside Junior-Senior High School, Omaha, Nebraska," *NASSP Bulletin,* vol. XLII, January, 1958, pp. 81–93.

NEVADA, LAS VEGAS

Indication of team teaching in progress.

NEW YORK, GLENS FALLS

Indication of the beginning of a project.

NEW YORK, HAMBURG

Some indication of team teaching in progress.

NEW YORK, HUNTINGTON

Profiles of Significant Schools: High Schools 1962, New York, Educational Facilities Laboratories, 1961, pp. 31 ff.

NEW YORK, NEW YORK

Limited application of team teaching in Hunter College High School.

NEW YORK, ONEONTA

Catskill Area Project in Small School Design, Oneonta, N.Y., The Catskill Project, State University College of Education, 1959.
    Chapters include discussions of multiple classes, flexible schedules, school aides, electronic communication, and shared services.
School Aides at Work, Oneonta, N.Y., The Catskill Project, State University College of Education, 1959.
    One of the best available discussions of the nonprofessional assistant.
Sharing Educational Services, Oneonta, N.Y., The Catskill Project, State University College of Education, 1960.

NEW YORK, SNYDER

"Large Group Instruction at Amherst," Snyder, N.Y., Amherst Central High School, December, 1960.

NEW YORK, SYOSSET

Price, John W., "More Experience with Utilizing a New School Plant at Syosset, New York in Contributing to Staff Use and Curriculum Development," *NASSP Bulletin,* vol. XLIII, January, 1959, pp. 167–180.
    Team teaching in a new school designed for flexibility. Many types of arrangements being used.
Price, John, William C. French, and Ernest R. Weinrich, "Some Influences of a New School on Planning Staff Use and Curriculum Development Are Studied in Syosset, New York," *NASSP Bulletin,* vol. LXII, January, 1958, pp. 154–164.

OHIO, CLEVELAND HEIGHTS

Intensive Study Toward Improved Classroom Instruction, Cleveland Heights, Ohio, Cleveland Heights City School District, 1960.
    A collection of bulletins, most of which were prepared during a summer workshop in 1960. A good example of careful and extensive preparation for a relatively small project.

OHIO, TOLEDO

Team teaching in progress in two new high schools.

OKLAHOMA, OKLAHOMA CITY

Some indication of team teaching.

OREGON, CORVALLIS

Bodine, Ivan, E. M. Hollister, and Harry Sackett, "A Contribution to Team Teaching," *NASSP Bulletin,* vol. XLVI, April, 1962, pp. 111–117. A description of how team teaching was used to teach a course in American Problems in the Corvallis Senior High School, Corvallis, Oregon. Special attention was given to large-group lecture techniques and the development of a curriculum.

OREGON, MILWAUKEE

Some indication of team teaching in progress.

OREGON, PORTLAND

Bushnell, Sue and Shirley Petery, "Madison Teachers Develop Team Teaching Approach," *The School Bulletin,* vol. XLV, Portland, Ore., June, 1960, pp. 8–9.

OREGON, SALEM

Indication of team teaching in progress.

PENNSYLVANIA, BERWYN

Indication of some team teaching here.

PENNSYLVANIA, COATESVILLE

"Project Pyramid: Phase II," Coatesville, Pa., Coatesville Area Schools, 1960.

PENNSYLVANIA, EASTON

Peterson, Carl H., "Easton Senior High School Team Teaching Program," Curriculum Publication SE-60-1, Easton, Pa., Easton-Forks Joint School System and Easton Area Joint High School System, 1960. A team teaching program, designed for gifted students, which crosses subject matter boundaries.

RHODE ISLAND, CRANSTON

Larson, Knute, "Cranston High School East Experiments in Team Teaching," *The Rhode Island Schoolmaster,* March, 1961, p. 6.

RHODE ISLAND, WARWICK

Some indication of team teaching in progress.

TENNESSEE, DAVIDSON COUNTY

Turney, David T., "A Study of the Classroom Use of Secretarial Help in the Public Schools of Davidson County, Tennessee," *NASSP Bulletin,* vol. XLIV, January, 1960, pp. 335–340.

TEXAS, HOUSTON

Fisher, Mildred Ogg, "Team Teaching in Houston," *English Journal,* vol. LI, December, 1962, pp. 628–331.
Team teaching in the S. P. Waltrip Senior High School.

TEXAS, SNYDER

Henry, C. D., "Snyder Public Schools Staff Utilization Project Summary Report," Snyder, Texas, Snyder Public Schools, January, 1960.
A report on the project after it was officially discontinued.
Johnson, Palmer O., William O. Nesbitt, and Dell Felder, "Snyder, Texas, Redeploys Students to Improve Staff Utilization," *NASSP Bulletin,* vol. XLIII, January, 1959, pp. 149–166.
McCollum, T. E., C. D. Henry, and Wm. O. Nesbitt, "Snyder, Texas, Continues Team Teaching," *NASSP Bulletin,* vol. XLV, January, 1961, pp. 261–265.
Nesbitt, William O., *An Experimental Study of the Relative Effectiveness on Learning in Selected High School Subjects of the Conventional Methods and a Composite of Procedures Involving Modern Educational Media in Addition to Classes of Varying Sizes, Team Teaching and Teacher Aides,* Austin, Texas, University of Texas, June, 1960.
This dissertation is the most complete study of the project available.
Nesbitt, William O. and Palmer O. Johnson, "Some Conclusions Drawn from the Snyder, Texas, Project," *NASSP Bulletin,* vol. XLIV, January, 1960, pp. 63–75.
This article gives first indication of the establishment of teams of teachers.
Yarbrough, C. L., and William O. Nesbitt, "Changes in Class Size, Teacher Time and the Use of Electronic and Mechanical Aids are Made in Snyder, Texas," *NASSP Bulletin,* vol. XLII, January, 1958, pp. 126–141.
First article on project. An attempt to give teachers more time for planning and to use large groups for instruction. Some use of closed-circuit television.

UTAH, HURRICANE

Clark, Gwyn R. and Matthew F. Noall, "Better Staff Utilization in Hurricane High School Through Language Arts Reorganization," in

Matthew F. Noall, "Utah Schools Conduct Variety of Studies Under Statewide Organization," *NASSP Bulletin,* vol. XLV, January, 1961, pp. 223–227.

Noall, Matthew F. and Maurice Nuttall, "Staff Utilization Through Language Arts Reorganization, Hurricane, Utah," *NASSP Bulletin,* vol. XLIV, January, 1959, pp. 148–155.
A different approach to team teaching in which six teachers work with 169 students within a flexible schedule which permits constant opportunity to reorganize for various instructional purposes.

"Report: Washington County School District Project for the Hurricane High School, 1959–60 School Year," Salt Lake City, Utah, Utah Central Research Committee, August, 1960.

UTAH, LOGAN

Noall, Matthew F. and Parry Wilson, "Paraprofessional Helpers in a Language Arts Program at the Logan City High School, Utah," *NASSP Bulletin,* vol. XLIV, January, 1960, pp. 172–177.
Use of lay readers.

WASHINGTON, BELLEVUE

Johnson, John, John Sorenson, Glen Holden, and Ekstedt, eds., "Experiments in Social Studies: Senior History, Bellevue Senior High School," Bellevue, Wash., Bellevue Senior High School.

WASHINGTON, SEATTLE

Two projects in operation—12th-grade English and 9th-grade English.

WASHINGTON, TACOMA

Some indication of team teaching in progress.

WISCONSIN, HALES CORNERS

Making Teaching and Learning Better: The Wisconsin Improvement Program, 1959–1961, Madison, Wis., Wisconsin Improvement Program, 1962.

WISCONSIN, JANESVILLE

"Team Teaching in Janesville," Janesville, Wis., Janesville Public Schools, May, 1961.

WISCONSIN, MILWAUKEE

Some indication of team teaching in progress.

WISCONSIN, RACINE

Making Teaching and Learning Better: The Wisconsin Improvement Program, 1959–1961, Madison, Wis., Wisconsin Improvement Program, 1962.

WISCONSIN, WAUSAU

Making Teaching and Learning Better: The Wisconsin Improvement Program, 1959–1961, Madison, Wis., Wisconsin Improvement Program, 1962.

WISCONSIN, WEST BEND

Dishon, Robert L., "Teaching Team Gets Test at West Bend High School," *The Milwaukee Journal,* April 10, 1960.
Making Teaching and Learning Better: The Wisconsin Improvement Program, 1959–1961, Madison, Wis., Wisconsin Improvement Program, 1962.

D. Universities

CALIFORNIA, CLAREMONT—CLAREMONT GRADUATE SCHOOL

Armstrong, Hubert, "Outline for Use in the Evaluation of the Ford Teaching Team Project under the Auspices of the Claremont Graduate School," Claremont, Calif., Claremont Graduate School, 1959.
Brownell, John A., *The Claremont Teaching Team Program,* Claremont, Calif., Claremont Graduate School, 1961.
Brownell, John A., ed., *First Annual Report to the Ford Foundation of the Claremont Team Teaching Program, 1959–1961,* Claremont, Calif., Claremont Graduate School, 1960.
Brownell, John A., ed., *Second Annual Report to the Ford Foundation by the Claremont Teaching Team Program for 1960–61,* Claremont, Calif., Claremont Graduate School, 1962.
Douglass, Malcolm P., "The Teaching Team in the Elementary School," Claremont, Calif., Claremont Graduate School, 1960.

CALIFORNIA, LOS ANGELES—UNIVERSITY OF SOUTHERN CALIFORNIA

Melbo, I. R. and Leonard Calvert, "The Southern California High School Specialist-Teacher Program—A New Two-Year Graduate Preparation," *The High School Journal,* vol. XLIII, February, 1960, pp. 164–167.

CALIFORNIA, PALO ALTO—STANFORD UNIVERSITY

"The Winds of Freedom: A New Program of Teacher Education at Stanford," *The High School Journal*, vol. XLIII, February, 1960, pp. 168–173.

ILLINOIS, CHICAGO—UNIVERSITY OF CHICAGO

"Chicago Initiates New Two-Year Graduate Programs for High-School Teachers," *The High School Journal*, vol. XLIII, February, 1960, pp. 196–201.

"School Improvement Program," *Newsletter*, Chicago, The University of Chicago Department of Education, November, 1958.

ILLINOIS, EVANSTON—NORTHWESTERN UNIVERSITY

McSwain, E. T., "Teacher Education for Tomorrow's Secondary Schools," *The High School Journal*, vol. XLIII, February, 1960, pp. 218–222.

ILLINOIS, URBANA—UNIVERSITY OF ILLINOIS

Jackson, David M., "A Search for Practical Means of Improving Instruction by Increasing Students' Responsibility for Their Own Learning at the University of Illinois High School," *NASSP Bulletin*, vol. XLIII, January, 1959, pp. 233–239.

INDIANA, SOUTH BEND—UNIVERSITY OF NOTRE DAME

Walsh, John E., "Teacher Education at Notre Dame," *The High School Journal*, vol. XLIII, February, 1960, pp. 271–276.

MARYLAND, BALTIMORE—JOHNS HOPKINS UNIVERSITY

Walton, John, "The Scholar-Teacher," *The High School Journal*, vol. XLIII, February, 1960, pp. 294–300.

MASSACHUSETTS, CAMBRIDGE—HARVARD UNIVERSITY

Keppel, Francis, Judson T. Shaplin, and Wade M. Robinson, "Recent Developments at the Harvard Graduate School of Education," *The High School Journal*, vol. XLIII, February, 1960, pp. 242–261.
    Describes teacher training programs at Harvard. In many cases trainees work as team members.

Perry, Paul A., "A Question of Quality," *Harvard Graduate School of Education Association Bulletin*, vol. VII, Summer, 1962, pp. 2–24.

SUPRAD: An Interim Report on the School and University Program for Research and Development 1957–1962, Cambridge, Mass., SUPRAD, 1962.

MICHIGAN, EAST LANSING—MICHIGAN STATE UNIVERSITY

Dean, Leland W., "Secondary School Teacher Preparation—An Integrated Approach," *The High School Journal,* vol. XLIII, February, 1960, pp. 174–177.

MICHIGAN, MOUNT PLEASANT—CENTRAL MICHIGAN COLLEGE

A *Cooperative Study for the Better Utilization of Teacher Competencies,* Mount Pleasant, Mich., Central Michigan College, 1955.
   A report of the first two years of teacher aide experimentation in Bay City, Michigan.
Park, Charles B., "A New Program in Teacher Education," *The High School Journal,* vol. XLIII, February, 1960, pp. 208–212.

NEW MEXICO, SILVER CITY—NEW MEXICO WESTERN COLLEGE

Saunders, Jack O. L. and Hazel Sechler, "Student Teachers on the Classroom Team," *The Elementary School Journal,* vol. LXI, October, 1960, pp. 32–34.

NEW YORK, ITHACA—CORNELL UNIVERSITY

Stutz, Frederick H., "The Cornell University Junior High School Project," *The High School Journal,* vol. XLIII, February, 1960, pp. 188–191.

NEW YORK, NEW YORK—BARNARD COLLEGE

"The Barnard Experiment in Teacher Education," *The High School Journal,* vol. XLIII, February, 1960, pp. 158–163.

NEW YORK, NEW YORK—NEW YORK UNIVERSITY

Heathers, Glen, "A Non-Grade Sequence in Elementary Mathematics," New York, The New York University School of Education, Experimental Teaching Center, July 15, 1960.
Heathers, Glen and Lou Kleinman, "A Proposed Program for the Preparation of Elementary Teachers with a Specialty in Mathematics, Science or Language Arts-Social Studies," New York, The New York University School of Education, Experimental Teaching Center, March 4, 1960.
Heathers, Glen and Lou Kleinman, "School Superintendents' Views on Elementary Teachers Who Are Prepared to Specialize in One Curricular Area," New York, The New York University School of Education, Experimental Teaching Center, July 8, 1960.
"888: Integrated Graduate Program for the Preparation of Elementary Teachers with a Specialty," New York, The New York University School of Education.

Steinberg, Samuel, "A Non-Grade-Level Sequence in Elementary Mathematics," New York, The New York University School of Education, Experimental Teaching Center, July 15, 1960.

NEW YORK, NEW YORK—YESHIVA UNIVERSITY

Fine, Benjamin, "Teachers for Tomorrow's Secondary Schools," *The High School Journal*, vol. XLIII, February, 1960, pp. 223–230.

NORTH CAROLINA, CHAPEL HILL—UNIVERSITY OF NORTH CAROLINA

"North Carolina's Fifth Year Program in Teacher Education," *The High School Journal*, vol. XLIII, February, 1960, pp. 262–270.
   Teacher trainee works as part of a team with large groups and TV.

NORTH CAROLINA, DURHAM—DUKE UNIVERSITY

Hulburt, Allan S. and William H. Cartwright, "The Duke University Cooperative Program in Teacher Education," *The High School Journal*, vol. XLIII, February, 1960, pp. 213–217.

PENNSYLVANIA, LOUISBERG—BUCKNELL UNIVERSITY

Smith, Wendell, J. Charles Jones, and Carl D. Hartzell, "University Leadership in Cooperative Research in the Schools of Its Area," *The High School Journal*, vol. XLIII, February, 1960, pp. 178–187.
   Upper Susquehanna Valley Program of Cooperative Research. Some team teaching in progress.

PENNSYLVANIA, PITTSBURGH—UNIVERSITY OF PITTSBURGH

"Coordinated Education Center Report for July 1, 1959-June 30, 1960," Pittsburgh, Pa., University of Pittsburgh.

RHODE ISLAND, PROVIDENCE—BROWN UNIVERSITY

Smith, Elmer R., "The Brown Plan of Teacher Education," *The High School Journal*, vol. XLIII, February, 1960, pp. 283–293.

TENNESSEE, NASHVILLE—GEORGE PEABODY COLLEGE FOR TEACHERS

Alexander, William M. and Bennie E. Carmichael, "Teacher Education George Peabody College for Teachers: Past, Present, and Future," *The High School Journal*, vol. XLIII, February, 1960, pp. 231–241.
   Describes the many ways they are working on staff utilization as part of their teacher training program.
Anderson, A. Edwin and John H. Banks, "Team Approaches to College Teaching," *Research Bulletin No. 5*, Nashville, Tenn., Peabody-Public School Cooperative Program, September, 1958.

An interesting approach to the use of instructional teams on the college level.

Basler, Roosevelt and David Turney, "Secretarial Help for Classroom Teachers," *Research Bulletin No. 1,* Nashville, Tenn., Peabody-Public School Cooperative Program, September, 1958.

Extensive experiment with the use of clerical aides.

Carmichael, Bennie and David Turney, "Learning about Learning Through Cooperative Research," *Educational Leadership,* vol. XVI, March, 1959, pp. 342–345.

Turney, David T., *The Instructional Secretary as Used by Classroom Teachers,* Nashville, Tenn., Peabody Research and Development Program, 1959.

TENNESSEE, NASHVILLE—VANDERBILT UNIVERSITY

Purdy, R. R., "The 'Breakthrough' in Teacher Education at Vanderbilt," *The High School Journal,* vol. XLIII, February, 1960, pp. 202–207.

WISCONSIN, MADISON—UNIVERSITY OF WISCONSIN

Boyan, Norman J., "Further Consideration of the Original Proposal for the Intern-Team at the Secondary School Level," Madison, Wis., The School of Education of the University of Wisconsin.

Boyan, Norman J., "A Proposal for the Establishment of the Intern-Team at the Secondary School Level," Madison, Wis., The School of Education of the University of Wisconsin.

Fowlkes, John Guy, "Some Observations on the Preparation of Teachers," *The High School Journal,* vol. XLIII, February, 1960, pp. 192–195.

Making Teaching and Learning Better: The Wisconsin Improvement Program, 1959–1961, Madison, Wis., Wisconsin Improvement Program, 1962.

An extensive description of their school-university program.

"Team Plan Wears Well, Program Teachers Report After First 3 Years of Experience," *The Wisconsin Improvement Program Reporter,* vol. III, no. 3, June, 1962.

Also see all other issues of *The Reporter.*

Index